THE HARVARD CLASSICS

The Five-Foot Shelf of Books

THE HARVARD CLASSICS

The Five-Foot Shelf of Books

THE HARVARD CLASSICS
EDITED BY CHARLES W. ELIOT, LL.D.

The Confessions *of* St. Augustine

TRANSLATED BY EDWARD B. PUSEY

The Imitation of Christ
By Thomas A. Kempis

TRANSLATED BY WILLIAM BENHAM

With *Introductions and Notes*
Volume 7

P. F. Collier & Son Corporation
NEW YORK

TABLE OF CONTENTS

INTRODUCTORY NOTE

AURELIUS AUGUSTINUS, better known as Saint Augustine, was born of poor parents in the small town of Thagaste in Numidia, North Africa, A.D. 354. His father, Patricius, a pagan of somewhat loose life, was converted to Christianity before his death; his mother Monnica, on account of her personal piety and her influence on her son, is one of the most revered women in the history of the Christian Church. Augustine was educated at the University of Carthage, and according to his own account belonged to a fast set and joined in their dissipations. While there he entered into a relation which lasted for fourteen years with a young woman who became the mother of his son Adeodatus; and he joined the heretical sect of the Manichæans, who professed to have received from their founder, Manes, a higher form of truth than that taught by Christ. At the close of his university career, which had been brilliant in spite of distractions, he returned to his native town, and first there, and later in Carthage and Rome, he practised as a teacher of rhetoric, training young lawyers in the art of pleading. By the time he was about twenty-seven he had begun to have doubts as to the validity of Manichæism, but it was not till 387, while he was Professor of Rhetoric in the University of Milan, that he was converted to Catholic Christianity, and received baptism. He now gave up his profession and became an ascetic, studying the foundations of the faith, writing, chiefly against his former sect, and conversing with a group of disciples, first at Rome and then in his native town. When he was on a visit to Hippo, not far from Thagaste, he was forced into the priesthood, and in 395 he became Bishop of Hippo, an office which he filled for the remaining thirty-five years of his life. Though he took a leading part in the activities of the African Church through all this time, and gradually became one of the most distinguished ecclesiastical figures in the Empire, the care of his diocese and the writing of his books formed his chief occupations. He continued to lead a life of extreme simplicity and self-denial, and in his episcopal establishment he trained a large number of disciples who became leaders in the Church. The strength of his hold on these younger men was due not merely to his intellectual ascendency, but also to the charm and sweetness of his disposition.

A large part of his literary activity was devoted to controversy with the heretics of his time, first the Manichæans, then the Donatists, and finally the Pelagians. It was in his writings against these last and most

3

important opponents that he elaborated his statement of the doctrines of Predestination, Irresistible Grace and Final Perseverance, through which he has left his chief mark upon the creeds of later times. The theology of the Schoolmen, such as Thomas Aquinas, and of the Calvinists of the Reformation, is built upon an Augustinian basis.

His two most important books are "The City of God" and the "Confessions." The former of these was provoked by the attacks upon Christianity, roused by the disasters that began to fall upon the Western Empire in the beginning of the fifth century; and Augustine replies by pointing out the failure of the heathen gods in former times to protect the peoples who trusted in them, and goes on to expose the evil influence of the belief in the old mythology, in a minute examination of its traditions and mysteries. The second part of the book deals with the history of the "City of Man," founded upon love of self, and of the "City of God," founded upon love of God and contempt of self. This work is a vast storehouse of the knowledge of the time, and is a monument not only to Augustine's great learning, but also to the keenest metaphysical mind of the age.

The "Confessions," here printed, speaks for itself. The earliest of autobiographies, it remains unsurpassed as a sincere and intimate record of a great and pious soul laid bare before God.

THE CONFESSIONS OF
ST. AUGUSTINE

THE FIRST BOOK

Confessions of the greatness and unsearchableness of God, of God's mercies in infancy and boyhood, and human wilfulness; of his own sins of idleness, abuse of his studies, and of God's gifts up to his fifteenth year.

*G*REAT *art Thou, O Lord, and greatly to be praised; great is Thy power, and Thy wisdom infinite.*[1] And Thee would man praise; man, but a particle of Thy creation; man, that bears about him his mortality, the witness of his sin, the witness that *Thou resistest the proud:*[2] yet would man praise Thee; he, but a particle of Thy creation. Thou awakest us to delight in Thy praise; for Thou madest us for Thyself, and our heart is restless, until it repose in Thee. Grant me, Lord, to know and understand which is first, to call on Thee or to praise Thee? and, again, to know Thee or to call on Thee? for who can call on Thee, not knowing Thee? for he that knoweth Thee not, may call on Thee as other than Thou art. Or, is it rather, that we call on Thee that we may know Thee? But *how shall they call on Him in whom they have not believed? or how shall they believe without a preacher?*[3] *and they that seek the Lord shall praise Him:*[4] for *they that seek shall find Him,*[5] and they that find shall praise Him. I will seek Thee, Lord, by calling on Thee; and will call on Thee, believing in Thee; for to us hast Thou been preached. My faith, Lord, shall call on Thee, which Thou hast given me, wherewith Thou hast inspired me, through the Incarnation of Thy Son, through the ministry of the Preacher.

And how shall I call upon my God, my God and Lord, since, when I call for Him, I shall be calling Him to myself? and what

[1] Ps. cxlv. 3; cxlvii. 5.   [2] Jas. iv. 6; 1 Pet. v. 5.   [3] Rom. x. 14.
[4] Ps. xxii. 26.   [5] Matt. vii. 7.

room is there within me, whither my God can come into me? whither can God come into me, God who made heaven and earth? is there, indeed, O Lord my God, aught in me that can contain Thee? do then heaven and earth, which Thou hast made, and wherein Thou hast made me, contain Thee? or, because nothing which exists could exist without Thee, doth therefore whatever exists contain Thee? Since, then, I too exist, why do I seek that Thou shouldest enter into me, who were not, wert Thou not in me? Why? because I am not gone down in hell, and yet Thou art there also. For *if I go down into hell, Thou art there.*[6] I could not be then, O my God, could not be at all, wert Thou not in me; or, rather, unless I were in Thee, *of whom are all things, by whom are all things, in whom are all things?*[7] Even so, Lord, even so. Whither do I call Thee, since I am in Thee? or whence canst Thou enter into me? for whither can I go beyond heaven and earth, that thence my God should come into me, who hath said, *I fill the heaven and the earth.*[8]

Do the heaven and earth then contain Thee, since thou fillest them? or dost Thou fill them and yet overflow, since they do not contain Thee? And whither, when the heaven and the earth are filled, pourest Thou forth the remainder of Thyself? or hast Thou no need that aught contain Thee, who containest all things, since what Thou fillest Thou fillest by containing it? for the vessels which Thou fillest uphold Thee not, since, though they were broken, Thou wert not poured out. And when Thou art *poured out*[9] on us, Thou art not cast down, but Thou upliftest us; Thou art not dissipated, but Thou gatherest us. But Thou who fillest all things, fillest Thou them with Thy whole self? or, since all things cannot contain Thee wholly, do they contain part of Thee? and all at once the same part? or each its own part, the greater more, the smaller less? And is, then, one part of Thee greater, another less? or, art Thou wholly everywhere, while nothing contains Thee wholly?

What art Thou then, my God? what, but the Lord God? *For who is Lord but the Lord? or who is God save our God?*[10] Most highest, most good, most potent, most omnipotent; most merciful, yet most just; most hidden, yet most present; most beautiful, yet

[6] Ps. cxxxix. 7. [7] Rom. xi. 36. [8] Jer. xxiii. 24. [9] Acts ii. 18. [10] Ps. xviii. 31.

most strong; stable, yet incomprehensible; unchangeable, yet all-changing; never new, never old; all-renewing, and *bringing age upon the proud, and they know it not;* ever working, ever at rest; still gathering, yet nothing lacking; supporting, filling, and over-spreading; creating, nourishing, and maturing; seeking, yet having all things. Thou lovest, without passion; art jealous, without anxiety; repentest, yet grievest not; art angry, yet serene; changest Thy works, Thy purpose unchanged; receivest again what Thou findest, yet didst never lose; never in need, yet rejoicing in gains; never covetous, yet exacting usury.[11] Thou receivest over and above, that Thou mayest owe; and who hath aught that is not Thine? Thou payest debts, owing nothing; remittest debts, losing nothing. And what have I now said, my God, my life, my holy joy? or what saith any man when he speaks of Thee? Yet woe to him that speaketh not, since mute are even the most eloquent.

Oh! that I might repose on Thee! Oh! that Thou wouldest enter into my heart, and inebriate it, that I may forget my ills, and embrace Thee, my sole good? What art Thou to me? In Thy pity, teach me to utter it. Or what am I to Thee that Thou demandest my love, and, if I give it not, art wroth with me, and threatenest me with grievous woes? Is it then a slight woe to love Thee not? Oh! for Thy mercies' sake, tell me, O Lord my God, what Thou art unto me. *Say unto my soul, I am thy salvation.*[12] So speak, that I may hear. Behold, Lord, my heart is before Thee; open Thou the ears thereof, and *say unto my soul, I am thy salvation.* After this voice let me haste, and take hold on Thee. Hide not Thy face from me. Let me die—lest I die—only let me see Thy face.

Narrow is the mansion of my soul; enlarge Thou it, that Thou mayest enter in. It is ruinous; repair Thou it. It has that within which must offend Thine eyes; I confess and know it. But who shall cleanse it? or to whom should I cry, save Thee? *Lord, cleanse me from my secret faults and spare Thy servant from the power of the enemy.*[13] *I believe, and therefore do I speak.*[14] Lord, Thou knowest. *Have I not confessed against myself my transgressions unto Thee, and Thou, my God, hast forgiven the iniquity of my heart?*[15] *I con-*

---

[11] Matt. xxv. 27, *supererogatur tibi.*   [12] Ps. xxxv. 3.   [13] Ps. xix. 12, 13.
[14] Ps. cxvi. 10.   [15] Ps. xxxii. 5.

tend not in judgment with Thee,[16] who art the truth; I fear to deceive myself; *lest mine iniquity lie unto itself.*[17] Therefore I contend not in judgment with Thee; *for if Thou, Lord, shouldest mark iniquities, O Lord, who shall abide it?*[18]

Yet suffer me to speak unto Thy mercy, me, *dust and ashes.*[19] Yet suffer me to speak, since I speak to Thy mercy, and not to scornful man. Thou too, perhaps, despisest me, yet wilt Thou *return and have compassion*[20] upon me. For what would I say, O Lord my God, but that I know not whence I came into this dying life (shall I call it?) or living death. Then immediately did the comforts of Thy compassion take me up, as I heard (for I remember it not) from the parents of my flesh, out of whose substance Thou didst sometime fashion me. Thus there received me the comforts of woman's milk. For neither my mother nor my nurses stored their own breasts for me; but Thou didst bestow the food of my infancy through them, according to Thine ordinance, whereby Thou distributest Thy riches through the hidden springs of all things. Thou also gavest me to desire no more than Thou gavest; and to my nurses willingly to give me what Thou gavest them. For they, with a heaven-taught affection, willingly gave me what they abounded with from Thee. For this my good from them, was good for them. Nor, indeed, from them was it, but through them; for from Thee, O God, are all good things, and *from my God is all my health*. This I since learned, Thou, through these Thy gifts, within me and without, proclaiming Thyself unto me. For then I knew but to suck; to repose in what pleased, and cry at what offended my flesh; nothing more.

Afterwards I began to smile; first in sleep, then waking: for so it was told me of myself, and I believed it; for we see the like in other infants, though of myself I remember it not. Thus, little by little, I became conscious where I was; and to have a wish to express my wishes to those who could content them, and I could not; for the wishes were within me, and they without; nor could they by any sense of theirs enter within my spirit. So I flung about at random limbs and voice, making the few signs I could, and such as I could, like, though in truth very little like, what I wished. And when I was not presently obeyed (my wishes being hurtful or unintelligible),

[16] Job ix. 3.   [17] Ps. xxvi. 12.—Vulg.   [18] Ps. cxxx. 3.   [19] Gen. xviii. 27.   [20] Jer. xii. 15.

then I was indignant with my elders for not submitting to me, with those owing me no service, for not serving me; and avenged myself on them by tears. Such have I learnt infants to be from observing them; and that I was myself such, they, all unconscious, have shown me better than my nurses who knew it.

And, lo! my infancy died long since, and I live. But Thou, Lord, who for ever livest, and in whom nothing dies: for before the foundation of the worlds, and before all that can be called "before," Thou art, and art God and Lord of all which Thou hast created: in Thee abide, fixed for ever, the first causes of all things unabiding; and of all things changeable, the springs abide in Thee unchangeable: and in Thee live the eternal reasons of all things unreasoning and temporal. Say, Lord, to me, Thy suppliant; say, all-pitying, to me, Thy pitiable one; say, did my infancy succeed another age of mine that died before it? was it that which I spent within my mother's womb? for of that I have heard somewhat, and have myself seen women with child? and what before that life again, O God my joy, was I any where or any body? For this have I none to tell me, neither father nor mother, nor experience of others, nor mine own memory. Dost Thou mock me for asking this, and bid me praise Thee and acknowledge Thee, for that I do know?

I acknowledge Thee, Lord of heaven and earth, and praise Thee for my first rudiments of being, and my infancy, whereof I remember nothing; for Thou hast appointed that man should from others guess much as to himself; and believe much on the strength of weak females. Even then I had being and life, and (at my infancy's close) I could seek for signs whereby to make known to others my sensations. Whence could such a being be, save from Thee, Lord? Shall any be his own artificer? or can there elsewhere be derived any vein, which may stream essence and life into us, save from Thee, O Lord, in whom essence and life are one? for Thou Thyself art supremely Essence and Life. *For Thou art most high, and art not changed,*[21] neither in Thee doth to-day come to a close; yet in Thee doth it come to a close; because all such things also are in Thee. For they had no way to pass away, unless Thou upheldest them. And since *Thy years fail not,*[22] Thy years are one to-day. How many

[21] Mal. iii. 6.   [22] Ps. cii. 27.

of ours and our fathers' years have flowed away through Thy "to-day," and from it received the measure and the mould of such being as they had; and still others shall flow away, and so receive the mould of their degree of being. But *Thou art still the same,*[23] and all things of to-morrow, and all beyond, and all of yesterday, and all behind it, Thou hast done to-day. What is it to me, though any comprehend not this? Let him also rejoice and say, *What thing is this.*[24] Let him rejoice even thus; and be content rather by not discovering to discover Thee, than by discovering not to discover Thee.

Hear, O God. Alas, for man's sin! So saith man, and Thou pitiest him; for Thou madest him, but sin in him Thou madest not. Who remindeth me of the sins of my infancy? *for in Thy sight none is pure from sin, not even the infant whose life is but a day upon the earth.*[25] Who remindeth me? doth not each little infant, in whom I see what of myself I remember not? What then was my sin? was it that I hung upon the breast and cried? for should I now so do for food suitable to my age, justly should I be laughed at and reproved. What I then did was worthy reproof; but since I could not understand reproof, custom and reason forbade me to be reproved. For those habits, when grown, we root out and cast away. Now no man, though he prunes, wittingly casts away what is good.[26] Or was it then good, even for a while, to cry for what, if given, would hurt? bitterly to resent, that persons free, and its own elders, yea, the very authors of its birth, served it not? that many besides, wiser than it, obeyed not the nod of its good pleasure? to do its best to strike and hurt, because commands were not obeyed, which had been obeyed to its hurt? The weakness then of infant limbs, not its will, is its innocence. Myself have seen and known even a baby envious; it could not speak, yet it turned pale and looked bitterly on its foster-brother. Who knows not this? Mothers and nurses tell you that they allay these things by I know not what remedies. Is that too innocence, when the fountain of milk is flowing in rich abundance, not to endure one to share it, though in extremest need, and whose very life as yet depends thereon? We bear gently with all this, not as being no or slight evils, but because they will disappear as years

[23] Ps. cii. 27.   [24] Exod. xvi. 15.   [25] Job xxv. 4.   [26] John xv. 2.

increase; for, though tolerated now, the very same tempers are utterly intolerable when found in riper years.

Thou, then, O Lord my God, who gavest life to this my infancy, furnishing thus with senses (as we see) the frame Thou gavest, compacting its limbs, ornamenting its proportions, and for its general good and safety, implanting in it all vital functions, Thou commandest me to praise Thee in these things, *to confess unto Thee, and sing unto Thy name, Thou most Highest.*[27] For Thou art God, Almighty and Good, even hadst Thou done nought but only this, which none could do but Thou; whose Unity is the mould of all things; who out of Thy own fairness makest all things fair; and orderest all things by Thy law. This age, then, Lord, whereof I have no remembrance, which I take on others' word, and guess from other infants that I have passed, true though the guess be, I am yet loth to count in this life of mine which I live in this world. For no less than that which I spent in my mother's womb, is it hid from me in the shadows of forgetfulness. But if *I was shapen in iniquity, and in sin did my mother conceive me,*[28] where, I beseech Thee, O my God, where, Lord, or when, was I Thy servant guiltless? But, lo! that period I pass by; and what have I now to do with that, of which I can recall no vestige?

Passing hence from infancy, I came to boyhood, or rather it came to me, displacing infancy. Nor did that depart,—(for whither went it?)—and yet it was no more. For I was no longer a speechless infant, but a speaking boy. This I remember; and have since observed how I learned to speak. It was not that my elders taught me words (as, soon after, other learning) in any set method; but I, longing by cries and broken accents and various motions of my limbs to express my thoughts, that so I might have my will, and yet unable to express all I willed, or to whom I willed, did myself, by the understanding which Thou, my God, gavest me, practise the sounds in my memory. When they named any thing, and as they spoke turned towards it, I saw and remembered that they called what they would point out by the name they uttered. And that they meant this thing and no other was plain from the motion of their body, the natural language, as it were, of all nations, expressed by the

[27] Ps. xcii. 1.   [28] Ps. li. 7.

countenance, glances of the eye, gestures of the limbs, and tones of the voice, indicating the affections of the mind, as it pursues, possesses, rejects, or shuns. And thus by constantly hearing words, as they occurred in various sentences, I collected gradually for what they stood; and having broken in my mouth to these signs, I thereby gave utterance to my will. Thus I exchanged with those about me these current signs of our wills, and so launched deeper into the stormy intercourse of human life, yet depending on parental authority and the beck of elders.

O God my God, what miseries and mockeries did I now experience, when obedience to my teachers was proposed to me, as proper in a boy, in order that in this world I might prosper, and excel in tongue-science, which should serve to the "praise of men," and to deceitful riches. Next I was put to school to get learning, in which I (poor wretch) knew not what use there was; and yet, if idle in learning, I was beaten. For this was judged right by our forefathers; and many, passing the same course before us, framed for us weary paths, through which we were fain to pass; multiplying toil and grief upon the sons of Adam. But, Lord, we found that men called upon Thee, and we learnt from them to think of Thee (according to our powers) as of some great One, who, though hidden from our senses, couldst hear and help us. For so I began, as a boy, to pray to Thee, my aid and refuge; and broke the fetters of my tongue to call on Thee, praying Thee, though small, yet with no small earnestness, that I might not be beaten at school. And when Thou heardst me not (*not thereby giving me over to folly*[29]), my elders, yea, my very parents, who yet wished me no ill, mocked my stripes, my then great and grievous ill.

Is there, Lord, any of soul so great, and cleaving to Thee with so intense affection (for a sort of stupidity will in a way do it); but is there any one who, from cleaving devoutly to Thee, is endued with so great a spirit, that he can think as lightly of the racks and hooks and other torments (against which, throughout all lands, men call on Thee with extreme dread), mocking at those by whom they are feared most bitterly, as our parents mocked the torments which we suffered in boyhood from our masters? For we feared not our tor-

[29] Ps. xxi. 3.—Vulg.

ments less; nor prayed we less to Thee to escape them. And yet we sinned, in writing or reading or studying less than was exacted of us. For we wanted not, O Lord, memory or capacity, whereof Thy will gave enough for our age; but our sole delight was play; and for this we were punished by those who yet themselves were doing the like. But elder folks' idleness is called "business"; that of boys, being really the same, is punished by those elders; and none commiserates either boys or men. For will any of sound discretion approve of my being beaten as a boy, because, by playing at ball, I made less progress in studies which I was to learn, only that, as a man, I might play more unbeseemingly? and what else did he who beat me? who, if worsted in some trifling discussion with his fellow-tutor, was more embittered and jealous than I when beaten at ball by a play-fellow?

And yet, I sinned herein, O Lord God, the Creator and Disposer of all things in nature, of sin the Disposer[30] only, O Lord my God, I sinned in transgressing the commands of my parents and those my masters. For what they, with whatever motive, would have me learn, I might afterwards have put to good use. For I disobeyed, not from a better choice, but from love of play, loving the pride of victory in my contests, and to have my ears tickled with lying fables, that they might itch the more; the same curiosity flashing from my eyes more and more, for the shows and games of my elders. Yet those who give these shows are in such esteem, that almost all wish the same for their children, and yet are very willing that they should be beaten, if those very games detain them from the studies, whereby they would have them attain to be the givers of them. Look with pity, Lord, on these things, and deliver us who call upon Thee now; deliver those too who call not on Thee yet, that they may call on Thee, and Thou mayest deliver them.

As a boy, then, I had already heard of an eternal life, promised us through the humility of the Lord our God stooping to our pride; and even from the womb of my mother, who greatly hoped in Thee, I was sealed with the mark of His cross and salted with His salt. Thou sawest, Lord, how while yet a boy, being seized on a time with sudden oppression of the stomach, and like near to death—Thou

[30] Ordinator.

sawest, my God (for Thou wert my keeper), with what eagerness
and what faith I sought, from the pious care of my mother and Thy
Church, the mother of us all, the baptism of Thy Christ my God and
Lord. Whereupon the mother of my flesh, being much troubled
(since, with a heart pure in Thy faith, she even more lovingly *tra-
vailed in birth*[31] of my salvation), would in eager haste have provided
for my consecration and cleansing by the health-giving sacraments,
confessing Thee, Lord Jesus, for the remission of sins, unless I had
suddenly recovered. And so, as if I must needs be again polluted
should I live, my cleansing was deferred, because the defilements of
sin would, after that washing, bring greater and more perilous guilt.
I then already believed: and my mother, and the whole household
except my father: yet did not he prevail over the power of my
mother's piety in me, that as he did not yet believe, so neither should
I. For it was her earnest care that Thou my God, rather than he,
shouldest be my father; and in this Thou didst aid her to prevail
over her husband, whom she, the better, obeyed, therein also obeying Thee, who hast so commanded.

I beseech Thee, my God, I would fain know, if so Thou willest,
for what purpose my baptism was then deferred? was it for my good
that the rein was laid loose, as it were, upon me, for me to sin? or
was it not laid loose? If not, why does it still echo in our ears on
all sides, "Let him alone, let him do as he will, for he is not yet
baptised?" but as to bodily health, no one says, "Let him be worse
wounded, for he is not yet healed." How much better then, had I
been at once healed; and then by my friends' diligence and my own,
my soul's recovered health had been kept safe in Thy keeping who
gavest it. Better truly. But how many and great waves of temptation seemed to hang over me after my boyhood! These my mother
foresaw; and preferred to expose to them the clay whence I might
afterwards be moulded, than the very cast, when made.

In boyhood itself, however (so much less dreaded for me than
youth), I loved not study, and hated to be forced to it. Yet I was
forced; and this was well done towards me, but I did not well; for,
unless forced, I had not learnt. But no one doth well against his
will, even though what he doth, be well. Yet neither did they well

[31] Gal. iv. 19.

who forced me, but what was well came to me from Thee, my God. For they were regardless how I should employ what they forced me to learn, except to satiate the insatiate desires of a wealthy beggary, and a shameful glory. But Thou, *by whom the very hairs of our head are numbered*,[32] didst use for my good the error of all who urged me to learn; and my own, who would not learn, Thou didst use for my punishment—a fit penalty for one, so small a boy and so great a sinner. So by those who did not well, Thou didst well for me; and by my own sin Thou didst justly punish me. For Thou hast commanded, and so it is, that every inordinate affection should be its own punishment.

But why did I so much hate the Greek, which I studied as a boy? I do not yet fully know. For the Latin I loved; not what my first masters, but what the so-called grammarians taught me. For those first lessons, reading, writing, and arithmetic, I thought as great a burden and penalty as any Greek. And yet whence was this too, but from the sin and vanity of this life, because *I was flesh, and a breath that passeth away and cometh not again?*[33] For those first lessons were better certainly, because more certain; by them I obtained, and still retain, the power of reading what I find written and myself writing what I will; whereas in the others, I was forced to learn the wanderings of one Æneas, forgetful of my own, and to weep for dead Dido, because she killed herself for love; the while, with dry eyes, I endured my miserable self dying among these things, far from Thee, O God my life.

For what more miserable than a miserable being who commiserates not himself; weeping the death of Dido for love to Æneas, but weeping not his own death for want of love to Thee, O God. Thou light of my heart, Thou bread of my inmost soul, Thou Power who givest vigour to my mind, who quickenest my thoughts, I loved Thee not. I committed fornication against Thee, and all around me thus fornicating there echoed, "Well done! well done!" *for the friendship of this world is fornication against Thee;*[34] and "Well done! well done!" echoes on till one is ashamed to be thus a man. And all this I wept not, I who wept for Dido slain, and "seeking by the sword a stroke and wound extreme," myself seeking the while a

[32] Matt. x. 30.   [33] Ps. lxxviii. 39.   [34] Jam. iv. 4.

worse extreme, the extremest and lowest of Thy creatures, having forsaken Thee, earth passing into the earth. And if forbid to read all this, I was grieved that I might not read what grieved me. Madness like this is thought a higher and a richer learning, than that by which I learned to read and write.

But now, my God, cry Thou aloud in my soul; and let Thy truth tell me, "Not so, not so. Far better was that first study." For, lo, I would readily forget the wanderings of Æneas and all the rest, rather than how to read and write. But over the entrance of the Grammar School is a veil drawn! true; yet is this not so much an emblem of aught recondite, as a cloak of error. Let not those, whom I no longer fear, cry out against me, while I confess to Thee, my God, whatever my soul will, and acquiesce in the condemnation of my evil ways, that I may love Thy good ways. Let not either buyers or sellers of grammar-learning cry out against me. For if I question them whether it be true that Æneas came on a time to Carthage, as the poet tells, the less learned will reply that they know not, the more learned that he never did. But should I ask with what letters the name "Æneas" is written, every one who has learnt this will answer me aright, as to the signs which men have conventionally settled. If again, I should ask which might be forgotten with least detriment to the concerns of life, reading and writing or these poetic fictions? who does not foresee what all must answer who have not wholly forgotten themselves? I sinned, then, when as a boy I preferred those empty to those more profitable studies, or rather loved the one and hated the other. "One and one, two;" "two and two, four;" this was to me a hateful singsong: "the wooden horse lined with armed men," and "the burning of Troy,"[35] and "Creusa's shade and sad similitude," were the choice spectacle of my vanity.

Why then did I hate the Greek classics, which have the like tales? For Homer also curiously wove the like fictions, and is most sweetly-vain, yet was he bitter to my boyish taste. And so I suppose would Virgil be to Grecian children, when forced to learn him as I was Homer. Difficulty, in truth, the difficulty of a foreign tongue, dashed, as it were, with gall all the sweetness of Grecian fable. For not one word of it did I understand, and to make me understand I

[35] *Æn.* 2.

was urged vehemently with cruel threats and punishments. Time was also (as an infant) I knew no Latin; but this I learned without fear or suffering, by mere observation, amid the caresses of my nursery and jests of friends, smiling and sportively encouraging me. This I learned without any pressure of punishment to urge me on, for my heart urged me to give birth to its conceptions which I could only do by learning words not of those who taught, but of those who talked with me; in whose ears also I gave birth to the thoughts, whatever I conceived. No doubt, then, that a free curiosity has more force in our learning these things, than a frightful enforcement. Only this enforcement restrains the rovings of that freedom, through Thy laws, O my God, Thy laws, from the master's cane to the martyr's trials, being able to temper for us a wholesome bitter, recalling us to Thyself from that deathly pleasure which lures us from Thee.

Hear, Lord, my prayer; let not my soul faint under Thy discipline, nor let me faint in confessing unto Thee all Thy mercies, whereby Thou hast drawn me out of all my most evil ways, that Thou mightest become a delight to me above all the allurements which I once pursued; that I may most entirely love Thee, and clasp Thy hand with all my affections, and Thou mayest yet rescue me from every temptation, even unto the end. For, lo, O Lord, my King and my God, for Thy service be whatever useful thing my childhood learned; for Thy service, that I speak, write, read, reckon. For Thou didst grant me Thy discipline, while I was learning vanities; and my sin of delighting in those vanities Thou hast forgiven. In them, indeed, I learnt many a useful word, but these may as well be learned in things not vain; and that is the safe path for the steps of youth.

But woe is thee, thou torrent of human custom! Who shall stand against thee? how long shalt thou not be dried up? how long roll the sons of Eve into that huge and hideous ocean, which even they scarcely overpass who climb the cross? Did not I read in thee of Jove the thunderer and the adulterer? both, doubtless, he could not be; but so the feigned thunder might countenance and pander to real adultery. And now which of our gowned masters lends a sober ear to one who from their own school cries out, "These were Homer's fictions, transferring things human to the gods; would he had

brought down things divine to us!" Yet more truly had he said,
"These are indeed his fictions; but attributing a divine nature to
wicked men, that crimes might be no longer crimes, and whoso com-
mits them might seem to imitate not abandoned men, but the
celestial gods."

And yet, thou hellish torrent, into thee are cast the sons of men
with rich rewards, for compassing such learning; and a great solem-
nity is made of it, when this is going on in the forum, within sight
of laws appointing a salary beside the scholar's payments, and thou
lashest thy rocks and roarest, "Hence words are learnt; hence eloquence; most necessary to gain your ends, or maintain opinions." As
if we should have never known such words as "golden shower,"
"lap," "beguile," "temples of the heavens," or others in that passage,
unless Terence had brought a lewd youth upon the stage, setting up
Jupiter as his example of seduction.

> "Viewing a picture, where the tale was drawn,
>   Of Jove's descending in a golden shower
>   To Danae's lap, a woman to beguile."

And then mark how he excites himself to lust as by celestial authority:

> "And what God? Great Jove,
>   Who shakes heaven's highest temples with his thunder,
>   And I, poor mortal man, not do the same!
>   I did it, and with all my heart I did it."

Not one whit more easily are the words learnt for all this vileness;
but by their means the vileness is committed with less shame. Not
that I blame the words, being, as it were, choice and precious vessels;
but that wine of error which is drunk to us in them by intoxicated
teachers; and if we, too, drink not, we are beaten, and have no sober
judge to whom we may appeal. Yet, O my God (in whose presence I now without hurt may remember this), all this unhappily I
learnt willingly with great delight, and for this was pronounced a
hopeful boy.

Bear with me, my God, while I say somewhat of my wit, Thy gift,
and on what dotage I wasted it. For a task was set me, troublesome
enough to my soul, upon terms of praise or shame, and fear of stripes,

to speak the words of Juno, as she raged and mourned that she could not

"This Trojan prince from Latium turn."

Which words I had heard that Juno never uttered; but we were forced to go astray in the footsteps of these poetic fictions, and to say in prose much what he expressed in verse. And his speaking was most applauded, in whom the passions of rage and grief were most pre-eminent, and clothed in the most fitting language, maintaining the dignity of the character. What is it to me, O my true life, my God, that my declamation was applauded above so many of my own age and class? is not all this smoke and wind? and was there nothing else whereon to exercise my wit and tongue? Thy praises, Lord, Thy praises might have stayed the yet tender shoot of my heart by the prop of Thy Scriptures; so had it not trailed away amid these empty trifles, a defiled prey for the fowls of the air. For in more ways than one do men sacrifice to the rebellious angels.

But what marvel that I was thus carried away to vanities, and went from Thy presence, O my God, when men were set before me as models, who, if in relating some action of theirs, in itself not ill, they committed some barbarism or solecism, being censured, were abashed; but when in rich and adorned and well-ordered discourse they related their own disordered life, being bepraised, they gloried? These things Thou seest, Lord, and holdest Thy peace; *long-suffering, and plenteous in mercy and truth.*[36] Wilt Thou hold Thy peace for ever? and even now Thou drawest out of this horrible gulf the soul that seeketh Thee, that thirsteth for Thy pleasures, *whose heart saith unto Thee, I have sought Thy face; Thy face, Lord, will I seek.*[37] For *darkened*[38] affections is removal from Thee. For it is not by our feet, or change of place, that men leave Thee, or return unto Thee. Or did that Thy younger son look out for horses or chariots, or ships, fly with visible wings, or journey by the motion of his limbs, that he might in a far country waste in riotous living all Thou gavest at his departure? a loving Father, when Thou gavest, and more loving unto him, when he returned empty. So then in lustful, that is, in darkened affections, is the true distance from Thy face.

[36] Ps. lxxxvi. 15.   [37] Ps. xxvii. 8.   [38] Rom. i. 21.

Behold, O Lord God, yea, behold patiently as Thou art wont, how carefully the sons of men observe the covenanted rules of letters and syllables received from those who spake before them, neglecting the eternal covenant of everlasting salvation received from Thee. Insomuch, that a teacher or learner of the hereditary laws of pronunciation will more offend men by speaking without the aspirate, of a *"uman* being," in despite of the laws of grammar, than if he, a "human being," hate a "human being" in despite of Thine. As if any enemy could be more hurtful than the hatred with which he is incensed against him; or could wound more deeply him whom he persecutes, than he wounds his own soul by his enmity. Assuredly no science of letters can be so innate as the record of conscience, "that he is doing to another what from another he would be loath to suffer." How deep are Thy ways, O God, Thou only great, *that sittest* silent on high[39] and by an unwearied law dispensing penal blindness to lawless desires. In quest of the fame of eloquence, a man standing before a human judge, surrounded by a human throng, declaiming against his enemy with fiercest hatred, will take heed most watchfully, lest, by an error of the tongue, he murder the word "human being"; but takes no heed, lest, through the fury of his spirit, he murder the real human being.

This was the world at whose gate unhappy I lay in my boyhood; this the stage where I had feared more to commit a barbarism, than having committed one, to envy those who had not. These things I speak and confess to Thee, my God; for which I had praise from them, whom I then thought it all virtue to please. For I saw not the abyss of vileness, wherein *I was cast away from Thine eyes.*[40] Before them what more foul than I was already, displeasing even such as myself? with innumerable lies deceiving my tutor, my masters, my parents, from love of play, eagerness to see vain shows and restlessness to imitate them! Thefts also I committed, from my parents' cellar and table, enslaved by greediness, or that I might have to give to boys, who sold me their play, which all the while they liked no less than I. In this play, too, I often sought unfair conquests, conquered myself meanwhile by vain desire of pre-eminence. And what could I so ill endure, or, when I detected it, upbraided I so fiercely,

---

[39] Is. xxxiii. 3.   [40] Ps. xxxi. 22.

as that I was doing to others? and for which if, detected, I was up-braided, I chose rather to quarrel than to yield. And is this the inno-cence of boyhood? Not so, Lord, not so; I cry Thy mercy, O my God. For these very sins, as riper years succeed, these very sins are transferred from tutors and masters, from nuts and balls and spar-rows, to magistrates and kings, to gold and manors and slaves, just as severer punishments displace the cane. It was the low stature then of childhood which Thou our King didst commend as an emblem of lowliness, when Thou saidst, *Of such is the kingdom of heaven.*[41]

Yet, Lord, to Thee, the Creator and Governor of the universe, most excellent and most good, thanks were due to Thee our God, even hadst Thou destined for me boyhood only. For even then I was, I lived, and felt; and had implanted providence over my well-being—a trace of that mysterious Unity whence I was derived: I guarded by the inward sense the entireness of my senses, and in these minute pursuits, and in my thoughts on things minute, I learnt to delight in truth, I hated to be deceived, had a vigorous memory, was gifted with speech, was soothed by friendship, avoided pain, base-ness, ignorance. In so small a creature, what was not wonderful, not admirable? But all are gifts of my God: it was not I who gave them me; and good these are, and these together are myself. Good, then, is He that made me, and He is my good; and before Him will I exult for every good which of a boy I had. For it was my sin, that not in Him, but in His creatures—myself and others—I sought for pleasures, sublimities, truths, and so fell headlong into sorrows, con-fusions, errors. Thanks be to Thee, my joy and my glory and my confidence, my God, thanks be to Thee for Thy gifts; but do Thou preserve them to me. For so wilt Thou preserve me, and those things shall be enlarged and perfected which Thou hast given me, and I myself shall be with Thee, since even to be Thou hast given me.

[41] Matt. xix. 14.

THE SECOND BOOK

Object of these Confessions. Further ills of idleness developed in his sixteenth year. Evils of ill society, which betrayed him into theft.

I WILL now call to mind my past foulness, and the carnal corruptions of my soul; not because I love them, but that I may love Thee, O my God. For love of Thy love I do it; reviewing my most wicked ways in the very bitterness of my remembrance, that Thou mayest grow sweet unto me (Thou sweetness never failing, Thou blissful and assured sweetness); and gathering me again out of that my dissipation, wherein I was torn piecemeal, while turned from Thee, the One Good, I lost myself among a multiplicity of things. For I even burnt in my youth heretofore, to be satiated in things below; and I dared to grow wild again, with these various and shadowy loves: *my beauty consumed away,* and I stank in Thine eyes; pleasing myself, and desirous to please in the eyes of men.

And what was it that I delighted in, but to love, and be beloved? but I kept not the measure of love, of mind to mind, friendship's bright boundary: but out of the muddy concupiscence of the flesh, and the bubblings of youth, mists fumed up which beclouded and overcast my heart, that I could not discern the clear brightness of love from the fog of lustfulness. Both did confusedly boil in me, and hurried my unstayed youth over the precipice of unholy desires, and sunk me in a gulf of flagitiousnesses. Thy wrath had gathered over me, and I knew it not. I was grown deaf by the clanking of the chain of my mortality, the punishment of the pride of my soul, and I strayed further from Thee, and Thou lettest me alone, and I was tossed about, and wasted, and dissipated, and I boiled over in my fornications, and Thou heldest Thy peace, O Thou my tardy joy! Thou then heldest Thy peace, and I wandered further and further from Thee, into more and more fruitless seed-plots of sorrows, with a proud dejectedness, and a restless weariness.

22

Oh! that some one had then attempered my disorder, and turned to account the fleeting beauties of these, the extreme points of Thy creation! had put a bound to their pleasureableness, that so the tides of my youth might have cast themselves upon the marriage shore, if they could not be calmed, and kept within the object of a family, as Thy law prescribes, O Lord: who this way formest the offspring of this our death, being able with a gentle hand to blunt the thorns which were excluded from Thy paradise? For Thy omnipotency is not far from us, even when we be far from Thee. Else ought I more watchfully to have heeded the voice from the clouds: *Nevertheless such shall have trouble in the flesh, but I spare you.*[1] And *it is good for a man not to touch a woman.*[2] And, *he that is unmarried thinketh of the things of the Lord, how he may please the Lord; but he that is married careth for the things of this world, how he may please his wife.*[3]

To these words I should have listened more attentively, and being severed *for the kingdom of heaven's sake,*[4] had more happily awaited Thy embraces; but I, poor wretch, foamed like a troubled sea, following the rushing of my own tide, forsaking Thee, and exceeded all Thy limits; yet I escaped not Thy scourges. For what mortal can? For Thou wert ever with me mercifully rigorous, and besprinkling with most bitter alloy all my unlawful pleasures: that I might seek pleasures without alloy. But where to find such, I could not discover, save in Thee, O Lord, who *teachest by sorrow,* and woundest us, to heal; and killest us, lest we die from Thee.[5] Where was I, and how far was I exiled from the delights of Thy house, in that sixteenth year of the age of my flesh, when the madness of lust (to which human shamelessness giveth free licence, though unlicensed by Thy laws) took the rule over me, and I resigned myself wholly to it? My friends meanwhile took no care by marriage to save my fall; their only care was that I should learn to speak excellently, and be a persuasive orator.

For that year were my studies intermitted: whilst after my return from Madaura (a neighbour city, whither I had journeyed to learn grammar and rhetoric), the expenses for a further journey to Carthage were being provided for me; and that, rather by the resolution

[1] Cor. vii. 28   [2] Ver. 1.   [3] Ver. 32, 33.   [4] Matt. xix. 12.   [5] Deut. xxxii. 29.

than the means of my father, who was but a poor freeman of Thagaste. To whom tell I this? not to Thee, my God; but before Thee to mine own kind, even to that small portion of mankind as may light upon these writings of mine. And to what purpose? that whosoever reads this, may think *out of what depths we are to cry unto Thee*.[6] For what is nearer to Thine ears than a confessing heart, and a life of faith? Who did not extol my father, for that beyond the ability of his means, he would furnish his son with all necessaries for a far journey for his studies' sake? For many far abler citizens did no such thing for their children. But yet this same father had no concern how I grew towards Thee, or how chaste I were; so that I were but copious in speech, however barren I were to Thy culture, O God, who art the only true and good Lord of Thy field, my heart.

But while in that my sixteenth year I lived with my parents, leaving all school for a while (a season of idleness being interposed through the narrowness of my parents' fortunes), the briers of unclean desires grew rank over my head, and there was no hand to root them out. When that my father saw me at the baths, now growing towards manhood, and endued with a restless youthfulness, he, as already hence anticipating his descendants, gladly told it to my mother; rejoicing in that tumult of the senses wherein the world forgetteth Thee its Creator, and becometh enamoured of Thy creature, instead of Thyself, through the fumes of that invisible wine of its self-will, turning aside and bowing down to the very basest things. But in my mother's breast Thou hadst already begun Thy temple, and the foundation of Thy holy habitation, whereas my father was as yet but a catechumen, and that but recently. She then was startled with a holy fear and trembling; and though I was not as yet baptised, feared for me those crooked ways in which they walk who *turn their back to Thee, and not their face*.[7]

Woe is me! and dare I say that Thou heldest Thy peace, O my God, while I wandered further from Thee? Didst Thou then indeed hold Thy peace to me? And whose but Thine were these words which by my mother, Thy faithful one, Thou sangest in my ears? Nothing whereof sunk into my heart, so as to do it. For she wished, and I remember in private with great anxiety warned me, "not to

[6] Ps. cxxx. 1.   [7] Jer. ii. 27.

commit fornication; but especially never to defile another man's wife." These seemed to me womanish advices, which I should blush to obey. But they were Thine, and I knew it not: and I thought Thou wert silent and that it was she who spake; by whom Thou wert not silent unto me; and in her wast despised by me, her son, *the son of Thy handmaid, Thy servant.*[8] But I knew it not; and ran headlong with such blindness, that amongst my equals I was ashamed of a less shamelessness, when I heard them boast of their flagitiousness, yea, and the more boasting, the more they were degraded: and I took pleasure, not only in the pleasure of the deed, but in the praise. What is worthy of dispraise but vice? But I made myself worse than I was, that I might not be dispraised; and when in any thing I had not sinned as the abandoned ones, I would say that I had done what I had not done, that I might not seem contemptible in proportion as I was innocent; or of less account, the more chaste.

Behold with what companions I walked the streets of Babylon, and wallowed in the mire thereof, as if in a bed of spices and precious ointments. And that I might cleave the faster to its very centre, the invisible enemy trod me down, and seduced me, for that I was easy to be seduced. Neither did the mother of my flesh (who had now *fled out of the centre of Babylon,*[9] yet went more slowly in the skirts thereof), as she advised me to chastity, so heed what she had heard of me from her husband, as to restrain within the bounds of conjugal affection (if it could not be pared away to the quick) what she felt to be pestilent at present and for the future dangerous. She heeded not this, for she feared lest a wife should prove a clog and hindrance to my hopes. Not those hopes of the world to come, which my mother reposed in Thee; but the hope of learning, which both my parents were too desirous I should attain; my father, because he had next to no thought of Thee, and of me but vain conceits; my mother, because she accounted that those usual courses of learning would not only be no hindrance, but even some furtherance towards attaining Thee. For thus I conjecture, recalling, as well as I may, the disposition of my parents. The reins, meantime, were slackened to me, beyond all temper of due severity, to spend my time in sport, yea, even unto dissoluteness in whatsoever I affected. And in all

[8] Ps. cxvi. 16.   [9] Jer. li. 6.

was a mist, intercepting from me, O my God, the brightness of Thy truth; and *mine iniquity burst out as from very fatness.*[10]

Theft is punished by Thy Law, O Lord, and the law written in the hearts of men, which iniquity itself effaces not. For what thief will abide a thief? not even a rich thief, one stealing through want. Yet I lusted to thieve, and did it, compelled by no hunger, nor poverty, but through a cloyedness of well-doing, and a pamperedness of iniquity. For I stole that, of which I had enough, and much better. Nor cared I to enjoy what I stole, but joyed in the theft and sin itself. A pear tree there was near our vineyard, laden with fruit, tempting neither for colour nor taste. To shake and rob this, some lewd young fellows of us went, late one night (having according to our pestilent custom prolonged our sports in the streets till then), and took huge loads, not for our eating, but to fling to the very hogs, having only tasted them. And this, but to do what we liked only, because it was misliked. Behold my heart, O God, behold my heart, which Thou hadst pity upon in the bottom of the bottomless pit. Now, behold let my heart tell Thee what it sought there, that I should be gratuitously evil, having no temptation to ill, but the ill itself. It was foul, and I loved it; I loved to perish, I loved mine own fault, not that for which I was faulty, but my fault itself, Foul soul, falling from Thy firmament to utter destruction: not seeking aught through the shame, but the shame itself!

For there is an attractiveness in beautiful bodies, in gold and silver, and all things; and in bodily touch, sympathy hath much influence, and each other sense hath his proper object answerably tempered. Worldly honour hath also its grace, and the power of overcoming, and of mastery; whence springs also the thirst for revenge. But yet, to obtain all these, we may not depart from Thee, O Lord, nor decline from Thy law. The life also which here we live hath its own enchantment, through a certain proportion of its own, and a correspondence with all things beautiful here below. Human friendship also is endeared with a sweet tie by reason of the unity formed of many souls. Upon occasion of all these, and the like, is sin committed, while through an immoderate inclination towards these goods of the lowest order, the better and higher are forsaken,—Thou,

[10] Ps. lxxiii. 7.

our Lord God, Thy truth, and Thy law. For these lower things have their delights, but not like my God, who made all things; for *in Him doth the righteous delight, and He is the joy of the upright in heart.*[11]

When, then, we ask why a crime was done, we believe it not, unless it appear that there might have been some desire of obtaining some of those which we called lower goods, or a fear of losing them. For they are beautiful and comely; although compared with those higher and beatific goods, they be abject and low. A man hath murdered another; why? he loved his wife or his estate; or would rob for his own livelihood; or feared to lose some such things by him; or, wronged, was on fire to be revenged. Would any commit murder upon no cause, delighted simply in murdering? who would believe it? for as for that furious and savage man, of whom it is said that he was gratuitously evil and cruel, yet is the cause assigned; "lest" (saith he) "through idleness hand or heart should grow inactive." And to what end? that, through that practice of guilt, he might, having taken the city, attain to honours, empire, riches, and be freed from fear of the laws, and his embarrassments from domestic needs, and consciousness of villainies. So then, not even Catiline himself loved his own villainies, but something else, for whose sake he did them.

What then did wretched I so love in thee, thou theft of mine, thou deed of darkness, in that sixteenth year of my age? Lovely thou wert not, because thou wert theft. But art thou any thing, that thus I speak to thee? Fair were the pears we stole, because they were Thy creation, Thou fairest of all, Creator of all, Thou good God; God, the sovereign good and my true good. Fair were those pears, but not them did my wretched soul desire; for I had store of better, and those I gathered, only that I might steal. For, when gathered, I flung them away, my only feast therein being my own sin, which I was pleased to enjoy. For if aught of those pears came within my mouth, what sweetened it was the sin. And now, O Lord my God, I enquire what in that theft delighted me; and behold it hath no loveliness; I mean not such loveliness as in justice and wisdom; nor such as is in the mind and memory, and senses, and animal life of

[11] Ps. lxiv. 10.

man; nor yet as the stars are glorious and beautiful in their orbs; or the earth, or sea, full of embryo-life, replacing by its birth that which decayeth; nay, nor even that false and shadowy beauty which belongeth to deceiving vices.

For so doth pride imitate exaltedness; whereas Thou alone art God exalted over all. Ambition, what seeks it, but honours and glory? whereas Thou alone art to be honoured above all, and glorious for evermore. The cruelty of the great would fain be feared; but who is to be feared but God alone, out of whose power what can be wrested or withdrawn? when, or where, or whither, or by whom? The tendernesses of the wanton would fain be counted love: yet is nothing more tender than Thy charity; nor is aught loved more healthfully than that Thy truth, bright and beautiful above all. Curiosity makes semblance of a desire of knowledge; whereas Thou supremely knowest all. Yea, ignorance and foolishness itself is cloaked under the name of simplicity and uninjuriousness; because nothing is found more single than Thee: and what less injurious, since they are his own works which injure the sinner? Yea, sloth would fain be at rest; but what stable rest besides the Lord? Luxury affects to be called plenty and abundance; but Thou art the fulness and never-failing plenteousness of incorruptible pleasures. Prodigality presents a shadow of liberality: but Thou art the most overflowing Giver of all good. Covetousness would possess many things: and Thou possessest all things. Envy disputes for excellency; what more excellent than Thou? Anger seeks revenge: who revenges more justly than Thou? Fear startles at things unwonted and sudden, which endanger things beloved, and takes forethought for their safety; but to Thee what unwonted or sudden, or who separateth from Thee what Thou lovest?[12] Or where but with Thee is unshaken safety? Grief pines away for things lost, the delight of its desires; because it would have nothing taken from it, as nothing can from Thee.

Thus doth the soul commit fornication, when she turns from Thee, seeking without Thee, what she findeth not pure and untainted, till she returns to Thee. Thus all pervertedly imitate Thee, who remove far from Thee, and lift themselves up against Thee. But even by thus imitating Thee, they imply Thee to be the Creator

[12] Rom. viii. 9.

of all nature; whence there is no place whither altogether to retire from Thee. What then did I love in that theft? and wherein did I even corruptly and pervertedly imitate my Lord? Did I wish even by stealth to do contrary to Thy law, because by power I could not, so that being a prisoner, I might mimic a maimed liberty by doing with impunity things unpermitted me, a darkened likeness of Thy Omnipotency? Behold, Thy servant, fleeing from his Lord, and obtaining a shadow.[13] O rottenness, O monstrousness of life, and depth of death! could I like what I might not, only because I might not?

What shall I render unto the Lord,[14] that, whilst my memory recalls these things, my soul is not affrighted at them? *I will love Thee, O Lord, and thank Thee, and confess unto Thy name;* because Thou hast forgiven me these so great and heinous deeds of mine. To Thy grace I ascribe it, and to Thy mercy, that Thou hast melted away my sins as it were ice. To Thy grace I ascribe also whatsoever I have not done of evil; for what might I not have done, who even loved a sin for its own sake? Yea, all I confess to have been forgiven me; both what evils I committed by own wilfulness, and what by Thy guidance I committed not. What man is he, who, weighing his own infirmity, dares to ascribe his purity and innocency to his own strength; that so he should love Thee the less, as if he had less needed Thy mercy, whereby Thou remittest sins to those that turn to Thee? For whosoever, called by Thee, followed Thy voice, and avoided those things which he reads me recalling and confessing of myself, let him not scorn me, who being sick was cured by that Physician, through whose aid it was that he was not, or rather was less, sick: and for this let him love Thee as much, yea and more; since by whom he sees me to have been recovered from such deep consumption of sin, by Him he sees himself to have been from the like consumption of sin preserved.

What fruit had I then (wretched man!) *in those things, of the remembrance whereof I am now ashamed?*[15] Especially, in that theft which I loved for the theft's sake; and it too was nothing, and therefore the more miserable I, who loved it. Yet alone I had not done it: such was I then, I remember, alone I had never done it. I loved then in it also the company of the accomplices, with whom I did it? I did not then love nothing else but the theft, yea rather

[13] Jonah i., iv. [14] Ps. cxvi. 12. [15] Rom. vi. 21.

I did love nothing else; for that circumstance of the company was also nothing. What is, in truth? who can teach me, save He that enlighteneth my heart, and discovereth its dark corners? What is it which hath come into my mind to enquire, and discuss, and consider? For had I then loved the pears I stole, and wished to enjoy them, I might have done it alone, had the bare commission of the theft sufficed to attain my pleasure; nor needed I have inflamed the itching of my desires by the excitement of accomplices. But since my pleasure was not in those pears, it was in the offence itself, which the company of fellow-sinners occasioned.

What then was this feeling? For of a truth it was too foul: and woe was me, who had it. But yet what was it? *Who can understand his errors?*[16] It was the sport, which as it were tickled our hearts, that we beguiled those who little thought what we were doing, and much disliked it. Why then was my delight of such sort that I did it not alone? Because none doth ordinarily laugh alone? ordinarily no one; yet laughter sometimes masters men alone and singly when no one whatever is with them, if any thing very ludicrous presents itself to their senses or mind. Yet I had not done this alone; alone I had never done it. Behold my God, before Thee, the vivid remembrance of my soul; alone, I had never committed that theft wherein what I stole pleased me not, but that I stole; nor had it alone liked me to do it, nor had I done it. O friendship too unfriendly! thou incomprehensible inveigler of the soul, thou greediness to do mischief out of mirth and wantonness, thou thirst of others' loss, without lust of my own gain or revenge: but when it is said, "Let's go, let's do it," we are ashamed not to be shameless.

Who can disentangle that twisted and intricate knottiness? Foul is it: I hate to think on it, to look on it. But Thee I long for, O Righteousness and Innocency, beautiful and comely to all pure eyes, and of a satisfaction unsating. With Thee is rest entire, and life imperturbable. Whoso enters into Thee, *enters into the joy of his Lord:*[17] and shall not fear, and shall do excellently in the All-Excellent. I sank away from Thee, and I wandered, O my God, too much astray from Thee my stay, in these days of my youth, and I became to myself a barren land.

[16] Ps. xix. 12.   [17] Matt. xxv. 21.

THE THIRD BOOK

His residence at Carthage from his seventeenth to his nineteenth year. Source of his disorders. Love of shows. Advance in studies, and love of wisdom. Distaste for Scripture. Led astray to the Manichæans. Refutation of some of their tenets. Grief of his mother Monnica at his heresy, and prayers for his conversion. Her vision from God, and answer through a Bishop.

TO CARTHAGE I came, where there sang all around me in my ears a cauldron of unholy loves. I loved not yet, yet I loved to love, and out of a deep-seated want, I hated myself for wanting not. I sought what I might love, in love with loving, and safety I hated, and a way without snares. For within me was a famine of that inward food, Thyself, my God; yet, through that famine I was not hungered; but was without all longing for incorruptible sustenance, not because filled therewith, but the more empty, the more I loathed it. For this cause my soul was sickly and full of sores, it miserably cast itself forth, desiring to be scraped by the touch of objects of sense. Yet if these had not a soul, they would not be objects of love. To love then, and to be beloved, was sweet to me; but more, when I obtained to enjoy the person I loved. I defiled, therefore, the spring of friendship with the filth of concupiscence, and I beclouded its brightness with the hell of lustfulness; and thus foul and unseemly, I would fain, through exceeding vanity, be fine and courtly. I fell headlong then into the love wherein I longed to be ensnared. My God, my Mercy, with how much gall didst Thou out of Thy great goodness besprinkle for me that sweetness? For I was both beloved, and secretly arrived at the bond of enjoying; and was with joy fettered with sorrow-bringing bonds, that I might be scourged with the iron burning rods of jealousy, and suspicion, and fears, and angers, and quarrels.

Stage-plays also carried me away, full of images of my miseries, and of fuel to my fire. Why is it, that man desires to be made sad, beholding doleful and tragical things, which yet himself would by no means suffer? yet he desires as a spectator to feel sorrow at them, and this very sorrow is his pleasure. What is this but a miserable madness? for a man is the more affected with these actions, the less free he is from such affections. Howsoever, when he suffers in his own person, it used to be styled misery; when he compassionates others, then it is mercy. But what sort of compassion is this for feigned and scenical passions? for the auditor is not called on to relieve, but only to grieve: and he applauds the actor of these fictions the more, the more he grieves. And if the calamities of those persons (whether of old times, or mere fiction) be so acted, that the spectator is not moved to tears, he goes away disgusted and criticising; but if he be moved to passion, he stays intent, and weeps for joy.

Are griefs then too loved? Verily all desire joy. Or whereas no man likes to be miserable, is he yet pleased to be merciful? which because it cannot be without passion, for this reason alone are passions loved? This also springs from that vein of friendship. But whither goes that vein? whither flows it? wherefore runs it into that torrent of pitch bubbling forth those monstrous tides of foul lustfulness, into which it is wilfully changed and transformed, being of its own will precipitated and corrupted from its heavenly clearness? Shall compassion then be put away? by no means. Be griefs then sometimes loved. But beware of uncleanness, O my soul, under the guardianship of my God, *the God of our fathers, who is to be praised and exalted above all for ever,*[1] beware of uncleanness. For I have not now ceased to pity; but then in the theatres I rejoiced with lovers when they wickedly enjoyed one another, although this was imaginary only in the play. And when they lost one another, as if very compassionate, I sorrowed with them, yet had my delight in both. But now I much more pity him that rejoiceth in his wickedness, than him who is thought to suffer hardship, by hissing some pernicious pleasure, and the loss of some miserable felicity. This certainly is the truer mercy, but in it grief delights not. For though he that grieves for the miserable, be commended for his office of charity; yet had he, who is genuinely compassionate, rather there were nothing for him to grieve for. For if good will be ill willed

[1] Song of the Three Children, ver. 3.

(which can never be), then may he, who truly and sincerely commiserates, wish there might be some miserable, that he might commiserate. Some sorrow may then be allowed, none loved. For thus dost Thou, O Lord God, who lovest souls far more purely than we, and hast more incorruptibly pity on them, yet are wounded with no sorrowfulness. *And who is sufficient for these things?*[2]

But I, miserable, then loved to grieve, and sought out what to grieve at, when in another's and that feigned and personated misery, that acting best pleased me, and attracted me the most vehemently, which drew tears from me. What marvel that an unhappy sheep straying from Thy flock, and impatient of Thy keeping, I became infected with a foul disease? And hence the love of griefs; not such as should sink deep into me; for I loved not to suffer, what I loved to look on; but such as upon hearing their fictions should lightly scratch the surface; upon which, as on envenomed nails, followed inflamed swelling, impostumes, and a putrified sore. My life being such, was it life, O my God?

And Thy faithful mercy hovered over me afar. Upon how grievous iniquities consumed I myself, pursuing a sacrilegious curiosity, that having forsaken Thee, it might bring me to the treacherous abyss, and the beguiling service of devils, to whom I sacrificed my evil actions, and in all these things Thou didst scourge me! I dared even, while Thy solemnities were celebrated within the walls of Thy church, to desire, and to compass a business deserving death for its fruits, for which Thou scourgedst me with grievous punishments, though nothing to my fault, O Thou my exceeding mercy, my God, my refuge from those terrible destroyers, among whom I wandered with a stiff neck, withdrawing further from Thee, loving mine own ways, and not Thine; loving a vagrant liberty.

Those studies also, which were accounted commendable, had a view to excelling in the courts of litigation; the more bepraised, the craftier. Such is men's blindness, glorying even in their blindness. And now I was chief in the rhetoric school, whereat I joyed proudly, and I swelled with arrogancy, though (Lord, Thou knowest) far quieter and altogether removed from the subvertings of those "Subverters" (for this ill-omened and devilish name was the very

[2] 2 Cor. ii. 16.

badge of gallantry) among whom I lived, with a shameless shame that I was not even as they. With them I lived, and was sometimes delighted with their friendship, whose doings I ever did abhor— i. e., their "subvertings," wherewith they wantonly persecuted the modesty of strangers, which they disturbed by a gratuitous jeering, feeding thereon their malicious mirth. Nothing can be liker the very actions of devils than these. What then could they be more truly called than "subverters"? themselves subverted and altogether perverted first, the deceiving spirits secretly deriding and seducing them, wherein themselves delight to jeer at, and deceive others.

Among such as these, in that unsettled age of mine, learned I books of eloquence, wherein I desired to be eminent, out of a damnable and vainglorious end, a joy in human vanity. In the ordinary course of study, I fell upon a certain book of Cicero, whose speech almost all admire, not so his heart. This book of his contains an exhortation to philosophy, and is called *"Hortensius."* But this book altered my affections, and turned my prayers to Thyself, O Lord; and made me have other purposes and desires. Every vain hope at once became worthless to me; and I longed with an incredibly burning desire for an immortality of wisdom, and began now to arise, that I might return to Thee. For not to sharpen my tongue (which thing I seemed to be purchasing with my mother's allowances, in that my nineteenth year, my father being dead two years before), not to sharpen my tongue did I employ that book; nor did it infuse into me its style, but its matter.

How did I burn then, my God, how did I burn to re-mount from earthly things to Thee, nor knew I what Thou wouldst do with me? For with Thee is wisdom. But the love of wisdom is in Greek called "philosophy," with which that book inflamed me. Some there be that seduce through philosophy, under a great, and smooth, and honourable name colouring and disguising their own errors: and almost all who in that and former ages were such, are in that book censured and set forth: there also is made plain that wholesome advice of Thy Spirit, by Thy good and devout servant: *Beware lest any man spoil you through philosophy and vain deceit, after the tradition of men, after the rudiments of the world, and not after*

Christ. For in Him dwelleth all the fulness of the Godhead bodily.[3]
And since at that time (Thou, O light of my heart, knowest) Apostolic Scripture was not known to me, I was delighted with that exhortation, so far only, that I was thereby strongly roused, and kindled, and inflamed to love, and seek, and obtain, and hold, and embrace not this or that sect, but wisdom itself whatever it were; and this alone checked me thus enkindled, that the name of Christ was not in it. For this name, according to Thy mercy, O Lord, this name of my Saviour Thy Son, had my tender heart, even with my mother's milk, devoutly drunk in, and deeply treasured; and whatsoever was without that name, though never so learned, polished, or true, took not entire hold of me.

I resolved then to bend my mind to the holy Scriptures, that I might see what they were. But behold, I see a thing not understood by the proud, nor laid open to children, lowly in access, in its recesses lofty, and veiled with mysteries; and I was not such as could enter into it, or stoop my neck to follow its steps. For not as I now speak, did I feel when I turned to those Scriptures; but they seemed to me unworthy to be compared to the stateliness of Tully: for my swelling pride shrunk from their lowliness, nor could my sharp wit pierce the interior thereof. Yet were they such as would grow up in a little one. But I disdained to be a little one; and, swollen with pride, took myself to be a great one.

Therefore I fell among men proudly doting, exceeding carnal and prating, in whose mouths were the snares of the Devil, limed with the mixture of the syllables of Thy name, and of our Lord Jesus Christ, and of the Holy Ghost, the Paraclete, our Comforter. These names departed not out of their mouth, but so far forth as the sound only and the noise of the tongue, for the heart was void of truth. Yet they cried out "Truth, Truth," and spake much thereof to me, yet *it was not in them:*[4] but they spake falsehood, not of Thee only (who truly art Truth), but even of those elements of this world, Thy creatures. And I indeed ought to have passed by even philosophers who spake truth concerning them, for love of Thee, my Father, supremely good, Beauty of all things beau-

[3] Col. ii. 8, 9.   [4] 1 John ii. 4.

tiful. O Truth, Truth, how inwardly did even then the marrow of my soul pant after Thee, when they often and diversly, and in many and huge books, echoed of Thee to me, though it was but an echo? And these were the dishes wherein to me, hungering after Thee, they, instead of Thee, served up the Sun and Moon, beautiful works of Thine, but yet Thy works, not Thyself, no nor Thy first works. For Thy spiritual works are before these corporeal works, celestial though they be, and shining. But I hungered and thirsted not even after those first works of Thine, but after Thee Thyself, the Truth, *in whom is no variableness, neither shadow of turning:*[5] yet they still set before me in those dishes, glittering fantasies, than which better were it to love this very sun (which is real to our sight at least), than those fantasies which by our eyes deceive our mind. Yet because I thought them to be Thee, I fed thereon; not eagerly, for Thou didst not in them taste to me as Thou art; for Thou wast not these emptinesses, nor was I nourished by them, but exhausted rather. Food in sleep shows very like our food awake; yet are not those asleep nourished by it, for they are asleep. But those were not even any way like to Thee, as Thou hast now spoken to me; for those were corporeal fantasies, false bodies, than which these true bodies, celestial or terrestrial, which with our fleshly sight we behold, are far more certain: these things the beasts and birds discern as well as we, and they are more certain than when we fancy them. And again, we do with more certainty fancy them, than by them conjecture other vaster and infinite bodies which have no being. Such empty husks was I then fed on; and was not fed. But Thou, my soul's Love, *in looking for whom I fail,*[6] that I may become strong, art neither those bodies which we see, though in heaven; nor those which we see not there; for Thou hast created them, nor dost Thou account them among the chiefest of Thy works. How far then art Thou from those fantasies of mine, fantasies of bodies which altogether are not, than which the images of those bodies, which are, are far more certain, and more certain still the bodies themselves, which yet Thou art not; no, nor the soul, which is the life of the bodies. So then, better and more certain is the life of the bodies than

5 James i. 17.   6 Ps. lxix. 3.

the bodies. But Thou art the life of souls, the life of lives, having life in Thyself; and changest not, life of my soul.

Where then wert Thou then to me, and how far from me? Far verily was I straying from Thee, barred from the very husks of the swine, whom with husks I fed. For how much better are the fables of poets and grammarians than these snares? For verses, and poems, and "Medea flying," are more profitable truly than these men's five elements, variously disguised, answering to five dens of darkness which have no being, yet slay the believer. For verses and poems I can turn to true food, and "Medea flying," though I did sing, I maintained not; though I heard it sung, I believed not: but those things I did believe. Woe, woe, by what steps was I brought down to *the depths of hell!*[7] toiling and turmoiling through want of Truth, since I sought after Thee, my God (to Thee I confess it, who hadst mercy on me, not as yet confessing), not according to the understanding by the mind, wherein Thou willedst that I should excel the beasts, but according to the sense of the flesh. But Thou wert more inward to me, than my most inward part; and higher than my highest. I lighted upon that bold woman, *simple and knoweth nothing,* shadowed out in Solomon, *sitting at the door, and saying, Eat ye bread of secrecies willingly, and drink ye stolen waters which are sweet:*[8] she seduced me, because she found my soul dwelling abroad in the eye of my flesh, and ruminating on such food as through it I had devoured.

For other than this, that which really is I knew not; and was, as it were through sharpness of wit, persuaded to assent to foolish deceivers, when they asked me, "whence is evil?" "is God bounded by a bodily shape, and has hairs and nails?" "are they to be esteemed righteous who had many wives at once, and did kill men, and sacrificed living creatures?"[9] At which I, in my ignorance, was much troubled, and departing from the truth, seemed to myself to be making towards it; because as yet I knew not that evil was nothing but a privation of good, until at last a thing ceases altogether to be; which how should I see, the sight of whose eyes reached only to bodies, and of my mind to a phantasm? And I knew not *God to*

[7] Prov. ix. 18.   [8] Prov. ix. 13-17.   [9] 1 Kings xviii. 40.

be a Spirit,[10] not one who hath parts extended in length and breadth, or whose being was bulk; for every bulk is less in a part than in the whole: and if it be infinite, it must be less in such part as is defined by a certain space, than in its infinitude; and so is not wholly every where, as Spirit, as God. And what that should be in us, by which we were like to God, and might in Scripture be rightly said to be *after the image of God,*[11] I was altogether ignorant.

Nor knew I that true inward righteousness which judgeth not according to custom, but out of the most rightful law of God Almighty, whereby the ways of places and times were disposed according to those times and places; itself meantime being the same always and every where, one thing in one place, and another in another; according to which Abraham, and Isaac, and Jacob, and Moses, and David, were righteous, and all those commended by the mouth of God; but were judged unrighteous by silly men, *judging out of man's judgment,*[12] and measuring by their own petty habits, the moral habits of the whole human race. As if in an armory, one ignorant what were adapted to each part should cover his head with greaves, or seek to be shod with a helmet, and complain that they fitted not: or as if on a day when business is publicly stopped in the afternoon, one were angered at not being allowed to keep open shop, because he had been in the forenoon; or when in one house he observeth some servant take a thing in his hand, which the butler is not suffered to meddle with; or something permitted out of doors, which is forbidden in the dining-room; and should be angry, that in one house, and one family, the same thing is not allotted every where, and to all. Even such are they who are fretted to hear something to have been lawful for righteous men formerly, which now is not; or that God, for certain temporal respects, commanded them one thing, and these another, obeying both the same righteousness: whereas they see, in one man, and one day, and one house, different things to be fit for different members, and a thing formerly lawful, after a certain time not so; in one corner permitted or commanded, but in another rightly forbidden and punished. Is justice therefore various or mutable? No, but the times, over which it presides, flow

[10] John iv. 24.   [11] Gen. i. 27.   [12] 1 Cor. iv. 3.

not evenly, because they are times. But men whose *days are few upon the earth*,[13] for that by their senses they cannot harmonise the causes of things in former ages and other nations, which they had no experience of, with these which they have experience of, whereas in one and the same body, day, or family, they easily see what is fitting for each member, and season, part, and person; to the one they take exceptions, to the other they submit.

These things I then knew not, nor observed; they struck my sight on all sides, and I saw them not. I indited verses, in which I might not place every foot every where, but differently in different metres; nor even in any one metre the self-same foot in all places. Yet the art itself, by which I indited, had not different principles for these different cases, but comprised all in one. Still I saw not how that righteousness, which good and holy men obeyed, did far more excellently and sublimely contain in one all those things which God commanded, and in no part varied; although in varying times it prescribed not every thing at once, but apportioned and enjoined what was fit for each. And I, in my blindness, censured the holy Fathers, not only wherein they made use of things present as God commanded and inspired them, but also wherein they were foretelling things to come, as God was revealing in them.

Can it at any time or place be unjust *to love God with all his heart, with all his soul, and with all his mind; and his neighbour as himself?*[14] Therefore are those foul offences which be against nature, to be every where and at all times detested and punished: such as were those of the men of Sodom; which should all nations commit, they should all stand guilty of the same crime, by the law of God, which hath not so made men that they should so abuse one another. For even that intercourse which should be between God and us is violated, when that same nature, of which He is Author, is polluted by perversity of lust. But those actions which are offences against the customs of men, are to be avoided according to the customs severally prevailing; so that a thing agreed upon, and confirmed, by custom or law of any city or nation, may not be violated at the lawless pleasure of any, whether native or foreigner. For any part which harmoniseth not with its whole, is of-

[13] Job xiv. 1.   [14] Matt. xxii. 37–39.

fensive. But when God commands a thing to be done, against the customs or compact of any people, though it were never by them done heretofore, it is to be done; and if intermitted, it is to be restored; and if never ordained, is now to be ordained. For lawful if it be for a king, in the state which he reigns over, to command that which no one before him, nor he himself heretofore, had commanded, and to obey him cannot be against the common weal of the state (nay, it were against it if he were not obeyed, for to obey princes is a general compact of human society); how much more unhesitatingly ought we to obey God, in all which He commands, the Ruler of all His creatures! For as among the powers in man's society, the greater authority is obeyed in preference to the lesser, so must God above all.

So in acts of violence, where there is a wish to hurt, whether by reproach or injury; and these either for revenge, as one enemy against another; or for some profit belonging to another, as the robber to the traveller; or to avoid some evil, as towards one who is feared; or through envy, as one less fortunate to one more so, or one well thriven in any thing, to him whose being on a par with himself he fears, or grieves at, or for the mere pleasure at another's pain, as spectators of gladiators, or deriders and mockers of others. These be the heads of iniquity, which spring from the lust of the flesh, of the eye,[15] or of rule, either singly, or two combined, or all together; and so do men live ill against the three, and seven, that psaltery *of ten strings*,[16] Thy Ten Commandments, O God, most high, and most sweet. But what foul offences can there be against Thee, who canst not be defiled? or what acts of violence against Thee, who canst not be harmed? But Thou avengest what men commit against themselves, seeing also when they sin against Thee, they do wickedly against their own souls, and *iniquity gives itself the lie*,[17] by corrupting and perverting their nature, which Thou hast created and ordained, or by an immoderate use of things allowed, or in *burning* in things unallowed, *to that use which is against nature;*[18] or are found guilty, raging with heart and tongue against Thee, *kicking against the pricks;*[19] or when, bursting the pale of human society, they boldly joy in self-willed combinations or divi-

[15] I John ii. 16.   [16] Ps. cxliv. 9.   [17] Ps. xxvi. 12.—Vulg.   [18] Rom. i.   [19] Acts ix. 5.

sions, according as they have any object to gain or subject of offence. And these things are done when Thou art forsaken, O Fountain of Life, who art the only and true Creator and Governor of the Universe, and by a self-willed pride, any one false thing is selected therefrom and loved. So then by a humble devoutness we return to Thee; and Thou cleansest us from our evil habits, and art merciful to their sins who confess, and *hearest the groaning of the prisoner,*[20] and loosest us from the chains which we made for ourselves, if we lift not up against Thee the horns of an unreal liberty, suffering the loss of all through covetousness of more, by loving more our own private good than Thee, the Good of all.

Amidst these offences of foulness and violence, and so many iniquities, are sins of men, who are on the whole making proficiency; which by those that judge rightly, are, after the rule of perfection, discommended, yet the persons commended, upon hope of future fruit, as in the green blade of growing corn. And there are some, resembling offences of foulness or violence, which yet are no sins; because they offend neither Thee, our Lord God, nor human society; when, namely, things fitting for a given period are obtained for the service of life, and we know not whether out of a lust of having; or when things are, for the sake of correction, by constituted authority punished, and we know not whether out of a lust of hurting. Many an action then which in men's sight is disapproved, is by Thy testimony approved; and many, by men praised are (Thou being witness) condemned: because the show of the action, and the mind of the doer, and the unknown exigency of the period, severally vary. But when Thou on a sudden commandest an unwonted and unthought of thing, yea, although Thou hast sometime forbidden it, and still for the time hidest the reason of Thy command, and it be against the ordinance of some society of men, who doubts but it is to be done, seeing that society of men is just which serves Thee? But blessed are they who know Thy commands! For all things were done by Thy servants; either to show forth something needful for the present, or to foreshow things to come.

These things I being ignorant of, scoffed at those Thy holy servants and prophets. And what gained I by scoffing at them, but to be

[20] Ps. cii. 20.

scoffed at by Thee, being insensibly and step by step drawn on to those follies, as to believe that a fig-tree wept when it was plucked, and the tree, its mother, shed milky tears? Which fig notwithstanding (plucked by some other's, not his own, guilt) had some (Manichæan) saint eaten, and mingled with his bowels, he should breathe out of it angels, yea, there shall burst forth particles of divinity, at every moan or groan in his prayer, which particles of the most high and true God had remained bound in that fig, unless they had been set at liberty by the teeth or belly of some "Elect" saint! And I, miserable, believed that more mercy was to be shown to the fruits of the earth than men, for whom they were created. For if any one an hungered, not a Manichæan, should ask for any, that morsel would seem as it were condemned to capital punishment, which should be given him.

And Thou *sentest Thine hand from above*,[21] and drewest my soul out of that profound darkness, my mother, thy faithful one, weeping to Thee for me, more than mothers weep the bodily deaths of their children. For she, by that faith and spirit which she had from Thee, discerned the death wherein I lay, and Thou heardest her, O Lord; Thou heardest her, and despisedst not her tears, when streaming down, they watered the ground under her eyes in every place where she prayed, yea Thou heardest her. For whence was that dream whereby Thou comfortedst her; so that she allowed me to live with her, and to eat at the same table in the house, which she had begun to shrink from, abhorring and detesting the blasphemies of my error? For she saw herself standing on a certain wooden rule, and a shining youth coming towards her, cheerful and smiling upon her, herself grieving, and overwhelmed with grief. But he having (in order to instruct, as is their wont not to be instructed) enquired of her the causes of her grief and daily tears, and she answering that she was bewailing my perdition, he bade her rest contented, and told her to look and observe, "That where she was, there was I also." And when she looked, she saw me standing by her in the same rule. Whence was this, but that Thine ears were towards her heart? O Thou Good omnipotent, who so carest for every one of

[21] Ps. cxliv. 7.

us, as if Thou caredst for him only; and so for all, as if they were but one!

Whence was this also, that when she had told me this vision, and I would fain bend it to mean, "That she rather should not despair of being one day what I was;" she presently, without any hesitation, replies: "No; for it was not told me that, 'where he, there thou also;' but· 'where thou, there he also' "? I confess to Thee, O Lord, that to the best of my remembrance (and I have oft spoken of this), that Thy answer, through my waking mother,— that she was not perplexed by the plausibility of my false interpretation, and so quickly saw what was to be seen, and which I certainly had not perceived before she spake,—even then moved me more than the dream itself, by which a joy to the holy woman, to be fulfilled so long after, was, for the consolation of her present anguish, so long before foresignified. For almost nine years passed, in which I wallowed in the mire of that deep pit, and the darkness of falsehood, often assaying to rise, but dashed down the more grievously. All which time that chaste, godly and sober widow (such as Thou lovest), now more cheered with hope, yet no whit relaxing in her weeping and mourning, ceased not at all hours of her devotions to bewail my case unto Thee. And her *prayers entered into Thy presence*,[22] and yet Thou sufferest me to be yet involved and reinvolved in that darkness.

Thou gavest her meantime another answer, which I call to mind; for much I pass by, hasting to those things which more press me to confess unto Thee, and much I do not remember. Thou gavest her then another answer, by a Priest of Thine, a certain Bishop brought up in Thy Church, and well studied in Thy books. Whom when this woman had entreated to vouchsafe to converse with me, refute my errors, unteach me ill things, and teach me good things (for this he was wont to do, when he found persons fitted to receive it), he refused, wisely, as I afterwards perceived. For he answered, that I was yet unteachable, being puffed up with the novelty of that heresy, and had already perplexed divers unskilful persons with captious questions, as she had told him: "but let him alone a while"

[22] Ps. lxxxviii. 1.

(saith he), "only pray God for him, he will of himself by reading find what that error is, and how great its impiety." At the same time he told her, how himself, when a little one, had by his seduced mother been consigned over to the Manichees, and had not only read, but frequently copied out almost all, their books, and had (without any argument or proof from any one) seen how much that sect was to be avoided; and had avoided it. Which when he had said, and she would not be satisfied, but urged him more, with entreaties and many tears, that he would see me and discourse with me; he, a little displeased at her importunity, saith ,"Go thy ways, and God bless thee, for it is not possible that the son of these tears should perish." Which answer she took (as she often mentioned in her conversations with me) as if it had sounded from Heaven.

THE FOURTH BOOK

Augustine's life from nineteen to eight-and-twenty; himself a Manichæan, and seducing others to the same heresy; partial obedience
amidst vanity and sin, consulting astrologers, only partially shaken
herein; loss of an early friend, who is converted by being baptised
when in a swoon; reflections on grief, on real and unreal friendship,
and love of fame; writes on "the fair and fit," yet cannot rightly,
though God had given him great talents, since he entertained wrong
notions of God; and so even his knowledge he applied ill.

FOR this space of nine years then (from my nineteenth year to
my eight-and-twentieth) we lived seduced and seducing, deceived and deceiving, in divers lusts; openly, by sciences
which they call liberal; secretly, with a false-named religion; here
proud, there superstitious, every where vain! Here, hunting after
the emptiness of popular praise, down even to theatrical applauses,
and poetic prizes, and strifes for grassy garlands, and the follies of
shows, and the intemperance of desires. There, desiring to be
cleansed from these defilements, by carrying food to those who were
called "elect" and "holy," out of which, in the workhouse of their
stomachs, they should forge for us Angels and Gods, by whom we
might be cleansed. These things did I follow, and practise with my
friends, deceived by me, and with me. Let the arrogant mock me,
and such as have not been, to their soul's health, stricken and cast
down by Thee, O my God; but I would still confess to Thee mine
own shame in Thy praise. Suffer me, I beseech Thee, and give me
grace to go over in my present remembrance the wanderings of my
forepassed time, and *to offer unto Thee the sacrifice of thanksgiving.*[1] For what am I to myself without Thee, but a guide to mine
own downfall? or what am I even at the best, but an infant sucking
the milk Thou givest, and feeding upon Thee, *the food that perisheth not?*[2] But what sort of man is any man, seeing he is but a man?
Let now the strong and the mighty laugh at us, but let us *poor and
needy*[3] confess unto Thee.

[1] Ps. xlix. 14.   [2] John vi. 27.   [3] Ps. lxxiii. 21.

45

In those years I taught rhetoric, and, overcome by cupidity, made sale of a loquacity to overcome by. Yet I preferred (Lord, Thou knowest) honest scholars (as they are accounted), and these I, without artifice, taught artifices, not to be practised against the life of the guiltless, though sometimes for the life of the guilty. And Thou, O God, from afar perceivedst me stumbling in that slippery course, and amid much smoke sending out some sparks of faithfulness, which I showed in that my guidance of *such as loved vanity, and sought after leasing,*[4] myself their companion. In those years I had one,—not in that which is called lawful marriage, but whom I had found out in a wayward passion, void of understanding; yet but one, remaining faithful even to her; in whom I in my own case experienced what difference there is betwixt the self-restraint of the marriage-covenant, for the sake of issue, and the bargain of a lustful love, where children are born against their parents' will, although, once born, they constrain love.

I remember also, that when I had settled to enter the lists for a theatrical prize, some wizard asked me what I would give him to win; but I, detesting and abhorring such foul mysteries, answered, "Though the garland were of imperishable gold, I would not suffer a fly to be killed to gain me it." For he was to kill some living creatures in his sacrifices, and by those honours to invite the devils to favour me. But this ill also I rejected, not out of a pure love for Thee, O God of my heart; for I knew not how to love Thee, who knew not how to conceive aught beyond a material brightness. And doth not a soul, sighing after such fictions, commit fornication against Thee, trust in things unreal, and *feed the wind?*[5] Still I would not forsooth have sacrifices offered to devils for me, to whom I was sacrificing myself by that superstition. For what else is it *to feed the wind,* but to feed them, that is, by going astray to become their pleasure and derision?

Those impostors then, whom they style Mathematicians, I consulted without scruple; because they seemed to use no sacrifice, nor to pray to any spirit for their divinations: which art, however, Christian and true piety consistently rejects and condemns. For, *it is a good thing to confess unto Thee,* and to say, *Have mercy upon*

[4] Is. xlii. 5; Matt. xii. 20; Ps. iv. 2.   [5] Hos. xii 1.

me, heal my soul, for I have sinned against Thee;[6] and not to abuse
Thy mercy for a license to sin, but to remember the Lord's words,
*Behold, thou art made whole, sin no more, lest a worse thing come
unto thee.*[7] All which wholesome advice they labour to destroy,
saying, "The cause of thy sin is inevitably determined in heaven;"
and "This did Venus, or Saturn, or Mars:" that man, forsooth, flesh
and blood, and proud corruption, might be blameless; while the
Creator and Ordainer of heaven and the stars is to bear the blame.
And who is He but our God? the very sweetness and well-spring of
righteousness, who *renderest to every man according to his works:
and a broken and contrite heart wilt Thou not despise.*[8]

There was in those days a wise man, very skilful in physic, and
renowned therein, who had with his own proconsular hand put the
Agonistic garland upon my distempered head, but not as a physician: for this disease Thou only curest, *who resistest the proud, and
givest grace to the humble.*[9] But didst Thou fail me even by that
old man, or forbear to heal my soul? For having become more ac-
quainted with him, and hanging assiduously and fixedly on his
speech (for though in simple terms, it was vivid, lively, and earnest), when he had gathered by my discourse that I was given to
the books of nativity-casters, he kindly and fatherly advised me to
cast them away, and not fruitlessly bestow a care and diligence, necessary for useful things, upon these vanities; saying, that he had in
his earliest years studied that art, so as to make it the profession
whereby he should live, and that, understanding Hippocrates, he
could soon have understood such a study as this; and yet he had
given it over, and taken to physic, for no other reason but that he
found it utterly false; and he, a grave man, would not get his living
by deluding people. "But thou," saith he, "hast rhetoric to maintain
thyself by, so that thou followest this of free choice, not of necessity: the more then oughtest thou to give me credit herein, who
laboured to acquire it so perfectly as to get my living by it alone."
Of whom when I had demanded, how then could many true things
be foretold by it, he answered me (as he could) "that the force of
chance, diffused throughout the whole order of things, brought

⁶ Ps. xli. 4.   ⁷ John v. 14.   ⁸ Rom. ii. 6; Matt. xvi. 27; Ps. li. 17.
⁹ 1 Pet. v. 5; Jam. iv. 6.

this about. For if when a man by haphazard opens the pages of some poet, who sang and thought of something wholly different, a verse oftentimes fell out, wondrously agreeable to the present business: it were not to be wondered at, if out of the soul of man, unconscious what takes place in it, by some higher instinct an answer should be given, by hap, not by art, corresponding to the business and actions of the demander."

And thus much, either from or through him, Thou conveyedst to me, and tracedst in my memory, what I might hereafter examine for myself. But at that time neither he, nor my dearest Nebridius, a youth singularly good and of a holy fear, who derided the whole body of divination, could persuade me to cast it aside, the authority of the authors swaying me yet more, and as yet I had found no certain proof (such as I sought) whereby it might without all doubt appear, that what had been truly foretold by those consulted was the result of haphazard, not of the art of the star-gazers.

In those years when I first began to teach rhetoric in my native town, I had made one my friend, but too dear to me, from a community of pursuits, of mine own age, and, as myself, in the first opening flower of youth. He had grown up a child with me, and we had been both school-fellows and play-fellows. But he was not yet my friend as afterwards, nor even then, as true friendship is; for true it cannot be, unless in such as Thou cementest together, cleaving unto Thee, by that *love which is shed abroad in our hearts by the Holy Ghost, which is given unto us.*[10] Yet was it but too sweet, ripened by the warmth of kindred studies: for, from the true faith (which he as a youth had not soundly and thoroughly imbibed), I had warped him also to those superstitious and pernicious fables, for which my mother bewailed me. With me he now erred in mind, nor could my soul be without him. But behold Thou wert close on the steps of Thy fugitives, at once *God of vengeance,*[11] and Fountain of mercies, turning us to Thyself by wonderful means; Thou tookest that man out of this life, when he had scarce filled up one whole year of my friendship, sweet to me above all sweetness of that my life.

Who can recount all Thy praises,[12] which he hath felt in his one

[10] Rom. v. 5.   [11] Ps. xciv. 1.   [12] Ps. cvi. 2.

self? What diddest Thou then, my God, and how unsearchable is the *abyss of Thy judgments?*[13] For long, sore sick of a fever, he lay senseless in a death-sweat; and his recovery being despaired of, he was baptised, unknowing; myself meanwhile little regarding, and presuming that his soul would retain rather what it had received of me, not what was wrought on his unconscious body. But it proved far otherwise; for he was refreshed, and restored. Forthwith, as soon as I could speak with him (and I could, so soon as he was able, for I never left him, and we hung but too much upon each other), I essayed to jest with him, as though he would jest with me at that baptism which he had received, when utterly absent in mind and feeling, but had now understood that he had received. But he so shrunk from me, as from an enemy; and with a wonderful and sudden freedom bade me, as I would continue his friend, forbear such language to him. I, all astonished and amazed, suppressed all my emotions till he should grow well, and his health were strong enough for me to deal with him as I would. But he was taken away from my frenzy, that with Thee he might be preserved for my comfort; a few days after, in my absence, he was attacked again by the fever, and so departed.

At this grief my heart was utterly darkened; and whatever I beheld was death. My native country was a torment to me, and my father's house a strange unhappiness; and whatever I had shared with him, wanting him, became a distracting torture. Mine eyes sought him every where, but he was not granted them; and I hated all places, for that they had not him; nor could they now tell me, "he is coming," as when he was alive and absent. I became a great riddle to myself, and I asked my soul, *why she was so sad, and why she disquieted me sorely:*[14] but she knew not what to answer me. And if I said, *Trust in God,* she very rightly obeyed me not; because that most dear friend, whom she had lost, was, being man, both truer and better than that phantasm she was bid to trust in. Only tears were sweet to me, for they succeeded my friend, in the dearest of my affections.

And now, Lord, these things are passed by, and time hath assuaged my wound. May I learn from Thee, who art Truth, and

[13] Ps. xxxvi. 2.   [14] Ps. xlii. 5.

approach the ear of my heart unto Thy mouth, that Thou mayest tell me why weeping is sweet to the miserable? Hast Thou, although present every where, cast away our misery far from Thee? And Thou abidest in Thyself, but we are tossed about in divers trials. And yet unless we mourned in Thine ears, we should have no hope left. Whence then is sweet fruit gathered from the bitterness of life, from groaning, tears, sighs, and complaints? Doth this sweeten it, that we hope Thou hearest? This is true of prayer, for therein is a longing to approach unto Thee. But is it also in grief for a thing lost, and the sorrow wherewith I was then overwhelmed? For I neither hoped he should return to life nor did I desire this with my tears; but I wept only and grieved. For I was miserable, and had lost my joy. Or is weeping indeed a bitter thing, and for very loathing of the things which we before enjoyed, does it then, when we shrink from them, please us?

But what speak I of these things? for now is no time to question, but to confess unto Thee. Wretched I was; and wretched is every soul bound by the friendship of perishable things; he is torn asunder when he loses them, and then he feels the wretchedness which he had ere yet he lost them. So was it then with me; I wept most bitterly, and found my repose in bitterness. Thus was I wretched, and that wretched life I held dearer than my friend. For though I would willingly have changed it, yet was I more unwilling to part with it than with him; yea, I know not whether I would have parted with it even for him, as is related (if not feigned) of Pylades and Orestes, that they would gladly have died for each other or together, not to live together being to them worse than death. But in me there had arisen some unexplained feeling, too contrary to this, for at once I loathed exceedingly to live and feared to die. I suppose, the more I loved him, the more did I hate, and fear (as a most cruel enemy) death, which had bereaved me of him: and I imagined it would speedily make an end of all men, since it had power over him. Thus was it with me, I remember. Behold my heart, O my God, behold and see into me; for well I remember it, O my Hope, who cleansest me from the impurity of such affections, directing *mine eyes towards Thee,* and *plucking my feet out of the snare*.[15] For I wondered that others, subject to death, did live, since he whom I loved, as if he should never die, was dead; and I wondered yet more that myself, who was to him a second self, could live, he being dead. Well said one of his friend, "Thou half of my soul;" for I felt that my soul and his soul were "one soul in two bodies:" and therefore was my life a horror to me, because I would not live halved. And therefore perchance I feared to die, lest he whom I had much loved should die wholly.

O madness, which knowest not how to love men, like men! O foolish man that I then was, enduring impatiently the lot of man! I fretted then, sighed, wept, was distracted; had neither rest nor counsel. For I bore about a shattered and bleeding soul, impatient of being borne by me, yet where to repose it, I found not. Not in calm groves, not in games and music, nor in fragrant spots, nor in curious banquetings, nor in the pleasures of the bed and the couch; nor (finally) in books or poesy, found it repose. All things looked ghastly, yea, the very light; whatsoever was not what he was, was revolting and hateful, except groaning and tears. For in those alone found I a little refreshment. But when my soul was withdrawn from them a huge load of misery weighed me down. To Thee, O Lord, it ought to have been raised, for Thee to lighten; I knew it; but neither could nor would; the more, since, when I thought of Thee, Thou wert not to me any solid or substantial thing. For Thou wert not Thyself, but a mere phantom, and my error was my God. If I offered to discharge my load thereon, that it might rest, it glided through the void, and came rushing down again on me; and I had remained to myself a hapless spot, where I could neither be, nor be from thence. For whither should my heart flee from my heart? Whither should I flee from myself? Whither not follow myself? And yet I fled out of my country; for so should mine eyes less look for him, where they were not wont to see him. And thus from Thagaste, I came to Carthage.

Times lose no time; nor do they roll idly by; through our senses they work strange operations on the mind. Behold, they went and came day by day, and by coming and going, introduced into my

[15] Ps. xxv. 14.

mind other imaginations and other remembrances; and little by little patched me up again with my old kind of delights, unto which that my sorrow gave way. And yet there succeeded, not indeed other griefs, yet the causes of other griefs. For whence had that former grief so easily reached my very inmost soul, but that I had poured out my soul upon the dust, in loving one that must die, as if he would never die? For what restored and refreshed me chiefly was the solaces of other friends, with whom I did love, what instead of Thee I loved; and this was a great fable, and protracted lie, by whose adulterous stimulus, our soul, which lay itching in our ears, was being defiled. But that fable would not die to me, so oft as any of my friends died. There were other things which in them did more take my mind; to talk and jest together, to do kind offices by turns; to read together honied books; to play the fool or be earnest together; to dissent at times without discontent, as a man might with his own self; and even with the seldomness of these dissentings, to season our more frequent consentings; sometimes to teach, and sometimes learn; long for the absent with impatience; and welcome the coming with joy. These and the like expressions, proceeding out of the hearts of those that loved and were loved again, by the countenance, the tongue, the eyes, and a thousand pleasing gestures, were so much fuel to melt our souls together, and out of many make but one.

This is it that is loved in friends; and so loved, that a man's conscience condemns itself, if he love not him that loves him again, or love not again him that loves him, looking for nothing from his person but indications of his love. Hence that mourning, if one die, and darkenings of sorrows, that steeping of the heart in tears, all sweetness turned to bitterness; and upon the loss of life of the dying, the death of the living. Blessed whoso loveth Thee, and his friend in Thee, and his enemy for Thee. For he alone loses none dear to him, to whom all are dear in Him who cannot be lost. And who is this but our God, the *God that made heaven and earth,* and *filleth them*,[16] because by filling them He created them? Thee none loseth, but who leaveth. And who leaveth Thee, whither goeth or whither fleeth he, but from Thee well-pleased, to Thee displeased?

[16] Gen. ii. 24; Jer. xxiii. 24.

For where doth he not find Thy law in his own punishment? *And Thy law is truth,*[17] and truth Thou.

Turn us, O God of Hosts, show us Thy countenance, and we shall be whole.[18] For whithersoever the soul of man turns itself, unless towards Thee, it is riveted upon sorrows, yea though it is riveted on things beautiful. And yet they, out of Thee, and out of the soul, were not, unless they were from Thee. They rise, and set; and by rising, they begin as it were to be; they grow, that they may be perfected; and perfected, they wax old and wither; and all grow not old, but all wither. So then when they rise and tend to be, the more quickly they grow that they may be, so much the more they haste not to be. This is the law of them. Thus much hast Thou allotted them, because they are portions of things, which exist not all at once, but by passing away and succeeding, they together complete that universe, whereof they are portions. And even thus is our speech completed by signs giving forth a sound: but this again is not perfected unless one word pass away when it hath sounded its part, that another may succeed. Out of all these things let my soul praise Thee, O God, Creator of all; yet let not my soul be riveted unto these things with the glue of love, through the senses of the body. For they go whither they were to go, that they might not be; and they rend her with pestilent longings, because she longs to be, yet loves to repose in what she loves. But in these things is no place of repose; they abide not, they flee; and who can follow them with the senses of the flesh? yea, who can grasp them, when they are hard by? For the sense of the flesh is slow, because it is the sense of the flesh; and thereby is it bounded. It sufficeth; for that it was made for; but it sufficeth not to stay things running their course from their appointed starting-place to the end appointed. For in Thy Word, by which they are created, they hear their decree, "hence and hitherto."

Be not foolish, O my soul, nor become deaf in the ear of thine heart with the tumult of thy folly. Hearken thou too. The Word itself calleth thee to return: and there is the place of rest imperturbable, where love is not forsaken, if itself forsaketh not. Behold, these things pass away, that others may replace them, and so this

17 Ps. cxix. 142; John xiv. 6.   18 Ps. lxxx. 19.

lower universe be completed by all his parts. But do I depart any whither? saith the Word of God. There fix thy dwelling, trust there whatsoever thou hast thence, O my soul, at least now thou art tired out with vanities. Entrust Truth, whatsoever thou hast from the Truth, and thou shalt lose nothing; and thy decay shall bloom again, and *all thy diseases be healed*,[19] and thy mortal parts be re-formed and renewed, and bound around thee: nor shall they lay thee whither themselves descend; but they shall stand fast with thee, and abide for ever before God, *who abideth* and standeth fast *for ever*.[20]

Why then be perverted and follow thy flesh? Be it converted and follow thee. Whatever by her thou hast sense of, is in part; and the whole, whereof these are parts, thou knowest not, and yet they delight thee. But had the sense of thy flesh a capacity for comprehending the whole, and not itself also, for thy punishment, been justly restricted to a part of the whole, thou wouldest, that whatsoever existeth at this present, should pass away, that so the whole might better please thee. For what we speak also, by the same sense of the flesh thou hearest; yet wouldest not thou have the syllables stay, but fly away, that others may come, and thou hear the whole. And so ever, when any one thing is made up of many, all of which do not exist together, all collectively would please more than they do severally, could all be perceived collectively. But far better than these is He who made all; and He is our God, nor doth He pass away, for neither doth aught succeed Him.

If bodies please thee, praise God on occasion of them, and turn back thy love upon their Maker; lest in these things which please thee, thou displease. If souls please thee, be they loved in God: for they too are mutable, but in Him are they firmly stablished; else would they pass, and pass away. In Him then be they beloved; and carry unto Him along with thee what souls thou canst, and say to them, "Him let us love, Him let us love: He made these, nor is He far off. For He did not make them, and so depart, but they are of Him, and in Him. See there He is, where truth is loved. He is within the very heart, yet hath the heart strayed from Him. *Go back into your heart, ye transgressors,* and cleave fast to Him that

[19] Ps. ciii. 3.   [20] 1 Pet. i. 23.

made you. Stand with Him, and ye shall stand fast. Rest in Him, and ye shall be at rest. Whither go ye in rough ways? Whither go ye? The good that you love is from Him; but it is good and pleasant through reference to Him, and justly shall it be embittered, because unjustly is anything loved which is from Him, if He be forsaken for it. To what end then would ye still and still walk these difficult and toilsome ways? There is no rest, where ye seek it. Seek what ye seek; but it is not there where ye seek. Ye seek a blessed life in the land of death; it is not there. For how should there be a blessed life where life itself is not?"

"But our true Life came down hither, and bore our death, and slew him, out of the abundance of His own life: and He thundered, calling aloud to us to return hence to Him into that secret place, whence He came forth to us, first into the virgin's womb, wherein he espoused the human creation, our mortal flesh, that it might not be for ever mortal, and thence *like a bridegroom coming out of his chamber, rejoicing as a giant to run his course.*[21] For He lingered not, but ran, calling aloud by words, deeds, death, life, descent, ascension; crying aloud to us to return unto Him. And He departed from our eyes, that we might return into our heart, and there find Him. For He departed, and lo, He is here. He would not be long with us, yet left us not; for He departed thither, whence He never parted, *because the world was made by Him.*[22] And *in this world He was, and into this world He came to save sinners,*[23] unto whom my soul confesseth, *and He healeth it, for it hath sinned against Him.*[24] *O ye sons of men, how long so slow of heart?*[25] Even now, after the descent of Life to you, will ye not ascend and live? But whither ascend ye, when ye are on high, and *set your mouth against the heavens?*[26] Descend, that ye may ascend, and ascend to God. For ye have fallen, by ascending against Him." Tell them this, that they may weep *in the valley of tears,*[27] and so carry them up with thee unto God; because out of His Spirit thou speakest thus unto them, if thou speakest, burning with the fire of charity.

These things I then knew not, and I loved these lower beauties, and I was sinking to the very depths, and to my friends I said, "Do

[21] Ps. xix. 5. [22] John i. 10. [23] 1 Tim. i. 15. [24] Ps. xli. 4. [25] Ps. iv. 3.—Vulg.
[26] Ps. lxxiii. 9. [27] Ps. lxxxiv. 6.

we love any thing but the beautiful? What then is the beautiful? and what is beauty? What is it that attracts and wins us to the things we love? for unless there were in them a grace and beauty, they could by no means draw us unto them." And I marked and perceived that in bodies themselves, there was a beauty, from their forming a sort of whole, and again, another from apt and mutual correspondence, as of a part of the body with its whole, or a shoe with a foot, and the like. And this consideration sprang up in my mind, out of my inmost heart, and I wrote "on the fair and fit," I think, two or three books. Thou knowest, O Lord, for it is gone from me; for I have them not, but they are strayed from me, I know not how.

But what moved me, O Lord my God, to dedicate these books unto Hierius, an orator of Rome, whom I knew not by face, but loved for the fame of his learning which was eminent in him, and some words of his I had heard, which pleased me? But more did he please me, for that he pleased others, who highly extolled him, amazed that out of a Syrian, first instructed in Greek eloquence, should afterwards be formed a wonderful Latin orator, and one most learned in things pertaining unto philosophy. One is commended, and, unseen, he is loved: doth this love enter the heart of the hearer from the mouth of the commender? Not so. But by one who loveth is another kindled. For hence he is loved who is commended, when the commender is believed to extol him with an unfeigned heart; that is, when one that loves him praises him.

For so did I then love men, upon the judgment of men, not Thine, O my God, in whom no man is deceived. But yet why not for qualities, like those of a famous charioteer, or fighter with the beasts in the theatre, known far and wide by a vulgar popularity, but far otherwise, and earnestly, and so as I would be myself commended? For I would not be commended or loved, as actors are (though I myself did commend and love them), but had rather be unknown, than so known; and even hated, than so loved. Where now are the impulses to such various and divers kinds of loves laid up in one soul? Why, since we are equally men, do I love in another what, if I did not hate, I should not spurn and cast from myself? For it holds not, that as a good horse is loved by him, who would not, though he might, be that horse, therefore the same may be said of an actor, who shares our nature. Do I then love in a man, what I hate to be, who am a man? Man himself is a great deep, whose very *hairs Thou numberest,* O Lord, *and they fall not to the ground without Thee.*[28] And yet are the hairs of his head easier to be numbered than are his feelings, and the beatings of his heart.

But that orator was of that sort whom I loved, as wishing to be myself such; and I erred through a swelling pride, and *was tossed about with every wind,*[29] but yet was steered by Thee, though very secretly. And whence do I know, and whence do I confidently confess unto Thee, that I had loved him more for the love of his commenders, than for the very things for which he was commended? Because, had he been unpraised, and these self-same men had dispraised him, and with dispraise and contempt told the very same things of him, I had never been so kindled and excited to love him. And yet the things had not been other, nor he himself other; but only the feelings of the relators. See where the impotent soul lies along, that is not yet stayed up by the solidity of truth! Just as the gales of tongues blow from the breast of the opinionative, so is it carried this way and that, driven forward and backward, and the light is overclouded to it, and the truth unseen. And lo, it is before us. And it was to me a great matter, that my discourse and labours should be known to that man: which should he approve, I were the more kindled, but if he disapproved, my empty heart, void of Thy solidity, had been wounded. And yet the "fair and fit," whereon I wrote to him, I dwelt on with pleasure, and surveyed it, and admired it, though none joined therein.

But I saw not yet, whereon this weighty matter turned in Thy wisdom, O Thou Omnipotent, *who only doest wonders;*[30] and my mind ranged through corporeal forms; and "fair," I defined and distinguished what is so in itself, and "fit," whose beauty is in correspondence to some other thing: and this I supported by corporeal examples. And I turned to the nature of the mind, but the false notion which I had of spiritual things, let me not see the truth. Yet the force of truth did of itself flash into mine eyes, and I turned

[28] Matt. x. 29, 30.   [29] Eph. iv. 14.   [30] Ps. cvi. 4.

away my panting soul from incorporeal substance to lineaments, and colours, and bulky magnitudes. And not being able to see these in the mind, I thought I could not see my mind. And whereas in virtue I loved peace, and in viciousness I abhorred discord; in the first I observed a unity, but in the other, a sort of division. And in that unity I conceived the rational soul, and the nature of truth and of the chief good to consist; but in this division I miserably imagined there to be some unknown substance of irrational life, and the nature of the chief evil, which should not only be a substance, but real life also, and yet not derived from Thee, O my God, of whom are all things. And yet that first I called a Monad, as it had been a soul without sex; but the latter a Duad;—anger, in deeds of violence, and in flagitiousness, lust; not knowing whereof I spake. For I had not known or learned that neither was evil a substance, nor our soul that chief and unchangeable good.

For as deeds of violence arise, if that emotion of the soul be corrupted, whence vehement action springs, stirring itself insolently and unrulily; and lusts, when that affection of the soul is ungoverned, whereby carnal pleasures are drunk in, so do errors and false opinions defile the conversation, if the reasonable soul itself be corrupted; as it was then in me, who knew not that it must be enlightened by another light, that it may be partaker of truth, seeing itself is not that nature of truth. *For Thou shalt light my candle, O Lord my God, Thou shalt enlighten my darkness:*[31] *and of Thy fulness have we all received, for Thou art the true light that lighteth every man that cometh into the world;*[32] *for in Thee there is no variableness, neither shadow of change.*[33]

But I pressed towards Thee, and was thrust from Thee, that I might taste of death: for *thou resistest the proud.*[34] But what prouder, than for me with a strange madness to maintain myself to be that by nature which Thou art? For whereas I was subject to change (so much being manifest to me, my very desire to become wise, being the wish, of worse to become better), yet chose I rather to imagine Thee subject to change, than myself not to be that which Thou art. Therefore I was repelled by Thee, and Thou resistedst my vain stiff-neckedness, and I imagined corporeal forms,

[31] Ps. xviii. 28.   [32] John i. 16, 9.   [33] Jam. i. 17.   [34] 1 Pet. v. 5; Jam. iv. 6.

and, myself flesh, I accused flesh; and, a *wind that passeth away, I returned not*[35] to Thee, but I passed on and on to things which have no being, neither in Thee, nor in me, nor in the body. Neither were they created for me by Thy truth, but by my vanity devised out of things corporeal. And I was wont to ask Thy faithful little ones, my fellow-citizens (from whom, unknown to myself, I stood exiled), I was wont, prating and foolishly, to ask them, "Why then doth the soul err which God created?" But I would not be asked, "Why then doth God err?" And I maintained that Thy unchangeable substance did err upon constraint, rather than confess that my changeable substance had gone astray voluntarily, and now, in punishment, lay in error.

I was then some six or seven and twenty years old when I wrote those volumes; revolving within me corporeal fictions, buzzing in the ears of my heart, which I turned, O sweet truth, to thy inward melody, meditating on the "fair and fit," and longing to stand and hearken to Thee, and *to rejoice greatly at the Bridegroom's voice,*[36] but could not; for by the voices of mine own errors, I was hurried abroad, and through the weight of my own pride, I was sinking into the lowest pit. For Thou didst not *make me to hear joy and gladness,* nor did *the bones exult which were not yet humbled.*[37]

And what did it profit me, that scarce twenty years old, a book of Aristotle, which they call the ten Predicaments, falling into my hands (on whose very name I hung, as on something great and divine, so often as my rhetoric master of Carthage, and others, accounted learned, mouthed it with cheeks bursting with pride), I read and understood it unaided? And on my conferring with others, who said that they scarcely understood it with very able tutors, not only orally explaining it, but drawing many things in sand, they could tell me no more of it than I had learned, reading it by myself. And the book appeared to me to speak very clearly of substances, such as "man," and of their qualities, as the figure of a man, of what sort it is; and stature, how many feet high; and his relationship, whose brother he is; or where placed; or when born; or whether he stands or sits; or be shod or armed; or does, or suffers anything; and all the innumerable things which might be ranged under these nine

[35] Ps. lxxviii. 39.   [36] John iii. 29.   [37] Ps. li. 8.

Predicaments, of which I have given some specimens, or under that chief Predicament of Substance.

What did all this further me, seeing it even hindered me? when, imagining whatever was, was comprehended under those ten Predicaments, I essayed in such wise to understand, O my God, Thy wonderful and unchangeable Unity also, as if Thou also hadst been subjected to Thine own greatness or beauty; so that (as in bodies) they should exist in Thee, as their subject: whereas Thou Thyself art Thy greatness and beauty; but a body is not great or fair in that it is a body, seeing that, though it were less great or fair, it should notwithstanding be a body. But it was falsehood which of Thee I conceived, not truth, fictions of my misery, not the realities of Thy Blessedness. For Thou hadst commanded, and it was done in me, that the *earth should bring forth briars and thorns to me,* and that *in the sweat of my brows I should eat my bread.*

And what did it profit me, that all the books I could procure of the so-called liberal arts, I, the vile slave of vile affections, read by myself, and understood? And I delighted in them, but knew not whence came all, that herein was true or certain. For I had my back to the light, and my face to the things enlightened; whence my face, with which I discerned the things enlightened, itself was not enlightened. Whatever was written, either on rhetoric, or logic, geometry, music, and arithmetic, by myself without much difficulty or any instructor, I understood, Thou knowest, O Lord my God; because both quickness of understanding, and acuteness in discerning, is Thy gift: yet did I not thence sacrifice to Thee. So then it served not to my use, but rather to my perdition, since I went about to get so good a *portion of my substance* into my own keeping; and I *kept not my strength for Thee,* but wandered from Thee *into a far country, to spend it upon harlotries.*[38] For what profited me good abilities, not employed to good uses? For I felt not that those arts were attained with great difficulty, even by the studious and talented, until I attempted to explain them to such; when he most excelled in them who followed me not altogether slowly.

But what did this further me, imagining that Thou, O Lord God, the Truth, wert a vast and bright body, and I a fragment of that

[38] Luke xv.; Ps. lviii. 10.—Vulg.

body? Perverseness too great! But such was I. Nor do I blush, O my God, to *confess to Thee Thy mercies towards me,* and to call upon Thee, who blushed not then to profess to men my blasphemies, and to bark against Thee. What profited me then my nimble wit in those sciences and all those most knotty volumes, unravelled by me, without aid from human instruction; seeing I erred so foully, and with such sacrilegious shamefulness, in the doctrine of piety? Or what hindrance was a far slower wit to Thy little ones, since they departed not far from Thee, that in the nest of Thy Church they might securely be fledged, and nourish the wings of charity, by the food of a sound faith. O Lord our God, *under the shadow of Thy wings let us hope;* protect us, and carry us. Thou wilt carry us both when little, and *even to hoar hairs wilt Thou carry us;*[39] for our firmness, when it is Thou, then is it firmness; but when our own, it is infirmity. Our good ever lives with Thee; from which when we turn away, we are turned aside. Let us now, O Lord, return, that we may not be overturned, because with Thee our good lives without any decay, which good art Thou; nor need we fear, lest there be no place whither to return, because we fell from it: for through our absence, our mansion fell not—Thy eternity.

[39] Is. xlvi. 4.

THE FIFTH BOOK

St. Augustine's twenty-ninth year. Faustus, a snare of Satan to many, made an instrument of deliverance to St. Augustine, by showing the ignorance of the Manichees on those things wherein they professed to have divine knowledge. Augustine gives up all thought of going further among the Manichees: is guided to Rome and Milan, where he hears St. Ambrose, leaves the Manichees, and becomes again a Catechumen in the Church Catholic.

ACCEPT the sacrifice of my confessions from the ministry of my tongue, which Thou hast formed and stirred up to confess unto Thy name. *Heal Thou all my bones, and let them say, O Lord, who is like unto Thee?*[1] For he who confesses to Thee doth not teach Thee what takes place within him; seeing a closed heart closes not out Thy eye, nor can man's hard-heartedness thrust back Thy hand: for Thou dissolvest it at Thy will in pity or in vengeance, *and nothing can hide itself from Thy heat*.[2] But let my soul praise Thee, that it may love Thee; and let it confess Thy own mercies to Thee, that it may praise Thee. Thy whole creation ceaseth not, nor is silent in Thy praises; neither the spirit of man with voice directed unto Thee, nor creation animate or inanimate, by the voice of those who meditate thereon: that so our souls may from their weariness arise towards Thee, leaning on those things which Thou hast created, and passing on to Thyself, who madest them wonderfully; and there is refreshment and true strength.

Let the restless, the godless, depart and flee from Thee; yet Thou seest them, and dividest the darkness. And behold, the universe with them is fair, though they are foul. And how have they injured Thee? or how have they disgraced Thy government, which, from the heaven to this lowest earth, is just and perfect? For whither fled they, when they fled from Thy presence?[3] or where dost not Thou find them? But they fled, that they might not see Thee seeing them, and, blinded, might stumble against Thee[4] (because *Thou*

---

[1] Ps. xxxv. 20.   [2] Ps. xix. 6.   [3] Ps. cxxxix. 7.   [4] Gen. xvi. 14.

forsakest nothing Thou hast made[5]); that the unjust, I say, might stumble upon Thee, and justly be hurt; withdrawing themselves from thy gentleness, and stumbling at Thy uprightness, and falling upon their own ruggedness. Ignorant, in truth, that Thou art every where, Whom no place encompasseth! and Thou alone art near, even to those that *remove far from Thee.*[6] Let them then be turned, and seek Thee; because not as they have forsaken their Creator, hast Thou forsaken Thy creation. Let them be turned and seek Thee; and behold, Thou art there in their heart, in the heart of those that confess to Thee, and cast themselves upon Thee, and weep in Thy bosom, after all their rugged ways. Then dost Thou gently wipe away their tears, and they weep the more, and joy in weeping; even for that Thou, Lord,—not man of flesh and blood, but—Thou, Lord, who madest them, re-makest and comfortest them. But where was I, when I was seeking Thee? And Thou wert before me, but I had gone away from Thee; nor did I find myself, how much less Thee!

I would lay open before my God that nine-and-twentieth year of mine age. There had then come to Carthage a certain Bishop of the Manichees, Faustus by name, a great snare of the Devil, and many were entangled by him through that lure of his smooth language: which though I did commend, yet could I separate from the truth of the things which I was earnest to learn: nor do I so much regard the service of oratory as the science which this Faustus, so praised among them, set before me to feed upon. Fame had before bespoken him most knowing in all valuable learning, and exquisitely skilled in the liberal sciences. And since I had read and well remembered much of the philosophers, I compared some things of theirs with those long fables of the Manichees, and found the former the more probable; even although they *could only prevail so far as to make judgment of this lower world, the Lord of it they could by no means find out.*[7] *For Thou art great, O Lord, and hast respect unto the humble, but the proud Thou beholdest afar off.*[8] Nor dost thou *draw near*, but to *the contrite in heart*,[9] nor art found by the proud, no, not though by curious skill they could number the stars

---

[5] Wisd. xi. 25, old vers.   [6] Ps. lxxiii. 27.   [7] Wisd. xiii. 9.   [8] Ps. cxxxviii. 6.
[9] Ps. xxxiv. 18.

and the sand, and measure the starry heavens, and track the courses of the planets.

For with their understanding and wit, which Thou bestowedst on them, they search out these things; and much have they found out; and foretold, many years before, eclipses of those luminaries, the sun and moon,—what day and hour, and how many digits,—nor did their calculation fail; and it came to pass as they foretold; and they wrote down the rules they had found out, and these are read at this day, and out of them do others foretell in what year and month of the year, and what day of the month, and what hour of the day, and what part of its light, moon or sun is to be eclipsed and so it shall be, as it is foreshowed. At these things men, that know not this art, marvel and are astonished, and they that know it, exult, and are puffed up; and by an ungodly pride departing from Thee, and failing of Thy light, they foresee a failure of the sun's light, which shall be, so long before, but see not their own, which is. For they search not religiously whence they have the wit, wherewith they search out this. And finding that Thou madest them, they give not themselves up to Thee, to preserve what Thou madest, nor sacrifice to Thee what they have made themselves; nor slay their own soaring imaginations, as *fowls of the air,* nor their own diving curiosities (wherewith, like the *fishes of the sea*[10] they wander over the unknown paths of the abyss), nor their own luxuriousness, as *beasts of the field,* that *Thou, Lord, a consuming fire,*[11] mayest burn up those dead cares of theirs, and recreate themselves immortally.

But they knew not the way, Thy Word,[12] by Whom Thou madest these things which they number, and themselves who number, and the sense whereby they perceive what they number, and the understanding, out of which they number; or that *of Thy wisdom there is no number.*[13] But the Only Begotten is Himself *made unto us wisdom, and righteousness, and sanctification,*[14] and was numbered among us, and *paid tribute unto Cæsar.*[15] They knew not this Way whereby to descend to Him from themselves, and by Him ascend unto Him. They knew not this way, and deemed themselves exalted amongst the stars and shining; and behold, they *fell upon the*

[10] Ps. viii. 7, 8.   [11] Deut. iv. 24.   [12] John i. 3.   [13] Ps. cxlvii. 5.
[14] 1 Cor. i. 30.   [15] Matt. xvii. 27.

earth, and their foolish heart was darkened.[16] They discourse many things truly concerning the creature; but Truth, Artificer of the creature, they seek not piously, and therefore find him not; or if they find him, *knowing Him to be God, they glorify Him not as God, neither are thankful, but become vain in their imaginations,* and *profess themselves to be wise,*[17] attributing to themselves what is Thine; and thereby with most perverse blindness, study to impute to Thee what is their own, forging lies of Thee who art the Truth, and *changing the glory of the uncorruptible God into an image made like corruptible man, and to birds, and four-footed beasts, and creeping things, changing Thy truth into a lie, and worshipping and serving the creature more than the Creator.*[18]

Yet many truths concerning the creature retained I from these men, and saw the reason thereof from calculations, the succession of times, and the visible testimonies of the stars; and compared them with the saying of Manichæus, which in his frenzy he had written most largely on these subjects; but discovered not any account of the solstices, or equinoxes, or the eclipses of the greater lights, nor whatever of this sort I had learned in the books of secular philosophy. But I was commanded to believe; and yet it corresponded not with what had been established by calculations and my own sight, but was quite contrary.

Doth then, O Lord God of Truth, whoso knoweth these things, therefore please Thee? Surely unhappy is he who knoweth all these, and knoweth not Thee: but happy whoso knoweth Thee, though he know not these. And whoso knoweth both Thee and them is not the happier for them, but for Thee only, if, *knowing Thee,* he *glorifies Thee as God, and is thankful, and becomes not vain in his imaginations.*[19] For as he is better off who knows how to possess a tree, and return thanks to Thee for the use thereof, although he know not how many cubits high it is, or how wide it spreads, than he that can measure it, and count all its boughs, and neither owns it, nor knows or loves its Creator: so a believer, whose all this world of wealth is, and *who having nothing, yet possesseth all things,*[20] by cleaving unto Thee, whom all things serve, though he know not even the circles of the Great Bear, yet is it folly to

[16] Is. xiv. 13; Rev. xii. 4; Rom. i. 21.   [17] Rom. i. 21.   [18] Rom. i. 23.
[19] Rom. i. 21.   [20] 2 Cor. vi. 10.

doubt but he is in a better state than one who can measure the
heavens, and number the stars, and poise the elements, yet neglecteth Thee *who hast made all things in number, weight, and measure.*[21]

But yet who bade that Manichæus write on these things also,
skill in which was no element of piety? For Thou hast said to man,
Behold piety and wisdom;[22] of which he might be ignorant, though
he had perfect knowledge of these things; but these things, since,
knowing not, he most impudently dared to teach, he plainly could
have no knowledge of piety. For it is vanity to make profession of
these worldly things even when known; but confession to Thee is
piety. Wherefore this wanderer to this end spake much of these
things, that convicted by those who had truly learned them, it might
be manifest what understanding he had in the other abstruser
things. For he would not have himself meanly thought of, but went
about to persuade men, "That the Holy Ghost, the Comforter and
Enricher of Thy faithful ones, was with plenary authority person-
ally within him." When then he was found out to have taught
falsely of the heaven and stars, and of the motions of the sun and
moon (although these things pertain not to the doctrine of religion),
yet his sacrilegious presumption would become evident enough,
seeing he delivered things which not only he knew not, but which
were falsified, with so mad a vanity of pride, that he sought to
ascribe them to himself, as to a divine person.

For when I hear any Christian brother ignorant of these things,
and mistaken on them, I can patiently behold such a man holding
his opinion; nor do I see that any ignorance as to the position or
character of the corporeal creation can injure him, so long as he
doth not believe any thing unworthy of Thee, O Lord, the Creator
of all. But it doth injure him, if he imagine it to pertain to the
form of the doctrine of piety, and will yet affirm that too stiffly
whereof he is ignorant. And yet is even such an infirmity, in the
infancy of faith, borne by our mother Charity, till the newborn
may *grow up unto a perfect man,* so as *not to be carried about with
every wind of doctrine.*[23] But in him who in such wise presumed
to be the teacher, source, guide, chief of all whom he could so per-

[21] Wisd. xi. 20.   [22] Job. xxviii. 28. LXX.   [23] Eph. iv. 13, 14.

suade, that whoso followed him thought that he followed, not a mere man, but Thy Holy Spirit; who would not judge that so great madness, when once convicted of having taught any thing false, were to be detested and utterly rejected? But I had not as yet clearly ascertained whether the vicissitudes of longer and shorter days and nights, and of day and night itself, with the eclipses of the greater lights, and whatever else of the kind I had read of in other books, might be explained consistently with his sayings; so that, if they by any means might, it should remain a question to me whether it were so or no; but I might, on account of his reputed sanctity, rest my credence upon his authority.

And for almost all those nine years, wherein with unsettled mind I had been their disciple, I had longed but too intensely for the coming of this Faustus. For the rest of the sect, whom by chance I had lighted upon, when unable to solve my objections about these things, still held out to me the coming of this Faustus, by conference with whom these and greater difficulties, if I had them, were to be most readily and abundantly cleared. When then he came, I found him a man of pleasing discourse, and who could speak fluently and in better terms, yet still but the self-same things which they were wont to say. But what availed the utmost neatness of the cup-bearer to my thirst for a more precious draught? Mine ears were already cloyed with the like, nor did they seem to me therefore better, because better said; or therefore true, because eloquent; nor the soul therefore wise, because the face was comely, and the language grace-ful. But they who held him out to me were no good judges of things; and therefore to them he appeared understanding and wise, because in words pleasing. I felt however that another sort of people were suspicious even of truth, and refused to assent to it, if de-livered in a smooth and copious discourse. But Thou, O my God, hadst already taught me by wonderful and secret ways, and there-fore I believe that Thou taughtest me, because it is truth, nor is there besides Thee any teacher of truth, where or whencesoever it may shine upon us. Of Thyself therefore had I now learned, that neither ought any thing to seem to be spoken truly, because eloquently; nor therefore falsely, because the utterance of the lips is inharmonious; nor, again, therefore true, because rudely delivered; or therefore false, because the language is rich; but that wisdom and folly are as wholesome and unwholesome food; and adorned or unadorned phrases as courtly or country vessels; either kind of meats may be served up in either kind of dishes.

That greediness then, wherewith I had of so long time expected that man, was delighted verily with his action and feeling when disputing, and his choice and readiness of words to clothe his ideas. I was then delighted, and, with many others and more than they, did I praise and extol him. It troubled me, however, that in the assembly of his auditors, I was not allowed to put in and communicate those questions that troubled me, in familiar converse with him. Which when I might, and with my friends began to engage his ears at such times as it was not unbecoming for him to discuss with me, and had brought forward such things as moved me; I found him first utterly ignorant of liberal sciences, save grammar, and that but in an ordinary way. But because he had read some of Tully's Orations, a very few books of Seneca, some things of the poets, and such few volumes of his own sect as were written in Latin and neatly, and was daily practised in speaking, he acquired a certain eloquence, which proved the more pleasing and seductive, because under the guidance of a good wit, and with a kind of natural gracefulness. Is it not thus, as I recall it, O Lord my God, Thou Judge of my conscience? before Thee is my heart, and my remembrance, Who didst at that time direct me by the hidden mystery of Thy providence, and didst set those shameful errors of mine before my face, that I might see and hate them.[24]

For after it was clear that he was ignorant of those arts in which I thought he excelled, I began to despair of his opening and solving the difficulties which perplexed me (of which indeed however ignorant, he might have held the truths of piety, had he not been a Manichee). For their books are fraught with prolix fable, of the heaven, and stars, sun, and moon, and I now no longer thought him able satisfactorily to decide what I much desired, whether, on comparison of these things with the calculations I had elsewhere read, the account given in the books of Manichæus were preferable, or at least as good. Which when I proposed to be considered and

[24] Ps. l. 21.

discussed, he, so far modestly, shrunk from the burthen. For he knew that he knew not these things, and was not ashamed to confess it. For he was not one of those talking persons, many of whom I had endured, who undertook to teach me these things, and said nothing. But this man had a heart, though not right towards Thee, yet neither altogether treacherous to himself. For he was not altogether ignorant of his own ignorance, nor would he rashly be entangled in a dispute, whence he could neither retreat nor extricate himself fairly. Even for this I liked him the better. For fairer is the modesty of a candid mind, than the knowledge of those things which I desired; and such I found him, in all the more difficult and subtile questions.

My zeal for the writings of Manichæus being thus blunted, and despairing yet more of their other teachers, seeing that in divers things which perplexed me, he, so renowned among them, had so turned out; I began to engage with him in the study of that literature, on which he also was much set (and which as rhetoric-reader I was at that time teaching young students at Carthage), and to read with him, either what himself desired to hear, or such as I judged fit for his genius. But all my efforts whereby I had purposed to advance in that sect, upon knowledge of that man, came utterly to an end; not that I detached myself from them altogether, but as one finding nothing better, I had settled to be content meanwhile with what I had in whatever way fallen upon, unless by chance something more eligible should dawn upon me. Thus that Faustus, to so many a snare of death, had now, neither willing nor witting it, begun to loosen that wherein I was taken. For Thy hands, O my God, in the secret purpose of Thy providence, did not forsake my soul; and out of my mother's heart's blood, through her tears night and day poured out, was a sacrifice offered for me unto Thee; and Thou didst deal with me by wondrous ways.[25] Thou didst it, O my God: for *the steps of a man are ordered by the Lord, and He shall dispose his way.*[26] Or how shall we obtain salvation, but from Thy hand, re-making what it made?

Thou didst deal with me, that I should be persuaded to go to Rome, and to teach there rather, what I was teaching at Carthage. And

[25] Joel. ii. 26.   [26] Ps. xxxvii. 23.

how I was persuaded to this, I will not neglect to confess to Thee: because herein also the deepest recesses of Thy wisdom, and Thy most present mercy to us, must be considered and confessed. I did not wish therefore to go to Rome, because higher gains and higher dignities were warranted me by my friends who persuaded me to this (though even these things had at that time an influence over my mind), but my chief and almost only reason was, that I heard that young men studied there more peacefully, and were kept quiet under a restraint of more regular discipline; so that they did not, at their pleasures, petulantly rush into the school of one whose pupils they were not, nor were even admitted without his permission. Whereas at Carthage there reigns among the scholars a most disgraceful and unruly licence. They burst in audaciously, and with gestures almost frantic, disturb all order which any one hath established for the good of his scholars. Divers outrages they commit, with a wonderful stolidity, punishable by law, did not custom uphold them; that custom evincing them to be the more miserable, in that they now do as lawful what by Thy eternal law shall never be lawful; and they think they do it unpunished, whereas they are punished with the very blindness whereby they do it, and suffer incomparably worse than what they do. The manners then which, when a student, I would not make my own, I was fain as a teacher to endure in others: and so I was well pleased to go where, all that knew it, assured me that the like was not done. But Thou, *my refuge and my portion in the land of the living;*[27] that I might change my earthly dwelling for the salvation of my soul, at Carthage didst goad me, that I might thereby be torn from it; and at Rome didst proffer me allurements, whereby I might be drawn thither, by men in love with a dying life, the one doing frantic, the other promising vain, things; and, to correct my steps, didst secretly use their and my own perverseness. For both they who disturbed my quiet were blinded with a disgraceful frenzy, and they who invited me elsewhere savoured of earth. And I, who here detested real misery, was there seeking unreal happiness.

But why I went hence, and went thither, Thou knewest, O God, yet showedst it neither to me, nor to my mother, who grievously

[27] Ps. cxlii. 5.

bewailed my journey, and followed me as far as the sea. But I deceived her, holding me by force, that either she might keep me back or go with me, and I feigned that I had a friend whom I could not leave, till he had a fair wind to sail. And I lied to my mother, and such a mother, and escaped: for this also hast Thou mercifully forgiven me, preserving me, thus full of execrable defilements, from the waters of the sea, for the water of Thy Grace; whereby when I was cleansed, the streams of my mother's eyes should be dried, with which for me she daily watered the ground under her face. And yet refusing to return without me, I scarcely persuaded her to stay that night in a place hard by our ship, where was an Oratory in memory of the blessed Cyprian. That night I privily departed, but she was not behind in weeping and prayer. And what, O Lord, was she with so many tears asking of Thee, but that Thou wouldst not suffer me to sail? But Thou, in the depth of Thy counsels and hearing the main point of her desire, regardedst not what she then asked, that Thou mightest make me what she ever asked. The wind blew and swelled our sails, and withdrew the shore from our sight; and she on the morrow was there, frantic with sorrow, and with complaints and groans filled Thine ears, who didst then disregard them; whilst through my desires, Thou wert hurrying me to end all desire, and the earthly part of her affection to me was chastened by the allotted scourge of sorrows. For she loved my being with her, as mothers do, but much more than many; and she knew not how great joy Thou wert about to work for her out of my absence. She knew not; therefore did she weep and wail, and by this agony there appeared in her the inheritance of Eve, with sorrow seeking what in sorrow she had brought forth. And yet, after accusing my treachery and hardheartedness, she betook herself again to intercede to Thee for me, went to her wonted place, and I to Rome.

And lo, there was I received by the scourge of bodily sickness, and I was going down to hell, carrying all the sins which I had committed, both against Thee, and myself, and others, many and grievous, over and above that bond of original sin, whereby *we all die in Adam*.[28] For Thou hadst not forgiven me any of these things

[28] 1 Cor. xv. 22.

in Christ, nor had He *abolished by His* cross *the enmity* which by
my sins I had incurred with Thee. For how should He, by the
crucifixion of a phantasm, which I believed Him to be? So true,
then, was the death of my soul, as that of His flesh seemed to me
false; and how true the death of His body, so false was the life of
my soul, which did not believe it. And now the fever heightening,
I was parting and departing for ever. For had I then parted hence,
whither had I departed, but into fire and torments, such as my
misdeeds deserved in the truth of Thy appointment? And this she
knew not, yet in absence prayed for me. But Thou, everywhere
present, heardest her where she was, and, where I was, hadst compassion upon me; that I should recover the health of my body,
though frenzied as yet in my sacrilegious heart. For I did not in
all that danger desire Thy baptism; and I was better as a boy, when
I begged it of my mother's piety, as I have before recited and confessed. But I had grown up to my own shame, and I madly scoffed
at the prescripts of Thy medicine, who wouldest not suffer me, being
such, to die a double death. With which wound had my mother's
heart been pierced, it could never be healed. For I cannot express
the affection she bare to me, and with how much more vehement
anguish she was now in labour of me in the spirit, than at her child-
bearing in the flesh.[29]

I see not then how she should have been healed, had such a death
of mine stricken through the bowels of her love. And where would
have been those her so strong and unceasing prayers, unintermitting
to Thee alone? But wouldest Thou, God of mercies, *despise* the
contrite and humbled heart[30] of that chaste and sober widow, so frequent in alms-deeds, so full of duty and service to Thy saints, no
day intermitting the oblation at Thine altar, twice a day, morning
and evening, without any intermission, coming to Thy church, not
for idle tattlings and old wives' *fables,*[31] but that she might hear
Thee in Thy discourses, and Thou her in her prayers. Couldest
Thou despise and reject from Thy aid the tears of such an one,
wherewith she begged of Thee not gold or silver, nor mutable or
passing good, but the salvation of her son's soul? Thou, by whose
gift she was such? Never, Lord. Yea, Thou wert at hand, and wert

[29] Gal. iv. 9.   [30] Ps. li. 17.   [31] 1 Tim. v. 10.

hearing and doing, in that order wherein Thou hadst determined before that it should be done. Far be it that Thou shouldest deceive her in Thy visions and answers, some whereof I have, some I have not mentioned, which she laid up in her faithful heart, and ever praying urged upon Thee, as Thine own handwriting. For Thou, *because Thy mercy endureth for ever,* vouchsafest to those to whom Thou forgivest all their debts, to become also a debtor by Thy promises.

Thou recoveredst me then of that sickness, and healedst the son of Thy handmaid, for the time in body, that he might live, for Thee to bestow upon him a better and more abiding health. And even then, at Rome, I joined myself to those deceiving and deceived "holy ones"; not with their disciples only (of which number was he, in whose house I had fallen sick and recovered); but also with those whom they call "The Elect." For I still thought "that it was not we that sin, but that I know not what other nature sinned in us"; and it delighted my pride, to be free from blame; and when I had done any evil, not to confess I had done any, *that Thou mightest heal my soul because it had sinned against Thee:*[32] but I loved to excuse it, and to accuse I know not what other thing, which was with me, but which I was not. But in truth it was wholly I, and mine impiety had divided me against myself: and that sin was the more incurable, whereby I did not judge myself a sinner; and execrable iniquity it was, that I had rather have Thee, Thee, O God Almighty, to be overcome in me to my destruction, than myself of Thee to salvation. Not as yet then hadst Thou *set a watch before my mouth, and a door of safe keeping around my lips, that my heart might not turn aside to wicked speeches,* to *make excuses of sins, with men that work iniquity: and,* therefore, was I still *united with their Elect.*[33]

But now despairing to make proficiency in that false doctrine, even those (with which if I should find no better, I had resolved to rest contented) I now held more laxly and carelessly. For there half arose a thought in me that those philosophers, whom they call Academics, were wiser than the rest, for that they held men ought to doubt everything, and laid down that no truth can be compre-

[32] Ps. xli. 4   [33] Ps. cxli. 3, 4.—Vulg.

hended by man: for so, not then understanding even their meaning, I also was clearly convinced that they thought, as they are commonly reported. Yet did I freely and openly discourage that host of mine from that over-confidence which I perceived him to have in those fables, which the books of Manichæus are full of. Yet I lived in more familiar friendship with them, than with others who were not of this heresy. Nor did I maintain it with my ancient eagerness; still my intimacy with that sect (Rome secretly harbouring many of them) made me slower to seek any other way: especially since I despaired of finding the truth, from which they had turned me aside, in Thy Church, O Lord of heaven and earth, Creator of all things visible and invisible: and it seemed to me unseemly to believe Thee to have the shape of human flesh, and to be bounded by the bodily lineaments of our members. And because, when I wished to think on my God, I knew not what to think of, but a mass of bodies (for what was not such did not seem to me to be any thing), this was the greatest, and almost only cause of my inevitable error.

For hence I believed Evil also to be some such kind of substance, and to have its own foul and hideous bulk; whether gross, which they called earth, or thin and subtile (like the body of the air), which they imagine to be some malignant mind, creeping through that earth. And because a piety, such as it was, constrained me to believe that the good God never created any evil nature, I conceived two masses, contrary to one another, both unbounded, but the evil narrower, the good more expansive. And from this pestilent beginning, the other sacrilegious conceits followed on me. For when my mind endeavoured to recur to the Catholic faith, I was driven back, since that was not the Catholic faith which I thought to be so. And I seemed to myself more reverential, if I believed of Thee, my God (to whom Thy mercies confess out of my mouth), as unbounded, at least on other sides, although on that where the mass of evil was opposed to Thee, I was constrained to confess Thee bounded; than if on all sides I should imagine Thee to be bounded by the form of a human body. And it seemed to me better to believe Thee to have created no evil (which to me ignorant seemed not some only, but a bodily substance, because I could not conceive of mind unless as a subtile body, and that diffused in definite spaces), than to believe the nature of evil, such as I conceived it, could come from Thee. Yea, and our Saviour Himself, Thy Only Begotten, I believed to have been reached forth (as it were) for our salvation, out of the mass of Thy most lucid substance, so as to believe nothing of Him, but what I could imagine in my vanity. His Nature then, being such, I thought could not be born of the Virgin Mary, without being mingled with the flesh: and how that which I had so figured to myself could be mingled, and not defiled, I saw not. I feared therefore to believe Him born in the flesh, lest I should be forced to believe Him defiled by the flesh. Now will Thy spiritual ones mildly and lovingly smile upon me, if they shall read these my confessions. Yet such was I.

Furthermore, what the Manichees had criticised in Thy Scriptures, I thought could not be defended; yet at times verily I had a wish to confer upon these several points with some one very well skilled in those books, and to make trial what he thought thereon: for the words of one Helpidius, as he spoke and disputed face to face against the said Manichees, had begun to stir me even at Carthage: in that he had produced things out of the Scriptures, not easily withstood, the Manichees' answer whereto seemed to me weak. And this answer they liked not to give publicly, but only to us in private. It was, that the Scriptures of the New Testament had been corrupted by I know not whom, who wished to engraff the law of the Jews upon the Christian faith: yet themselves produced not any uncorrupted copies. But I, conceiving of things corporeal only, was mainly held down, vehemently oppressed and in a manner suffocated by those "masses"; panting under which after the breath of Thy truth, I could not breathe it pure and untainted.

I began then diligently to practise that for which I came to Rome, to teach rhetoric; and first, to gather some to my house, to whom, and through whom, I had begun to be known; when lo, I found other offences committed in Rome, to which I was not exposed in Africa. True, those "subvertings" by profligate young men were not here practised, as was told me: but on a sudden, said they, to avoid paying their master's stipend, a number of youths plot together, and remove to another;—breakers of faith, who for love of money hold justice cheap. These also *my heart hated,* though not *with a perfect hatred*:[34] for perchance I hated them more because I was to suffer by them, than because they did things utterly unlawful. Of a truth such are base persons, and they go a whoring from Thee, loving these fleeting mockeries of things temporal, and filthy lucre, which fouls the hand that grasps it; hugging the fleeting world, and despising Thee, who abidest, and recallest, and forgivest the adulteress soul of man, when she returns to Thee. And now I hate such depraved and crooked persons, though I love them if corrigible, so as to prefer to money the learning which they acquire, and to learning, Thee, O God, the truth and fulness of assured good, and most pure peace. But then I rather for my own sake misliked them evil, than liked and wished them good for Thine.

When therefore they of Milan had sent to Rome to the prefect of the city, to furnish them with a rhetoric reader for their city, and send him at the public expense, I made application (through those very persons, intoxicated with Manichæan vanities, to be freed wherefrom I was to go, neither of us however knowing it) that Symmachus, then prefect of the city, would try me by setting me some subject, and so send me. To Milan I came, to Ambrose the Bishop, known to the whole world as among the best of men, Thy devout servant; whose eloquent discourse did then plentifully dispense unto Thy people the flour of Thy wheat, the gladness of Thy oil, and the sober inebriation of Thy wine.[35] To him was I unknowing led by Thee, that by him I might knowingly be led to Thee. That man of God received me as a father, and showed me an Episcopal kindness on my coming. Thenceforth I began to love him, at first indeed not as a teacher of the truth (which I utterly despaired of in Thy Church), but as a person kind towards myself. And I listened diligently to him preaching to the people, not with that intent I ought, but, as it were, trying his eloquence, whether it answered the fame thereof, or flowed fuller or lower than was reported; and I hung on his words attentively; but of the matter I was as a careless and scornful looker-on; and I was delighted with the sweetness of his discourse, more recondite, yet in manner less winning and harmonious, than that of Faustus. Of the matter, how-

34 Ps. cxxxix. 22.   35 Ps. iv. 7; civ. 15.

ever, there was no comparison; for the one was wandering amid
Manichæan delusions, the other teaching salvation most soundly.
But *salvation is far from sinners,*[36] such as I then stood before him;
and as yet was I drawing nearer by little and little, and uncon-
sciously.

For though I took no pains to learn what he spake, but only to
hear how he spake (for that empty care alone was left me, despairing of a way, open for man, to Thee), yet together with the words
which I would choose, came also into my mind the things which
I would refuse; for I could not separate them. And while I opened
my heart to admit "how eloquently he spake," there also entered
"how truly he spake;" but this by degrees. For first, these things
also had now begun to appear to me capable of defence; and the
Catholic faith, for which I had thought nothing could be said against
the Manichees' objections, I now thought might be maintained
without shamelessness; especially after I had heard one or two
places of the Old Testament resolved, and ofttimes *"in a figure,"*[37]
which when I understood literally, I was slain spiritually. Very
many places then of those books having been explained, I now
blamed my despair, in believing that no answer could be given to
such as hated and scoffed at the Law and the Prophets. Yet did I
not therefore then see that the Catholic way was to be held, because
it also could find learned maintainers, who could at large and with
some show of reason answer objections; nor that what I held was
therefore to be condemned, because both sides could be maintained.
For the Catholic cause seemed to me in such sort not vanquished,
as still not as yet to be victorious.

Hereupon I earnestly bent my mind, to see if in any way I could
by any certain proof convict the Manichees of falsehood. Could I
once have conceived a spiritual substance, all their strongholds had
been beaten down, and cast utterly out of my mind; but I could
not. Notwithstanding, concerning the frame of this world, and the
whole of nature, which the senses of the flesh can reach to, as I more
and more considered and compared things, I judged the tenets of
most of the philosophers to have been much more probable. So then
after the manner of the Academics (as they are supposed) doubting

[36] Ps. cxix. 155.   [37] 1 Cor. xiii. 12; 2 Cor. iii. 6.

of everything, and wavering between all, I settled so far, that the Manichees were to be abandoned; judging that, even while doubting, I might not continue in that sect, to which I already preferred some of the philosophers; to which philosophers notwithstanding, for that they were without the saving Name of Christ, I utterly refused to commit the cure of my sick soul. I determined therefore so long to be a Catechumen in the Catholic Church, to which I had been commended by my parents, till something certain should dawn upon me, whither I might steer my course.

THE SIXTH BOOK

Arrival of Monnica at Milan; her obedience to St. Ambrose, and his value for her; St. Ambrose's habits; Augustine's gradual abandonment of error; finds that he has blamed the Church Catholic wrongly; desire of absolute certainty, but struck with the contrary analogy of God's natural Providence; how shaken in his worldly pursuits; God's guidance of his friend Alypius; Augustine debates with himself and his friends about their mode of life; his inveterate sins, and dread of judgment.

O THOU, my hope from my youth,[1] where wert Thou to me, and whither wert Thou gone? Hadst not Thou created me, and separated me from the beasts of the field, and fowls of the air? Thou hadst made me wiser, yet did I walk in darkness, and in slippery places, and sought Thee abroad out of myself, and found not the God of my heart; and had come into the depths of the sea, and distrusted and despaired of ever finding truth. My mother had now come to me, resolute through piety, following me over sea and land, in all perils confiding in Thee. For in perils of the sea, she comforted the very mariners (by whom passengers unacquainted with the deep, use rather to be comforted when troubled), assuring them of a safe arrival, because Thou hadst by a vision assured her thereof. She found me in grievous peril, through despair of ever finding truth. But when I had discovered to her that I was now no longer a Manichee, though not yet a Catholic Christian, she was not overjoyed, as at something unexpected; although she was now assured concerning that part of my misery, for which she bewailed me as one dead, though to be reawakened by Thee, carrying me forth upon the *bier* of her thoughts, that Thou mightest say to the *son of the widow, Young man, I say unto thee, Arise; and he should revive, and begin to speak, and thou shouldest deliver him to his mother.*[2] Her heart then was shaken with no tumultuous exultation, when she heard that what she daily desired of Thee was

[1] Ps. lxxi. 5.   [2] Luke vii. 14, 15.

79

already in so great part realised; in that, though I had not yet attained the truth, I was rescued from falsehood; but, as being assured, that Thou, who hadst promised the whole, wouldest one day give the rest, most calmly, and with a heart full of confidence, she replied to me, "She believed in Christ, that before she departed this life, she should see me a Catholic believer." Thus much to me. But to Thee, Fountain of mercies, poured she forth more copious prayers and tears, that Thou wouldest hasten Thy help, and enlighten my darkness; and she hastened the more eagerly to the Church, and hung upon the lips of Ambrose, praying for *the fountain of that water, which springeth up unto life everlasting.*[3] But that man she loved *as an angel of God,* because she knew that by him I had been brought for the present to that doubtful state of faith I now was in, through which she anticipated most confidently that I should pass from sickness unto health, after the access, as it were, of a sharper fit, which physicians call "the crisis."

When then my mother had once, as she was wont in Afric, brought to the Churches built in memory of the Saints, certain cakes, and bread and wine, and was forbidden by the door-keeper; so soon as she knew that the Bishop had forbidden this, she so piously and obediently embraced his wishes, that I myself wondered how readily she censured her own practice, rather than discuss his prohibition. For wine-bibbing did not lay siege to her spirit, nor did love of wine provoke her to hatred of the truth, as it doth too many (both men and women), who revolt at a lesson of sobriety, as men well drunk at a draught mingled with water. But she, when she had brought her basket with the accustomed festival-food, to be but tasted by herself, and then given away, never joined therewith more than one small cup of wine, diluted according to her own abstemious habits, which for courtesy she would taste. And if there were many churches of the departed saints that were to be honoured in that manner, she still carried round that same one cup, to be used every where; and this, though not only made very watery, but unpleasantly heated with carrying about, she would distribute to those about her by small sips; for she sought there devotion, not pleasure. So soon, then, as she found this custom to be forbidden by that

[3] John iv. 14.

famous preacher and most pious prelate, even to those that would use it soberly, lest so an occasion of excess might be given to the drunken; and for that these, as it were, anniversary funeral solemnities did much resemble the superstition of the Gentiles, she most willingly forbare it: and for a basket filled with fruits of the earth, she had learned to bring to the Churches of the martyrs a breast filled with more purified petitions, and to give what she could to the poor; that so the communication of the Lord's Body might be there rightly celebrated, where, after the example of His Passion, the martyrs had been sacrificed and crowned. But yet it seems to me, O Lord my God, and thus thinks my heart of it in Thy sight, that perhaps she would not so readily have yielded to the cutting off of this custom, had it been forbidden by another, whom she loved not as Ambrose, whom, for my salvation, she loved most entirely; and he her again, for her most religious conversation, whereby in good works, *so fervent in spirit,* she was constant at church; so that, when he saw me, he often burst forth into her praises; congratulating me that I had such a mother; not knowing what a son she had in me, who doubted of all these things, and imagined the way to life could not be found out.

Nor did I yet groan in my prayers, that Thou wouldest help me; but my spirit was wholly intent on learning, and restless to dispute. And Ambrose himself, as the world counts happy, I esteemed a happy man, whom personages so great held in such honour; only his celibacy seemed to me a painful course. But what hope he bore within him, what struggles he had against the temptations which beset his very excellencies, or what comfort in adversities, and what sweet joys Thy Bread had for the hidden mouth of his spirit, when chewing the cud thereof, I neither could conjecture, nor had experienced. Nor did he know the tides of my feelings, or the abyss of my danger. For I could not ask of him, what I would as I would, being shut out both from his ear and speech by multitudes of busy people, whose weaknesses he served. With whom when he was not taken up (which was but a little time), he was either refreshing his body with the sustenance absolutely necessary, or his mind with reading. But when he was reading, his eye glided over the pages, and his heart searched out the sense, but his voice and tongue were at rest. Ofttimes when we had come (for no man was forbidden to enter, nor was it his wont that any who came should be announced to him), we saw him thus reading to himself, and never otherwise; and having long sat silent (for who durst intrude on one so intent?) we were fain to depart, conjecturing that in the small interval which he obtained, free from the din of others' business, for the recruiting of his mind, he was loth to be taken off; and perchance he dreaded lest if the author he read should deliver any thing obscurely, some attentive or perplexed hearer should desire him to expound it, or to discuss some of the harder questions; so that his time being thus spent, he could not turn over so many volumes as he desired; although the preserving of his voice (which a very little speaking would weaken) might be the truer reason for his reading to himself. But with what intent soever he did it, certainly in such a man it was good.

I however certainly had no opportunity of enquiring what I wished of that so holy oracle of Thine, his breast, unless the thing might be answered briefly. But those tides in me, to be poured out to him, required his full leisure, and never found it. I heard him indeed every Lord's day, *rightly expounding the Word of truth*[4] among the people; and I was more and more convinced that all the knots of those crafty calumnies, which those our deceivers had knit against the Divine Books, could be unravelled. But when I understood withal, that *"man, created by Thee after Thine own image,"* was not so understood by Thy spiritual sons, whom of the Catholic Mother Thou hast born again through grace as though they believed and conceived of Thee as bounded by human shape (although what a spiritual substance should be I had not even a faint or shadowy notion); yet, with joy I blushed at having so many years barked not against the Catholic faith, but against the fictions of carnal imaginations. For so rash and impious had I been, that what I ought by enquiring to have learned, I had pronounced on, condemning. For Thou, Most High, and most near; most secret, and most present; Who hast not limbs some larger, some smaller, but art wholly every where, and no where in space, art not of such

[4] 2 Tim. ii. 15.

corporeal shape, yet hast Thou made man after Thine own image; and behold, from head to foot is he contained in space.

Ignorant then how this Thy image should subsist, I should have knocked and proposed the doubt, how it was to be believed, not insultingly opposed it, as if believed. Doubt, then, what to hold for certain, the more sharply gnawed my heart, the more ashamed I was, that so long deluded and deceived by the promise of certainties, I had with childish error and vehemence, prated of so many uncertainties. For that they were falsehoods became clear to me later. However I was certain that they were uncertain, and that I had formerly accounted them certain, when with a blind contentiousness, I accused Thy Catholic Church, whom I now discovered, not indeed as yet to teach truly, but at least not to teach that for which I had grievously censured her. So I was confounded, and converted; and I joyed, O my God, that the One Only Church, the body of Thine Only Son (wherein the name of Christ had been put upon me as an infant), had no taste for infantine conceits; nor in her sound doctrine maintained any tenet which should confine Thee, the Creator of all, in space, however great and large, yet bounded every where by the limits of a human form.

I joyed also that the old Scriptures of the law and the Prophets were laid before me, not now to be perused with that eye to which before they seemed absurd, when I reviled Thy holy ones for so thinking, whereas indeed they thought not so: and with joy I heard Ambrose in his sermons to the people, oftentimes most diligently recommend this text for a rule, *The letter killeth, but the Spirit giveth life*,[5] whilst he drew aside the mystic veil, laying open spiritually what, according to the letter, seemed to teach something unsound; teaching herein nothing that offended me, though he taught what I knew not as yet, whether it were true. For I kept my heart from assenting to any thing, fearing to fall headlong; but by hanging in suspense I was the worse killed. For I wished to be as assured of the things I saw not, as I was that seven and three are ten. For I was not so mad as to think that even this could not be comprehended; but I desired to have other things as clear as this, whether

[5] 2 Cor. iii. 6.

things corporeal, which were not present to my senses, or spiritual, whereof I knew not how to conceive, except corporeally. And by believing might I have been cured, that so the eyesight of my soul being cleared, might in some way be directed to Thy truth, which abideth always, and in no part faileth. But as it happens that one who has tried a bad physician, fears to trust himself with a good one, so was it with the health of my soul, which could not be healed but by believing, and lest it should believe falsehoods, refused to be cured; resisting Thy hands, who hast prepared the medicines of faith, and hast applied them to the diseases of the whole world, and given unto them so great authority.

Being led, however, from this to prefer the Catholic doctrine, I felt that her proceeding was more unassuming and honest, in that she required to be believed things not demonstrated (whether it was that they could in themselves be demonstrated but not to certain persons, or could not at all be), whereas among the Manichees our credulity was mocked by a promise of certain knowledge, and then so many most fabulous and absurd things were imposed to be believed, because they could not be demonstrated. Then Thou, O Lord, little by little with most tender and most merciful hand, touching and composing my heart, didst persuade me—considering what innumerable things I believed, which I saw not, nor was present while they were done, as so many things in secular history, so many reports of places and of cities, which I had not seen; so many of friends, so many of physicians, so many continually of other men, which unless we should believe, we should do nothing at all in this life; lastly, with how unshaken an assurance I believed of what parents I was born, which I could not know, had I not believed upon hearsay—considering all this, Thou didst persuade me, that not they who believed Thy Books (which Thou hast established in so great authority among almost all nations), but they who believed them not, were to be blamed; and that they were not to be heard who should say to me, "How knowest thou those Scriptures to have been imparted unto mankind by the Spirit of the one true and most true God?" For this very thing was of all most to be believed, since no contentiousness of blasphemous questionings, of all that multitude which I had read in the self-contradicting philosophers, could wring this belief from me, "That Thou art" whatsoever Thou wert (what I knew not), and "That the government of human things belongs to Thee."

This I believed, sometimes more strongly, more weakly otherwhiles; yet I ever believed both that Thou wert, and hadst a care of us; though I was ignorant, both what was to be thought of Thy substance, and what way led or led back to Thee. Since then we were too weak by abstract reasonings to find out truth: and for this very cause needed the authority of Holy Writ; I had now begun to believe that Thou wouldest never have given such excellency of authority to that Writ in all lands, hadst Thou not willed thereby to be believed in, thereby sought. For now what things, sounding strangely in the Scripture, were wont to offend me, having heard divers of them expounded satisfactorily, I referred to the depths of the mysteries, and its authority appeared to me the more venerable, and more worthy of religious credence, in that, while it lay open to all to read, it reserved the majesty of its mysteries within its profounder meaning, stooping to all in the great plainness of its words and lowliness of its style, yet calling forth the intensest application of such as are not light of heart; that so it might receive all in its open bosom, and through narrow passages waft over towards Thee some few, yet many more than if it stood not aloft on such a height of authority, nor drew multitudes within its bosom by its holy lowliness. These things I thought on, and Thou wert with me; I sighed, and Thou heardest me; I wavered, and Thou didst guide me; I wandered through the broad way of the world, and Thou didst not forsake me.

I panted after honours, gains, marriage; and Thou deridest me. In these desires I underwent most bitter crosses, Thou being the more gracious, the less Thou sufferedst aught to grow sweet to me, which was not Thou. Behold my heart, O Lord, who wouldest I should remember all this, and confess to Thee. Let my soul cleave unto Thee, now that Thou hast freed it from that fast-holding birdlime of death. How wretched was it! and Thou didst irritate the feeling of its wound, that forsaking all else, it might be converted unto Thee, who art above all, and without whom all things would be nothing; be converted, and be healed. How miserable was I then, and how didst Thou deal with me, to make me feel my misery on that day, when I was preparing to recite a panegyric of the Emperor, wherein I was to utter many a lie, and lying, was to be applauded by those who knew I lied, and my heart was panting with these anxieties, and boiling with the feverishness of consuming thoughts. For, passing through one of the streets of Milan, I observed a poor beggar, then, I suppose, with a full belly, joking and joyous: and I sighed, and spoke to the friends around me, of the many sorrows of our frenzies; for that by all such efforts of ours, as those wherein I then toiled, dragging along, under the goading of desire, the burthen of my own wretchedness, and, by dragging, augmenting it, we yet looked to arrive only at that very joyousness whither that beggar-man had arrived before us, who should never perchance attain it. For what he had obtained by means of a few begged pence, the same was I plotting for by many a toilsome turning and winding; the joy of a temporary felicity. For he verily had not the true joy; but yet I with those my ambitious designs was seeking one much less true. And certainly he was joyous, I anxious; he void of care, I full of fears. But should any ask me, had I rather be merry or fearful? I would answer, merry. Again, if he asked had I rather be such as he was, or what I then was? I should choose to be myself, though worn with cares and fears; but out of wrong judgment; for, was it the truth? For I ought not to prefer myself to him, because more learned than he, seeing I had no joy therein, but sought to please men by it; and that not to instruct, but simply to please. Wherefore also Thou didst break my bones with the staff of Thy correction.

Away with those then from my soul who say to her, "It makes a difference whence a man's joy is. That beggar-man joyed in drunkenness; Thou desiredst to joy in glory." What glory, Lord? That which is not in Thee. For even as his was no true joy, so was that no true glory: and it overthrew my soul more. He that very night should digest his drunkenness; but I had slept and risen again with mine, and was to sleep again, and again to rise with it, how many days, Thou, God, knowest. But "it doth make a difference whence a man's joy is." I know it, and the joy of a faithful hope lieth incomparably beyond such vanity. Yea, and so was he then beyond me:

for he verily was the happier; not only for that he was thoroughly drenched in mirth, I disembowelled with cares: but he, by fair wishes, had gotten wine; I, by lying, was seeking for empty, swelling praise. Much to this purpose said I then to my friends: and I often marked in them how it fared with me; and I found it went ill with me, and grieved, and doubled that very ill; and if any prosperity smiled on me, I was loth to catch at it, for almost before I could grasp it, it flew away.

These things we, who are living as friends together, bemoaned together, but chiefly and most familiarly did I speak thereof with Alypius and Nebridius, of whom Alypius was born in the same town with me, of persons of chief rank there, but younger than I. For he had studied under me, both when I first lectured in our town, and afterwards at Carthage, and he loved me much, because I seemed to him kind, and learned; and I him, for his great toward-liness to virtue, which was eminent enough in one of no greater years. Yet the whirlpool of Carthaginian habits (amongst whom those idle spectacles are hotly followed) had drawn him into the madness of the Circus. But while he was miserably tossed therein, and I, professing rhetoric there, had a public school, as yet he used not my teaching, by reason of some unkindness risen betwixt his father and me. I had found then how deadly he doted upon the Circus, and was deeply grieved that he seemed likely, nay, or had thrown away so great promise: yet had I no means of advising or with a sort of constraint reclaiming him, either by the kindness of a friend, or the authority of a master. For I supposed that he thought of me as did his father; but he was not such; laying aside then his father's mind in that matter, he began to greet me, come sometimes into my lecture-room, hear a little, and be gone.

I however had forgotten to deal with him, that he should not through a blind and headlong desire of vain pastimes, undo so good a wit. But Thou, O Lord, who guidest the course of all Thou hast created, hadst not forgotten him, who was one day to be among Thy children, Priest and Dispenser of Thy Sacrament; and that his amendment might plainly be attributed to Thyself, Thou effectedst it through me, but unknowingly. For as one day I sat in my accus-tomed place, with my scholars before me, he entered, greeted me, sat down, and applied his mind to what I then handled. I had by chance a passage in hand, which while I was explaining, a likeness from the Circensian races occurred to me, as likely to make what I would convey pleasanter and plainer, seasoned with biting mockery of those whom that madness had enthralled; God, Thou knowest that I then thought not of curing Alypius of that infection. But he took it wholly to himself, and thought that I said it simply for his sake. And whence another would have taken occasion of offence with me, that right-minded youth took as a ground of being offended at himself, and loving me more fervently. For Thou hadst said it long ago, and put it into Thy book, *Rebuke a wise man and he will love thee*.[6] But I had not rebuked him, but Thou, who employest all, knowing or not knowing, in that order which Thyself knowest (and that order is just), didst of my heart and tongue make burning coals, by which to set on fire the hopeful mind, thus languishing, and so cure it. Let him be silent in Thy praises, who considers not Thy mercies, which confess unto Thee out of my inmost soul. For he upon that speech burst out of that pit so deep, wherein he was wilfully plunged, and was blinded with its wretched pastimes; and he shook his mind with a strong self-command; whereupon all the filths of the Circensian pastimes flew off from him, nor came he again thither. Upon this, he prevailed with his unwilling father that he might be my scholar. He gave way, and gave in. And Alypius beginning to be my hearer again, was involved in the same superstition with me, loving in the Manichees that show of continency which he supposed true and unfeigned. Whereas it was a senseless and seducing continency, ensnaring precious souls, unable as yet to reach the depth of virtue, yet readily beguiled with the surface of what was but a shadowy and counterfeit virtue.

He, not forsaking that secular course which his parents had charmed him to pursue, had gone before me to Rome, to study law, and there he was carried away incredibly with an incredible eagerness after the shows of gladiators. For being utterly averse to and detesting such spectacles, he was one day by chance met by divers of his acquaintance and fellow-students coming from dinner, and they with a familiar violence haled him, vehemently refusing and resist-

[6] Prov. ix. 8.

ing, into the Amphitheatre, during these cruel and deadly shows, he thus protesting: "Though you hale my body to that place, and there set me, can you force me also to turn my mind or my eyes to those shows? I shall then be absent while present, and so shall overcome both you and them." They hearing this, led him on nevertheless, desirous perchance to try that very thing, whether he could do as he said. When they were come thither, and had taken their places as they could, the whole place kindled with that savage pastime. But he, closing the passages of his eyes, forbade his mind to range abroad after such evils; and would he had stopped his ears also! For in the fight, when one fell, a mighty cry of the whole people striking him strongly, overcome by curiosity, and as if prepared to despise and be superior to it whatsoever it were, even when seen, he opened his eyes, and was stricken with a deeper wound in his soul than the other, whom he desired to behold, was in his body; and he fell more miserably than he upon whose fall that mighty noise was raised, which entered through his ears, and unlocked his eyes, to make way for the striking and beating down of a soul, bold rather than resolute, and the weaker, in that it had presumed on itself, which ought to have relied on Thee. For so soon as he saw that blood, he therewith drunk down savageness; nor turned away, but fixed his eye, drinking in frenzy, unawares, and was delighted with that guilty fight, and intoxicated with the bloody pastime. Nor was he now the man he came, but one of the throng he came unto, yea, a true associate of theirs that brought him thither. Why say more? He beheld, shouted, kindled, carried thence with him the madness which should goad him to return not only with them who first drew him thither, but also before them, yea and to draw in others. Yet thence didst Thou with a most strong and most merciful hand pluck him, and taughtest him to have confidence not in himself, but in Thee. But this was after.

But this was already being laid up in his memory to be a medicine hereafter. So was that also, that when he was yet studying under me at Carthage, and was thinking over at mid-day in the market-place what he was to say by heart (as scholars use to practise), Thou sufferedst him to be apprehended by the officers of the market-plao for a thief. For no other cause, I deem, didst Thou, our God, suffer it but that he who was hereafter to prove so great a man, should already begin to learn that in judging of causes, man was not readily to be condemned by man out of a rash credulity. For as he was walking up and down by himself before the judgment-seat, with his note-book and pen, lo, a young man, a lawyer, the real thief, privily bringing a hatchet, got in, unperceived by Alypius, as far as the leaden gratings which fence in the silversmiths' shops, and began to cut away the lead. But the noise of the hatchet being heard, the silversmiths beneath began to make a stir, and sent to apprehend whomever they should find. But he hearing their voices, ran away, leaving his hatchet, fearing to be taken with it. Alypius now, who had not seen him enter, was aware of his going, and saw with what speed he made away. And being desirous to know the matter, entered the place; where finding the hatchet, he was standing, wondering and considering it, when behold, those that had been sent, find him alone with the hatchet in his hand, the noise whereof had startled and brought them thither. They seize him, hale him away, and gathering the dwellers in the market-place together, boast of having taken a notorious thief, and so he was being led away to be taken before the judge.

But thus far was Alypius to be instructed. For forthwith, O Lord, Thou succouredst his innocency, whereof Thou alone wert witness. For as he was being led either to prison or to punishment, a certain architect met them, who had the chief charge of the public buildings. Glad they were to meet him especially, by whom they were wont to be suspected of stealing the goods lost out of the market-place, as though to show him at last by whom these thefts were committed. He, however, had divers times seen Alypius at a certain senator's house, to whom he often went to pay his respects; and recognising him immediately, took him aside by the hand, and enquiring the occasion of so great a calamity, heard the whole matter, and bade all present, amid much uproar and threats, to go with him. So they came to the house of the young man who had done the deed. There, before the door, was a boy so young as to be likely, not apprehending any harm to his master, to disclose the whole. For he had attended his master to the market-place. Whom so soon as Alypius remembered, he told the architect: and he showing the hatchet to the boy, asked him "Whose that was?" "Ours," quoth he presently: and being further questioned, he discovered every thing. Thus the crime being transferred to that house, and the multitude ashamed, which had begun to insult over Alypius, he who was to be a dispenser of Thy Word, and an examiner of many causes in Thy Church, went away better experienced and instructed.

Him then I had found at Rome, and he clave to me by a most strong tie, and went with me to Milan, both that he might not leave me, and might practise something of the law he had studied, more to please his parents than himself. There he had thrice sat as Assessor, with an uncorruptness much wondered at by others, he wondering at others rather who could prefer gold to honesty. His character was tried besides, not only with the bait of covetousness, but with the goad of fear. At Rome he was Assessor to the count of the Italian Treasury. There was at that time a very powerful senator, to whose favours many stood indebted, many much feared. He would needs, by his usual power, have a thing allowed him which by the laws was unallowed. Alypius resisted it: a bribe was promised; with all his heart he scorned it: threats were held out; he trampled upon them: all wondering at so unwonted a spirit, which neither desired the friendship, nor feared the enmity of one so great and so mightily renowned for innumerable means of doing good or evil. And the very Judge, whose councillor Alypius was, although also unwilling it should be, yet did not openly refuse, but put the matter off upon Alypius, alleging that he would not allow him to do it: for in truth had the Judge done it, Alypius would have decided otherwise. With this one thing in the way of learning was he well-nigh seduced, that he might have books copied for him at Prætorian prices, but consulting justice, he altered his deliberation for the better; esteeming equity whereby he was hindered more gainful than the power whereby he were allowed. These are slight things, *but he that is faithful in little, is faithful also in much.*[7] Nor can that any how be void, which proceeded out of the mouth of Thy Truth: *If ye have not been faithful in the unrighteous Mammon, who will commit to your trust true riches? And if ye have not been faithful in that which is another man's, who shall give you that which is your*

[7] Luke xvi. 10.

own?[8] He being such, did at that time cleave to me, and with me wavered in purpose, what course of life was to be taken.

Nebridius also, who having left his native country near Carthage, yea and Carthage itself, where he had much lived, leaving his excellent family-estate and house, and a mother behind, who was not to follow him, had come to Milan, for no other reason but that with me he might live in a most ardent search after truth and wisdom. Like me he sighed, like me he wavered, an ardent searcher after true life, and a most acute examiner of the most difficult questions. Thus were there the mouths of three indigent persons, sighing out their wants one to another, and *waiting upon Thee that Thou mightest give them their meat in due season.*[9] And in all the bitterness which by Thy mercy followed our worldly affairs, as we looked towards the end, why we should suffer all this, darkness met us; and we turned away groaning, and saying, *How long shall these things be?* This too we often said; and so saying forsook them not, for as yet there dawned nothing certain, which, these forsaken, we might embrace.

And I, viewing and reviewing things, most wondered at the length of time from that my nineteenth year, wherein I had begun to kindle with the desire of wisdom, settling when I had found her, to abandon all the empty hopes and lying frenzies of vain desires. And lo, I was now in my thirtieth year, sticking in the same mire, greedy of enjoying things present, which passed away and wasted my soul; while I said to myself, "To-morrow I shall find it; it will appear manifestly, and I shall grasp it; Faustus the Manichee will come, and clear every thing! O you great men, ye Academicians, it is true then, that no certainty can be attained for the ordering of life! Nay, let us search the more diligently, and despair not. Lo, things in the ecclesiastical books are not absurd to us now, which sometimes seemed absurd, and may be otherwise taken, and in a good sense. I will take my stand, where, as a child, my parents placed me, until the clear truth be found out. But where shall it be sought or when? Ambrose has no leisure; we have no leisure to read; where shall we find even the books? Whence, or when procure them? from whom borrow them? Let set times be appointed, and certain hours be ordered

[8] Luke xvi. 11, 12.   [9] Ps. cxlv. 15

for the health of our soul. Great hope has dawned; the Catholic Faith teaches not what we thought, and vainly accused it of; her instructed members hold it profane to believe God to be bounded by the figure of a human body: and do we doubt to 'knock,' that the rest 'may be opened'? The forenoons our scholars take up; what do we during the rest? Why not this? But when then pay we court to our great friends, whose favour we need? When compose what we may sell to scholars? When refresh ourselves, unbending our minds from this intenseness of care?"

"Perish every thing, dismiss we these empty vanities, and betake ourselves to the one search for truth! Life is vain, death uncertain; if it steals upon us on a sudden, in what state shall we depart hence? and where shall we learn what here we have neglected? and shall we not rather suffer the punishment of this negligence? What, if death itself cut off and end all care and feeling? Then must this be ascertained. But God forbid this! It is no vain and empty thing, that the excellent dignity of the authority of the Christian Faith hath overspread the whole world. Never would such and so great things be by God wrought for us, if with the death of the body the life of the soul came to an end. Wherefore delay then to abandon worldly hopes, and give ourselves wholly to seek after God and the blessed life? But wait! Even those things are pleasant; they have some, and no small sweetness. We must not lightly abandon them, for it were a shame to return again to them. See, it is no great matter now to obtain some station, and then what should we more wish for? We have store of powerful friends; if nothing else offer, and we be in much haste, at least a presidentship may be given us: and a wife with some money, that she increase not our charges: and this shall be the bound of desire. Many great men, and most worthy of imitation, have given themselves to the study of wisdom in the state of marriage."

While I went over these things, and these winds shifted and drove my heart this way and that, time passed on, but I delayed to turn to the Lord; and from day to day deferred to live in Thee, and deferred not daily to die in myself. Loving a happy life, I feared it in its own abode, and sought it, by fleeing from it. I thought I should be too miserable, unless folded in female arms; and of the medicine of Thy mercy to cure that infirmity I thought not, not having tried it. As for continency, I supposed it to be in our own power (though in myself I did not find that power), being so foolish as not to know what is written, *None can be continent unless Thou give it*;[10] and that Thou wouldest give it, if with inward groanings I did knock at Thine ears, and with a settled faith did cast my care on Thee.

Alypius indeed kept me from marrying; alleging that so could we by no means with undistracted leisure live together in the love of wisdom, as we had long desired. For himself was even then most pure in this point, so that it was wonderful; and that the more, since in the outset of his youth he had entered into that course, but had not stuck fast therein; rather had he felt remorse and revolting at it, living thenceforth until now most continently. But I opposed him with the examples of those who as married men had cherished wisdom, and served God acceptably, and retained their friends, and loved them faithfully. Of whose greatness of spirit I was far short; and bound with the disease of the flesh and its deadly sweetness, drew along my chain, dreading to be loosed, and as if my wound had been fretted, put back his good persuasions, as it were the hand of one that would unchain me. Moreover, by me did the serpent speak unto Alypius himself, by my tongue weaving and laying in his path pleasurable snares, wherein his virtuous and free feet might be entangled.

For when he wondered that I, whom he esteemed not slightly, should stick so fast in the birdlime of that pleasure, as to protest (so oft as we discussed it) that I could never lead a single life; and urged in my defence when I saw him wonder, that there was great difference between his momentary and scarce-remembered knowledge of that life, which so he might easily despise, and my continued acquaintance whereto if but the honourable name of marriage were added, he ought not to wonder why I could not contemn that course; he began also to desire to be married; not as overcome with desire of such pleasure, but out of curiosity. For he would fain know, he said, what that should be, without which my life, to him so pleasing, would to me seem not life but a punishment. For his mind, free from that chain, was amazed at my thraldom; and through that

10 Wisd. viii. 2.—Vulg.

amazement was going on to a desire of trying it, thence to the trial itself, and thence perhaps to sink into that bondage whereat he wondered, seeing he was willing to *make a covenant with death*;[11] and *he that loves danger, shall fall into it.*[12] For whatever honour there be in the office of well-ordering a married life, and a family, moved us but slightly. But me for the most part the habit of satisfying an insatiable appetite tormented, while it held me captive; him, an admiring wonder was leading captive. So were we, until Thou, O Most High, not forsaking our dust, commiserating us miserable, didst come to our help, by wondrous and secret ways.

Continual effort was made to have me married. I wooed, I was promised, chiefly through my mother's pains, that so once married, the health-giving baptism might cleanse me, towards which she rejoiced that I was being daily fitted, and observed that her prayers, and Thy promises, were being fulfilled in my faith. At which time verily, both at my request and her own longing, with strong cries of heart she daily begged of Thee, that Thou wouldest by a vision discover unto her something concerning my future marriage; Thou never wouldest. She saw indeed certain vain and fantastic things, such as the energy of the human spirit, busied thereon, brought together; and these she told me of, not with that confidence she was wont, when Thou showedst her any thing, but slighting them. For she could, she said, through a certain feeling, which in words she could not express, discern betwixt Thy revelations, and the dreams of her own soul. Yet the matter was pressed on, and a maiden asked in marriage, two years under the fit age; and as pleasing, was waited for.

And many of us friends conferring about, and detesting the turbulent turmoils of human life, had debated and now almost resolved on living apart from business and the bustle of men; and this was to be thus obtained; we were to bring whatever we might severally procure, and make one household of all; so that through the truth of our friendship nothing should belong especially to any; but the whole thus derived from all, should as a whole belong to each, and all to all. We thought there might be some ten persons in this society; some of whom were very rich, especially Romanianus our

[11] Is. xxviii. 15.   [12] Ecclus. iii. 27.

townsman, from childhood a very familiar friend of mine, whom the grievous perplexities of his affairs had brought up to court; who was the most earnest for this project; and therein was his voice of great weight, because his ample estate far exceeded any of the rest. We had settled also that two annual officers, as it were, should provide all things necessary, the rest being undisturbed. But when we began to consider whether the wives, which some of us already had, others hoped to have, would allow this, all that plan, which was being so well moulded, fell to pieces in our hands, was utterly dashed and cast aside. Thence we betook us to sighs, and groans, and our steps to follow the *broad and beaten ways* of the world;[13] for many thoughts were in our heart, *but Thy counsel standeth for ever.*[14] Out of which counsel Thou didst deride ours, and preparedst Thine own; purposing to *give us meat in due season, and to open Thy hand, and to fill our souls with blessing.*[15]

Meanwhile my sins were being multiplied, and my concubine being torn from my side as a hindrance to my marriage, my heart which clave unto her was torn and wounded and bleeding. And she returned to Afric, vowing unto Thee never to know any other man, leaving with me my son by her. But unhappy I, who could not imitate a very woman, impatient of delay, inasmuch as not till after two years was I to obtain her I sought, not being so much a lover of marriage as a slave to lust, procured another, though no wife, that so by the servitude of an enduring custom, the disease of my soul might be kept up and carried on in its vigour, or even augmented, into the dominion of marriage. Nor was that my wound cured, which had been made by the cutting away of the former, but after inflammation and most acute pain, it mortified, and my pains became less acute, but more desperate.

To Thee be praise, glory to Thee, Fountain of mercies. I was becoming more miserable, and Thou nearer. Thy right hand was continually ready to pluck me out of the mire, and to wash me throughly, and I knew it not; nor did any thing call me back from a yet deeper gulf of carnal pleasures, but the fear of death, and of Thy judgment to come; which amid all my changes, never departed from my breast. And in my disputes with my friends Alypius and Neb-

13 Matt. vii. 13.   14 Ps. xxxiii. 11.   15 Ps. cxlv. 15, 16.

ridius of the nature of good and evil, I held that Epicurus had in my mind won the palm, had I not believed that after death there remained a life for the soul, and places of requital according to men's deserts, which Epicurus would not believe. And I asked, "were we immortal, and to live in perpetual bodily pleasures, without fear of losing it, why should we not be happy, or what else should we seek?" not knowing that great misery was involved in this very thing, that, being thus sunk and blinded, I could not discern that light of excellence and beauty, to be embraced for its own sake, which the eye of flesh cannot see, and is seen by the inner man. Nor did I, unhappy, consider from what source it sprung, that even on these things, foul as they were, I with pleasure discoursed with my friends, nor could I, even according to the notions I then had of happiness, be happy without friends, amid what abundance soever of carnal pleasures. And yet these friends I loved for themselves only, and I felt that I was beloved of them again for myself only.

O crooked paths! Woe to the audacious soul, which hoped, by forsaking Thee, to gain some better thing! Turned it hath, and turned again, upon back, sides, and belly, yet all was painful; and Thou alone rest. And behold, Thou art at hand, and deliverest us from our wretched wanderings, and placest us in Thy way, and dost comfort us, and say, "Run; I will carry you; yea I will bring you through; there also will I carry you."

THE SEVENTH BOOK

Augustine's thirty-first year; gradually extricated from his errors, but still with material conceptions of God; much aided by an argument of Nebridius; sees that the cause of sin lies in free-will, rejects the Manichæan heresy, but can not altogether embrace the doctrine of the Church; recovered from the belief in Astrology, but miserably perplexed about the origin of evil; is led to find in the Platonists the seeds of the doctrine of the Divinity of the WORD, but not of His humiliation; hence he obtains clearer notions of God's majesty, but, not knowing Christ to be the Mediator, remains estranged from Him; all his doubts removed by the study of Holy Scripture, especially St. Paul.

DECEASED was now that my evil and abominable youth, and I was passing into early manhood; the more defiled by vain things as I grew in years, who could not imagine any substance, but such as is wont to be seen with these eyes. I thought not of Thee, O God, under the figure of a human body; since I began to hear aught of wisdom, I always avoided this; and rejoiced to have found the same in the faith of our spiritual mother, Thy Catholic Church. But what else to conceive Thee I knew not. And I, a man, and such a man, sought to conceive of Thee the sovereign, only, true God; and I did in my inmost soul believe that Thou wert incorruptible, and uninjurable, and unchangeable; because though not knowing whence or how, yet I saw plainly, and was sure, that that which may be corrupted must be inferior to that which cannot; what could not be injured I preferred unhesitatingly to what could receive injury; the unchangeable to things subject to change. My heart passionately cried out against all my phantoms, and with this one blow I sought to beat away from the eye of my mind all that unclean troop which buzzed around it. And lo, being scarce put off, in the twinkling of an eye they gathered again thick about me, flew against my face, and beclouded it; so that though not under the form of the human body, yet was I constrained to conceive of Thee (that incorruptible, uninjurable, and unchangeable, which I preferred before the corruptible, and injurable, and change-able) as being in space, whether infused into the world, or diffused infinitely without it. Because whatsoever I conceived, deprived of this space, seemed to me nothing, yea altogether nothing, not even a void, as if a body were taken out of its place, and the place should remain empty of any body at all, of earth and water, air and heaven, yet would it remain a void place, as it were a spacious nothing.

I then being thus gross-hearted, nor clear even to myself, what-soever was not extended over certain spaces, nor diffused, nor con-densed, nor swelled out, or did not or could not receive some of these dimensions, I thought to be altogether nothing. For over such forms as my eyes are wont to range, did my heart then range: nor yet did I see that this same notion of the mind, whereby I formed those very images, was not of this sort, and yet it could not have formed them, had not itself been some great thing. So also did I endeavour to conceive of Thee, Life of my life, as vast, through in-finite spaces on every side penetrating the whole mass of the uni-verse, and beyond it, every way, through unmeasurable boundless spaces; so that the earth should have Thee, the heaven have Thee, all things have Thee, and they be bounded in Thee, and Thou bounded nowhere. For that as the body of this air which is above the earth, hindereth not the light of the sun from passing through it, penetrating it, not by bursting or by cutting, but by filling it wholly: so I thought the body not of heaven, air, and sea only, but of the earth too, previous to Thee, so that in all its parts, the greatest as the smallest, it should admit Thy presence, by a secret inspiration within and without, directing all things which Thou hast created. So I guessed, only as unable to conceive aught else, for it was false. For thus should a greater part of the earth contain a greater portion of Thee, and a less, a lesser: and all things should in such sort be full of Thee, that the body of an elephant should contain more of Thee than that of a sparrow, by how much larger it is and takes up more room; and thus shouldest Thou make the several portions of Thyself present unto the several portions of the world, in fragments, large to the large, petty to the petty. But such are not Thou. But not as yet hadst Thou enlightened my darkness.

It was enough for me, Lord, to oppose to those deceived deceivers,

and dumb praters, since Thy word sounded not out of them;—
that was enough which long ago, while we were yet at Carthage,
Nebridius used to propound, at which all we that heard it were
staggered: "That said nation of darkness, which the Manichees are
wont to set as an opposing mass over against Thee, what could it
have done unto Thee, hadst Thou refused to fight with it? For, if
they answered, 'it would have done Thee some hurt,' then shouldest
Thou be subject to injury and corruption: but if 'it could do Thee no
hurt,' then was no reason brought for Thy fighting with it; and fighting in such wise, as that a certain portion or member of Thee, or
offspring of Thy very Substance, should be mingled with opposed
powers, and natures not created by Thee, and be by them so far corrupted and changed to the worse, as to be turned from happiness
into misery, and need assistance, whereby it might be extricated and
purified; and that this offspring of Thy Substance was the soul,
which being enthralled, defiled, corrupted, Thy Word free, pure and
whole might relieve; that Word itself being still corruptible because
it was of one and the same Substance. So then, should they affirm
Thee, whatsoever Thou art, that is, Thy Substance whereby Thou
art, to be incorruptible, then were all these sayings false and execrable; but if corruptible, the very statement showed it to be false
and revolting." This argument then of Nebridius sufficed against
those who deserved wholly to be vomited out of the overcharged
stomach; for they had no escape, without horrible blasphemy of heart
and tongue, thus thinking and speaking of Thee.

But I also as yet, although I held and was firmly persuaded that
Thou our Lord the true God, who madest not only our souls, but our
bodies, and not only our souls and bodies, but all beings, and all
things wert undefilable and unalterable, and in no degree mutable;
yet understood I not, clearly and without difficulty, the cause of evil.
And yet whatever it were, I perceived it was in such wise to be
sought out, as should not constrain me to believe the immutable God
to be mutable, lest I should become that evil I was seeking out. I
sought it out then, thus far free from anxiety, certain of the untruth
of what these held, from whom I shrunk with my whole heart: for
I saw, that through enquiring the origin of evil, they were filled with

evil, in that they preferred to think that Thy substance did suffer ill than their own did commit it.

And I strained to perceive what I now heard, that freewill was the cause of our doing ill, and Thy just judgment of our suffering ill. But I was not able clearly to discern it. So then endeavouring to draw my soul's vision out of that deep pit, I was again plunged therein, and endeavouring often, I was plunged back as often. But this raised me a little into Thy light, that I knew as well that I had a will, as that I lived: when then I did will or nill any thing, I was most sure that no other than myself did will and nill: and I all but saw that there was the cause of my sin. But what I did against my will, I saw that I suffered rather than did, and I judged not to be my fault, but my punishment; whereby however, holding Thee to be just, I speedily confessed myself to be not unjustly punished. But again I said, Who made me? Did not my God, who is not only good, but goodness itself? Whence then came I to will evil and nill good, so that I am thus justly punished? who set this in me, and ingrafted into me this plant of bitterness, seeing I was wholly formed by my most sweet God? If the devil were the author, whence is that same devil? And if he also by his own perverse will, of a good angel became a devil, whence, again, came in him that evil will whereby he became a devil, seeing the whole nature of angels was made by that most good Creator? By these thoughts I was again sunk down and choked; yet not brought down to that hell of error (where no man confesseth unto Thee), to think rather that Thou dost suffer ill, than that man doth it.[1]

For I was in such wise striving to find out the rest, as one who had already found that the incorruptible must needs be better than the corruptible: and Thee therefore, whatsoever Thou wert, I confessed to be incorruptible. For never soul was, nor shall be able to conceive any thing which may be better than Thou, who art the sovereign and the best good. But since most truly and certainly, the incorruptible is preferable to the corruptible (as I did now prefer it), then, wert Thou not incorruptible, I could in thought have arrived at something better than my God. Where then I saw the incor-

[1] Ps. vi. 5.

ruptible to be preferable to the corruptible, there ought I to seek for Thee, and there observe "wherein evil itself was;" that is whence corruption comes, by which Thy substance can by no means be impaired. For corruption does no ways impair our God; by no will, by no necessity, by no unlooked-for chance: because He is God, and what He wills is good, and Himself is that good; but to be corrupted is not good. Nor art Thou against Thy will constrained to any thing, since Thy will is not greater than Thy power. But greater should it be, were Thyself greater than Thyself. For the will and power of God is God Himself. And what can be unlooked for by Thee, who knowest all things? Nor is there any nature in things, but Thou knowest it. And what should we more say, "why that substance which God is should not be corruptible," seeing if it were so, it should not be God?

And I sought "whence is evil," and sought in an evil way; and saw not the evil in my very search. I set now before the sight of my spirit the whole creation, whatsoever we can see therein (as sea, earth, air, stars, trees, mortal creatures); yea, and whatever in it we do not see, as the firmament of heaven, all angels moreover, and all the spiritual inhabitants thereof. But these very beings, as though they were bodies, did my fancy dispose in place, and I made one great mass of Thy creation, distinguished as to the kinds of bodies; some, real bodies, some, what myself had feigned for spirits. And this mass I made huge, not as it was (which I could not know), but as I thought convenient, yet every way finite. But Thee, O Lord, I imagined on every part environing and penetrating it, though every way infinite: as if there were a sea, every where, and on every side, through unmeasured space, one only boundless sea, and it contained within it some sponge, huge, but bounded; that sponge must needs, in all its parts, be filled from that unmeasurable sea: so conceived I Thy creation, itself finite, full of Thee, the Infinite; and I said, Behold God, and behold what God hath created; and God is good, yea, most mightily and incomparably better than all these: but yet He, the Good, created them good; and see how He environeth and fulfils them. Where is evil then, and whence, and how crept it in hither? What is its root, and what its seed? Or hath it no being? Why then fear we and avoid what is not? Or if we fear it idly, then is that very fear evil, whereby the soul is thus idly goaded and racked. Yea, and so much a greater evil, as we have nothing to fear, and yet do fear. Therefore either is that evil which we fear, or else evil is, that we fear. Whence is it then? seeing God, the Good, hath created all these things good. He indeed, the greater and chiefest Good, hath created these lesser goods; still both Creator and created, all are good. Whence is evil? Or, was there some evil matter of which He made, and formed, and ordered it, yet left something in it which He did not convert into good? Why so then? Had He no right to turn and change the whole, so that no evil should remain in it, seeing He is Almighty? Lastly, why should He make any thing at all of it, and not rather by the same All-mightiness cause it not to be at all? Or, could it then be against His will? Or if it were from eternity, why suffered He it so to be for infinite spaces of times past, and was pleased so long after to make something out of it? Or if He were suddenly pleased now to effect somewhat, this rather should the All-mighty have effected, that this evil matter should not be, and He alone be, the whole, true, sovereign, and infinite Good. Or if it was not good that He who was good should not also frame and create something that were good, then, that evil matter being taken away and brought to nothing, He might form good matter, whereof to create all things. For He should not be All-mighty, if He might not create something good without the aid of that matter which Himself had not created. These thoughts I revolved in my miserable heart, overcharged with most gnawing cares, lest I should die ere I had found the truth; yet was the faith of Thy Christ, our Lord and Saviour, professed in the Church Catholic, firmly fixed in my earth, in many points, indeed, as yet unformed, and fluctuating from the rule of doctrine; yet did not my mind utterly leave it, but rather daily took in more and more of it.

By this time also had I rejected the lying divinations and impious dotages of the astrologers. Let Thine own mercies, out of my very inmost soul, confess unto Thee for this also, O my God.[2] For Thou, Thou altogether (for who else calls us back from the death of all errors, save the Life which cannot die, and the Wisdom which needing no light enlightens the minds that need it, whereby the universe

----

[2] Ps. cvi. 8.—Vulg.

is directed, down to the whirling leaves of trees?),—Thou madest provision for my obstinacy wherewith I struggled against Vindicianus,[3] an acute old man, and Nebridius, a young man of admirable talents; the first vehemently affirming, and the latter often (though with some doubtfulness) saying, "That there was no such art whereby to foresee things to come, but that men's conjectures were a sort of lottery, and that out of many things which they said should come to pass, some actually did, unawares to them who spake it, who stumbled upon it, through their oft speaking." Thou providest then a friend for me, no negligent consulter of the astrologers; nor yet well skilled in those arts, but (as I said) a curious consulter with them, and yet knowing something, which he said he had heard of his father, which how far it went to overthrow the estimation of that art, he knew not. This man then, Firminus by name, having had a liberal education, and well taught in Rhetoric, consulted me, as one very dear to him, what, according to his so-called constellations, I thought on certain affairs of his, wherein his worldly hopes had risen, and I, who had herein now begun to incline towards Nebridius' opinion, did not altogether refuse to conjecture, and tell him what came into my unresolved mind: but added, that I was now almost persuaded that these were but empty and ridiculous follies. Thereupon he told me that his father had been very curious in such books, and had a friend as earnest in them as himself, who with joint study and conference fanned the flame of their affections to these toys, so that they would observe the moments whereat the very dumb animals, which bred about their houses, gave birth, and then observed the relative position of the heavens, thereby to make fresh experiments in this so-called art. He said then that he had heard of his father, that what time his mother was about to give birth to him, Firminus, a woman-servant of that friend of his father's was also with child, which could not escape her master, who took care with most exact diligence to know the births of his very puppies. And so it was that (the one for his wife, and the other for his servant, with the most careful observation, reckoning days, hours, nay, the lesser divisions of the hours) both were delivered at the same instant; so that both were constrained to allow the same con-

[3] See Book IV., p. 50.

stellations, even to the minutest points, the one for his son, the other for his new-born slave. For so soon as the women began to be in labour, they each gave notice to the other what was fallen out in their houses, and had messengers ready to send to one another so soon as they had notice of the actual birth, of which they had easily provided, each in his own province, to give instant intelligence. Thus then the messengers of the respective parties met, he averred, at such an equal distance from either house, that neither of them could make out any difference in the position of the stars, or any other minutest points; and yet Firminus, born in a high estate in his parents' house, ran his course through the gilded paths of life, was increased in riches, raised to honours; whereas that slave continued to serve his masters, without any relaxation of his yoke, as Firminus, who knew him, told me.

Upon hearing and believing these things, told by one of such credibility, all that my resistance gave way; and first I endeavoured to reclaim Firminus himself from that curiosity, by telling him that upon inspecting his constellations, I ought, if I were to predict truly, to have seen in them parents eminent among their neighbours, a noble family in its own city, high birth, good education, liberal learning. But if that servant had consulted me upon the same constellations, since they were his also, I ought again (to tell him too truly) to see in them a lineage the most abject, a slavish condition, and every thing else utterly at variance with the former. Whence then, if I spake the truth, I should, from the same constellations, speak diversely, or if I spake the same, speak falsely: thence it followed most certainly that whatever, upon consideration of the constellations, was spoken truly, was spoken not out of art, but chance; and whatever spoken falsely, was not out of ignorance in the art, but the failure of the chance.

An opening thus made, ruminating with myself on the like things, that no one of those dotards (who lived by such a trade, and whom I longed to attack, and with derision to confute) might urge against me that Firminus had informed me falsely, or his father him; I bent my thoughts on those that are born twins, who for the most part come out of the womb so near one to other, that the small interval (how much force soever in the nature of things folk may pretend it to have) cannot be noted by human observation, or be at all expressed in those figures which the astrologer is to inspect, that he may pronounce truly. Yet they cannot be true: for looking into the same figures, he must have predicted the same of Esau and Jacob, whereas the same happened not to them. Therefore he must speak falsely; or if truly, then, looking into the same figures, he must not give the same answer. Not by art, then, but by chance, would he speak truly. For Thou, O Lord, most righteous Ruler of the Universe, while consulters and consulted know it not, dost by Thy hidden inspiration effect that the consulter should hear what, according to the hidden deservings of souls, he ought to hear, out of the unsearchable depth of Thy just judgment, to Whom let no man say, What is this? Why that? Let him not so say, for he is man.

Now then, O my Helper, hadst thou loosed me from those fetters: and I sought "whence is evil," and found no way. But thou sufferedst me not by any fluctuations of thought to be carried away from the Faith whereby I believed Thee both to be, and Thy substance to be unchangeable, and that Thou hast a care of, and wouldest judge men, and that in Christ, Thy Son, our Lord, and the holy Scriptures, which the authority of Thy Catholic Church pressed upon me, Thou hadst set the way of man's salvation, to that life which is to be after this death. These things being safe and immovably settled in my mind, I sought anxiously "whence was evil?" What were the pangs of my teeming heart, what groans, O my God! yet even there were Thine ears open, and I knew it not: and when in silence I vehemently sought, those silent contritions of my soul were strong cries unto Thy mercy. Thou knewest what I suffered, and no man. For, what was that which was thence through my tongue distilled into the ears of my most familiar friends? Did the whole tumult of my soul, for which neither time nor utterance[4] sufficed, reach them? Yet went up the whole to Thy hearing, all which I roared out from the groanings of my heart; and my desire was before Thee, and the light of mine eyes was not with me: for that was within, I without: nor was that confined to place, but I was intent on things contained in place, but there found I no resting-place, nor did they so receive me, that I could say, "It

[4] Ps. xxxvii. 9–11.—Vulg.

is enough," "it is well": nor did they yet suffer me to turn back, where it might be well enough with me. For to these things was I superior, but inferior to Thee; and Thou art my true joy when subjected to Thee, and Thou hadst subjected to me what Thou createdst below me. And this was the true temperament, and middle region of my safety, to remain in Thy Image, and by serving Thee, rule the body. But when I rose proudly against Thee, and *ran against the Lord with my neck, with the thick bosses of my buckler*,[5] even these inferior things were set above me, and pressed me down, and no where was there respite or space for breathing. They met my sight on all sides by heaps and troops, and in thought the images thereof presented themselves unsought, as I would return to Thee, as if they would say unto me, "Whither goest thou, unworthy and defiled?" And these things had grown out of my wound; for Thou "humbledst the proud like one that is wounded,"[6] and through my own swelling was I separated from Thee; yea, my pride-swollen face closed up mine eyes.

But Thou, Lord, *abidest for ever,* yet not for ever art Thou angry with us; because Thou pitiest our dust and ashes and it was pleasing in Thy sight to reform my deformities and by inward goads didst Thou rouse me, that I should be ill at ease, until Thou wert manifested to my inward sight. Thus, by the secret hand of Thy medicining was my swelling abated, and the troubled and bedimmed eye-sight of my mind, by the smarting anointings of healthful sorrows, was from day to day healed.

And Thou, willing first to show me how Thou *resistest the proud, but givest grace unto the humble,*[7] and by how great an act of Thy Mercy Thou hadst traced out to men the way of humility, in that Thy WORD was made flesh, and dwelt among men:—Thou procuredst for me, by means of one puffed up with most unnatural pride, certain books of the Platonists, translated from Greek into Latin. And therein I read, not indeed in the very words, but to the very same purpose, enforced by many and divers reasons, that *In the beginning was the Word, and the Word was with God, and the Word was God: the Same was in the beginning with God: all things were made by Him, and without Him was nothing made:*

[5] Job xv. 26.   [6] Ps. lxxxviii. 11.—Vulg.   [7] Jam. iv. 6; 1 Pet. v. 5.

that which was made by Him is life, and the life was the light of men, and the light shineth in the darkness, and the darkness comprehended it not.[8] And that the soul of man, though it *bears witness to the light,* yet itself *is not that light;* but the Word of God, being God, *is that true light that lighteth every man that cometh into the world.*[9] And that *He was in the world, and the world was made by Him, and the world knew Him not.*[10] But that *He came unto His own, and His own received him not;*[11] *but as many as received Him, to them gave He power to become the sons of God, as many as believed in His name;*[12] this I read not there.

Again I read there, that *God the Word was born not of flesh, nor of blood, nor of the will of man, nor of the will of the flesh, but of God.*[13] But that *the Word was made flesh, and dwelt among us,*[14] I read not there. For I traced in those books that it was many and divers ways said, that *the Son was in the form of the Father, and thought it not robbery to be equal with God,* for that naturally He was the Same Substance. But that *He emptied himself, taking the form of a servant, being made in the likeness of men, and found in fashion as a man, humbled Himself, and became obedient unto death, and that the death of the cross: wherefore God exalted Him* from the dead *and gave Him a name above every name, that at the name of Jesus every knee should bow, of things in heaven, and things in earth, and things under the earth; and that every tongue should confess that the Lord Jesus Christ is in the Glory of God the Father;*[15] those books have not. For that before all times and above all times Thy Only-Begotten Son remaineth unchangeable, co-eternal with Thee, and that *of His fulness souls receive,*[16] that they may be blessed; and that by participation of wisdom abiding in them, they are renewed, so as to be wise, is there. But that *in due time He died for the ungodly;*[17] and that *Thou sparedst not Thine Only Son, but deliveredst Him for us all,*[18] is not there. *For Thou hiddest these things from the wise, and revealedst them to babes;* that they *that labour and are heavy laden might come unto Him, and He refresh them,* because *He is meek and lowly in heart;*[19] and *the meek He directeth in judgment, and the gentle He teacheth His ways,*[20] beholding our

[8] John i. 1–5.   [9] *Ib.* 9.   [10] *Ib.* 10.   [11] *Ib.* 11.   [12] *Ib.* 12.   [13] *Ib.* 13.   [14] *Ib.* 14.
[15] Phil. ii. 6–11.   [16] John i. 16.   [17] Rom. v. 6.   [18] *Ib.* viii. 32.
[19] Matt. xi., 25, 28, 29.   [20] Ps. xxv. 9.

loneliness and trouble, and forgiving all our sins.[21] But such as are lifted up in the lofty walk of some would-be sublimer learning, hear not Him, saying, *Learn of Me, for I am meek and lowly in heart, and ye shall find rest to your souls.*[22] *Although they knew God, yet they glorify Him not as God, nor are thankful, but wax vain in their thoughts; and their foolish heart is darkened; professing that they were wise, they became fools.*[23]

And therefore did I read there also, that they had *changed the glory of Thy incorruptible nature* into idols and divers shapes, *into the likeness of the image of corruptible man, and birds, and beasts, and creeping things;*[24] namely, into that Egyptian food for which Esau lost his birthright,[25] for that Thy first-born people worshipped the head of a four-footed beast instead of Thee;[26] turning in heart back towards Egypt; and bowing Thy image, their own soul, before the image of *a calf that eateth hay.*[27] These things found I here, but I fed not on them. For it pleased Thee, O Lord, to take away the reproach of diminution from Jacob, *that the elder should serve the younger:*[28] and Thou calledst the Gentiles into Thine inheritance. And I had come to Thee from among the Gentiles; and I set my mind upon the gold which Thou willedst Thy people to take from Egypt, seeing Thine it was, wheresoever it were.[29] And to the Athenians Thou saidst by Thy Apostle, *that in Thee we live, move, and have our being, as one of their own poets had said.*[30] And verily these books came from thence. But I set not my mind on the idols of Egypt, *whom they served with Thy gold,*[31] *who changed the truth of God into a lie, and worshipped and served the creature more than the Creator.*[32]

And being thence admonished to return to myself, I entered even into my inward self, Thou being my Guide: and able I was, for Thou wert become my Helper. And I entered and beheld with the eye of my soul (such as it was), above the same eye of my soul, above my mind, the Light Unchangeable. Not this ordinary light, which all flesh may look upon, nor as it were a greater of the same kind, as though the brightness of this should be manifold brighter, and with its greatness take up all space. Not such was this light, but

[21] *Ib.* 18.   [22] Matt xi. 29.   [23] Rom. i. 21, 22.   [24] Rom. i. 23.   [25] Gen. xxv. 33, 34   [26] Ex. xxxii. 1–6.   [27] Ps. cvi. 20.   [28] Rom. ix. 13.   [29] Ex. iii. 22; xi. 2.   [30] Acts xvii. 28.   [31] Hos. ii. 8.   [32] Rom. i. 25.

other, yea, far other from all these. Nor was it above my soul, as oil is above water, nor yet as heaven above earth: but above to my soul, because It made me; and I below It, because I was made by it. He that knows the Truth, knows what that Light is; and he that knows It, knows eternity. Love knoweth it. O Truth Who art Eternity! and Love Who art Truth! and Eternity Who art Love! Thou art my God, to Thee do I sigh night and day. Thee when I first knew, Thou liftedst me up, that I might see there was what I might see, and that I was not yet such as to see. And Thou didst beat back the weakness of my sight, streaming forth Thy beams of light upon me most strongly, and I trembled with love and awe: and I perceived myself to be far off from Thee, in the region of unlikeness, as if I heard this Thy voice from on high: "I am the food of grown men; grow and thou shalt feed upon Me; nor shalt thou convert Me, like the food of thy flesh, into thee, but thou shalt be converted into Me." And I learned, that *Thou for iniquity chastenest man, and Thou madest my soul to consume away like a spider.*[33] And I said, "Is Truth therefore nothing because it is not diffused through space finite or infinite?" And Thou criedst to me from afar: "Yea, verily, *I AM that I AM.*"[34] And I heard, as the heart heareth, nor had I room to doubt, and I should sooner doubt that I live than that Truth is not, *which is clearly seen, being understood by those things which are made.*[35]

And I beheld the other things below Thee, and I perceived that they neither altogether are, nor altogether are not, for they are, since they are from Thee, but are not, because they are not, what Thou art. For that truly is which remains unchangeably. *It is good then for me to hold fast unto God;*[36] for if I remain not in Him, I cannot in myself; but *He remaining in Himself, reneweth all things.*[37] *And Thou art the Lord* my God since Thou *standest not in need of my goodness.*[38]

And it was manifested unto me, that those things be good which yet are corrupted; which neither were they sovereignly good, nor unless they were good could be corrupted: for if sovereignly good, they were incorruptible, if not good at all, there were nothing in

---

[33] Ps. xxxix. 11. [34] Exod. iii. 14. [35] Rom. i. 20.
[36] Ps. lxxiii. 28 [37] Wisd. vii. 27. [38] Ps. xvi. 1.

them to be corrupted. For corruption injures, but unless it diminished goodness, it could not injure. Either then corruption injures not, which cannot be; or which is most certain, all which is corrupted is deprived of good. But if they be deprived of all good, they shall cease to be. For if they shall be, and can now no longer be corrupted, they shall be better than before, because they shall abide incorruptibly. And what more monstrous than to affirm things to become better by losing all their good? Therefore, if they shall be deprived of all good, they shall no longer be. So long therefore as they are, they are good: therefore whatsoever is, is good. That evil then which I sought, whence it is, is not any substance: for were it a substance, it should be good. For either it should be an incorruptible substance, and so a chief good: or a corruptible substance; which unless it were good, could not be corrupted. I perceived therefore, and it was manifested to me that Thou madest all things good, nor is there any substance at all, which Thou madest not; and for that Thou madest not all things equal, therefore are all things; because each is good, and altogether very good, because our God *made all things very good.*[39]

And to Thee is nothing whatsoever evil: yea, not only to Thee, but also to Thy creation as a whole, because there is nothing without, which may break in, and corrupt that order which Thou hast appointed it. But in the parts thereof some things, because unharmonising with other some, are accounted evil: whereas those very things harmonise with others, and are good; and in themselves are good. And all these things which harmonise not altogether, do yet with the inferior part, which we call Earth, having its own cloudy and windy sky harmonising with it. Far be it then that I should say, "These things should not be:" for should I see nought but these, I should indeed long for the better; but still must even for these alone praise Thee; for that Thou art to be *praised,* do show *from the earth, dragons, and all deeps, fire, hail, snow, ice, and stormy wind which fulfil Thy word; mountains and all hills, fruitful trees, and all cedars; beasts, and all cattle, creeping things, and flying fowls; kings of the earth, and all people, princes, and all judges of the earth; young men and maidens, old men and young,*

[39] Gen. i. 31; Eccli. xxxix. 21.

praise Thy Name. But when, from heaven, these *praise Thee, praise Thee, our God, in the heights, all Thy angels, all Thy hosts, sun and moon, all the stars and light, the Heaven of heavens, and the waters that be above the heavens, praise Thy Name;*[40] I did not now long for things better because I conceived of all: and with a sounder judgment I apprehended that the things above were better than these below, but all together better than those above by themselves.

There is no soundness in them, whom aught of Thy creation displeaseth: as neither in me, when much which Thou hast made, displeased me. And because my soul durst not be displeased at my God, it would fain not account that Thine, which displeased it. Hence it had gone into the opinion of two substances, and had no rest, but talked idly. And returning thence, it had made to itself a God, through infinite measures of all space; and thought it to be Thee, and placed it in its heart; and had again become the temple of its own idol, to Thee abominable. But after Thou hadst soothed my head, unknown to me, and closed *mine eyes that they should not behold vanity,*[41] I ceased somewhat of my former self, and my frenzy was lulled to sleep; and I awoke in Thee, and saw Thee infinite, but in another way, and this sight was not derived from the flesh.

And I looked back on other things; and I saw that they owed their being to Thee; and were all bounded in Thee: but in a different way; not as being in space; but because Thou containest all things in Thine hand in Thy Truth; and all things are true so far as they be; nor is there any falsehood unless when that is thought to be, which is not. And I saw that all things did harmonise, not with their places only, but with their seasons. And that Thou, who only art Eternal, didst not begin to work after innumerable spaces of times spent; for that all spaces of times, both which have passed, and which shall pass, neither go nor come, but through Thee, working, and abiding.

And I perceived and found it nothing strange, that bread which is pleasant to a healthy palate is loathsome to one distempered: and to sore eyes light is offensive, which to the sound is delightful. And Thy righteousness displeaseth the wicked; much more the viper and reptiles, which Thou hast created good, fitting in with the inferior

[40] Ps. cxlviii. 1–12.   [41] Ps. cxix. 37.

portions of Thy Creation, with which the very wicked also fit in; and that the more, by how much they be unlike Thee; but with the superior creatures by how much they become more like to Thee. And I enquired what iniquity was, and found it to be no substance, but the perversion of the will, turned aside from Thee, O God, the Supreme, towards these lower things, and *casting out its bowels*, and puffed up outwardly.

And I wondered that I now loved Thee, and no phantasm for Thee. And yet did I not press on to enjoy my God; but was borne up to Thee by Thy beauty, and soon borne down from Thee by mine own weight, sinking with sorrow into these inferior things. This weight was carnal custom. Yet dwelt there with me a remembrance of Thee; nor did I any way doubt that there was One to whom I might cleave, but that I was not yet such as to cleave to Thee: for that *the body which is corrupted presseth down the soul, and the earthly tabernacle weigheth down the mind that museth upon many things*.[42] And most certain I was, *that Thy invisible works from the creation of the world are clearly seen, being understood by the things that are made, even Thy eternal power and Godhead*.[43] For examining whence it was that I admired the beauty of bodies celestial or terrestrial; and what aided me in judging soundly on things mutable, and pronouncing, "This ought to be thus, this not;" examining, I say, whence it was that I so judged, seeing I did so judge, I had found the unchangeable and true Eternity of Truth above my changeable mind. And thus by degrees I passed from bodies to the soul, which through the bodily senses perceives; and thence to its inward faculty, to which the bodily senses represent things external, whitherto reach the faculties of beasts; and thence again to the reasoning faculty, to which what is received from the senses of the body is referred to be judged. Which finding itself also to be in me a thing variable, raised itself up to its own understanding, and drew away my thoughts from the power of habit, withdrawing itself from those troops of contradictory phantasms; that so it might find what that light was whereby it was bedewed, when, without all doubting, it cried out, "That the unchangeable was to be preferred to the changeable;" whence also it knew That

[42] Wisd. ix. 15.   [43] Rom. i. 20.

Unchangeable, which, unless it had in some way known, it had had no sure ground to prefer it to the changeable. And thus with the flash of one trembling glance it arrived at THAT WHICH IS. And then I saw Thy *invisible things understood by the things which are made.*[44] But I could not fix my gaze thereon; and my infirmity being struck back, I was thrown again on my wonted habits, carrying along with me only a loving memory thereof, and a longing for what I had, as it were, perceived the odour of, but was not yet able to feed on.

Then I sought a way of obtaining strength sufficient to enjoy Thee; and found it not, until I embraced *that Mediator betwixt God and men, the Man Christ Jesus,*[45] *who is over all, God blessed for evermore,*[46] calling unto me, and saying, *I am the way, the truth, and the life,*[47] and mingling that food which I was unable to receive, with our flesh. *For, the Word was made flesh,*[48] that Thy wisdom, whereby Thou createdst all things, might provide milk for our infant state. For I did not hold to my Lord Jesus Christ, I, humbled, to the humble; nor knew I yet whereto His infirmity would guide us. For Thy Word, the Eternal Truth, far above the higher parts of Thy Creation, raises up the subdued unto Itself: but in this lower world built for Itself a lowly habitation of our clay, whereby to abase from themselves such as would be subdued, and bring them over to Himself; allaying their swelling, and fomenting their love; to the end they might go on no further in self-confidence, but rather consent to become weak, seeing before their feet the Divinity weak by taking our *coats of skin;*[49] and wearied, might cast themselves down upon It, and It rising, might lift them up.

But I thought otherwise; conceiving only of my Lord Christ as of a man of excellent wisdom, whom no one could be equalled unto; especially, for that being wonderfully born of a Virgin, He seemed, in conformity therewith, through the Divine care for us, to have attained that great eminence of authority, for an ensample of despising things temporal for the obtaining of immortality. But what mystery there lay in *"The Word was made flesh,"* I could not even imagine. Only I had learnt out of what is delivered to us in writing

[44] Rom. i. 20.   [45] 1 Tim. ii. 5.   [46] Rom. ix. 5.   [47] John xiv. 6.
[48] John i. 14.   [49] Gen. iii. 21.

of Him that He did eat, and drink, sleep, walk, rejoiced in spirit, was sorrowful, discoursed; that flesh did not cleave by itself unto Thy Word but with the human soul and mind. All know this who know the unchangeableness of Thy Word, which I now knew, as far as I could, nor did I at all doubt thereof. For, now to move the limbs of the body by will, now not, now to be moved by some affection, now not, now to deliver wise sayings through human signs, now to keep silence, belong to soul and mind subject to variation. And should these things be falsely written of Him, all the rest also would risk the charge, nor would there remain in those books any saving faith for mankind. Since then they were written truly, I acknowledged a perfect man to be in Christ; not the body of a man only, nor, with the body, a sensitive soul without a rational, but very man; whom, not only as being a form of Truth, but for a certain great excellency of human nature and a more perfect participation of wisdom, I judged to be preferred before others. But Alypius imagined the Catholics to believe God to be so clothed with flesh, that besides God and flesh, there was no soul at all in Christ, and did not think that a human mind was ascribed to him. And because he was well persuaded that the actions recorded of Him could only be performed by a vital and a rational creature, he moved the more slowly towards the Christian Faith. But understanding afterwards that this was the error of the Apollinarian heretics, he joyed in and was conformed to the Catholic Faith. But somewhat later, I confess, did I learn how in that saying, *The Word was made flesh,* the Catholic Truth is distinguished from the falsehood of Photinus. For the rejection of heretics makes the tenets of Thy Church and sound doctrine to stand out more clearly. *For there must also be heresies, that the approved may be made manifest among the weak.*[50]

But having then read those books of the Platonists, and thence been taught to search for incorporeal truth, I saw Thy *invisible things, understood by those things which are made;*[51] and though cast back, I perceived what that was which through the darkness of my mind I was hindered from contemplating, being assured, "That Thou wert, and wert infinite, and yet not diffused in space, finite or infinite; and that Thou truly art who art the same ever, in no

[50] 1 Cor. xi. 19.   [51] Rom. i. 20.

part nor motion varying; and that all other things are from Thee, on this most sure ground alone, that they are." Of these things I was assured, yet too unsure to enjoy Thee. I prated as one well skilled; but had I not sought Thy way in Christ our Saviour, I had proved to be, not skilled, but killed. For now I had begun to wish to seem wise, being filled with mine own punishment, yet I did not mourn, but rather scorn, puffed up with knowledge.[52] For where was that charity building upon the *foundation* of humility, *which is Christ Jesus?*[53] or when should these books teach me it? Upon these, I believe, Thou therefore willedst that I should fall, before I studied Thy Scriptures, that it might be imprinted on my memory how I was affected by them; and that afterwards when my spirits were tamed through Thy books, and my wounds touched by Thy healing fingers, I might discern and distinguish between presumption and confession; between those who saw whither they were to go, yet saw not the way, and the way that leadeth not to behold only but to dwell in the beatific country. For had I first been formed in Thy Holy Scriptures, and hadst Thou in the familiar use of them grown sweet unto me, and had I then fallen upon those other volumes, they might perhaps have withdrawn me from the solid ground of piety, or, had I continued in that healthful frame which I had thence imbibed, I might have thought that it might have been obtained by the study of those books alone.

Most eagerly then did I seize that venerable writing of Thy Spirit: and chiefly the Apostle Paul. Whereupon those difficulties vanished away, wherein he once seemed to me to contradict himself, and the text of his discourse not to agree with the testimonies of the Law and the Prophets. And the face of that pure word appeared to me one and the same; and I learned to *rejoice with trembling.*[54] So I began; and whatsoever truth I had read in those other books, I found here amid the praise of Thy Grace; that whoso sees, may not *so glory as if he had not received,*[55] not only what he sees, but also that he sees (*for what hath he, which he hath not received?*), and that he may be not only admonished to behold Thee, *Who art* ever *the same, but also healed,* to hold Thee, and that *he who cannot see afar off,* may yet walk on the way, whereby he may arrive, and behold, and

---

[52] I Cor. viii. I.   [53] *Ibid*. iii. II.   [54] Ps. ii. II.   [55] I Cor. iv. 7.

hold Thee. For, though a man *be delighted with the law of God after the inner man*,[56] what shall he do with that *other law in his members which warreth against the law of his mind, and bringeth him into captivity to the law of sin which is in his members?*[57] For, *Thou art righteous, O Lord, but we have sinned and committed iniquity, and have done wickedly*,[58] and Thy hand is grown heavy upon us, and *we are justly delivered over* unto that ancient sinner, the king of death; because he persuaded our will to be like his will, whereby *he abode not in Thy truth. What shall wretched man do? who shall deliver him from the body of this death, but only Thy Grace, through Jesus Christ our Lord*,[59] whom Thou hast begotten co-eternal, and *formedst in the beginning of Thy ways*,[60] *in whom the prince of this world found nothing worthy of death*,[61] yet killed he Him; and *the handwriting, which was contrary to us, was blotted out?*[62] This those writings contain not. Those pages present not the image of this piety, the tears of confession, *Thy sacrifice, a troubled spirit, a broken and a contrite heart*,[63] the salvation of the people, the *Bridal City*,[64] *the earnest of the Holy Ghost*,[65] *the Cup of our Redemption*.[66] No man sings there. *Shall not my soul be submitted unto God? for of Him cometh my salvation. For He is my God and my salvation, my guardian, I shall no more be moved*.[67] No one there hears Him call, *Come unto Me, all ye that labour*.[68] They scorn to *learn of Him, because He is meek and lowly in heart; for these things hast Thou hid from the wise and prudent, and hast revealed them unto babes*.[69] For it is one thing, from the mountain's shaggy top to see the land of peace, and to find no way thither;[70] and in vain to essay through ways unpassable, opposed and beset by fugitives and deserters, under their captain *the lion and the dragon:* and another to keep on the way that leads thither, guarded by the host of the heavenly General; where they spoil not who have deserted the heavenly army; for they avoid it, as very torment. These things did wonderfully sink into my bowels, when I read that *least of Thy Apostles*,[71] and had meditated upon Thy works, and trembled exceedingly.

---

[56] Rom. vii. 22.   [57] Rom. vii. 23.   [58] Song of the Three Children, 4 *et seq*.
[59] Rom. vii. 24.   [60] Prov. viii. 22.   [61] John xiv. 30.   [62] Col. ii. 14.
[63] Ps. li. 17.   [64] Rev. xxi. 2.   [65] 2 Cor. v. 5.   [66] Ps. cxvi. 13.
[67] Ps. lxii. 1, 2.   [68] Matt. xi. 28.   [69] Ver. 29.   [70] Deut. xxxii. 49.   [71] 1 Cor. xv. 9.

THE EIGHTH BOOK

Augustine's thirty-second year. He consults Simplicianus: from him hears
the history of the conversion of Victorinus, and longs to devote himself entirely to God, but is mastered by his old habits; is still further roused by the history of St. Antony, and the conversion of two
courtiers; during a severe struggle hears a voice from heaven, opens
Scripture, and is converted, with his friend Alypius. His mother's
vision fulfilled.

O MY God, let me, with thanksgiving, remember, and confess unto Thee Thy mercies on me. *Let my bones* be bedewed with Thy love, and let them *say unto Thee, Who
is like unto Thee, O Lord?*[1] *Thou hast broken my bonds in sunder,
I will offer unto Thee the sacrifice of thanksgiving.*[2] And how Thou
hast broken them, I will declare; and all who worship Thee, when
they hear this, shall say, "Blessed be the Lord in heaven and in earth,
great and wonderful is His name." Thy words had stuck fast in my
heart, and *I was hedged round about on all sides by Thee.*[3] Of Thy
eternal life I was now certain, though I saw it in a figure and as
through a glass.[4] Yet I had ceased to doubt that there was an incorruptible substance, whence was all other substance; nor did I now
desire to be more certain of Thee, but more steadfast in Thee. But
for my temporal life, all was wavering, and *my heart had to be
purged from the old leaven.*[5] *The Way,*[6] the Saviour Himself, well
pleased me, but as yet I shrunk from going through its straitness.
And Thou didst put into my mind, and it seemed good in my
eyes, to go to Simplicianus, who seemed to me a good servant of
Thine; and Thy grace shone in him. I had heard also that from
his very youth he had lived most devoted unto Thee. Now he was
grown into years; and by reason of so great age spent in such zealous
following of Thy ways, he seemed to me likely to have learned much
experience; and so he had. Out of which store I wished that he

---

[1] Ps. xxxv. 10.   [2] Ps. cxvi. 16, 17.   [3] Job. i. 10.   [4] 1 Cor. xiii. 12.
[5] 1 Cor. v. 7.   [6] John xiv. 6.

would tell me (setting before him my anxieties) which were the fittest way for one in my case to walk in Thy paths.

For, I saw the church full; and one went this way, and another that way. But I was displeased that I led a secular life; yea now that my desires no longer inflamed me, as of old, with hopes of honour and profit, a very grievous burden it was to undergo so heavy a bondage. For, in comparison of Thy sweetness, *and the beauty of Thy house which I loved,*[7] those things delighted me no longer. But still I was enthralled with the love of woman; nor did the Apostle forbid me to marry, although he advised me to something better, chiefly wishing *that all men were as himself was.*[8] But I being weak, chose the more indulgent place; and because of this alone, was tossed up and down in all beside, faint and wasted with withering cares, because in other matters I was constrained against my will to conform myself to a married life, to which I was given up and enthralled. I had heard from the mouth of the Truth, *that there were some eunuchs which had made themselves eunuchs for the kingdom of heaven's sake: but,* saith He, *let him who can receive it, receive it.*[9] *Surely vain are all men who are ignorant of God, and could not out of the good things which are seen, find out Him who is good.*[10] But I was no longer in that vanity; I had surmounted it; and by the common witness of all Thy creatures had found Thee our Creator, and Thy Word, God with Thee, and together with Thee one God, by whom Thou createdst all things. There is yet another kind of ungodly, *who knowing God, glorified Him not as God, neither were thankful.*[11] Into this also I had fallen, but *Thy right hand upheld me,*[12] and took me thence, and Thou placedst me where I might recover. For Thou hast said unto man, *Behold, the fear of the Lord is wisdom,*[13] and, *Desire not to seem wise,*[14] because they *who affirmed themselves to be wise, became fools.*[15] But I had now *found the goodly pearl, which, selling all that I had,*[16] I ought to have *bought,* and I hesitated.

To Simplicianus then I went, the father of Ambrose (a Bishop now) in receiving Thy grace, and whom Ambrose truly loved as a father. To him I related the mazes of my wanderings. But when

[7] Ps. xxxvi. 8.   [8] 1 Cor. vii. 8.   [9] Matt. xix. 12.   [10] Wisd. xiii. 1.
[11] Rom. i. 21.   [12] Ps. xviii. 35.   [13] Job. xxviii. 28.   [14] Prov. iii. 7.
[15] Rom. i. 22.   [16] Matt. xiii. 46.

I mentioned that I had read certain books of the Platonists, which Victorinus, sometime Rhetoric Professor of Rome (who had died a Christian, as I had heard), had translated into Latin, he testified his joy that I had not fallen upon the writings of other philosophers, full of *fallacies and deceits, after the rudiments of this world,*[17] whereas the Platonists many ways led to the belief in God and His Word. Then to exhort me to the humility of Christ, *hidden from the wise, and revealed to little ones,*[18] he spoke of Victorinus himself, whom while at Rome he had most intimately known: and of him he related what I will not conceal. For it contains great *praise of Thy grace,* to be confessed unto Thee, how that aged man, most learned and skilled in the liberal sciences, and who had read, and weighed so many works of the philosophers; the instructor of so many noble Senators, who also, as a monument of his excellent discharge of his office, had (which men of this world esteem a high honour) both deserved and obtained a statue in the Roman Forum; he, to that age a worshipper of idols, and a partaker of the sacrilegious rites, to which almost all the nobility of Rome were given up, and had inspired the people with the love of

> "Anubis, barking Deity, and all
> The monster Gods of every kind, who fought
> 'Gainst Neptune, Venus, and Minerva":

whom Rome once conquered, now adored, all which the aged Victorinus had with thundering eloquence so many years defended; —he now blushed not to be the child of Thy Christ, and the newborn babe of Thy fountain; submitting his neck to the yoke of humility, and subduing his forehead to the reproach of the Cross.

O Lord, Lord, *Which hast bowed the heavens and come down, touched the mountains and they did smoke,*[19] by what means didst Thou convey Thyself into that breast? He used to read (as Simplicianus said) the holy Scripture, most studiously sought and searched into all the Christian writings, and said to Simplicianus (not openly, but privately and as a friend), "Understand that I am already a Christian." Whereto he answered, "I will not believe it, nor will I rank you among Christians, unless I see you in the Church of

17 Col. ii. 8.   18 Matt. xi. 25.   19 Ps. cxliv. 5.

Christ." The other, in banter replied, "Do walls then make Christians?" And this he often said, that he was already a Christian; and Simplicianus as often made the same answer, and the conceit of the "walls" was by the other as often renewed. For he feared to offend his friends, proud dæmon-worshippers, from the height of whose Babylonian dignity, as from *cedars of Libanus*,[20] which *the Lord* had not *yet broken down,* he supposed the weight of enmity would fall upon him. But after that by reading and earnest thought he had gathered firmness, and feared to be *denied by Christ before the holy angels, should he now be afraid to confess Him before men*,[21] and appeared to himself guilty of a heavy offence, in being ashamed of the Sacraments of the humility of Thy Word, and not being ashamed of the sacrilegious rites of those proud dæmons, whose pride he had imitated and their rites adopted, he became bold-faced against vanity, and shame-faced towards the truth, and suddenly and unexpectedly said to Simplicianus (as himself told me), "Go we to the Church; I wish to be made a Christian." But he, not containing himself for joy, went with him. And having been admitted to the first Sacrament and become a Catechumen, not long after he further gave in his name, that he might be regenerated by baptism, Rome wondering, the Church, rejoicing. The proud *saw, and were wroth; they gnashed with their teeth, and melted away.*[22] But the *Lord* God *was the hope* of Thy servant, and *he regarded not vanities and lying* madness.[23]

To conclude, when the hour was come for making profession of his faith (which at Rome they, who are about to approach to Thy grace, deliver, from an elevated place, in the sight of all the faithful, in a set form of words committed to memory), the presbyters, he said, offered Victorinus (as was done to such as seemed likely through bashfulness to be alarmed) to make his profession more privately: but he chose rather to profess his salvation in the presence of the holy multitude. "For it was not salvation that he taught in rhetoric, and yet that he had publicly professed: how much less then ought he, when pronouncing Thy word, to dread Thy meek flock, who, when delivering his own words, had not feared a mad multitude!" When, then, he went up to make his profession, all,

[20] Ps. xxix. 5.   [21] Luke ix. 26.   [22] Ps. cxii. 10.   [23] Ps. xxxi. 6, 40, etc.

as they knew him, whispered his name one to another with the voice of congratulation. And who there knew him not? and there ran a low murmur through all the mouths of the rejoicing multitude, Victorinus! Victorinus! Sudden was the burst of rapture, that they saw him; suddenly were they hushed that they might hear him. He pronounced the true faith with an excellent boldness, and all wished to draw him into their very heart: yea by their love and joy they drew him thither, such were the hands wherewith they drew him.

Good God! what takes place in man that he should more rejoice at the salvation of a soul despaired of, and freed from greater peril, than if there had always been hope of him, or the danger had been less? For so Thou also, merciful Father, *dost more rejoice over one penitent than over ninety-nine just persons that need no repentance.*[24] And with much joyfulness do we hear, so often as we hear with what joy *the sheep which had strayed is brought back upon the shepherd's shoulder,* and *the groat is restored to Thy treasury, the neighbours rejoicing with the woman who found it;*[25] and the joy of the solemn service of Thy house forceth to tears, when in Thy house it is read of Thy *younger son, that he was dead, and liveth again; had been lost, and is found.* For Thou *rejoicest* in us, and in Thy holy angels, holy through holy charity. For Thou art ever the same; for all things which abide not the same nor for ever, Thou for ever knowest in the same way.

What then takes place in the soul, when it is more delighted at finding or recovering the things it loves, than if it had ever had them? yea, and other things witness hereunto; and all things are full of witnesses, crying out, "So is it." The conquering commander triumphant; yet had he not conquered unless he had fought; and the more peril there was in the battle, so much the more joy is there in the triumph. The storm tosses the sailors, threatens shipwreck; all wax pale at approaching death; sky and sea are calmed, and they are exceedingly joyed, as having been exceeding afraid. A friend is sick, and his pulse threatens danger; all who long for his recovery are sick in mind with him. He is restored, though as yet he walks not with his former strength; yet there is such joy, as was not, when

[24] Luke xv. 7.   [25] Ver. 5-9.

before he walked sound and strong. Yea, the very pleasures of human life men acquire by difficulties, not those only which fall upon us unlooked for, and against our wills, but even by self-chosen, and pleasure-seeking trouble. Eating and drinking have no pleasure, unless there precede the pinching of hunger and thirst. Men, given to drink, eat certain salt meats, to procure a troublesome heat, which the drink allaying, causes pleasure. It is also ordered that the affianced bride should not at once be given, lest as a husband he should hold cheap whom, as betrothed, he sighed not after.

This law holds in foul and accursed joy; this in permitted and lawful joy; this in the very purest perfection of friendship; this, in him *who was dead, and lived again; had been lost and was found.* Every where the greater joy is ushered in by the greater pain. What means this, O Lord my God, whereas Thou art everlastingly joy to Thyself, and some things around Thee evermore rejoice in Thee? What means this, that this portion of things thus ebbs and flows alternately displeased and reconciled? Is this their allotted measure? Is this all Thou hast assigned to them, whereas from the highest heavens to the lowest earth, from the beginning of the world to the end of ages, from the angel to the worm, from the first motion to the last, Thou settest each in its place, and realisest each in their season, every thing good after its kind? Woe is me! how high art Thou in the highest, and how deep in the deepest! and Thou never departest, and we scarcely return to Thee.

Up, Lord, and do; stir us up, and recall us; kindle and draw us; inflame, grow sweet unto us; let us now love, *let us run.*[26] Do not many, out of a deeper hell of blindness than Victorinus, return to Thee, approach, and are enlightened, receiving that *Light,* which *they who receive, receive power from Thee to become Thy sons?*[27] But if they be less known to the nations, even they that know them, joy less for them. For when many joy together, each also has more exuberant joy; for that they are kindled and inflamed one by the other. Again, because those known to many, influence the more towards salvation, and lead the way with many to follow. And therefore do they also who preceded them much rejoice not in them, because they rejoice not in them alone. For far be it, that in Thy taber-

[26] Cant. i. 4.   [27] John i. 12.

nacle the persons of the rich should be accepted before the poor, or the noble before the ignoble; seeing rather *Thou hast chosen the weak things of the world to confound the strong; and the base things of this world, and the things despised hast Thou chosen, and those things which are not, that Thou mightest bring to nought things that are.*[28] And yet even that *least of* Thy *Apostles,*[29] by whose tongue Thou soundedest forth these words, when through his warfare, Paulus the Proconsul, his pride conquered, was made to pass under the *easy yoke* of Thy Christ, and became a provincial of the great King; he also for his former name Saul, was pleased to be called Paul, in testimony of so great a victory. For the enemy is more overcome in one, of whom he hath more hold; by whom he hath hold of more. But the proud he hath more hold of, through their nobility; and by them, of more through their authority. By how much the more welcome then the heart of Victorinus was esteemed, which the devil had held as an impregnable possession, the tongue of Victorinus, with which mighty and keen weapon he had slain many; so much the more abundantly ought Thy sons to rejoice, for that our King *hath bound the strong man,*[30] and they saw his *vessels taken from him and cleansed,* and *made meet for Thy honour;*[31] and become *serviceable for the Lord, unto every good work.*[32]

But when that man of Thine, Simplicianus, related to me this of Victorinus, I was on fire to imitate him; for for this very end had he related it. But when he had subjoined also, how in the days of the Emperor Julian a law was made, whereby Christians were forbidden to teach the liberal sciences or oratory; and how he, obeying this law, chose rather to give over the wordy school than Thy *Word,* by which Thou *makest eloquent the tongues of the dumb;*[33] he seemed to me not more resolute than blessed, in having thus found opportunity to wait on Thee only. Which thing I was sighing for, bound as I was, not with another's irons, but by my own iron will. My will the enemy held, and thence had made a chain for me, and bound me. For of a froward will, was a lust made; and a lust served, became custom; and custom not resisted, became necessity. By which links, as it were, joined together (whence I called it a

[28] 1 Cor. i. 27, 28.   [29] 1 Cor. xv. 9.   [30] Matt. xii. 29.   [31] Luke xi. 22, 25.
[32] Tim. ii. 21.   [33] Wisd. x. 21.

chain) a hard bondage held me enthralled. But that new will which had begun to be in me, freely to serve Thee, and to wish to enjoy Thee, O God, the only assured pleasantness, was not yet able to overcome my former wilfulness, strengthened by age. Thus did my two wills, one new, and the other old, one carnal, the other spiritual, struggle within me; and by their discord, undid my soul.

Thus I understood, by my own experience, what I had read, how *the flesh lusteth against the spirit and the spirit against the flesh.*[34] Myself verily either way; yet more myself, in that which I approved in myself, than in that which in myself I disapproved.[35] For in this last, it was now for the more part not myself, because in much I rather endured against my will, than acted willingly. And yet it was through me, that custom had obtained this power of warring against me, because I had come willingly, whither I willed not. And who has any right to speak against it, if just punishment follow the sinner? Nor had I now any longer my former plea, that I therefore as yet hesitated to be above the world and serve Thee, for that the truth was not altogether ascertained to me; for now it too was. But I, still under service to the earth, refused to fight under Thy banner, and feared as much to be freed of all encumbrances, as we should fear to be encumbered with it. Thus with the baggage of this present world was I held down pleasantly, as in sleep; and the thoughts wherein I meditated on Thee were like the efforts of such as would awake, who yet overcome with a heavy drowsiness, are again drenched therein. And as no one would sleep for ever, and in all men's sober judgment waking is better, yet a man for the most part, feeling a heavy lethargy in all his limbs, defers to shake off sleep, and, though half displeased, yet even, after it is time to rise, with pleasure yields to it, so was I assured that much better were it for me to give myself up to Thy charity, than to give myself over to mine own cupidity; but though the former course satisfied me and gained the mastery, the latter pleased me and held me mastered. Nor had I any thing to answer Thee calling to me, *Awake thou that sleepest, and arise from the dead, and Christ shall give thee light.*[36] And when Thou didst on all sides show me that what Thou saidst was true, I, convicted by the truth, had noth-

[34] Gal. v. 17. [35] Rom. vii. 18. [36] Eph. v. 14.

ing at all to answer, but only those dull and drowsy words, "Anon, anon," "presently," "leave me but a little." But "presently, presently," had no present, and my "little while" went on for a long while; in vain *I delighted in Thy law according to the inner man, when another law in my members rebelled against the law of my mind, and led me captive under the law of sin which was in my members.*[37] For the law of sin is the violence of custom, whereby the mind is drawn and holden, even against its will; but deservedly, for that it willingly fell into it. *Who then should deliver me thus wretched from the body of this death, but Thy grace only, through Jesus Christ our Lord?*[38]

And how Thou didst deliver me out of the bonds of desire, wherewith I was bound most straitly to carnal concupiscence, and out of the drudgery of worldly things, I will now declare, and confess unto Thy name, *O Lord, my helper and my Redeemer.*[39] Amid increasing anxiety, I was doing my wonted business, and daily sighing unto Thee. I attended Thy Church, whenever free from the business under the burden of which I groaned. Alypius was with me, now after the third sitting released from his law business, and waiting to whom to sell his counsel, as I sold the skill of speaking, if indeed teaching can impart it. Nebridius had now, in consideration of our friendship, consented to teach under Verecundus, a citizen and a grammarian of Milan, and a very intimate friend of us all; who urgently desired, and by the right of friendship challenged from our company, such faithful aid as he greatly needed. Nebridius then was not drawn to this by any desire of advantage (for he might have made much more of his learning had he so willed), but as a most kind and gentle friend, he would not be wanting to a good office, and slight our request. But he acted herein very discreetly, shunning to become known to personages great according to this world, avoiding the distraction of mind thence ensuing, and desiring to have it free and at leisure, as many hours as might be, to seek, or read, or hear something concerning wisdom.

Upon a day then, Nebridius being absent (I recollect not why), lo, there came to see me and Alypius, one Pontitianus, our countryman so far as being an African, in high office in the Emperor's

[37] Rom. vii. 22.   [38] Ver. 24, 25.   [39] Ps. xix. 14.

court. What he would with us, I know not, but we sat down to converse, and it happened that upon a table for some game, before us, he observed a book, took, opened it, and contrary to his expectation, found it the Apostle Paul; for he had thought it some of those books which I was wearing myself in teaching. Whereat smiling, and looking at me, he expressed his joy and wonder that he had on a sudden found this book, and this only before my eyes. For he was a Christian, and baptised, and often bowed himself before Thee our God in the Church, in frequent and continued prayers. When then I had told him that I bestowed very great pains upon those Scriptures, a conversation arose (suggested by his account) on Antony the Egyptian monk; whose name was in high reputation among Thy servants, though to that hour unknown to us. Which when he discovered, he dwelt the more upon that subject, informing and wondering at our ignorance of one so eminent. But we stood amazed, hearing Thy wonderful works most fully attested, in times so recent, and almost in our own, wrought in the true Faith and Church Catholic. We all wondered; we, that they were so great, and he, that they had not reached us.

Thence his discourse turned to the flocks in the monasteries, and their holy ways, a sweet-smelling savour unto Thee, and the fruitful deserts of the wilderness, whereof we knew nothing. And there was a monastery at Milan, full of good brethren, without the city walls, under the fostering care of Ambrose, and we knew it not. He went on with his discourse, and we listened in intent silence. He told us then how one afternoon at Triers, when the Emperor was taken up with the Circensian games, he and three others, his companions, went out to walk in gardens near the city walls, and there as they happened to walk in pairs, one went apart with him, and the other two wandered by themselves; and these, in their wanderings, lighted upon a certain cottage, inhabited by certain of Thy servants, *poor in spirit, of whom is the kingdom of heaven,*[40] and there they found a little book containing the life of Antony. This one of them began to read, admire and kindle at it; and as he read, to meditate on taking up such a life, and giving over his secular service to serve Thee. And these two were of those whom they style agents for the public

[40] Matt. v. 3.

affairs. Then suddenly, filled with an holy love, and a sober shame, in anger with himself he cast his eyes upon his friend, saying, "Tell me, I pray thee, what would we attain by all these labours of ours? what aim we at? what serve we for? Can our hopes in court rise higher than to be the Emperor's favourites? and in this, what is there not brittle, and full of perils? and by how many perils arrive we at a greater peril? and when arrive we thither? But a friend of God, if I wish it, I become now at once." So spake he. And in pain with the travail of a new life, he turned his eyes again upon the book, and read on, and was changed inwardly, where Thou sawest, and his mind was stripped of the world, as soon appeared. For as he read and rolled up and down the waves of his heart, he stormed at himself a while, then discerned, and determined on a better course; and now being Thine, said to his friend, "Now have I broken loose from those our hopes, and am resolved to serve God; and this, from this hour, in this place, I begin upon. If thou likest not to imitate me, oppose not." The other answered, he would cleave to him, to partake so glorious a reward, so glorious a service. Thus both being now Thine, were *building* the *tower* at the necessary *cost,* the *forsaking all that they had, and following Thee.*[41] Then Pontitianus and the other with him, that had walked in other parts of the garden, came in search of them to the same place; and finding them, reminded them to return, for the day was now far spent. But they relating their resolution and purpose, and how that will was begun and settled in them, begged them, if they would not join, not to molest them. But the others, though nothing altered from their former selves, did yet bewail themselves (as he affirmed), and piously congratulated them, recommending themselves to their prayers; and so, with hearts lingering on the earth, went away to the palace. But the other two, fixing their heart on heaven, remained in the cottage. And both had affianced brides, who when they heard hereof, also dedicated their virginity unto God.

Such was the story of Pontitianus; but Thou, O Lord, while he was speaking, didst turn me round towards myself, taking me from behind my back where I had placed me, unwilling to observe myself; and setting me before my face, that I might see how foul I was, how crooked and defiled, bespotted and ulcerous. And I beheld and

[41] Luke xiv. 26-35.

stood aghast; and whither to flee from myself I found not. And if I sought to turn mine eye from off myself, he went on with his relation, and Thou again didst set me over against myself, and thrustedst me before my eyes, that *I might find out mine iniquity, and hate it.*[42] I had known it, but made as though I saw it not, winked at it, and forgot it.

But now, the more ardently I loved those whose healthful affections I heard of, that they had resigned themselves wholly to Thee to be cured, the more did I abhor myself, when compared with them. For many of my years (some twelve) had now run out with me since my nineteenth, when, upon the reading of Cicero's Hortensius, I was stirred to an earnest love of wisdom; and still I was deferring to reject mere earthly felicity, and give myself to search out that, whereof not the finding only, but the very search, was to be preferred to the treasures and kingdoms of the world, though already found, and to the pleasures of the body, though spread around me at my will. But I wretched, most wretched, in the very commencement of my early youth, had begged chastity of Thee, and said, "Give me chastity and continency, only not yet." For I feared lest Thou shouldest hear me soon, and soon cure me of the disease of concupiscence, which I wished to have satisfied, rather than extinguished. And I had wandered through crooked ways in a sacrilegious superstition, not indeed assured thereof, but as preferring it to the others which I did not seek religiously, but opposed maliciously.

I had thought that I therefore deferred from day to day to reject the hopes of this world, and follow Thee only, because there did not appear aught certain, whither to direct my course. And now was the day come wherein I was to be laid bare to myself, and my conscience was to upbraid me. "Where art thou now, my tongue? Thou saidst that for an uncertain truth thou likedst not to cast off the baggage of vanity; now, it is certain, and yet that burden still oppresseth thee, while they who neither have worn themselves out with seeking it, nor for ten years and more have been thinking thereon, have had their shoulders lightened, and received wings to fly away." Thus was I gnawed within, and exceedingly confounded with a horrible shame, while Pontitianus was so speaking. And he having brought to a close his tale and the business he came for, went his way; and I

[42] Ps. xxxvi. 2.

into myself. What said I not against myself? with what scourges of condemnation lashed I not my soul, that it might follow me, striving to go after Thee! Yet it drew back; refused, but excused not itself. All arguments were spent and confuted; there remained a mute shrinking; and she feared, as she would death, to be restrained from the flux of that custom, whereby she was wasting to death.

Then in this great contention of my inward dwelling, which I had strongly raised against my soul, in *the chamber*[43] of my heart, troubled in mind and countenance, I turned upon Alypius. "What ails us?" I exclaim: "what is it? what heardest thou? The unlearned start up and *take heaven by force,*[44] and we with our learning, and without heart, lo, where we wallow in flesh and blood! Are we ashamed to follow, because others are gone before, and not ashamed not even to follow?" Some such words I uttered, and my fever of mind tore me away from him, while he, gazing on me in astonishment, kept silence. For it was not my wonted tone; and my forehead, cheeks, eyes, colour, tone of voice, spake my mind more than the words I uttered. A little garden there was to our lodging, which we had the use of, as of the whole house; for the master of the house, our host, was not living there. Thither had the tumult of my breast hurried me, where no man might hinder the hot contention wherein I had engaged with myself, until it should end as Thou knewest, I knew not. Only I was healthfully distracted and dying, to live; knowing what evil thing I was, and not knowing what good thing I was shortly to become. I retired then into the garden, and Alypius, on my steps. For his presence did not lessen my privacy; or how could he forsake me so disturbed? We sate down as far removed as might be from the house. I was troubled in spirit, most vehemently indignant that I entered not into Thy will and covenant, O my God, which *all my bones cried out* unto me to enter, and praised it to the skies. And therein we enter not by ships, or chariots, or feet, no, move not so far as I had come from the house to that place where we were sitting. For, not to go only, but to go in thither was nothing else but to will to go, but to will resolutely and thoroughly; not to turn and toss, this way and that, a maimed and half-divided will, struggling, with one part sinking as another rose.

[43] Is. xxvi. 20; Matt. vi. 6.   [44] Matt. vi. 12.

Lastly, in the very fever of my irresoluteness, I made with my body many such motions as men sometimes would, but cannot, if either they have not the limbs, or these be bound with bands, weakened with infirmity, or any other way hindered. Thus, if I tore my hair, beat my forehead, if locking my fingers I clasped my knees; I willed, I did it. But I might have willed, and not done it; if the power of motion in my limbs had not obeyed. So many things then I did, when "to will" was not in itself "to be able"; and I did not what both I longed incomparably more to do, and which soon after, when I should will, I should be able to do; because soon after, when I should will, I should will thoroughly. For in these things the ability was one with the will, and to will was to do; and yet was it not done: and more easily did my body obey the weakest willing of my soul, in moving its limbs at its nod, than the soul obeyed itself to accomplish in the will alone this its momentous will.

Whence is this monstrousness? and to what end? Let Thy mercy gleam that I may ask, if so be the secret penalties of men, and those darkest pangs of the sons of Adam, may perhaps answer me. Whence is this monstrousness? and to what end? The mind commands the body, and it obeys instantly; the mind commands itself, and is resisted. The mind commands the hand to be moved; and such readiness is there, that command is scarce distinct from obedience. Yet the mind is mind, the hand is body. The mind commands the mind, its own self, to will and yet it doth not. Whence this monstrousness? and to what end? It commands itself, I say, to will, and would not command, unless it willed, and what it commands is not done. But it willeth not entirely: therefore doth it not command entirely. For so far forth it commandeth, as it willeth; and, so far forth is the thing commanded, not done, as it willeth not. For the will commandeth that there be a will; not another, but itself. But it doth not command entirely, therefore what it commandeth, is not. For were the will entire, it would not even command it to be, because it would already be. It is therefore no monstrousness partly to will, partly to nill, but a disease of the mind, that it doth not wholly rise, by truth up-borne, borne down by custom. And therefore are there two wills, for that one of them is not entire: and what the one lacketh, the other hath.

Let them perish from Thy presence,[45] O God, as perish *vain talkers and seducers*[46] of the soul: who observing that in deliberating there were two wills, affirm that there are two minds in us of two kinds, one good, the other evil. Themselves are truly evil, when they hold these evil things: and themselves shall become good when they hold the truth and assent unto the truth, that Thy Apostle may say to them, *Ye were sometimes darkness, but now light in the Lord.*[47] But they, wishing to be light, not *in the Lord,* but in themselves, imagining the nature of the soul to be that which God is, are made more gross darkness through a dreadful arrogancy; for that they *went back farther from Thee, the true Light that enlighteneth every man that cometh into the world.*[48] Take heed what you say, and blush for shame: *draw near unto Him and be enlightened, and your faces shall not be ashamed.*[49] Myself when I was deliberating upon the serving the Lord my God now, as I had long purposed, it was I who willed, I who nilled, I, I myself. I neither willed entirely, nor nilled entirely. Therefore was I at strife with myself, and rent asunder by myself. And this rent befell me against my will, and yet indicated, not the presence of another mind, but the punishment of my own. *Therefore it was no more I that wrought it, but sin that dwelt in me;*[50] the punishment of a sin more freely committed, in that I was a son of Adam.

For if there be so many contrary natures as there be conflicting wills, there shall now be not two only, but many. If a man deliberate whether he should go to their conventicle or to the theatre, these Manichees cry out, Behold, here are two natures: one good, draws this way; another bad, draws back that way. For whence else is this hesitation between conflicting wills? But I say that both be bad: that which draws to them, as that which draws back to the theatre. But they believe not that will to be other than good, which draws to them. What then if one of us should deliberate, and amid the strife of his two wills be in a strait, whether he should go to the theatre or to our church? would not these Manichees also be in a strait what to answer? For either they must confess (which they fain would not) that the will which leads to our church is good, as well as theirs,

45 Ps. lxviii. 2.   46 Tit. i. 10.   47 Eph. v. 8.
48 John i. 9.   49 Ps. xxxiv. 5.   50 Rom. vii. 17.

who have received and are held by the mysteries of theirs: or they must suppose two evil natures, and two evil souls conflicting in one man, and it will not be true, which they say, that there is one good and another bad; or they must be converted to the truth, and no more deny that where one deliberates, one soul fluctuates between contrary wills.

Let them no more say then, when they perceive two conflicting wills in one man, that the conflict is between two contrary souls, of two contrary substances, from two contrary principles, one good, and the other bad. For Thou, O true God, dost disprove, check, and convict them; as when, both wills being bad, one deliberates whether he should kill a man by poison or by the sword; whether he should seize this or that estate of another's, when he cannot both; whether he should purchase pleasure by luxury, or keep his money by covetousness; whether he go to the circus or the theatre, if both be open on one day; or thirdly, to rob another's house, if he have the opportunity; or, fourthly, to commit adultery, if at the same time he have the means thereof also; all these meeting together in the same juncture of time, and all being equally desired, which cannot at one time be acted: for they rend the mind amid four, or even (amid the vast variety of things desired) more, conflicting wills, nor do they yet allege that there are so many divers substances. So also in wills which are good. For I ask them, is it good to take pleasure in reading the Apostle? or good to take pleasure in a sober Psalm? or good to discourse on the Gospel? They will answer to each, "It is good." What then if all give equal pleasure, and all at once? Do not divers wills distract the mind, while he deliberates which he should rather choose? yet are they all good, and are at variance till one be chosen, whither the one entire will may be borne, which before was divided into many. Thus also, when, above, eternity delights us, and the pleasure of temporal good holds us down below, it is the same soul which willeth not this or that with an entire will; and therefore is rent asunder with grievous perplexities, while out of truth it sets this first, but out of habit sets not that aside.

Thus soul-sick was I, and tormented, accusing myself much more severely than my wont, rolling and turning me in my chain, till that were wholly broken, whereby I now was but just, but still was, held. And Thou, O Lord, pressedst upon me in my inward parts by a severe mercy, redoubling the lashes of fear and shame, lest I should again give way, and not bursting that same slight remaining tie, it should recover strength, and bind me the faster. For I said within myself, "Be it done now, be it done now," and as I spake, I all but enacted it: I all but did it, and did it not: yet sunk not back to my former state, but kept my stand hard by, and took breath. And I essayed again, and wanted somewhat less of it, and somewhat less, and all but touched, and laid hold of it; and yet came not at it, nor touched nor laid hold of it; hesitating to die to death and to live to life: and the worse whereto I was inured, prevailed more with me than the better whereto I was unused: and the very moment wherein I was to become other than I was, the nearer it approached me, the greater horror did it strike into me; yet did it not strike me back, nor turned me away, but held me in suspense.

The very toys of toys, and vanities of vanities, my ancient mistresses, still held me; they plucked my fleshly garment, and whispered softly, "Dost thou cast us off? and from that moment shall we no more be with thee for ever? and from that moment shall not this or that be lawful for thee for ever?" And what was it which they suggested in that I said, "this or that," what did they suggest, O my God? Let Thy mercy turn it away from the soul of Thy servant. What defilements did they suggest! what shame! And now I much less than half heard them, and not openly showing themselves and contradicting me, but muttering as it were behind my back, and privily plucking me, as I was departing, but to look back on them. Yet they did retard me, so that I hesitated to burst and shake myself free from them, and to spring over whither I was called; a violent habit saying to me, "Thinkest thou, thou canst live without them?"

But now it spake very faintly. For on that side whither I had set my face, and whither I trembled to go, there appeared unto me the chaste dignity of Continency, serene, yet not relaxedly, gay, honestly alluring me to come and doubt not; and stretching forth to receive and embrace me, her holy hands full of multitudes of good examples: there were so many young men and maidens here, a multitude of youth and every age, grave widows and aged virgins; and Continence herself in all, not barren, but a *fruitful mother of children* of joys, by Thee her Husband, O Lord. And she smiled on me with a persuasive mockery, as would she say, "Canst not thou what these youths, what these maidens can? or can they either in themselves, and not rather in the Lord their God? The Lord their God gave me unto them. Why standest thou in thyself, and so standest not? cast thyself upon Him, fear not He will not withdraw Himself that thou shouldest fall; cast thyself fearlessly upon Him, He will receive, and will heal thee." And I blushed exceedingly, for that I yet heard the muttering of those toys, and hung in suspense. And she again seemed to say, "Stop thine ears against *those* thy unclean *members on the earth,* that they may be *mortified. They tell thee of delights, but not as doth the law of the Lord thy God."* [51] This controversy in my heart was self against self only. But Alypius sitting close by my side, in silence waited the issue of my unwonted emotion.

But when a deep consideration had from the secret bottom of my soul drawn together and heaped up all my misery in the sight of my heart; there arose a mighty storm, bringing a mighty shower of tears. Which that I might pour forth wholly, in its natural expressions, I rose from Alypius: solitude was suggested to me as fitter for the business of weeping; so I retired so far that even his presence could not be a burden to me. Thus was it then with me, and he perceived something of it; for something I suppose I had spoken, wherein the tones of my voice appeared choked with weeping, and so had risen up. He then remained where we were sitting, most extremely aston-ished. I cast myself down I know not how, under a certain fig-tree, giving full vent to my tears; and the floods of mine eyes gushed out an *acceptable sacrifice to Thee.* And, not indeed in these words, yet to this purpose, spake I much unto Thee: *and Thou, O Lord, how long? how long, Lord, wilt Thou be angry, for ever?*[52] *Remember not our former iniquities,*[53] for I felt that I was held by them. I sent up these sorrowful words: How long, how long, "to-morrow, and to-morrow?" Why not now? why not is there this hour an end to my uncleanness?

So was I speaking and weeping in the most bitter contrition of my heart, when, lo! I heard from a neighbouring house a voice, as of

[51] Ps. cix. 85. Old Ver.   [52] Ps. vi. 4.   [53] Ps. lxxix. 5, 8.

boy or girl, I know not, chanting, and oft repeating, "Take up and read; Take up and read." Instantly, my countenance altered, I began to think most intently whether children were wont in any kind of play to sing such words: nor could I remember ever to have heard the like. So checking the torrent of my tears, I arose; interpreting it to be no other than a command from God to open the book, and read the first chapter I should find. For I had heard of Antony, that coming in during the reading of the Gospel, he received the admonition, as if what was being read was spoken to him: *Go, sell all that thou hast, and give to the poor, and thou shalt have treasure in heaven, and come and follow me:*[54] and by such oracle he was forthwith converted unto Thee. Eagerly then I returned to the place where Alypius was sitting; for there had I laid the volume of the Apostle when I arose thence. I seized, opened, and in silence read that section on which my eyes first fell: *Not in rioting and drunkenness, not in chambering and wantonness, not in strife and envying; but put ye on the Lord Jesus Christ, and make not provision for the flesh,*[55] *in concupiscence.* No further would I read; nor needed I: for instantly at the end of this sentence, by a light as it were of serenity infused into my heart, all the darkness of doubt vanished away.

Then putting my finger between, or some other mark, I shut the volume, and with a calmed countenance made it known to Alypius. And what was wrought in him, which I knew not, he thus showed me. He asked to see what I had read: I showed him; and he looked even further than I had read, and I knew not what followed. This followed, *him that is weak in the faith, receive;*[56] which he applied to himself, and disclosed to me. And by this admonition was he strengthened; and by a good resolution and purpose, and most corresponding to his character, wherein he did always very far differ from me, for the better, without any turbulent delay he joined me. Thence we go in to my mother; we tell her; she rejoiceth: we relate in order how it took place; she leaps for joy, and triumpheth, and blessed Thee, *Who art able to do above that which we ask or think;*[57] for she perceived that Thou hadst given her more for me, than she was wont to beg by her pitiful and most sorrowful groanings. For thou convertedst me unto Thyself, so that I sought neither wife,

[54] Matt. xix. 21.   [55] Rom. xiii. 13, 14.   [56] Rom. xiv. 1.   [57] Eph. iii. 20.

nor any hope of this world, standing in that rule of faith, where Thou hadst showed me unto her in a vision, so many years before. And Thou didst *convert her mourning into joy*[58] much more plentiful than she had desired, and in a much more precious and purer way than she erst required, by having grandchildren of my body.

[58] Ps. xxx. 11.

THE NINTH BOOK

Augustine determines to devote his life to God, and to abandon his profession of Rhetoric, quietly however; retires to the country to prepare himself to receive the grace of Baptism, and is baptised with Alypius, and his son Adeodatus. At Ostia, in his way to Africa, his mother Monnica dies, in her fifty-sixth year, the thirty-third of Augustine. Her life and character.

O LORD, I am Thy servant; I am Thy servant, and the son of Thy handmaid. Thou hast broken my bonds in sunder. I will offer to Thee the sacrifice of praise.[1] Let my heart and my tongue praise Thee; yea, let *all my bones say, O Lord, who is like unto Thee?* Let them say, and answer Thou me, and *say unto my soul, I am thy salvation?*[2] Who am I, and what am I? What evil have not been either my deeds, or if not my deeds, my words, or if not my words, my will? But Thou, O Lord, art good and merciful, and Thy right hand had respect unto the depth of my death, and from the bottom of my heart emptied that abyss of corruption. And this Thy whole gift was, to nill what I willed, and to will what Thou willedst. But where through all those years, and out of what low and deep recess was my free-will called forth in a moment, whereby to submit my neck to Thy *easy yoke,*[3] and my shoulders unto Thy *light burden, O Christ Jesus, my Helper and my Redeemer?*[4] How sweet did it at once become to me, to want the sweetness of those toys! and what I feared to be parted from, was now a joy to part with. For Thou didst cast them forth from me, Thou true and highest sweetness. Thou castest them forth, and for them enteredst in Thyself, sweeter than all pleasure, though not to flesh and blood; brighter than all light, but more hidden than all depths, higher than all honour, but not to the high in their own conceits. Now was my soul free from the biting cares of canvassing and getting, and weltering in filth, and scratching off the itch of

[1] Ps. cxvi. 16, 17.　　[2] Ps. xxxv. 10.　　[3] Matt. xi. 30.　　[4] Ps. xix. 4.

138

lust. And my infant tongue spake freely to Thee, my brightness, and my riches, and my health, the Lord my God.

And I resolved in Thy sight, not tumultuously to tear, but gently to withdraw, the service of my tongue from the marts of lip-labour: that the young, no students in Thy law, nor in Thy peace, but in lying dotages and law-skirmishes, should no longer buy at my mouth arms for their madness. And very seasonably, it now wanted but very few days unto the Vacation of the Vintage, and I resolved to endure them, then in a regular way to take my leave, and having been purchased by Thee, no more to return for sale. Our purpose then was known to Thee; but to men, other than our own friends, was it not known. For we had agreed among ourselves not to let it out abroad to any: although to us, now ascending from the *valley of tears,* and singing that *song of degrees,* Thou hadst given *sharp arrows,* and *destroying coals* against the *subtle tongue,* which as though advising for us, would thwart, and would out of love devour us, as it doth its meat.

Thou hadst pierced our hearts with Thy charity, and we carried Thy words as it were fixed in our entrails: and the examples of Thy servants, whom for black Thou hadst made bright, and for dead, alive, being piled together in the receptacle of our thoughts, kindled and burned up that our heavy torpor, that we should not sink down to the abyss; and they fired us so vehemently, that all the blasts of *subtle tongues* from gainsayers might only inflame us the more fiercely, not extinguish us. Nevertheless, because for *Thy Name's* sake which Thou hast hallowed throughout the earth, this our vow and purpose might also find some to commend it, it seemed like ostentation not to wait for the vacation now so near, but to quit beforehand a public profession, which was before the eyes of all; so that, all looking on this act of mine, and observing how near was the time of vintage which I wished to anticipate, would talk much of me, as if I had desired to appear some great one. And what end had it served me, that people should repute and dispute upon my purpose, and that *our good should be evil spoken of.*[5]

Moreover, it had at first troubled me that in this very summer my lungs began to give way, amid too great literary labour, and to

[5] Rom. xiv. 16.

breathe deeply with difficulty and by the pain in my chest to show that they were injured, and to refuse any full or lengthened speaking; this had troubled me, for it almost constrained me of necessity to lay down that burden of teaching, or, if I could be cured and recover, at least to intermit it. But when the full wish for leisure, that I might see *how that Thou art the Lord*,[6] arose, and was fixed, in me; my God, Thou knowest, I began even to rejoice that I had this secondary, and that no feigned, excuse, which might something moderate the offence taken by those who, for their sons' sake, wished me never to have the freedom of Thy sons. Full then of such joy, I endured till that interval of time were run; it may have been some twenty days, yet they were endured manfully; endured, for the covetousness which aforetime bore a part of this heavy business, had left me, and I remained alone, and had been overwhelmed, had not patience taken its place. Perchance, some of Thy servants, my brethren, may say that I sinned in this, that with a heart fully set on Thy service, I suffered myself to sit even one hour in the chair of lies. Nor would I be contentious. But hast not Thou, O most merciful Lord, pardoned and remitted this sin also, with my other most horrible and deadly sins, in the holy water?

Verecundus was worn down with care about this our blessedness, for that being held back by bonds, whereby he was most straitly bound, he saw that he should be severed from us. For himself was not yet a Christian, his wife one of the faithful; and yet hereby, more rigidly than by any other chain, was he let and hindered from the journey which we had now essayed. For he would not, he said, be a Christian on any other terms than on those he could not. However, he offered us courteously to remain at his country-house so long as we should stay there. Thou, O Lord, shalt reward him *in the resurrection of the just*,[7] seeing Thou hast already given him *the lot* of the righteous.[8] For although in our absence, being now at Rome, he was seized with bodily sickness, and therein being made a Christian, and one of the faithful, he departed this life; yet *hadst Thou mercy not on him only, but on us also*:[9] lest remembering the exceeding kindness of our friend towards us, yet unable to number him among Thy flock, we should be agonised with intolerable sorrow.

[6] Ps. xlvi. 10.   [7] Luke xiv. 14.   [8] Ps. cxxv. 3.   [9] Phil. ii. 27.

Thanks unto Thee, our God, we are Thine: Thy suggestions and consolations tell us, Faithful in promises, Thou now requitest Verecundus for his country-house of Cassiacum, where from the fever of the world we reposed in Thee, with the eternal freshness of Thy Paradise: for that Thou hast forgiven him his sins upon earth, in that rich mountain, that mountain which yieldeth milk, Thine own mountain.

He then had at that time sorrow, but Nebridius joy. For although he also, not being yet a Christian, had fallen into the pit of that most pernicious error, believing the flesh of Thy Son to be a phantom: yet emerging thence, he believed as we did; not as yet endued with any Sacraments of Thy Church, but a most ardent searcher out of truth. Whom, not long after our conversion and regeneration by Thy Baptism, being also a faithful member of the Church Catholic, and serving Thee in perfect chastity and continence amongst his people in Africa, his whole house having through him first been made Christian, didst Thou release from the flesh; and now he lives in Abraham's bosom. Whatever that be, which is signified by that bosom, there lives my Nebridius, my sweet friend, and Thy child, O Lord, adopted of a freed man: there he liveth. For what other place is there for such a soul? There he liveth, whereof he asked much of me, a poor inexperienced man. Now lays he not his ear to my mouth, but his spiritual mouth unto Thy fountain, and drinketh as much as he can receive, wisdom in proportion to his thirst, endlessly happy. Nor do I think that he is so inebriated therewith, as to forget me; seeing Thou, Lord, Whom he drinketh, art mindful of us. So were we then, comforting Verecundus, who sorrowed, as far as friendship permitted, that our conversion was of such sort; and exhorting him to become faithful, according to his measure, namely, of a married estate; and awaiting Nebridius to follow us, which, being so near, he was all but doing: and so, lo! those days rolled by at length; for long and many they seemed, for the love I bare to the easeful liberty, that I might sing to Thee from my inmost marrow, *My heart hath said unto Thee, I have sought Thy face: Thy face, Lord, will I seek.*[10]

Now was the day come wherein I was in deed to be freed of my Rhetoric Professorship, whereof in thought I was already freed. And

[10] Ps. xxvii. 8.

it was done. Thou didst rescue my tongue, whence Thou hadst before rescued my heart. And I blessed Thee, rejoicing; retiring with all mine to the villa. What I there did in writing, which was now enlisted in Thy service, though still, in this breathing-time as it were, panting from the school of pride, my books may witness, as well what I debated with others, as what with myself alone, before Thee: what with Nebridius, who was absent, my Epistles bear witness. And when shall I have time to rehearse all Thy great benefits towards us at that time, especially when hasting on to yet greater mercies? For my remembrance recalls me, and pleasant is it to me, O Lord, to confess to Thee, by what inward goads Thou tamedst me; and how Thou hast evened me, *lowering the mountains and hills of my high imaginations, straightening my crookedness, and smoothing my rough ways;* and how Thou also subduest the brother of my heart, Alypius, unto the Name of Thy Only Begotten, our Lord and Saviour Jesus Christ, which he would not at first vouchsafe to have inserted in our writings. For rather would he have them savour of the lofty *cedars* of the Schools, which *the Lord* hath now *broken down,*[11] than of the wholesome herbs of the Church, the antidote against serpents.

Oh, in what accents spake I unto Thee, my God, when I read the Psalms of David, those faithful songs, and sounds of devotion, which allow of no swelling spirit, as yet a Catechumen, and a novice in Thy real love, resting in that villa, with Alypius a Catechumen, my mother cleaving to us, in female garb with masculine faith, with the tranquillity of age, motherly love, Christian piety! Oh, what accents did I utter unto Thee in those Psalms, and how was I by them kindled towards Thee, and on fire to rehearse them, if possible, through the whole world, against the pride of mankind! And yet they are sung through the whole world, nor can *any hide himself from Thy heat.*[12] With what vehement and bitter sorrow was I angered at the Manichees! and again I pitied them for that they knew not those Sacraments, those medicines, and were mad against the antidote which might have recovered them of their madness. How I would they had then been somewhere near me, and without

[11] Ps. xxix. 5.   [12] Ps. xix. 6.

my knowing that they were there, could have beheld my countenance, and heard my words, when I read the fourth Psalm in that
time of my rest, and how that Psalm wrought upon me, *When I
called, the God of my righteousness heard me; in tribulation Thou
enlargedst me. Have mercy upon me, O Lord, and hear my prayer.*[13]
Would that what I uttered on these words, they could hear, without my knowing whether they heard, lest they should think I spake
it for their sakes! Because in truth neither should I speak the same
things, nor in the same way, if I perceived that they heard and
saw me; nor if I spake them would they so receive them, as when I
spake by and for myself before Thee, out of the natural feelings of
my soul.

I trembled for fear, and again kindled with hope, and with rejoicing in Thy mercy, O Father; and all issued forth both by mine eyes
and voice, when Thy good Spirit turning unto us, said, *O ye sons of
men, how long slow of heart? why do ye love vanity, and seek after
leasing?*[14] For I had *loved vanity, and sought after leasing.*[15] *And
Thou, O Lord,* hadst already *magnified Thy Holy One, raising Him
from the dead, and setting Him at Thy right hand,*[16] whence *from on
high* He should *send* His *promise,* the *Comforter, the Spirit of
truth.*[17] And He had already sent Him, but I knew it not; He had
sent Him, because He was now magnified, rising again from the
dead, and ascending into heaven.[18] For till then, *the Spirit was not
yet given, because Jesus was not yet glorified.*[19] And the prophet
cries out, *How long, slow of heart? why do ye love vanity, and seek
after leasing? Know this, that the Lord hath magnified His Holy
One.* He cries out, *How long?* He cries out, *Know this:* and I so
long, not knowing, *loved vanity, and sought after leasing:* and
therefore I heard and trembled, because it was spoken unto such as
I remembered myself to have been. For in those phantoms which I
had held for truths, was there *vanity and leasing;* and I spake aloud
many things earnestly and forcibly, in the bitterness of my remembrance. Which would they had heard, who yet *love vanity and seek
after leasing!* They would perchance have been troubled, and have

[13] Ps. iv. 1. Old Vers.   [14] Ps. iv. 2. Old Vers.   [15] Ver. 3.
[16] Eph. i. 20.   [17] Luke xxix. 49; John xiv. 16, 17.   [18] Acts ii. 1-4.
[19] John vii. 39.

vomited it up; and *Thou wouldest hear them when they cried unto Thee;* for by a true death in the flesh did He die for us, who now *intercedeth unto Thee for us.*[20]

I further read, *Be angry, and sin not.*[21] And how was I moved, O my God, who had now learned to be angry at myself for things past, that I might not sin in time to come! Yea, to be justly angry; for that it was not another nature of a people of darkness which sinned for me, as they say who are not angry at themselves, and *treasure up* wrath *against the day of* wrath, *and of the revelation of Thy just judgment.*[22] Nor were my *good things* now without, nor sought with the eyes of flesh in that earthly sun; for they that would have joy from without soon become vain, and waste themselves on the things seen and temporal, and in their famished thoughts do lick their very shadows. Oh that they were wearied out with their famine, and said, *Who will show us good things?*[23] And we would say, and they hear, *The light of Thy countenance is sealed upon us.*[24] For we are not *that light which enlighteneth every man,*[25] but we are enlightened by Thee; that *having been sometimes darkness, we may be light in Thee.*[26] Oh that they could see the eternal Internal, which having tasted, I was grieved that I could not show It them, so long as they brought me their heart in their eyes roving abroad from Thee, while they said, *Who will show us good things?*[27] For there, where I was *angry* within myself *in my chamber,* where I was inwardly pricked, where I had sacrificed, slaying my old man and commencing the purpose of a new life, *putting my trust in Thee,*[28]—there hadst Thou begun to grow sweet unto me, and *hadst put gladness in my heart.*[29] And I cried out, as I read this outwardly, finding it inwardly. Nor would I be multiplied with worldly goods; wasting away time, and wasted by time; whereas I had in Thy eternal Simple Essence other *corn, and wine, and oil.*

And with a loud cry of my heart I cried out in the next verse, O *in peace,* O for *The Self-same!* O what said he, *I will lay me down and sleep,*[30] for who shall hinder us, when *cometh to pass that saying which is written, Death is swallowed up in victory?*[31] And Thou surpassingly are the Self-same, Who *art not changed;* and in Thee is rest which forgetteth all toil, for there is none other with Thee, nor

[20] Rom. viii. 34.   [21] Eph. iv. 26.   [22] Rom. ii. 5.   [23] Ps. iv. 6.   [24] *Ibid.*
[25] John i. 9.   [26] Eph. v. 8.   [27] Ps. iv. 6.   [28] Ver. 5.
[29] Ps. iv. 7.   [30] Ver. 8.   [31] 1 Cor. xv. 54.

are we to seek those many other things, which are not what Thou art: but Thou Lord, *alone* hast *made me dwell in hope*. I read, and kindled; nor found I what to do to those deaf and dead, of whom myself had been, a pestilent person, a bitter and a blind bawler against those writings, which are honied with the honey of heaven, and lightsome with Thine own light: and I was consumed with zeal at the enemies of this Scripture.

When shall I recall all which passed in those holy-days? Yet neither have I forgotten, nor will I pass over the severity of Thy scourge, and the wonderful swiftness of Thy mercy. Thou didst then torment me with pain in my teeth; which when it had come to such height that I could not speak, it came into my heart to desire all my friends present to pray for me to Thee, the God of all manner of health. And this I wrote on wax, and gave it to them to read. Presently so soon as with humble devotion we had bowed our knees, that pain went away. But what pain? or how went it away? I was affrighted, O my Lord, my God, for from infancy I had never experienced the like. And the power of Thy Nod was deeply conveyed to me, and rejoicing in faith, I praised Thy Name. And that faith suffered me not to be at ease about my past sins, which were not yet forgiven me by Thy baptism.

The vintage-vacation ended, I gave notice to the Milanese to provide their scholars with another master to sell words to them; for that I had both made choice to serve Thee, and through my difficulty of breathing and pain in my chest was not equal to the Professorship. And by letters I signified to Thy Prelate, the holy man Ambrose, my former errors and present desires, begging his advice what of Thy Scriptures I had best read, to become readier and fitter for receiving so great grace. He recommended Isaiah the Prophet: I believe, because he above the rest is a more clear fore-shower of the Gospel and of the calling of the Gentiles. But I, not understanding the first lesson in him, and imagining the whole to be like it, laid it by, to be resumed when better practised in our Lord's own words.

Thence, when the time was come wherein I was to give in my name, we left the country and returned to Milan. It pleased Alypius also to be with me born again in Thee, being already clothed with the humility befitting Thy Sacraments; and a most valiant tamer of the body, so as, with unwonted venture, to wear the frozen ground of Italy with his bare feet. We joined with us the boy Adeodatus, born after the flesh of my sin. Excellently hadst Thou made him. He was not quite fifteen, and in wit surpassed many grave and learned men. I confess unto Thee Thy gifts, O Lord my God, Creator of all, and abundantly able to reform our deformities: for I had no part in that boy, but the sin. For that we brought him up in Thy discipline, it was Thou, none else, had inspired us with it. I confess unto Thee Thy gifts. There is a book of ours entitled *The Master;* it is a dialogue between him and me. Thou knowest that all there ascribed to the person conversing with me were his ideas, in his sixteenth year. Much besides, and yet more admirable, I found in him. That talent struck awe into me. And who but Thou could be the workmaster of such wonders? Soon didst Thou take his life from the earth: and I now remember him without anxiety, fearing nothing for his childhood or youth, or his whole self. Him we joined with us, our contemporary in grace, to be brought up in Thy discipline; and we were baptised, and anxiety for our past life vanished from us. Nor was I sated in those days with the wondrous sweetness of considering the depth of Thy counsels concerning the salvation of mankind. How did I weep, in Thy Hymns and Canticles, touched to the quick by the voices of Thy sweet-attuned Church! The voices flowed into mine ears, and the Truth distilled into my heart, whence the affections of my devotion overflowed, and tears ran down, and happy was I therein.

Not long had the Church of Milan begun to use this kind of consolation and exhortation, the brethren zealously joining with harmony of voice and hearts. For it was a year, or not much more, that Justina, mother to the Emperor Valentinian, a child, persecuted Thy servant Ambrose, in favour of her heresy, to which she was seduced by the Arians. The devout people kept watch in the Church, ready to die with their Bishop Thy servant. There my mother Thy handmaid, bearing a chief part of those anxieties and watchings, lived for prayer. We, yet unwarmed by the heat of Thy Spirit, still were stirred up by the sight of the amazed and disquieted city. Then it was first instituted that after the manner of the Eastern Churches, Hymns and Psalms should be sung, lest the people should wax faint through the tediousness of sorrow: and from that day to this the custom is retained, divers (yea, almost all) Thy congregations, throughout other parts of the world, following herein.

Then didst Thou by a vision discover to Thy forenamed Bishop where the bodies of Gervasius and Protasius the martyrs lay hid (whom Thou hadst in Thy secret treasury stored uncorrupted so many years), whence Thou mightest seasonably produce them to repress the fury of a woman, but an Empress. For when they were discovered and dug up, and with due honour translated to the Ambrosian Basilica, not only they who were vexed with unclean spirits (the devils confessing themselves) were cured, but a certain man who had for many years been blind, a citizen, and well known to the city, asking and hearing the reason of the people's confused joy, sprang forth, desiring his guide to lead him thither. Led thither, he begged to be allowed to touch with his handkerchief the bier of Thy *saints, whose death is precious in Thy sight.*[32] Which when he had done, and put to his eyes, they were forthwith opened. Thence did the fame spread, thence Thy praises glowed, shone; thence the mind of that enemy, though not turned to the soundness of believing, was yet turned back from her fury of persecuting. Thanks to Thee, O my God. Whence and whither hast Thou thus led my remembrance, that I should confess these things also unto Thee? which great though they be, I had passed by in forgetfulness. And yet then, when *the odour of Thy ointments was so fragrant,* did we not *run after Thee.*[33] Therefore did I more weep among the singing of Thy Hymns, formerly sighing after Thee, and at length breathing in Thee, as far as the breath may enter into this our house of grass.

Thou *that makest men to dwell of one mind in one house,*[34] didst join with us Euodius also, a young man of our own city. Who being an officer of Court, was before us converted to Thee and baptised: and quitting his secular warfare, girded himself to Thine. We were together, about to dwell together in our devout purpose. We sought where we might serve Thee most usefully, and were together returning to Africa: whitherward being as far as Ostia, my mother departed this life. Much I omit, as hastening much. Receive my confessions and thanksgivings, O my God, for innumerable things whereof I

[32] Ps. cxvi. 15.   [33] Cant. i. 2, 3.   [34] Ps. lxviii. 6.

am silent. But I will not omit whatsoever my soul would bring forth concerning that Thy handmaid, who brought me forth, both in the flesh, that I might be born to this temporal light, and in heart, that I might be born to Light eternal. Not her gifts, but Thine in her, would I speak of; for neither did she make nor educate herself. Thou createdst her; nor did her father and mother know what a one should come from them. And the sceptre of Thy Christ, the discipline of Thine only Son, in a Christian house, a good member of Thy Church, educated her in Thy fear. Yet for her good discipline was she wont to commend not so much her mother's diligence, as that of a certain decrepit maid-servant, who had carried her father when a child, as little ones used to be carried at the backs of elder girls. For which reason, and for her great age, and excellent conversation, was she, in that Christian family, well respected by its heads. Whence also the charge of her master's daughters was entrusted to her, to which she gave diligent heed, restraining them earnestly, when necessary, with a holy severity, and teaching them with a grave discretion. For, except at those hours wherein they were most temperately fed at their parents' table, she would not suffer them, though parched with thirst, to drink even water; preventing an evil custom, and adding this wholesome advice: "Ye drink water now, because you have not wine in your power; but when you come to be married, and be made mistresses of cellars and cupboards, you will scorn water, but the custom of drinking will abide." By this method of instruction, and the authority she had, she refrained the greediness of childhood, and moulded their very thirst to such an excellent moderation that what they should not, that they would not.

And yet (as Thy handmaid told me her son) there had crept upon her a love of wine. For when (as the manner was) she, as though a sober maiden, was bidden by her parents to draw wine out of the hogshead, holding the vessel under the opening, before she poured the wine into the flagon, she sipped a little with the tip of her lips; for more her instinctive feelings refused. For this she did, not out of any desire of drink, but out of the exuberance of youth, whereby, it boils over in mirthful freaks, which in youthful spirits are wont to be kept under by the gravity of their elders. And thus by adding to that little, daily littles (*for whoso despiseth little things shall fall by little and little*[35]) she had fallen into such a habit as greedily to drink off her little cup brim-full almost of wine. Where was then that discreet old woman, and that her earnest countermanding? Would aught avail against a secret disease, if Thy healing hand, O Lord, watched not over us? Father, mother, and governors absent, Thou present, who createdst, who callest, who also by those set over us, workest something towards the salvation of our souls, what didst Thou then, O my God? how didst Thou cure her? how heal her? didst Thou not out of another soul bring forth a hard and a sharp taunt, like a lancet out of Thy secret store, and with one touch remove all that foul stuff? For a maid-servant with whom she used to go to the cellar, falling to words (as it happens) with her little mistress, when alone with her, taunted her with this fault, with most bitter insult, calling her wine-bibber. With which taunt, she, stung to the quick, saw the foulness of her fault, and instantly condemned and forsook it. As flattering friends pervert, so reproachful enemies mostly correct. Yet not what by them Thou doest, but what themselves purposed, dost Thou repay them. For she in her anger sought to vex her young mistress, not to amend her; and did it in private, for that the time and place of the quarrel so found them; or lest herself also should have anger, for discovering it thus late. But Thou, Lord, Governor of all in heaven and earth, who turnest to Thy purposes the deepest currents, and the ruled turbulence of the tide of times, didst by the very unhealthiness of one soul heal another; lest any, when he observes this, should ascribe it to his own power, even when another, whom he wished to be reformed, is reformed through words of his.

Brought up thus modestly and soberly, and made subject rather by Thee to her parents, than by her parents to Thee, so soon as she was of marriageable age, being bestowed upon a husband, she served him as her lord; and did her diligence to win him unto Thee, preaching Thee unto him by her conversation; by which Thou ornamentedst her, making her reverently amiable, and admirable unto her husband. And she so endured the wronging of her bed as never to have any quarrel with her husband thereon. For she looked for

[35] Ecclus. xix. 1.

Thy mercy upon him, that believing in Thee, he might be made chaste. But besides this, he was fervid, as in his affections, so in anger: but she had learnt not to resist an angry husband, not in deed only, but not even in word. Only when he was smoothed and tranquil, and in a temper to receive it, she would give an account of her actions, if haply he had overhastily taken offence. In a word, while many matrons, who had milder husbands, yet bore even in their faces marks of shame, would in familiar talk blame their husbands' lives, she would blame their tongues, giving them, as in jest, earnest advice: "That from the time they heard the marriage writings read to them, they should account them as indentures, whereby they were made servants; and so, remembering their condition, ought not to set themselves up against their lords." And when they, knowing what a choleric husband she endured, marvelled that it had never been heard, nor by any token perceived, that Patricius had beaten his wife, or that there had been any domestic difference between them, even for one day, and confidentially asking the reason, she taught them her practice above mentioned. Those wives who observed it found the good, and returned thanks; those who observed it not, found no relief, and suffered.

Her mother-in-law also, at first by whisperings of evil servants incensed against her, she so overcame by observance and persevering endurance and meekness, that she of her own accord discovered to her son the meddling tongues whereby the domestic peace betwixt her and her daughter-in-law had been disturbed, asking him to correct them. Then, when in compliance with his mother, and for the well-ordering of the family, and the harmony of its members, he had with stripes corrected those discovered, at her will who had discovered them, she promised the like reward to any who, to please her, should speak ill of her daughter-in-law to her: and none now venturing, they lived together with a remarkable sweetness of mutual kindness.

This great gift also Thou bestowedst, O my God, my mercy, upon that good handmaid of Thine, in whose womb Thou createdst me, that between any disagreeing and discordant parties where she was able, she showed herself such a peace-maker, that hearing on both sides most bitter things, such as swelling and indigested choler uses to break out into, when the crudities of enmities are breathed out in sour discourses to a present friend against an absent enemy, she never would disclose aught of the one unto the other, but what might tend to their reconcilement. A small good this might appear to me, did I not to my grief know numberless persons, who through some horrible and wide-spreading contagion of sin, not only disclose to persons mutually angered things said in anger, but add withal things never spoken, whereas to humane humanity, it ought to seem a light thing not to foment or increase ill will by ill words, unless one study withal by good words to quench it. Such was she, Thyself, her most inward Instructor, teaching her in the school of the heart.

Finally, her own husband, towards the very end of his earthly life, did she gain unto Thee; nor had she to complain of that in him as a believer, which before he was a believer she had borne from him. She was also the servant of Thy servants; whosoever of them knew her, did in her much praise and honour and love Thee; for that through the witness of the fruits of a holy conversation they perceived Thy presence in her heart. For she had been *the wife of one man,* had *requited her parents, had governed her house* piously, *was well reported of her good works, had brought up children,*[36] so often *travailing in birth of them,*[37] as she saw them swerving from Thee. Lastly, of all of us Thy servants, O Lord (whom on occasion of Thy own gift Thou sufferest to speak), us, who before her sleeping in Thee lived united together, having received the grace of Thy baptism, did she so take care of, as though she had been mother of us all; so served us, as though she had been child to us all.

The day now approaching whereon she was to depart this life (which day Thou well knewest, we knew not), it came to pass, Thyself, as I believe, by Thy secret ways so ordering it, that she and I stood alone, leaning in a certain window, which looked into the garden of the house where we now lay, at Ostia; where removed from the din of men, we were recruiting from the fatigues of a long journey, for the voyage. We were discoursing then together, alone, very sweetly; and *forgetting those things which are behind, and reaching forth unto those things which are before,*[38] we were enquiring between ourselves in the presence of the Truth, which

36 Tim. v. 4, 9, 10   37 Gal. iv. 19.   38 Phil. iii. 13.

Thou art, of what sort the eternal life of the saints was to be, *which eye hath not seen, nor ear heard, nor hath it entered into the heart of man.*[39] But yet we gasped with the mouth of our heart, after those heavenly streams of Thy fountain, *the fountain of life,* which is *with Thee;*[40] that being bedewed thence according to our capacity, we might in some sort meditate upon so high a mystery.

And when our discourse was brought to that point, that the very highest delight of the earthly senses, in the very purest material light, was, in respect of the sweetness of that life, not only not worthy of comparison, but not even of mention; we raising up ourselves with a more glowing affection towards the "Self-same," did by degrees pass through all things bodily, even the very heaven whence sun and moon and stars shine upon the earth; yea, we were soaring higher yet, by inward musing, and discourse, and admiring of Thy works; and we came to our own minds, and went beyond them, that we might arrive at that region of never-failing plenty, where *Thou feedest Israel*[41] for ever with the food of truth, and where life is the *Wisdom by whom all* these *things are made,* and what have been, and what shall be, and she is not made, but is, as she hath been, and so shall she be ever; yea rather, to "have been," and "hereafter to be," are not in her, but only "to be," seeing she is eternal. For to "have been," and to "be hereafter," are not eternal. And while we were discoursing and panting after her, we slightly touched on her with the whole effort of our heart; and we sighed, and there we leave bound *the first fruits of the Spirit;*[42] and returned to vocal expressions of our mouth, where the word spoken has beginning and end. And what is like unto Thy Word, our Lord, who *endureth in Himself* without becoming old, and *maketh all things new?*[43]

We were saying then: If to any the tumult of the flesh were hushed, hushed the images of earth, and waters, and air, hushed also the poles of heaven, yea the very soul be hushed to herself, and by not thinking on self surmount self, hushed all dreams and imaginary revelations, every tongue and every sign, and whatsoever exists only in transition, since if any could hear, all these say, *We made not ourselves, but He made us that abideth for ever*—If then

[39] 1 Cor. ii. 9.   [40] Ps. xxxvi. 9.   [41] Ps. lxxx. 1.   [42] Rom. viii. 22.   [43] Wisd. vii. 27.

having uttered this, they too should be hushed, having roused only
our ears to Him who made them, and He alone speak, not by them,
but by Himself, that we may hear His Word, not through any
tongue of flesh, nor Angel's voice, nor sound of thunder, nor in the
dark riddle of a similitude, but might hear Whom in these things
we love, might hear His Very Self without these (as we two now
strained ourselves, and in swift thought touched on that Eternal
Wisdom which abideth over all):—could this be continued on, and
other visions of kind far unlike be withdrawn, and this one ravish,
and absorb, and wrap up its beholder amid these inward joys, so
that life might be for ever like that one moment of understanding
which now we sighed after; were not this, *Enter into thy Master's
joy?*[44] And when shall that be? When *we shall all rise again,
though we shall not all be changed?*[45]

Such things was I speaking, and even if not in this very manner,
and these same words, yet Lord, Thou knowest that in that day
when we were speaking of these things, and this world with all its
delights became, as we spake, contemptible to us, my mother said,
"Son, for mine own part I have no further delight in any thing in
this life. What I do here any longer, and to what end I am here,
I know not, now that my hopes in this world are accomplished. One
thing there was for which I desired to linger for a while in this
life, that I might see thee a Catholic Christian before I died. My
God hath done this for me more abundantly, that I should now see
thee withal, despising earthly happiness, become His servant: what
do I here?"

What answer I made her unto these things, I remember not. For
scarce five days after, or not much more, she fell sick of a fever; and
in that sickness one day she fell into a swoon, and was for a while
withdrawn from these visible things. We hastened round her; but
she was soon brought back to her senses; and looking on me and
my brother standing by her, said to us enquiringly, "Where was
I?" And then looking fixedly on us, with grief amazed: "Here,"
saith she, "shall you bury your mother." I held my peace and refrained weeping; but my brother spake something, wishing, for
her, as the happier lot, that she might die, not in a strange place,

[44] Matt. xxv. 21.   [45] I Cor. xv. 51.—Vulg., etc.

but in her own land. Whereat, she with anxious look, checking him
with her eyes, for that he still *savoured such things,* and then looking upon me: "Behold," saith she, "what he saith:" and soon after
to us both, "Lay," she saith, "this body any where; let not the care
for that any way disquiet you: this only I request, that you would
remember me at the Lord's altar, wherever you be." And having delivered this sentiment in what words she could she held her peace,
being exercised by her growing sickness.

But I, considering Thy gifts, Thou unseen God, which Thou in-
stillest into the hearts of Thy faithful ones, whence wondrous fruits
do spring, did rejoice and give thanks to Thee, recalling what I
before knew, how careful and anxious she had ever been as to her
place of burial, which she had provided and prepared for herself by
the body of her husband. For because they had lived in great harmony together, she also wished (so little can the human mind embrace things divine) to have this addition to that happiness, and
to have it remembered among men, that after her pilgrimage beyond the seas, what was earthly of this united pair had been permitted to be united beneath the same earth. But when this emptiness had through the fulness of Thy goodness begun to cease in her
heart, I knew not, and rejoiced admiring what she had so disclosed
to me; though indeed in that our discourse also in the window,
when she said, "What do I here any longer?" there appeared no
desire of dying in her own country. I heard afterwards also, that
when we were now at Ostia, she with a mother's confidence, when
I was absent, one day discoursed with certain of my friends about
the contempt of this life, and the blessing of death: and when they
were amazed at such courage which Thou hadst given to a woman,
and asked, "Whether she were not afraid to leave her body so far
from her own city?" she replied, "Nothing is far to God; nor was
it to be feared lest at the end of the world, He should not recognise
whence He were to raise me up." On the ninth day then of her
sickness, and the fifty-sixth year of her age, and the three-and-
thirtieth of mine, was that religious and holy soul freed from the
body.

I closed her eyes; and there flowed withal a mighty sorrow into
my heart, which was overflowing into tears; mine eyes at the same

time, by the violent command of my mind, drank up their fountain wholly dry; and woe was me in such a strife! But when she breathed her last, the boy Adeodatus burst out into a loud lament; then, checked by us all, held his peace. In like manner also a childish feeling in me, which was, through my heart's youthful voice, finding its vent in weeping, was checked and silenced. For we thought it not fitting to solemnise that funeral with tearful lament, and groanings; for thereby do they for the most part express grief for the departed, as though unhappy, or altogether dead; whereas she was neither unhappy in her death, nor altogether dead. Of this we were assured on good grounds, the testimony of her good conversation and her *faith unfeigned*.

What then was it which did grievously pain me within, but a fresh wound wrought through the sudden wrench of that most sweet and dear custom of living together? I joyed indeed in her testimony, when, in that her last sickness, mingling her endearments with my acts of duty, she called me "dutiful," and mentioned, with great affection of love, that she never had heard any harsh or reproachful sound uttered by my mouth against her. But yet, O my God, Who madest us, what comparison is there betwixt that honour that I paid to her, and her slavery for me? Being then forsaken of so great comfort in her, my soul was wounded, and that life rent asunder as it were, which, of hers and mine together, had been made but one.

The boy then being stilled from weeping, Euodius took up the Psalter, and began to sing, our whole house answering him, the Psalm, *I will sing of mercy and judgment to Thee, O Lord.*[46] But hearing what we were doing, many brethren and religious women came together; and whilst they (whose office it was) made ready for the burial, as the manner is, I (in a part of the house, where I might properly), together with those who thought not fit to leave me, discoursed upon something fitting the time; and by this balm of truth assuaged that torment, known to Thee, they unknowing and listening intently, and conceiving me to be without all sense of sorrow. But in Thy ears, where none of them heard, I blamed the weakness of my feelings, and refrained my flood of grief, which

[46] Ps. ci.

gave way a little unto me; but again came, as with a tide, yet not so as to burst out into tears, nor to a change of countenance; still I knew what I was keeping down in my heart. And being very much displeased that these human things had such power over me, which in the due order and appointment of our natural condition must needs come to pass, with a new grief I grieved for my grief, and was thus worn by a double sorrow.

And behold, the corpse was carried to the burial; we went and returned without tears. For neither in those prayers which we poured forth unto Thee, when the Sacrifice of our ransom was offered for her, when now the corpse was by the grave's side, as the manner there is, previous to its being laid therein, did I weep even during those prayers; yet was I the whole day in secret heavily sad, and with troubled mind prayed Thee, as I could, to heal my sorrow, yet Thou didst not; impressing, I believe, upon my memory by this one instance, how strong is the bond of all habit, even upon a soul, which now feeds upon no deceiving Word. It seemed also good to me to go and bathe, having heard that the bath had its name (balneum) from the Greek βαλανειον, for that it drives sadness from the mind. And this also I confess unto Thy mercy, *Father of the fatherless,*[47] that I bathed, and was the same as before I bathed. For the bitterness of sorrow could not exude out of my heart. Then I slept, and woke up again, and found my grief not a little softened; and as I was alone in my bed, I remembered those true verses of Thy Ambrose. For Thou art the

> "Maker of all, the Lord,
>   And Ruler of the height,
> Who, robing day in light, hast poured
>   Soft slumbers o'er the night,
>
> "That to our limbs the power
>   Of toil may be renew'd,
> And hearts be rais'd that sink and cower,
>   And sorrows be subdu'd."

And then by little and little I recovered my former thoughts of Thy handmaid, her holy conversation towards Thee, her holy ten-

[47] Ps. lxviii. 5.

derness and observance towards us, whereof I was suddenly deprived: and I was minded to weep in Thy sight, for her and for myself, in her behalf and in my own. And I gave way to the tears which I before restrained, to overflow as much as they desired; reposing my heart upon them; and it found rest in them, for it was in Thy ears not in those of man, who would have scornfully interpreted my weeping. And now, Lord, in writing I confess it unto Thee. Read it, who will, and interpret it, how he will: and if he finds sin therein, that I wept my mother for a small portion of an hour (the mother who for the time was dead to mine eyes, who had for many years wept for me that I might live in Thine eyes), let him not deride me; but rather, if he be one of large charity, let him weep himself for my sins unto Thee, the Father of all the brethren of Thy Christ.

But now, with a heart cured of that wound, wherein it might seem blameworthy for an earthly feeling, I pour out unto Thee, our God, in behalf of that Thy handmaid, a far different kind of tears, flowing from a spirit shaken by the thoughts of the dangers of every soul *that dieth in Adam.*[48] And although she having been quickened in Christ, even before her release from the flesh, had lived to the praise of Thy name for her faith and conversation; yet dare I not say that from what time Thou regeneratedst her by baptism, no word issued from her mouth against Thy Commandment.[49] Thy Son, the Truth, hath said, *Whosoever shall say unto his brother, Thou fool, shall be in danger of hell fire.*[50] And woe be even unto the commendable life of men, if, laying aside mercy, Thou shouldest examine it. But because Thou art not extreme in enquiring after sins, we confidently hope to find some place with Thee. But whosoever reckons up his real merits to Thee, what reckons he up to Thee but Thine own gifts? O that men would know themselves to be men; *and that he that glorieth would glory in the Lord.*[51]

I therefore, O my Praise and my Life, God of my heart, laying aside for a while her good deeds, for which I give thanks to Thee with joy, do now beseech Thee for the sins of my mother. Hearken unto me, I entreat Thee, by the Medicine of our wounds, Who hung upon the tree, and now *sitting at Thy right hand maketh interces-*

[48] 1 Cor. xv. 22. [49] Matt. xii. 36. [50] Matt. v. 22. [51] 1 Cor. x. 17.

sion to Thee for us.[52] I know that she dealt mercifully, and from her heart *forgave her debtors their debts; do Thou also forgive her debts,*[53] what ever she may have contracted in so many years, since the water of salvation. Forgive her, Lord, forgive, I beseech Thee; *enter not into the judgment with her.*[54] *Let Thy mercy be exalted above Thy justice,*[55] since Thy words are true, and *Thou hast promised mercy unto the merciful,*[56] which thou gavest them to be, *who wilt have mercy on whom Thou wilt have mercy; and wilt have compassion on whom Thou hast had compassion.*[57]

And, I believe, Thou hast already done what I ask; but *accept, O Lord, the free-will offerings of my mouth.*[58] For she, the day of her dissolution now at hand, took no thought to have her body sumptuously wound up, or embalmed with spices; nor desired she a choice monument, or to be buried in her own land. These things she enjoined us not; but desired only to have her name commemorated at Thy Altar, which she had served without intermission of one day: whence she knew that holy Sacrifice to be dispensed, by which the *hand-writing that was against us is blotted out;*[59] through which the enemy was triumphed over, who summing up our offences, and seeking what to lay to our charge, *found nothing in Him,*[60] in Whom we conquer. Who shall restore to Him the innocent blood? Who repay Him the price wherewith He bought us, and so take us from Him. Unto the Sacrament of which our ransom, Thy handmaid bound her soul by the bond of faith. Let none sever her from Thy protection: let neither *the lion nor the dragon*[61] interpose himself by force or fraud. For she will not answer that she owes nothing, lest she be convicted and seized by the crafty accuser: but she will answer that *her sins are forgiven* her by Him, to Whom none can repay that price which He, Who owed nothing, paid for us.

May she rest then in peace with the husband before and after whom she had never any; whom she obeyed, *with patience bringing forth fruit*[62] unto Thee, that she might win him also unto Thee. And inspire, O Lord my God, inspire Thy servants my brethren, Thy sons my masters, whom with voice and heart, and pen I serve, that so many as shall read these Confessions, may at Thy Altar re-

[52] Rom. viii. 34.   [53] Matt. xviii. 35; vi. 12.   [54] Ps. cxliii. 2.   [55] James ii. 13.
[56] Matt. v. 7.   [57] Rom. ix. 15.   [58] Ps. cxix. 108.   [59] Col. ii. 14.
[60] John xiv. 30.   [61] Ps. xci. 1.   [62] Luke viii. 15.

member Monnica Thy handmaid, with Patricius, her sometimes husband, by whose bodies Thou broughtest me into this life, how, I know not. May they with devout affection remember my parents in this transitory light, my brethren under Thee our Father in our Catholic Mother, and my fellow-citizens in that eternal Jerusalem which Thy pilgrim people sigheth after from their Exodus, even unto their return thither. That so my mother's last request of me, may, through my Confessions, more than through my prayers, be, through the prayers of many, more abundantly fulfilled to her.

THE TENTH BOOK

Having in the former books spoken of himself before his receiving the grace of Baptism, in this Augustine confesses what he then was. But first, he enquires by what faculty we can know God at all, whence he enlarges on the mysterious character of the memory, wherein God, being made known, dwells, but which could not discover Him. Then he examines his own trials under the triple division of temptation, "lust of the flesh, lust of the eyes, and pride"; what Christian continency prescribes as to each. On Christ the Only Mediator, who heals and will heal all infirmities.

LET me know Thee, O Lord, who knowest me; *let me know Thee, as I am known.*[1] Power of my soul, enter into it, and fit it for Thee, that Thou mayest have and hold it *without spot or wrinkle.*[2] This is my hope, *therefore do I speak;*[3] and in this hope do I rejoice, when I rejoice healthfully. Other things of this life are the less to be sorrowed for, the more they are sorrowed for; and the more to be sorrowed for, the less men sorrow for them. For behold, *Thou lovest the truth,*[4] and *he that doth it, cometh to the light.*[5] This would I do in my heart before Thee in confession: and in my writing, before many witnesses.

And from Thee, O Lord, *unto whose eyes*[6] the abyss of man's conscience is naked, what could be hidden in me though I would not confess it? For I should hide Thee from me, not me from Thee. But now, for that my groaning is witness, that I am displeased with myself, Thou shinest out, and art pleasing, and beloved, and longed for; that I may be ashamed of myself, and renounce myself, and choose Thee, and neither please Thee nor myself, but in Thee. To Thee therefore, O Lord, am I open, whatever I am; and with what fruit I confess unto Thee, I have said. Nor do I it with words and sounds of the flesh, but with the words of my soul, and the cry of the thought which Thy ear knoweth. For

[1] I Cor. xiii. 12.   [2] Eph. v. 27.   [3] Ps. cxvi. 10.   [4] Ps. li. 6.   [5] John iii. 20.
[6] Heb. iv. 13.

when I am evil, then to confess to Thee is nothing else than to be displeased with myself; but when holy, nothing else than not to ascribe it to myself: because Thou, O Lord, *blessest the godly*,[7] but first Thou *justifiest him when ungodly*.[8] My confession then, O my God, in Thy sight, is made silently, and not silently. For in sound, it is silent; in affection, it cries aloud. For neither do I utter any thing right unto men, which Thou hast not before heard from me; nor dost Thou hear any such thing from me, which Thou hast not first said unto me.

What then have I to do with men, that they should hear my confessions—as if they could *heal all my infirmities*[9]—a race, curious to know the lives of others, slothful to amend their own? Why seek they to hear from me what I am; who will not hear from Thee what themselves are? And how know they, when from myself they hear of myself, whether I say true; seeing *no man knows what is in man, but the spirit of man which is in him?*[10] But if they hear from Thee of themselves, they cannot say, "The Lord lieth." For what is it to hear from Thee of themselves, but to know themselves? and who knoweth and saith, "It is false," unless himself lieth? But because *charity believeth all things*[11] (that is, among those whom knitting unto itself it maketh one), I also, O Lord, will in such wise confess unto Thee, that men may hear, to whom I cannot demonstrate whether I confess truly; yet they believe me, whose ears charity openeth unto me.

But do Thou, my inmost Physician, make plain unto me what object I may gain by doing it. For the confessions of my past sins, which Thou hast *forgiven and covered*,[12] that Thou mightest bless me in Thee, changing my soul by Faith and Thy Sacrament, when read and heard, stir up the heart, that it sleep not in despair and say "I cannot," but awake in the love of Thy mercy and the sweetness of Thy grace, whereby whoso *is weak, is strong,* when by it he became conscious of his own weakness. And the good delight to hear of the past evils of such as are now freed from them, not because they are evils, but because they have been and are not. With what object, then, O Lord my God, to Whom my conscience daily con-

[7] Ps. v. 12.   [8] Rom. iv. 5.   [9] Ps. ciii. 3.   [10] 1 Cor. ii. 11.   [11] *Ibid*. xiii. 7.
[12] Ps. xxxii. 1.

fesseth, trusting more in the hope of Thy mercy than in her own innocency, with what object, I pray, do I by this book confess to men also in Thy presence what I now am, not what I have been? For that other object I have seen and spoken of. But what I now am, at the very time of making these confessions, divers desire to know, who have or have not known me, who have heard from me or of me; but their ear is not at my heart, where I am, whatever I am. They wish then to hear me confess what I am within; whither neither their eye, nor ear, nor understanding can reach; they wish it, as ready to believe—but will they know? For charity, whereby they are good, telleth them that in my confessions I lie not; and she in them, believeth me.

But for what object would they hear this? Do they desire to joy with me, when they hear how near, by Thy gift, I approach unto Thee? and to pray for me, when they shall hear how much I am held back by my own weight? To such will I discover myself. For it is no mean object, O Lord my God, *that by many thanks should be given* to Thee *on our behalf,*[13] and Thou be by many entreated for us. Let the brotherly mind love in me what Thou teachest is to be loved, and lament in me what Thou teachest is to be lamented. Let a brotherly, not a stranger, mind, not that of the *strange children, whose mouth talketh of vanity, and their right hand is a right hand of iniquity,*[14] but that brotherly mind which when it approveth rejoiceth for me, and when it disapproveth me, is sorry for me; because whether it approveth or disapproveth, it loveth me. To such will I discover myself: they will breathe freely at my good deeds, sigh for my ill. My good deeds are Thine appointments and Thy gifts; my evil ones are my offences, and Thy judgments. Let them breathe freely at the one, sigh at the other; and let hymns and weeping go up into Thy sight out of the hearts of my brethren, Thy *censers.*[15] And do Thou, O Lord, be pleased with the incense of Thy holy temple, *have mercy upon me according to Thy great mercy for Thine own name's sake;*[16] and no ways forsaking what Thou hast begun, perfect my imperfections.

This is the object of my confessions of what I am, not of what I have been, to confess this, not before Thee only, in a secret

[13] 1 Cor. ii. 11.   [14] Ps. cxliv. 11.   [15] Rev. viii. 3.   [16] Ps. li. 1.

exultation with trembling,[17] and a secret sorrow with hope; but in the ears also of the believing sons of men, sharers of my joy, and partners in my mortality, my fellow-citizens, and fellow-pilgrims, who are gone before, or are to follow on, companions of my way. These are Thy servants, my brethren, whom Thou willest to be Thy sons; my masters, whom Thou commandest me to serve, if I would live with Thee, of Thee. But this Thy Word were little, did it only command by speaking and not go before in performing. This then I do in deed and word, this I do *under Thy wings;* in over great peril, were not my soul subdued unto Thee under Thy wings, and my infirmity known unto Thee. I am a little one, but my Father ever liveth, and my Guardian is *sufficient for me.* For he is the same who begat me, and defends me: and Thou Thyself art all my good; Thou, Almighty, Who art with me, yea, before I am with Thee. To such then whom Thou commandest me to serve will I discover, not what I have been, but what I now am and what I yet am. *But neither do I judge myself.*[18] Thus therefore I would be heard.

For Thou, Lord, dost judge me:[19] because, although *no man knoweth the things of a man, but the spirit of a man which is in him,* yet is there something of man, which neither *the spirit of man that is in him,* itself *knoweth.*[20] But Thou, Lord, knowest all of him, Who hast made him. Yet I, though in Thy sight I despise myself, and account myself *dust and ashes;* yet know I something of Thee, which I know not of myself. And truly, *now we see through a glass darkly,* not *face to face*[21] as yet. So long therefore as *I be absent from Thee,*[22] I am more present with myself than with Thee, and yet know I Thee that Thou art in no ways passible; but I, what temptations I can resist, what I cannot, I know not. And there is hope, because *Thou art faithful, Who wilt not suffer us to be tempted above that we are able; but wilt with the temptation also make a way to escape, that we may be able to bear it.*[23] I will confess then what I know of myself, I will confess also what I know not of myself. And that because what I do know of myself, I know by Thy shining upon me; and what I know not of myself, so long

[17] Ps. ii. 11. [18] 1 Cor. iv. 3. [19] *Ibid.* [20] *Ibid.* ii. 11. [21] *Ibid.* xiii. 12. [22] 2 Cor. v. 6. [23] 1 Cor. x. 3.

know I not it, until *my darkness be made as the noon-day*[24] in Thy countenance.

Not with doubting, but with assured consciousness, do I love Thee, Lord. Thou hast stricken my heart with Thy word, and I loved Thee. Yea also *heaven and earth, and all that therein is,* behold on every side they bid me love Thee; nor cease to say so unto all, *that they may be without excuse.* But more deeply *wilt Thou have mercy on whom Thou wilt have mercy, and wilt have compassion on whom Thou hast had compassion:*[25] else in deaf ears do the heaven and the earth speak Thy praises. But what do I love, when I love Thee? not beauty of bodies, nor the fair harmony of time, nor the brightness of the light, so gladsome to our eyes, nor sweet melodies of varied songs, nor the fragrant smell of flowers, and ointments, and spices, not manna and honey, not limbs acceptable to embracements of flesh. None of these I love, when I love my God; and yet I love a kind of light, and melody, and fragrance, and meat, and embracement when I love my God, the light, melody, fragrance, meat, embracement of my inner man: where there shineth unto my soul what space cannot contain and there soundeth what time beareth not away, and there smelleth what breathing disperseth not, and there tasteth what eating diminisheth not, and there clingeth what satiety divorceth not. This is it which I love when I love my God.

And what is this? I asked the earth, and it answered me, "I am not He;" and whatsoever are in it confessed the same. I asked the sea and the deeps, and the living creeping things, and they answered, "We are not Thy God, seek above us." I asked the moving air; and the whole air with his inhabitants answered, "Anaximenes was deceived, I am not God." I asked the heavens, sun, moon, stars, "Nor (say they) are we the God whom thou seekest." And I replied unto all the things which encompass the door of my flesh: "Ye have told me of my God, that ye are not He; tell me something of Him." And they cried out with a loud voice, "He made us." My questioning them, was my thoughts on them: and their form of beauty gave the answer. And I turned myself unto myself, and said to myself, "Who art thou?" And I answered, "A man." And behold, in me there present themselves to me soul, and body, one without, the

[24] Isa. lviii. 10.   [25] Rom. i. 20; ix. 15.

other within. By which of these ought I to seek my God? I had sought Him in the body from earth to heaven, so far as I could send messengers, the beams of mine eyes. But the better is the inner, for to it as presiding and judging, all the bodily messengers reported the answers of heaven and earth, and all things therein, who said, "We are not God, but He made us." These things did my inner man know by the ministry of the outer: I the inner knew them; I, the mind, through the senses of my body. I asked the whole frame of the world about my God; and it answered me, "I am not He, but He made me."

Is not this corporeal figure apparent to all whose senses are perfect? why then speaks it not the same to all? Animals small and great see it, but they cannot ask it: because no reason is set over their senses to judge on what they report. But men can ask, so that *the invisible things of God are clearly seen, being understood by the things that are made;*[26] but by love of them, they are made subject unto them: and subjects cannot judge. Nor yet do the creatures answer such as ask, unless they can judge: nor yet do they change their voice (*i. e.,* their appearance), if one man only sees, another seeing asks, so as to appear one way to this man, another way to that; but appearing the same way to both, it is dumb to this, speaks to that; yea rather it speaks to all; but they only understand, who compare its voice received from without, with the truth within. For truth saith unto me, "Neither heaven, nor earth, nor any other body is thy God." This, their very nature saith to him that seeth them: "They are a mass; a mass is less in a part thereof than in the whole." Now to thee I speak, O my soul, thou art my better part: for thou quickenest the mass of my body, giving it life, which no body can give to a body: but thy God is even unto thee the Life of thy life.

What then do I love, when I love my God? who is He above the head of my soul? By my very soul will I ascend to Him. I will pass beyond that power whereby I am united to my body, and fill its whole frame with life. Nor can I by that power find my God; for so *horse and mule that have no understanding,*[27] might find Him; seeing it is the same power, whereby even their bodies

[26] Rom. i. 20.   [27] Ps. xxxii. 9.

live. But another power there is, not that only whereby I animate, but that too whereby I imbue with sense my flesh, which the Lord hath framed for me: commanding the eye not to hear, and the ear not to see; but the eye, that through it I should see, and the ear, that through it I should hear; and to the other senses severally, what is to each their own peculiar seats and offices; which, being divers, I the one mind, do through them enact. I will pass beyond this power of mine also; for this also have the horse and mule, for they also perceive through the body.

I will pass then beyond this power of my nature also, rising by degrees unto Him who made me. And I come to the fields and spacious palaces of my memory, where are the treasures of innumerable images, brought into it from things of all sorts perceived by the senses. There is stored up, whatsoever besides we think, either by enlarging or diminishing, or any other way varying those things which the sense hath come to; and whatever else hath been committed and laid up, which forgetfulness hath not yet swallowed up and buried. When I enter there, I require what I will to be brought forth, and something instantly comes; others must be longer sought after, which are fetched, as it were, out of some inner receptacle; others rush out in troops, and while one thing is desired and required, they start forth, as who should say, "Is it perchance I?" These I drive away with the hand of my heart, from the face of my remembrance; until what I wish for be unveiled, and appear in sight, out of its secret place. Other things come up readily, in unbroken order, as they are called for; those in front making way for the following; and as they make way, they are hidden from sight, ready to come when I will. All which takes place when I repeat a thing by heart.

There are all things preserved distinctly and under general heads, each having entered by its own avenue: as light, and all colours and forms of bodies by the eyes; by the ears all sorts of sounds; all smells by the avenue of the nostrils; all tastes by the mouth; and by the sensation of the whole body, what is hard or soft; hot or cold; smooth or rugged; heavy or light; either outwardly or inwardly to the body. All these doth that great harbour of the memory receive in her numberless secret and inexpressible windings, to be forthcoming, and brought out at need; each entering in by his own gate, and there laid up. Nor yet do the things themselves enter in; only the images of the things perceived are there in readiness, for thought to recall. Which images, how they are formed, who can tell, though it doth plainly appear by which sense each hath been brought in and stored up? For even while I dwell in darkness and in silence, in my memory I can produce colours, if I will, and discern betwixt black and white, and what others I will: nor yet do sounds break in and disturb the image drawn in by my eyes, which I am reviewing, though they also are there, lying dormant, and laid up, as it were, apart. For these too I call for, and forthwith they appear. And though my tongue be still, and my throat mute, so can I sing as much as I will; nor do those images of colours, which notwithstanding be there, intrude themselves and interrupt, when another store is called for, which flowed in by the ears. So the other things, piled in and up by the other senses, I recall at my pleasure, Yea, I discern the breath of lilies from violets, though smelling nothing; and I prefer honey to sweet wine, smooth before rugged, at the time neither tasting nor handling, but remembering only.

These things do I within, in that vast court of my memory. For there are present with me, heaven, earth, sea, and whatever I could think on therein, besides what I have forgotten. There also meet I with myself, and recall myself, and when, where, and what I have done, and under what feelings. There be all which I remember, either on my own experience, or others' credit. Out of the same store do I myself with the past continually combine fresh and fresh likenesses of things which I have experienced, or, from what I have experienced, have believed: and thence again infer future actions, events and hopes, and all these again I reflect on, as present. "I will do this or that," say I to myself, in that great receptacle of my mind, stored with the images of things so many and so great, "and this or that will follow." "O that this or that might be!" "God avert this or that!" So speak I to myself: and when I speak, the images of all I speak of are present, out of the same treasury of memory; nor would I speak of any thereof, were the images wanting.

Great is this force of memory, excessive great, O my God; a large and boundless chamber! who ever sounded the bottom thereof?

yet is this a power of mine, and belongs unto my nature; nor do I myself comprehend all that I am. Therefore is the mind too strait to contain itself. And where should that be, which it containeth not of itself? Is it without it, and not within? how then doth it not comprehend itself? A wonderful admiration surprises me, amazement seizes me upon this. And men go abroad to admire the heights of mountains, the mighty billows of the sea, the broad tides of rivers, the compass of the ocean, and the circuits of the stars, and pass themselves by; nor wonder that when I spake of all these things, I did not see them with mine eyes, yet could not have spoken of them, unless I then actually saw the mountains, billows, rivers, stars which I had seen, and that ocean which I believe to be, inwardly in my memory, and that, with the same vast spaces between, as if I saw them abroad. Yet did not I by seeing draw them into myself, when with mine eyes I beheld them; nor are they themselves with me, but their images only. And I know by what sense of the body each was impressed upon me.

Yet not these alone does the unmeasurable capacity of my memory retain. Here also is all, learnt of the liberal sciences and as yet unforgotten; removed as it were to some inner place, which is yet no place: nor are they the images thereof, but the things themselves. For, what is literature, what the art of disputing, how many kinds of questions there be, whatsoever of these I know, in such manner exists in my memory, as that I have not taken in the image, and left out the thing, or that it should have sounded and passed away like a voice fixed on the ear by that impress, whereby it might be recalled, as if it sounded, when it no longer sounded; or as a smell while it passes and evaporates into air affects the sense of smell, whence it conveys into the memory an image of itself, which remembering, we renew, or as meat, which verily in the belly hath now no taste, and yet in the memory still in a manner tasteth; or as any thing which the body by touch perceiveth, and which when removed from us, the memory still conceives. For those things are not transmitted into the memory, but their images only are with an admirable swiftness caught up, and stored as it were in wondrous cabinets, and thence wonderfully by the act of remembering, brought forth.

But now when I hear that there be three kinds of questions, "Whether the thing be? what it is? of what kind it is?" I do indeed hold the images of the sounds of which those words be composed, and that those sounds, with a noise passed through the air, and now are not. But the things themselves which are signified by those sounds, I never reached with any sense of my body, nor even discerned them otherwise than in my mind; yet in my memory have I laid up not their images, but themselves. Which how they entered into me, let them say if they can; for I have gone over all the avenues of my flesh, but cannot find by which they entered. For the eyes say, "if those images were coloured, we reported of them." The ears say, "if they sound, we gave knowledge of them." The nostrils say, "if they smell, they passed by us." The taste says, "unless they have a savour, ask me not." The touch says, "if it have not size, I handled it not; if I handled it not, I gave no notice of it." Whence and how entered these things into my memory? I know not how. For when I learned them, I gave no credit to another man's mind, but recognized them in mine; and approving them for true, I commended them to it, laying them up as it were, whence I might bring them forth when I willed. In my heart then they were, even before I learned them, but in my memory they were not. Where then? or wherefore, when they were spoken, did I acknowledge them, and said, "So is it, it is true," unless that they were already in the memory, but so thrown back and buried as it were in deeper recesses, that had not the suggestion of another drawn them forth I had perchance been unable to conceive of them?

Wherefore we find, that to learn these things whereof we imbibe not the images by our senses, but perceive within by themselves, without images, as they are, is nothing else, but by conception to receive, and by marking to take heed that those things which the memory did before contain at random and unarranged, be laid up at hand as it were in that same memory where before they lay unknown, scattered and neglected, and so readily occur to the mind familiarised to them. And how many things of this kind does my memory bear which have been already found out, and as I said, placed as it were at hand, which we are said to have learned and come to know; which were I for some short space of time to cease to call to mind, they are again so buried, and glide back, as it were, into the deeper recesses, that they must again, as if new, be thought out thence, for other abode they have none: but they must be drawn together again, that they may be known: that is to say, they must as it were be collected together from their dispersion: whence the word "cogitation" is derived. For *cogo* (collect) and *cogito* (re-collect) have the same relation to each other as *ago* and *agito, facio* and *factito*. But the mind hath appropriated to itself this word (cogi-tation), so that, not what is "collected" any how, but what is "re-collected," *i.e.*, brought together, in the mind, is properly said to be cogitated, or thought upon.

The memory containeth also reasons and laws innumerable of numbers and dimensions, none of which hath any bodily sense impressed; seeing they have neither colour, nor sound, nor taste, nor smell, nor touch. I have heard the sound of the words whereby when discussed they are denoted: but the sounds are other than the things. For the sounds are other in Greek than in Latin; but the things are neither Greek, nor Latin, nor any other language. I have seen the lines of architects, the very finest, like a spider's thread; but those are still different, they are not the images of those lines which the eye of flesh showed me: he knoweth them, whosoever without any conception whatsoever of a body, recognises them within himself. I have perceived also the numbers of the things with which we number all the senses of my body; but those numbers wherewith we number are different, nor are they the images of these, and therefore they indeed are. Let him who seeth them not, deride me for saying these things, and I will pity him, while he derides me.

All these things I remember, and how I learnt them I remember. Many things also most falsely objected against them have I heard, and remember; which though they be false, yet is it not false that I remember them; and I remember also that I have discerned betwixt those truths and these falsehoods objected to them. And I perceive that the present discerning of these things is different from remembering that I oftentimes discerned them, when I often thought upon them. I both remember then to have often under-stood these things; and what I now discern and understand, I lay up in my memory, that hereafter I may remember that I understood it now. So then I remember also to have remembered; as if hereafter I shall call to remembrance, that I have now been able to remember these things, by the force of memory shall I call it to remembrance.

The same memory contains also the affections of my mind, not in the same manner that my mind itself contains them, when it feels them; but far otherwise, according to a power of its own. For without rejoicing I remember myself to have joyed; and without sorrow do I recollect my past sorrow. And that I once feared, I review without fear; and without desire call to mind a past desire. Sometimes, on the contrary, with joy do I remember my fore-past sorrow, and with sorrow, joy. Which is not wonderful, as to the body; for mind is one thing, body another. If I therefore with joy remember some past pain of body, it is not so wonderful. But now seeing this very memory itself is mind (for when we give a thing in charge, to be kept in memory, we say, "See that you keep it in mind;" and when we forget, we say, "It did not come to my mind," and, "It slipped out of my mind," calling the memory itself the mind); this being so, how is it that when with joy I remember my past sorrow, the mind hath joy, the memory hath sorrow; the mind upon the joyfulness which is in it, is joyful, yet the memory upon the sadness which is in it, is not sad? Does the memory perchance not belong to the mind? Who will say so? The memory then is, as it were, the belly of the mind, and joy and sadness, like sweet and bitter food; which, when committed to the memory, are, as it were, passed into the belly, where they may be stowed, but cannot taste. Ridiculous it is to imagine these to be alike; and yet are they not utterly unlike.

But, behold, out of my memory I bring it, when I say there be four perturbations of the mind, desire, joy, fear, sorrow; and whatever I can dispute thereon, by dividing each into its subordinate species, and by defining it, in my memory find I what to say, and thence do I bring it: yet am I not disturbed by any of these perturbations, when by calling them to mind, I remember them; yea, and before I recalled and brought them back, they were there; and therefore could they, by recollection, thence be brought. Perchance, then, as meat is by chewing the cud brought up out of the belly, so by recollection these out of the memory. Why then does not the disputer, thus recollecting, taste in the mouth of his musing the sweetness of joy, or the bitterness of sorrow? Is the comparison unlike in this, because not in all respects like? For who would willingly speak thereof, if so oft as we name grief or fear, we should be compelled to be sad or fearful? And yet could we not speak of them, did we not find in our memory, not only the sounds of the names according to the images impressed by the senses of the body, but notions of the very things themselves which we never received by any avenue of the body, but which the mind itself perceiving by the experience of its own passions, committed to the memory, or the memory of itself retained, without being committed unto.

But whether by images or no, who can readily say? Thus, I name a stone, I name the sun, the things themselves not being present to my senses, but their images to my memory. I name a bodily pain, yet it is not present with me, when nothing aches: yet unless its image were present in my memory, I should not know what to say thereof, nor in discoursing discern pain from pleasure. I name bodily health; being sound in body, the thing itself is present with me; yet, unless its image also were present in my memory, I could by no means recall what the sound of this name should signify. Nor would the sick, when health were named, recognise what were spoken, unless the same image were by the force of memory retained, although the thing itself were absent from the body. I name numbers whereby we number; and not their images, but themselves are present in my memory. I name the image of the sun, and that image is present in my memory. For I recall not the image of its image, but the image itself is present to me, calling it to mind. I name memory, and I recognize what I name. And where do I recognise it, but in the memory itself? Is it also present to itself by its image, and not by itself?

What, when I name forgetfulness, and withal recognise what I name? whence should I recognize it, did I not remember it? I speak not of the sound of the name, but of the thing which it signifies: which if I had forgotten I could not recognise what that sound signifies. When then I remember memory, memory itself is, through itself, present with itself: but when I remember forgetfulness, there

are present both memory and forgetfulness; memory whereby I remember, forgetfulness which I remember. But what is forgetfulness, but the privation of memory? How then is it present that I
remember it, since when present I cannot remember? But if what
we remember we hold it in memory, yet, unless we did remember
forgetfulness, we could never at the hearing of the name recognise
the thing thereby signified, then forgetfulness is retained by memory.
Present then it is, that we forget not, and being so, we forget. It
is to be understood from this that forgetfulness, when we remember
it, is not present to the memory by itself, but by its image: because
if it were present by itself, it would not cause us to remember, but to
forget. Who now shall search out this? who shall comprehend
how it is?

Lord, I, truly, toil therein, yea and toil in myself; I am become
a heavy soil requiring over much *sweat of the brow*. For we are not
now searching out the regions of heaven, or measuring the distances
of the stars, or enquiring the balancings of the earth. It is I myself
who remember, I the mind. It is not so wonderful, if what I myself
am not, be far from me. But what is nearer to me than myself?
And lo, the force of mine own memory is not understood by me;
though I cannot so much as name myself without it. For what shall
I say, when it is clear to me that I remember forgetfulness? Shall I
say that that is not in my memory, which I remember? or shall I
say that forgetfulness is for this purpose in my memory, that I
might not forget? Both were most absurd. What third way is there?
How can I say that the image of forgetfulness is retained by my
memory, not forgetfulness itself, when I remember it? How could
I say this either, seeing that when the image of any thing is impressed on the memory, the thing itself must needs be first present,
whence that image may be impressed? For thus do I remember
Carthage, thus all places where I have been, thus men's faces whom
I have seen, and things reported by the other senses; thus the health
or sickness of the body. For when these things were present, my
memory received from them images, which, being present with me,
I might look on and bring back in my mind, when I remembered
them in their absence. If then this forgetfulness is retained in the
memory through its image, not through itself, then plainly itself was

once present, that its image might be taken. But when it was present, how did it write its image in the memory, seeing that forgetfulness by its presence effaces even what it finds already noted? And yet, in whatever way, although that way be past conceiving and explaining, yet certain am I that I remember forgetfulness itself also, whereby what we remember is effaced.

Great is the power of memory, a fearful thing, O my God, a deep and boundless manifoldness; and this thing is the mind, and this am I myself. What am I then, O my God? What nature am I? A life various and manifold, and exceeding immense. Behold in the plains, and caves, and caverns of my memory, innumerable and innumerably full of innumerable kinds of things, either through images, as all bodies; or by actual presence, as the arts; or by certain notions or impressions, as the affections of the mind, which, even when the mind doth not feel, the memory retaineth, while yet whatsoever is in the memory is also in the mind—over all these do I run, I fly; I dive on this side and on that, as far as I can, and there is no end. So great is the force of memory, so great the force of life, even in the mortal life of man. What shall I do then, O Thou my true life, my God? I will pass even beyond this power of mine which is called memory: yea, I will pass beyond it, that I may approach unto Thee, O sweet Light. What sayest Thou to me? See, I am mounting up through my mind towards Thee who abidest above me. Yea, I now will pass beyond this power of mine which is called memory, desirous to arrive at Thee, whence Thou mayest be arrived at; and to cleave unto Thee, whence one may cleave unto Thee. For even beasts and birds have memory; else could they not return to their dens and nests, nor many other things they are used unto: nor indeed could they be used to any thing, but by memory. I will pass then beyond memory also, that I may arrive at Him who hath separated me from the four-footed beasts and made me wiser than the fowls of the air, I will pass beyond memory also, and where shall I find Thee, Thou truly good and certain sweetness? And where shall I find Thee? If I find Thee without my memory, then do I not retain Thee in my memory. And how shall I find Thee, if I remember Thee not?

For the woman that had lost her groat, and sought it with a

light; unless she had remembered it, she had never found it.[28] For when it was found, whence should she know whether it were the same, unless she remembered it? I remember to have sought and found many a thing; and this I thereby know, that when I was seeking any of them, and was asked, "Is this it?" "Is that it?" so long said I "No," until that were offered me which I sought. Which had I not remembered (whatever it were) though it were offered me, yet should I not find it, because I could not recognize it. And so it ever is, when we seek and find any lost thing. Notwithstanding, when any thing is by chance lost from the sight, not from the memory (as any visible body), yet its image is still retained within, and it is sought until it be restored to sight; and when it is found, it is recognized by the image which is within: nor do we say that we have found what was lost, unless we recognize it; nor can we recognize it, unless we remember it. But this was lost to the eyes, but retained in the memory.

But what when the memory itself loses any thing, as falls out when we forget and seek that we may recollect? Where in the end do we search, but in the memory itself? and there, if one thing be perchance offered instead of another, we reject it, until what we seek meets us; and when it doth, we say, "This is it;" which we should not unless we recognized it, nor recognize it unless we remembered it. Certainly then we had forgotten it. Or, had not the whole escaped us, but by the part whereof we had hold, was the lost part sought for; in that the memory felt that it did not carry on together all which it was wont, and maimed, as it were, by the curtailment of its ancient habit, demanded the restoration of what it missed? For instance, if we see or think of some one known to us, and having forgotten his name, try to recover it; whatever else occurs, connects itself not therewith; because it was not wont to be thought upon together with him, and therefore is rejected, until that present itself, whereon the knowledge reposes equably as its wonted object. And whence does that present itself, but out of the memory itself? for even when we recognize it, on being reminded by another, it is thence it comes. For we do not believe it as something new, but, upon recollection, allow what was named to be right. But were it utterly blotted out of the mind, we should not remember it, even

[28] Luke xv. 8.

when reminded. For we have not as yet utterly forgotten that, which we remember ourselves to have forgotten. What then we have utterly forgotten, though lost, we cannot even seek after.

How then do I seek Thee, O Lord? For when I seek Thee, my God, I seek a happy life. *I will seek Thee, that my soul may live.* For my body liveth by my soul; and my soul by Thee. How then do I seek a happy life, seeing I have it not, until I can say, where I ought to say it, "It is enough"? How seek I it? By remembrance, as though I had forgotten it, remembering that I had forgotten it? Or, desiring to learn it as a thing unknown, either never having known, or so forgotten it, as not even to remember that I had forgotten it? is not a happy life what all will, and no one altogether wills it not? where have they known it, that they so will it? where seen it, that they so love it? Truly we have it, how, I know not. Yea, there is another way, wherein when one hath it, then is he happy; and there are, who are blessed in hope. These have it in a lower kind, than they who have it in very deed; yet are they better off than such as are happy neither in deed nor in hope. Yet even these, had they it not in some sort, would not so will to be happy, which that they do will, is most certain. They have known it then, I know not how, and so have it by some sort of knowledge, what, I know not, and am perplexed whether it be in the memory, which if it be, then we have been happy once; whether all severally, or in that man who first sinned, *in whom also we all died,*[29] and from whom we are all born with misery, I now enquire not; but only, whether the happy life be in the memory? For neither should we love it, did we not know it. We hear the name, and we all confess that we desire the thing; for we are not delighted with the mere sound. For when a Greek hears it in Latin, he is not delighted, not knowing what is spoken; but we Latins are delighted, as would he too, if he heard it in Greek; because the thing itself is neither Greek nor Latin, which Greeks and Latins, and men of all other tongues, long for so earnestly. Known therefore it is to all, for could they with one voice be asked, "would they be happy?" they would answer without doubt, "they would." And this could not be, unless the thing itself whereof it is the name were retained in their memory.

[29] i Cor. xv. 22.

But is it so, as one remembers Carthage who hath seen it? No. For a happy life is not seen with the eye, because it is not a body. As we remember numbers then? No. For these, he that hath in his knowledge, seeks not further to attain unto; but a happy life we have in our knowledge and therefore love it, and yet still desire to attain it, that we may be happy. As we remember eloquence then? No. For although upon hearing this name also, some call to mind the thing, who still are not yet eloquent, and many who desire to be so, whence it appears that it is in their knowledge; yet these have by their bodily senses observed others to be eloquent, and been delighted, and desire to be the like (though indeed they would not be delighted but for some inward knowledge thereof, nor wish to be the like, unless they were thus delighted); whereas a happy life, we do by no bodily sense experience in others. As then we remember joy? Perchance; for my joy I remember, even when sad, as a happy life, when unhappy; nor did I ever with bodily sense see, hear, smell, taste, or touch my joy; but I experienced it in my mind, when I rejoiced; and the knowledge of it clave to my memory, so that I can recall it with disgust sometimes, at others with longing, according to the nature of the things, wherein I remember myself to have joyed. For even from foul things have I been immersed in a sort of joy; which now recalling, I detest and execrate; otherwise in good and honest things, which I recall with longing, although perchance no longer present; and therefore with sadness I recall former joy.

Where then and when did I experience my happy life, that I should remember, and love, and long for it? Nor is it I alone, or some few besides, but we all would fain be happy; which, unless by some certain knowledge we knew, we should not with so certain a will desire. But how is this, that if two men be asked whether they would go to the wars, one, perchance, would answer that he would, the other, that he would not; but if they were asked whether they would be happy, both would instantly without any doubting say they would; and for no other reason would the one go to the wars, and the other not, but to be happy. Is it perchance that as one looks for his joy in this thing, another in that, all agree in their desire of being happy, as they would (if they were asked) that they wished to have joy, and this joy they call a happy life? Although then one obtains this joy by one means, another by another, all have one end, which they strive to attain, namely, joy. Which being a thing which all must say they have experienced, it is therefore found in the memory, and recognised whenever the name of a happy life is mentioned.

Far be it, Lord, far be it from the heart of Thy servant who here confesseth unto Thee, far be it, that, be the joy what it may, I should therefore think myself happy. For there is a *joy* which is *not* given *to the ungodly*,[30] but to those who love Thee for Thine own sake, whose joy Thou Thyself art. And this is the happy life, to rejoice to Thee, of Thee, for Thee; this is it, and there is no other. For they who think there is another, pursue some other and not the true joy. Yet is not their will turned away from some semblance of joy.

It is not certain then that all wish to be happy, inasmuch as they who wish not to joy in Thee, which is the only happy life, do not truly desire the happy life. Or do all men desire this, but *because the flesh lusteth against the Spirit, and the Spirit against the flesh, that they cannot do what they would*,[31] they fall upon that which they can, and are content therewith; because, what they are not able to do, they do not will so strongly as would suffice to make them able? For I ask any one, had he rather joy in truth, or in falsehood? They will as little hesitate to say "in the truth," as to say "that they desire to be happy," for a happy life is joy in the truth: for this is a joying in Thee, Who art *the Truth*,[32] O God *my light, health of my countenance, my God*.[33] This is the happy life which all desire; this life which alone is happy, all desire; to joy in the truth all desire. I have met with many that would deceive; who would be deceived, no one. Where then did they know this happy life, save where they knew the truth also? For they love it also, since they would not be deceived. And when they love a happy life, which is no other than joying in the truth, then also do they love the truth; which yet they would not love, were there not some notice of it in their memory. Why then joy they not in it? why are they not happy? because they are more strongly taken up with other things which have more power to make them miserable, than that which they so faintly remember to make them

[30] Is. xlviii. 22.   [31] Gal. v. 17.   [32] John xiv. 6.   [33] Ps. xxvii. 1; xlii. 11.

happy. For there is yet a little light in men; let them walk, let them *walk, that the darkness overtake them not.*[34]

But why doth "truth generate hatred" and the *man of thine,*[35] preaching the truth, become an enemy to them? whereas a happy life is loved, which is nothing else but joying in the truth; unless that truth is in that kind loved, that they who love any thing else would gladly have that which they love to be the truth: and because they would not be deceived, would not be convinced that they are so? Therefore do they hate the truth for that thing's sake which they love instead of the truth. They love truth when she enlightens, they hate her when she reproves. For since they would not be deceived, and would deceive, they love her when she discovers herself unto them, and hate her when she discovers them. Whence she shall so repay them, that they who would not be made manifest by her, she both against their will makes manifest, and herself becometh not manifest unto them. Thus, thus, yea thus doth the mind of man, thus blind and sick, foul and ill-favoured, wish to be hidden, but that aught should be hidden from it, it wills not. But the contrary is requited it, that itself should not be hidden from the Truth; but the Truth is hid from it. Yet even thus miserable, it had rather joy in truths than in falsehoods. Happy then will it be, when, no distraction interposing, it shall joy in that only Truth, by Whom all things are true.

See what a space I have gone over in my memory seeking Thee, O Lord; and I have not found Thee, without it. Nor have I found any thing concerning Thee, but what I have kept in memory, ever since I learnt Thee. For since I learnt Thee, I have not forgotten Thee. For where I found Truth, there found I my God, the Truth Itself; which since I learnt, I have not forgotten. Since then I learnt Thee, Thou residest in my memory; and there do I find Thee, when I call Thee to remembrance, and delight in Thee. These be my holy delights, which Thou hast given me in Thy mercy, having regard to my poverty.

But where in my memory residest Thou, O Lord, where residest Thou there? what manner of lodging hast Thou framed for Thee? what manner of sanctuary hast Thou builded for Thee? Thou hast

[34] John xii. 35.   [35] John viii. 40.

given this honour to my memory, to reside in it; but in what quarter of it Thou residest, that am I considering. For in thinking on Thee, I passed beyond such parts of it as the beasts also have, for I found Thee not there among the images of corporeal things: and I came to those parts to which I committed the affections of my mind, nor found Thee there. And I entered into the very seat of my mind (which it hath in my memory, inasmuch as the mind remembers itself also), neither wert Thou there: for as Thou art not a corporeal image, nor the affection of a living being (as when we rejoice, condole, desire, fear, remember, forget, or the like); so neither art Thou the mind itself; because Thou art the Lord God of the mind; and all these are changed, but Thou remainest unchangeable over all, and yet hast vouchsafed to dwell in my memory, since I learnt Thee. And why seek I now in what place thereof Thou dwellest, as if there were places therein? Sure I am, that in it Thou dwellest, since I have remembered Thee ever since I learnt Thee, and there I find Thee, when I call Thee to remembrance.

Where then did I find Thee, that I might learn Thee? For in my memory Thou wert not, before I learned Thee. Where then did I find Thee, that I might learn Thee, but in Thee above me? Place there is none; *we go backward and forward,*[36] and there is no place. Every where, O Truth, dost Thou give audience to all who ask counsel of Thee, and at once answerest all, though on manifold matters they ask Thy counsel. Clearly dost Thou answer, though all do not clearly hear. All consult Thee on what they will, though they hear not always what they will. He is Thy best servant who looks not so much to hear that from Thee which himself willeth, as rather to will that which from Thee he heareth.

Too late loved I Thee, O Thou Beauty of ancient days, yet ever new! too late I love Thee! And behold, Thou wert within, and I abroad, and there I searched for Thee; deformed I, plunging amid those fair forms which Thou hadst made. Thou wert with me, but I was not with Thee. Things held me far from Thee, which, unless they were in Thee, were not at all. Thou calledst and shoutedst, and burstest my deafness. Thou flashedst, shonest, and scatteredst my blindness. Thou breathedst odours, and *I drew in breath* and *pant*

[36] Job xxiii. 8, 9.

for Thee. I tasted, and *hunger and thirst.* Thou touchedst me, and I burned for Thy peace.

When I shall with my whole self cleave to Thee, I shall no where have sorrow or labour; and my life shall wholly live, as wholly full of Thee. But now since whom Thou fillest, Thou liftest up, because I am not full of Thee I am a burden to myself. Lamentable joys strive with joyous sorrows: and on which side is the victory, I know not. Woe is me! Lord, have pity on me. My evil sorrows strive with my good joys; and on which side is the victory, I know not. Woe is me! Lord, have pity on me. Woe is me! lo! I hide not my wounds; Thou art the Physician, I the sick; Thou merciful, I miserable. *Is not the life of man upon earth all trial?*[37] Who wishes for troubles and difficulties? Thou commandest them to be endured, not to be loved. No man loves what he endures, though he love to endure. For though he rejoices that he endures, he had rather there were nothing for him to endure. In adversity I long for prosperity, in prosperity I fear adversity. What middle place is there betwixt these two, where *the life of man is* not *all trial?* Woe to the prosperities of the world, once and again, through fear of adversity, and corruption of joy! Woe to the adversities of the world, once and again, and the third time, from the longing for prosperity, and because adversity itself is a hard thing, and lest it shatter endurance. Is not the *life of man upon earth all trial:* without any interval?

And all my hope is no where but in Thy exceeding great mercy. Give what Thou enjoinest, and enjoin what Thou wilt. Thou enjoinest us continency; and *when I knew,* saith one, *that no man can be continent, unless God give it, this also was a part of wisdom to know whose gift she is.*[38] By continency verily are we bound up and brought back into One, whence we were dissipated into many. For too little doth he love Thee, who loves any thing with Thee, which he loveth not for Thee. O love, who ever burnest and never consumest! O charity, my God! kindle me. Thou enjoinest continency: give me what Thou enjoinest, and enjoin what Thou wilt.

Verily Thou enjoinest me continency from the *lust of the flesh, the lust of the eyes, and the ambition of the world.*[39] Thou enjoinest continency from concubinage; and for wedlock itself. Thou hast

[37] Job. vii. 1.—Old Vulg.   [38] Wisd. viii. 21.   [39] 1 John ii. 16.

counselled something better than what Thou hast permitted. And since Thou gavest it, it was done, even before I became a dispenser of Thy Sacrament. But there yet live in my memory (whereof I have much spoken) the images of such things as my ill custom there fixed, which haunt me, strengthless when I am awake: but in sleep, not only so as to give pleasure, but even to obtain assent, and what is very like reality. Yea, so far prevails the illusion of the image, in my soul and in my flesh, that, when asleep, false visions persuade to that which when waking, the true cannot. Am I not then myself, O Lord my God? And yet there is so much difference betwixt myself and myself, within that moment wherein I pass from waking to sleeping, or return from sleeping to waking! Where is reason then, which, awake, resisteth such suggestions? And should the things themselves be urged on it, it remaineth unshaken. Is it clasped up with the eyes? is it lulled asleep with the senses of the body? And whence is it that often even in sleep we resist, and mindful of our purpose, and abiding most chastely in it, yield no assent to such enticements? And yet so much difference there is, that when it happeneth otherwise, upon waking we return to peace of conscience; and by this very difference discover that we did not, what yet we be sorry that in some way it was done in us.

Art Thou not mighty, God Almighty, so as to *heal all the diseases of my soul,*[40] and by Thy more abundant grace to quench even the impure motions of my sleep! Thou wilt increase, Lord, Thy gifts more and more in me, that my soul may follow me to Thee, disentangled from the bird-lime of concupiscence; that it rebel not against itself, and even in dreams not only not, through images of sense, commit those debasing corruptions, even to pollution of the flesh, but not even to consent unto them. For that nothing of this sort should have, over the pure affections even of a sleeper, the very least influence, not even such as a thought would restrain—to work this, not only during life, but even at my present age is not hard for the Almighty, Who art *able to do above all that we ask or think.*[41] But what I yet am in this kind of my evil, have I confessed unto my good Lord; *rejoicing with trembling,*[42] in that which Thou hast given me, and bemoaning that wherein I am still imperfect; hoping that Thou

40 Ps. ciii. 3.   41 Eph. iii. 20.   42 Ps. ii. 11.

wilt perfect Thy mercies in me, even to perfect peace, which my outward and inward man shall have with Thee, when *death shall be
swallowed up in victory*.[43]

There is another *evil of the day*,[44] which I would were *sufficient for
it*. For by eating and drinking we repair the daily decays of our
body, until Thou *destroy both belly and meat*,[45] when Thou shalt
slay my emptiness with a wonderful fulness, and *clothe this corruptible with* an eternal *incorruption*.[46] But now the necessity is
sweet unto me, against which sweetness I fight, that I be not taken
captive; and carry on a daily war by fastings; often *bringing my
body into subjection*,[47] and my pains are removed by pleasure. For
hunger and thirst are in a manner pains; they burn and kill like a
fever, unless the medicine of nourishments come to our aid. Which
since it is at hand through the consolations of Thy gifts, with which
land, and water, and air serve our weakness, our calamity is termed
gratification.

This hast Thou taught me, that I should set myself to take food as
physic. But while I am passing from the discomfort of emptiness to
the content of replenishing, in the very passage the snare of concupiscence besets me. For that passing, is pleasure, nor is there any
other way to pass thither, whither we needs must pass. And health
being the cause of eating and drinking, there joineth itself as an
attendant a dangerous pleasure, which mostly endeavours to go before it, so that I may for her sake do what I say I do, or wish to do,
for health's sake. Nor have each the same measure; for what is
enough for health, is too little for pleasure. And oft it is uncertain
whether it be the necessary care of the body which is yet asking for
sustenance, or whether a voluptuous deceivableness of greediness is
proffering its services. In this uncertainty the unhappy soul rejoiceth,
and therein prepares an excuse to shield itself, glad that it appeareth
not what sufficeth for the moderation of health, that under the cloak
of health, it may disguise the matter of gratification. These temptations I daily endeavour to resist, and I call on Thy right hand, and to
Thee do I refer my perplexities; because I have as yet no settled
counsel herein.

I hear the voice of my God commanding, *Let not your hearts be*

43 1 Cor. xv. 54.   44 Matt. vi. 34.   45 1 Cor. vi. 13.   46 1 Cor. xv. 54.   47 *Ibid*. ix. 27.

overcharged with surfeiting and drunkenness.[48] Drunkenness is far from me; Thou wilt have mercy, that it come not near me. But full feeding sometimes creepeth upon Thy servant; Thou wilt have mercy, that it may be far from me. For *no one can be continent unless Thou give it.*[49] Many things Thou givest us, praying for them; and what good soever we have received before we prayed, from Thee we received it; yea to the end we might afterwards know this, did we before receive it. Drunkard was I never, but drunkards have I known made sober by Thee. From Thee then it was, that they who never were such, should not so be, as from Thee it was, that they who have been, should not ever so be; and from Thee it was, that both might know from Whom it was. I hear another voice of Thine. *Go not after thy lusts, and from thy pleasure turn away.*[50] Yea by Thy favour have I heard that which I have much loved; *neither if we eat, shall we abound; neither if we eat not, shall we lack;*[51] which is to say, neither shall the one make me plenteous nor the other miserable. I heard also another, *for I have learned in whatsoever state I am, therewith to be content; I know how to abound, and how to suffer need. I can do all things through Christ that strengtheneth me.*[52] Behold a soldier of the heavenly camp, not the dust which we are. But *remember,*[53] Lord, *that we are dust,* and that of *dust Thou hast made man;*[54] and he *was lost and is found.*[55] Nor could he of himself do this, because he whom I so loved, saying this through the inbreathing of Thy inspiration, was of the same dust. *I can do all things* (saith he) *through Him that strengtheneth me.* Strengthen me, that *I can.* Give what Thou enjoinest, and enjoin what Thou wilt. He confesses to have received, and when *he glorieth, in the Lord he glorieth.*[56] Another have I heard begging that he might receive. *Take from me* (saith he) *the desires of the belly;*[57] whence it appeareth, O my holy God, that Thou givest, when that is done which Thou commandest to be done. Thou hast taught me, good Father, that *to the pure, all things are pure;* but that *it is evil unto the man that eateth with offence;*[58] and, that *every creature of Thine is good, and nothing to be refused, which is received with thanks-*

[48] Luke xxi. 34.   [49] Wisd. viii. 21.   [50] Ecclus. xviii. 30.   [51] 1 Cor. viii. 8.
[52] Phil. iv. 11-13.   [53] Ps. ciii. 14.   [54] Gen. iii. 19.   [55] Luke xv. 32.
[56] 1 Cor. i. 30, 31.   [57] Ecclus. xxiii. 6.   [58] Rom. xiv. 20.

giving;[59] and that *meat commendeth us not to God;*[60] and, that *no man should judge us in meat or drink;*[61] and, that *he which eateth, let him not despise him that eateth not; and let him not that eateth not, judge him that eateth.*[62] These things have I learned, thanks be to Thee, praise to Thee, my God, my Master, knocking at my ears, enlightening my heart; deliver me out of all temptation. I fear not uncleanness of meat, but the uncleanness of lusting. I know that Noah was permitted to eat all kind of flesh that was good for food;[63] that Elijah was fed with flesh;[64] that John, endued with an admirable abstinence, was not polluted by feeding on living creatures, locusts. I know also that Esau was deceived by lusting for lentiles;[65] and that David blamed himself for desiring a draught of water;[66] and that our King was tempted, not concerning flesh, but bread.[67] And therefore the people in the wilderness also deserved to be reproved, not for desiring flesh, but because, in the desire of food, they murmured against the Lord.[68]

Placed then amid these temptations, I strive daily against concupiscence in eating and drinking. For it is not of such nature that I can settle on cutting it off once for all, and never touching it afterward, as I could of concubinage. The bridle of the throat then is to be held attempered between slackness and stiffness. And who is he, O Lord, who is not some whit transported beyond the limits of necessity? whoever he is, he is a great one; let him make Thy Name great. But I am not such, for *I am a sinful man.*[69] Yet do I too magnify Thy name; and *He maketh intercession to Thee*[70] for my sins who *hath overcome the world;*[71] numbering me among the *weak members or His body;*[72] because *Thine eyes have seen* that of Him which is *imperfect, and in Thy book shall all be written.*[73]

With the allurements of smells, I am not much concerned. When absent, I do not miss them; when present, I do not refuse them; yet ever ready to be without them. So I seem to myself; perchance I am deceived. For that also is a mournful darkness whereby my abilities within are hidden from me; so that my mind making

[59] 1 Tim. iv. 4. [60] 1 Cor. viii. 8. [61] Col. ii. 16. [62] Rom. xiv. 3.
[63] Gen. ix. 3. [64] 1 Kings xvii. 6. [65] Gen. xxv. 34. [66] 2 Sam. xxiii. 15-17.
[67] Matt. iv. 3. [68] Numb. xi. [69] Luke v. 8. [70] Rom. viii. 34. [71] John xvi. 33.
[72] 1 Cor. xii. 22. [73] Ps. cxxxix. 16.

enquiry into herself of her own powers, ventures not readily to believe herself; because even what is in it is mostly hidden unless experience reveal it. And no one ought to be secure in that life, the whole whereof is called *a trial*,[74] that he who hath been capable of worse to be made better, may not likewise of better be made worse. Our only hope, only confidence, only assured promise is Thy mercy.

The delights of the ear had more firmly entangled and subdued me; but Thou didst loosen and free me. Now, in those melodies which Thy words breathe soul into, when sung with a sweet and attuned voice, I do little repose; yet not so to be held thereby, but that I can disengage myself when I will. But with the words which are their life and whereby they find admission into me, themselves seek in my affections a place of some estimation, and I can scarcely assign them one suitable. For at one time I seem to myself to give them more honour than is seemly, feeling our minds to be more holily and fervently raised unto a flame of devotion, by the holy words themselves when thus sung, than when not; and that the several affections of our spirit, by a sweet variety, have their own proper measures in the voice and singing, by some hidden correspondence wherewith they are stirred up. But this contentment of the flesh, to which the soul must not be given over to be enervated doth oft beguile me, the sense not so waiting upon reason as patiently to follow her; but having been admitted merely for her sake, it strives even to run before her, and lead her. Thus in these things I unawares sin, but afterwards am aware of it.

At other times, shunning over-anxiously this very deception, I err in too great strictness; and sometimes to that degree, as to wish the whole melody of sweet music which is used to David's Psalter, banished from my ears, and the Church's too; and that mode seems to me safer, which I remember to have been often told me of Athanasius. Bishop of Alexandria, who made the reader of the psalm utter it with so slight inflection of voice, that it was nearer speaking than singing. Yet again, when I remember the tears I shed at the Psalmody of Thy Church, in the beginning of my recovered faith; and how at this time I am moved not with the singing, but with the things sung, when they are sung with a clear voice and modulation

[74] Job vii. 1.—Vulg.

most suitable, I acknowledge the great use of this institution. Thus I fluctuate between peril of pleasure and approved wholesomeness; inclined the rather (though not as pronouncing an irrevocable opinion) to approve of the usage of singing in the church; that so by the delight of the ears the weaker minds may rise to the feeding of devotion. Yet when it befalls me to be more moved with the voice than the words sung, I confess to have sinned penally, and then had rather not hear music. See now my state: weep with me, and weep for me, ye, whoso regulate your feelings within, as that good action ensues. For you who do not act, these things touch not you. But Thou, O Lord my God, hearken; behold, and see, and *have mercy and heal me*,[75] Thou, in whose presence I have become a problem to myself; and *that is my infirmity*.[76]

There remains the pleasure of these eyes of my flesh, on which to make my confessions in the hearing of the ears of Thy temple, these brotherly and devout ears: and so to conclude the temptations of the *lust of the flesh,* which yet assail me, *groaning earnestly, and desiring to be clothed upon with my house from heaven*.[77] The eyes love fair and varied forms, and bright and soft colours. Let not these occupy my soul; let God rather occupy it, *who made these* things, *very good*[78] indeed, yet is He my good, not they. And these affect me, waking, the whole day, nor is any rest given me from them, as there is from musical, sometimes in silence, from all voices. For this queen of colours, the light, bathing all which we behold, wherever I am through the day, gliding by me in varied forms, soothes me when engaged on other things, and not observing it. And so strongly doth it entwine itself, that if it be suddenly withdrawn, it is with longing sought for, and if absent long, saddeneth the mind.

O Thou Light, which Tobias saw, when these eyes closed he taught his son the way of life;[79] and himself went before with the feet of charity, never swerving. Or which Isaac saw, when his fleshly *eyes being heavy*[80] and closed by old age, it was vouchsafed him, not knowingly, to bless his sons, but by blessing to know them. Or which Jacob saw, when he also, blind through great age, with illumined heart, in the persons of his sons shed light on the different races of

---

[75] Ps. vi. 3.   [76] Ps. lxxvii. 10.   [77] 2 Cor. v. 2.   [78] Gen. i. 31.
[79] Tob. iv.   [80] Gen. xxvii.

the future people, in them foresignified; and laid his hands, mystically crossed upon his grandchildren by Joseph, not as their father by his outward eye corrected them, but as himself inwardly discerned.[81] This is the light, it is one, and all are one, who see and love it. But that corporeal light whereof I spake, it seasoneth the life of this world for her blind lovers with an enticing and dangerous sweetness. But they who know how to praise Thee for it, "O All-creating Lord," take it up in Thy hymns, and are not taken up with it in their sleep. Such would I be. These seductions of the eyes I resist, lest my feet wherewith I walk upon Thy way be ensnared; and I lift up mine invisible eyes to Thee that Thou wouldest *pluck my feet out of the snare.*[82] Thou dost ever and anon pluck them out, for they are ensnared. Thou ceasest not to pluck them out, while I often entangle myself in the snares on all sides aid: because *Thou that keepest Israel neither slumber nor sleep.*[83]

What innumerable toys, made by divers arts and manufactures in our apparel, shoes, utensils and all sort of works, in pictures also in divers images, and these far exceeding all necessary and moderate use and all pious meaning, have men added to tempt their own eyes withal; outwardly following what themselves make, inwardly forsaking Him by whom themselves were made, and destroying that which themselves have been made! But I, my God and my Glory, do hence also sing a hymn to Thee, and do consecrate praise to Him who consecrateth me, because beautiful patterns which through men's souls are conveyed into their cunning hands, come from that Beauty, which is above our souls, which my soul day and night sigheth after. But the framers and followers of the outward beauties derive thence the rule of judging of them, but not of using them. And He is there, though they perceive Him not, that so they might not wander, but *keep their strength for Thee,*[84] and not scatter it abroad upon pleasurable wearinesses. And I, though I speak and see this, entangle my steps with these outward beauties; but Thou pluckest me out, O Lord, Thou pluckest me out; *because Thy lovingkindness is before my eyes.*[85] For I am taken miserably, and Thou pluckest me out mercifully; sometimes not perceiving it, when I

[81] Gen. xlviii.   [82] Ps. xxv. 15.   [83] Ps. cxxi. 4.   [84] Ps. lviii.—Vulg.
[85] Ps. xxv. 3.

had but lightly lighted upon them; otherwhiles with pain, because I had stuck fast in them.

To this is added another form of temptation more manifoldly dangerous. For besides that concupiscence of the flesh which consisteth in the delight of all senses and pleasures, wherein it slaves, who *go far from Thee*,[86] waste and *perish,* the soul hath, through the same senses of the body, a certain vain and curious desire, veiled under the title of knowledge and learning, not of delighting in the flesh, but of making experiments through the flesh. The seat whereof being in the appetite of knowledge, and sight being the sense chiefly used for attaining knowledge, it is in Divine language called *The lust of the eyes*.[87] For to see, belongeth properly to the eyes; yet we use this word of the other senses also, when we employ them in seeking knowledge. For we do not say, hark how it flashes, or smell how it glows, or taste how it shines, or feel how it gleams; for all these are said to be seen. And yet we say not only, see how it shineth, which the eyes alone can perceive; but also, see how it soundeth, see how it smelleth, see how it tasteth, see how hard it is. And so the general experience of the senses, as was said, is called *The lust of the eyes,* because the office of seeing, wherein the eyes hold the prerogative, the other senses by the way of similitude take to themselves when they make search after any knowledge.

But by this may more evidently be discerned, wherein pleasure and wherein curiosity is the object of the senses; for pleasure seeketh objects beautiful, melodious, fragrant, savoury, soft; but curiosity, for trial's sake, the contrary as well, not for the sake of suffering annoyance, but out of the lust of making trial and knowing them. For what pleasure hath it, to see in a mangled carcase what will make you shudder? and yet if it be lying near, they flock thither, to be made sad, and to turn pale. Even in sleep they are afraid to see it. As if when awake, any one forced them to see it, or any report of its beauty drew them thither! Thus also in the other senses, which it were long to go through. From this disease of curiosity are all those strange sights exhibited in the theatre. Hence men go on to search out the hidden powers of nature (which is besides our end), which to know profits not, and wherein men desire nothing but to

[86] Ps. lxxiii. 27.   [87] 1 John ii. 16.

know. Hence also, if with that same end of perverted knowledge magical arts be enquired by. Hence also in religion itself, is God tempted, when signs and wonders are demanded of Him, not desired for any good end, but merely to make trial of.

In this so vast wilderness, full of snares and dangers, behold many of them, I have cut off, and thrust out of my heart, as Thou hast given me, O God of my salvation. And yet when dare I say, since so many things of this kind buzz on all sides about our daily life— when dare I say that nothing of this sort engages my attention or causes in me an idle interest? True, the theatres do not now carry me away, nor care I to know the courses of the stars, nor did my soul ever consult ghosts departed; all sacrilegious mysteries I detest. From Thee, O Lord my God, to whom I owe humble and single-hearted service, by what artifices and suggestions doth the enemy deal with me to desire some sign! But I beseech Thee by our King, and by our pure and holy country, Jerusalem, that as any consenting thereto is far from me, so may it ever be further and further. But when I pray Thee for the salvation of any, my end and intention is far different. Thou givest and wilt give me to *follow Thee* willingly, doing what Thou *wilt*.[88]

Notwithstanding, in how many most petty and contemptible things is our curiosity daily tempted, and how often we give way, who can recount? How often do we begin as it were tolerating people telling vain stories, lest we offend the weak; then by degrees we take interest therein! I go not now to the circus to see a dog coursing a hare; but in the field, if passing, that coursing peradventure will distract me even from some weighty thought, and draw me after it: not that I turn aside the body of my beast, yet still incline my mind thither. And unless Thou, having made me see my infirmity, didst speedily admonish me either through the sight itself, by some contemplation to rise towards Thee, or altogether to despise and pass it by, I dully stand fixed therein. What, when sitting at home, a lizard catching flies, or a spider entangling them rushing into her nets, ofttimes takes my attention? Is the thing different, because they are but small creatures? I go on from them to praise Thee the wonderful Creator and Orderer of all, but this does not

[88] John xxi. 22.

first draw my attention. It is one thing to rise quickly, another not to fall. And of such things is my life full; and my one hope is Thy wonderful great mercy. For when our heart becomes the receptacle of such things and is overcharged with throngs of this abundant vanity, then are our prayers also thereby often interrupted and distracted, and whilst in Thy presence we direct the voice of our heart to Thine ears, this so great concern is broken off, by the rushing in of I know not what idle thoughts. Shall we then account this also among things of slight concernment, or shall aught bring us back to hope, save Thy complete mercy, since Thou hast begun to change us?

And Thou knowest how far Thou hast already changed me, who first healedst me of the lust of vindicating myself, that so Thou mightest *forgive all* the rest of my *iniquities, and heal all my infirmities,* and *redeem my life from corruption, and crown me with mercy and pity, and satisfy my desire with good things;*[89] who didst curb my pride with Thy fear, and tame my neck to Thy *yoke.* And now I bear it and it is *light*[90] unto me, because so hast Thou promised, and hast made it; and verily so it was, and I knew it not, when I feared to take it.

But, O Lord, Thou alone Lord without pride, because Thou art the only true Lord, who hast no Lord; hath this third kind of temptation also ceased from me, or can it cease through this whole life? To wish, namely, to be feared and loved of men, for no other end, but that we may have a joy therein which is no joy? A miserable life this and a foul boastfulness? Hence especially it comes that men do neither purely love nor fear Thee. And therefore *dost Thou resist the proud, and givest grace to the humble:*[91] yea, Thou thunderest down upon the ambitions of the world, and *the foundations of the mountains tremble.*[92] Because now certain offices of human society make it necessary to be loved and feared of men, the adversary of our true blessedness layeth hard at us, every where spreading his snares of "well-done, well-done;" that greedily catching at them, we may be taken unawares, and sever our joy from Thy truth, and set it in the deceivingness of men; and be pleased at being loved and feared, not for Thy sake, but in Thy stead: and thus having been

[89] Ps. ciii. 3-5.　　[90] Matt. xi. 30.　　[91] Jam. iv. 6.　　[92] Ps. xviii. 7.

made like him, he may have them for his own, not in the bands of charity, but in the bonds of punishment: who purposed to *set his throne in the north,*[93] that dark and chilled they might serve him pervertedly and crookedly imitating Thee. But we, O Lord, behold we are Thy *little flock;*[94] possess us as Thine, stretch Thy wings over us, and let us fly under them. Be Thou our glory; let us be loved for Thee, and Thy word feared in us. Who would be praised of men when Thou blamest, will not be defended of men when Thou judgest; nor delivered when Thou condemnest. But when—not *the sinner is praised in the desires of his soul,*[95] nor he *blessed who doth ungodlily,*[96] but—a man is praised for some gift which Thou hast given him, and he rejoices more at the praise for himself than that he hath the gift for which he is praised, he also is praised, while Thou dispraisest; and better is he who praised than he who is praised. For the one took pleasure in the gift of God in man; the other was better pleased with the gift of man, than of God.

By these temptations we are assailed daily, O Lord: without ceasing are we assailed. Our daily *furnace*[97] is the tongue of men. And in this way also Thou commandest us continence. Give what Thou enjoinest, and enjoin what Thou wilt. Thou knowest on this matter the groans of my heart, and the floods of mine eyes. For I cannot learn how far I am more cleansed from this plague, and I much fear my *secret sins,*[98] which Thine eyes know, mine do not. For in other kinds of temptations I have some sort of means of examining myself; in this, scarce any. For, in refraining my mind from the pleasures of the flesh and idle curiosity, I see how much I have attained to, when I do without them; foregoing, or not having them. For then I ask myself how much more or less troublesome it is to me not to have them? Then, riches, which are desired, that they may serve to some one or two or all of the three concupiscences,[99] if the soul cannot discern whether, when it hath them, it despiseth them, they may be cast aside, that so it may prove itself. But to be without praise, and therein essay our powers, must we live ill, yea so abandonedly and atrociously, that no one should know without detesting us? What greater madness can be said or thought of? But if praise

[93] Is. xiv. 13, 14.   [94] Luke xii. 32.   [95] Ps. ix. 29.—Vulg.   [96] Ps. x. 3.   [97] Prov. xxvii. 21.   [98] Ps. xix. 12.   [99] 1 John ii. 16.

useth and ought to accompany a good life and good works, we ought as little to forego its company, as good life itself. Yet I know not whether I can well or ill be without any thing, unless it be absent.

What then do I confess unto Thee in this kind of temptation, O Lord? What, but that I am delighted with praise, but with truth itself, more than with praise? For were it proposed to me, whether I would, being frenzied in error on all things, be praised by all men, or being consistent and most settled in the truth be blamed by all, I see which I should choose. Yet fain would I that the approbation of another should not even increase my joy for any good in me. Yet I own, it doth increase it, and not so only, but dispraise doth diminish it. And when I am troubled at this my misery, an excuse occurs to me, which of what value it is, Thou God knowest, for it leaves me uncertain. For since Thou has commanded us not continency alone, that is, from what things to refrain our love, but righteousness also, that is, whereon to bestow it, and hast willed us to love not Thee only, but our neighbour also; often, when pleased with intelligent praise, I seem to myself to be pleased with the proficiency or towardliness of my neighbour, or to be grieved for evil in him, when I hear him dispraise either what he understands not, or is good. For sometimes I am grieved at my own praise, either when those things be praised in me, in which I mislike myself, or even lesser and slight goods are more esteemed than they ought. But again how know I whether I am therefore thus affected, because I would not have him who praiseth me differ from me about myself; not as being influenced by concern for him, but because those same good things which please me in myself, please me more when they please another also? For some how I am not praised when my judgment of myself is not praised; forasmuch as either those things are praised, which displease me; or those more, which please me less. Am I then doubtful of myself in this matter?

Behold, in Thee, O Truth, I see that I ought not to be moved at my own praises, for my own sake, but for the good of my neighbour. And whether it be so with me, I know not. For herein I know less of myself than of Thee. I beseech now, O my God, discover to me myself also, that I may confess unto my brethren, who are to pray for me, wherein I find myself maimed. Let me examine myself again more diligently. If in my praise I am moved with the good of my neighbour, why am I less moved if another be unjustly dispraised than if it be myself? Why am I more stung by reproach cast upon myself, than at that cast upon another, with the same injustice, before me? Know I not this also? or is it at last that I *deceive myself*,[100] and do not the truth before Thee in my heart and tongue? This madness put far from me, O Lord, lest mine own mouth be to me the *sinner's oil to make fat my head*.[101] *I am poor and needy*;[102] yet best, while in hidden groanings I displease myself, and seek Thy mercy, until what is lacking in my defective state be renewed and perfected, on to that peace which the eye of the proud knoweth not.

Yet the word which cometh out of the mouth, and deeds known to men, bring with them a most dangerous temptation through the love of praise: which to establish a certain excellency of our own, solicits and collects men's suffrages. It tempts, even when it is reproved by myself in myself, on the very ground that it is reproved; and often glories more vainly of the very contempt of vainglory; and so it is no longer contempt of vainglory, whereof it glories; for it doth not contemn when it glorieth.

Within also, within is another evil, arising out of a like temptation; whereby men become vain, pleasing themselves in themselves, though they please not, or displease or care not to please others. But pleasing themselves, they much displease Thee, not only taking pleasure in things not good, as if good, but in Thy good things, as though their own; or even if as Thine, yet as though for their own merits; or even if as though from Thy grace, yet not with brotherly rejoicing, but envying that grace to others. In all these and the like perils and travails, Thou seest the trembling of my heart; and I rather feel my wounds to be cured by Thee, than not inflicted by me.

Where hast Thou not walked with me, O Truth, teaching me what to beware, and what to desire; when I referred to Thee what I could discover here below, and consulted Thee? With my outward senses, as I might, I surveyed the world and observed the life, which my body hath from me, and these my senses. Thence entered I the

[100] Gal. vi. 3; 1 John i. 8.   [101] Ps. cxli. 5.   [102] Ps. cix. 22.

recesses of my memory, those manifold and spacious chambers, wonderfully furnished with innumerable stores; and I considered, and stood aghast; being able to discern nothing of these things without Thee, and finding none of them to be Thee. Nor was I myself, who found out these things, who went over them all, and laboured to distinguish and to value every thing according to its dignity, taking some things upon the report of my senses, questioning about others which I felt to be mingled with myself, numbering and distinguishing the reporters themselves, and in the large treasure-house of my memory revolving some things, storing up others, drawing out others. Nor yet was I myself when I did this, *i. e.,* that my power whereby I did it, neither was it Thou, for Thou art the abiding light, which I consulted concerning all these, whether they were, what they were, and how to be valued; and I heard Thee directing and commanding me; and this I often do, this delights me; and as far as I may be freed from necessary duties, unto this pleasure have I recourse. Nor in all these which I run over consulting Thee can I find any safe place for my soul, but in Thee; whither my scattered members may be gathered, and nothing of me depart from Thee. And sometimes Thou admittest me to an affection, very unusual, in my inmost soul; rising to a strange sweetness, which if it were perfected in me, I know not what in it would not belong to the life to come. But through my miserable encumbrances I sink down again into these lower things, and am swept back by former custom, and am held, and greatly weep, but am greatly held. So much doth the burden of a bad custom weigh us down. Here I can stay, but would not; there I would, but cannot; both ways, miserable.

Thus then have I considered the sicknesses of my sins in that threefold concupiscence, and have called Thy right hand to my help. For with a wounded heart have I beheld Thy brightness, and stricken back I said, "Who can attain thither? *I am cast away from the sight of Thine eyes.*"[103] Thou art the Truth who presidest over all, but I through my covetousness would not indeed forego Thee, but would with Thee possess a lie; as no man would in such wise speak falsely, as himself to be ignorant of the truth. So then I lost Thee, because Thou vouchsafest not to be possessed with a lie.

[103] Ps. xxxi. 22.

Whom could I find to reconcile me to Thee? was I to have recourse to Angels? by what prayers, by what sacraments? Many endeavouring to return unto Thee, and of themselves unable, have, as I hear, tried this, and fallen into the desire of curious visions, and been accounted worthy to be deluded. For they, being high minded, sought Thee by the pride of learning, swelling out rather than smiting upon their breasts, and so by the agreement of their heart, drew unto themselves the *princes of the air,*[104] the fellow-conspirators of their pride, by whom, through magical influences, they were deceived, seeking a mediator, by whom they might be purged, and there was none. For the devil it was, *transforming himself into an Angel of light.*[105] And it much enticed proud flesh, that he had no body of flesh. For they were mortal, and sinners; but Thou, Lord, to whom they proudly sought to be reconciled, art immortal, and without sin. But, a mediator between God and man must have something like to God, something like to men; lest being in both like to man, he should be far from God: or if in both like God, too unlike man: and so not be a mediator. That deceitful mediator then, by whom in Thy secret judgments pride deserved to be deluded, hath one thing in common with man, that is sin; another he would seem to have in common with God; and not being clothed with the mortality of flesh, would vaunt himself to be immortal. But since *the wages of sin is death,*[106] this hath he in common with men, that with them he should be condemned to death.

But the true Mediator, Whom in Thy secret mercy Thou hast showed to the humble, and sentest, that by His example also they might learn that same humility, that *Mediator between God and man, the Man Christ Jesus,*[107] appeared betwixt mortal sinners and the immortal Just One; mortal with men, just with God: that because the wages of righteousness is life and peace, He might by a righteousness conjoined with God make void that death of sinners, now made righteous, which He willed to have in common with them. Hence He was showed forth to holy men of old; that so they, through faith in His Passion to come, as we through faith of it passed, might be saved. For as Man, He was a Mediator; but as the

[104] Eph. ii. 2.   [105] 2 Cor. xi. 14.   [106] Rom. vi. 20.   [107] 1 Tim. ii. 5.

Word, not in the middle between God and man, because equal to God, and God with God, and together one God.

How hast Thou loved us, good Father, who *sparedst not Thine only Son, but deliveredst Him up for us ungodly!*[108] How hast Thou loved us, for whom *He that thought it no robbery to be equal with Thee, was made subject even to the death of the cross,*[109] He alone, *free among the dead,*[110] *having power to lay down his life, and power to take it again:*[111] for us to Thee both Victor and Victim, and therefore Victor, because the Victim; for us to Thee Priest and Sacrifice, and therefore Priest because the Sacrifice; making us to Thee, of servants, sons, by being born of Thee, and serving us. Well then is my hope strong in Him, that Thou *wilt heal all my infirmities,*[112] by Him Who *sitteth at Thy right hand and maketh intercession for us;*[113] else should I despair. For many and great are my infirmities, many they are, and great; but Thy medicine is mightier. We might imagine that Thy Word was far from any union with man, and despair of ourselves, unless He had been *made flesh and dwelt among us.*[114]

Affrighted with my sins and the burden of my misery, I had cast in my heart, and had purposed to *flee to the wilderness:*[115] but Thou forbadest me, and strengthenedst me, saying, *Therefore Christ died for all, that they which live may now no longer live unto themselves, but unto Him that died for them.*[116] See, Lord, I *cast my care upon Thee,*[117] that I may live, and *consider wondrous things out of Thy law.*[118] Thou knowest my unskilfulness, and my infirmities; teach me, and heal me. He, Thine only Son, *in Whom are hid all the treasures of wisdom and knowledge,*[119] hath redeemed me with His blood. *Let not the proud speak evil of me;*[120] because I meditate on my Ransom, and eat and drink, and communicate it; and *poor, desired to be satisfied* from Him, amongst those that *eat and are satisfied, and they shall praise the Lord who seek Him.*[121]

[108] Rom. viii. 32.   [109] Phil. ii. 6, 8.
[110] Ps. lxxxviii. 5.   [111] John x. 18.   [112] Ps. cii. 3.   [113] Rom. viii. 34.
[114] John i. 12.   [115] Ps. lv. 7.   [116] 2 Cor. v. 15.   [117] Ps. lv. 22.   [118] Ps. cxix. 18.
[119] Col. ii. 3.   [120] Ps. cxix. 122.—Vulg.   [121] Ps. xxii. 26.

THE IMITATION OF CHRIST

BY

THOMAS À KEMPIS

TRANSLATED BY

REV. WILLIAM BENHAM

INTRODUCTORY NOTE

THE treatise "Of the Imitation of Christ" appears to have been originally written in Latin early in the fifteenth century. Its exact date and its authorship are still a matter of debate. Manuscripts of the Latin version survive in considerable numbers all over Western Europe, and they, with the vast list of translations and of printed editions, testify to its almost unparalleled popularity. One scribe attributes it to St. Bernard of Clairvaux; but the fact that it contains a quotation from St. Francis of Assisi, who was born thirty years after the death of St. Bernard, disposes of this theory. In England there exist many manuscripts of the first three books, called "Musica Ecclesiastica," frequently ascribed to the English mystic Walter Hilton. But Hilton seems to have died in 1395, and there is no evidence of the existence of the work before 1400. Many manuscripts scattered throughout Europe ascribe the book to Jean le Charlier de Gerson, the great Chancellor of the University of Paris, who was a leading figure in the Church in the earlier part of the fifteenth century. The most probable author, however, especially when the internal evidence is considered, is Thomas Haemmerlein, known also as Thomas à Kempis, from his native town of Kempen, near the Rhine, about forty miles north of Cologne. Haemmerlein, who was born in 1379 or 1380, was a member of the order of the Brothers of Common Life, and spent the last seventy years of his life at Mount St. Agnes, a monastery of Augustinian canons in the diocese of Utrecht. Here he died on July 26, 1471, after an uneventful life spent in copying manuscripts, reading, and composing, and in the peaceful routine of monastic piety.

With the exception of the Bible, no Christian writing has had so wide a vogue or so sustained a popularity as this. And yet, in one sense, it is hardly an original work at all. Its structure it owes largely to the writings of the medieval mystics, and its ideas and phrases are a mosaic from the Bible and the Fathers of the early Church. But these elements are interwoven with such delicate skill and a religious feeling at once so ardent and so sound, that it promises to remain, what it has been for five hundred years, the supreme call and guide to spiritual aspiration.

CONTENTS

BOOK I

BOOK II

BOOK III

BOOK IV

THE IMITATION OF CHRIST

THE FIRST BOOK

ADMONITIONS PROFITABLE FOR THE SPIRITUAL LIFE

CHAPTER I

OF THE IMITATION OF CHRIST, AND OF CONTEMPT OF THE WORLD
AND ALL ITS VANITIES

*H*E *that followeth me shall not walk in darkness,*[1] saith the Lord. These are the words of Christ; and they teach us how far we must imitate His life and character, if we seek true illumination, and deliverance from all blindness of heart. Let it be our most earnest study, therefore, to dwell upon the life of Jesus Christ.

2. His teaching surpasseth all teaching of holy men, and such as have His Spirit find therein *the hidden manna.*[2] But there are many who, though they frequently hear the Gospel, yet feel but little longing after it, because they have not the mind of Christ. He, therefore, that will fully and with true wisdom understand the words of Christ, let him strive to conform his whole life to that mind of Christ.

3. What doth it profit thee to enter into deep discussion concerning the Holy Trinity, if thou lack humility, and be thus displeasing to the Trinity? For verily it is not deep words that make a man holy and upright; it is a good life which maketh a man dear to God. I had rather feel contrition than be skilful in the definition thereof. If thou knewest the whole Bible, and the sayings of all the philosophers, what should all this profit thee without the love and grace of

---

[1] John viii. 12.   [2] Revelations ii. 17.

God? *Vanity of vanities, all is vanity,* save to love God, and Him only to serve. That is the highest wisdom, to cast the world behind us, and to reach forward to the heavenly kingdom.

4. It is vanity then to seek after, and to trust in, the riches that shall perish. It is vanity, too, to covet honours, and to lift up ourselves on high. It is vanity to follow the desires of the flesh and be led by them, for this shall bring misery at the last. It is vanity to desire a long life, and to have little care for a good life. It is vanity to take thought only for the life which now is, and not to look forward to the things which shall be hereafter. It is vanity to love that which quickly passeth away, and not to hasten where eternal joy abideth.

5. Be ofttimes mindful of the saying,[3] *The eye is not satisfied with seeing, nor the ear with hearing.* Strive, therefore, to turn away thy heart from the love of the things that are seen, and to set it upon the things that are not seen. For they who follow after their own fleshly lusts, defile the conscience, and destroy the grace of God.

CHAPTER II

OF THINKING HUMBLY OF ONESELF

THERE is naturally in every man a desire to know, but what profiteth knowledge without the fear of God? Better of a surety is a lowly peasant who serveth God, than a proud philosopher who watcheth the stars and neglecteth the knowledge of himself. He who knoweth himself well is vile in his own sight; neither regardeth he the praises of men. If I knew all the things that are in the world, and were not in charity, what should it help me before God, who is to judge me according to my deeds?

2. Rest from inordinate desire of knowledge, for therein is found much distraction and deceit. Those who have knowledge desire to appear learned, and to be called wise. Many things there are to know which profiteth little or nothing to the soul. And foolish out of measure is he who attendeth upon other things rather than those which serve to his soul's health. Many words satisfy not the soul,

[3] Ecclesiastes i. 8.

but a good life refresheth the mind, and a pure conscience giveth great confidence towards God.

3. The greater and more complete thy knowledge, the more severely shalt thou be judged, unless thou hast lived holily. Therefore be not lifted up by any skill or knowledge that thou hast; but rather fear concerning the knowledge which is given to thee. If it seemeth to thee that thou knowest many things, and understandest them well, know also that there are many more things which thou knowest not. *Be not high-minded,* but rather confess thine ignorance. Why desirest thou to lift thyself above another, when there are found many more learned and more skilled in the Scripture than thou? If thou wilt know and learn anything with profit, love to be thyself unknown and to be counted for nothing.

4. That is the highest and most profitable lesson, when a man truly knoweth and judgeth lowly of himself. To account nothing of one's self, and to think always kindly and highly of others, this is great and perfect wisdom. Even shouldest thou see thy neighbour sin openly or grievously, yet thou oughtest not to reckon thyself better than he, for thou knowest not how long thou shalt keep thine integrity. All of us are weak and frail; hold thou no man more frail than thyself.

CHAPTER III

OF THE KNOWLEDGE OF TRUTH

HAPPY is the man whom Truth by itself doth teach, not by figures and transient words, but as it is in itself.[1] Our own judgment and feelings often deceive us, and we discern but little of the truth. What doth it profit to argue about hidden and dark things, concerning which we shall not be even reproved in the judgment, because we knew them not? Oh, grievous folly, to neglect the things which are profitable and necessary, and to give our minds to things which are curious and hurtful! Having eyes, we see not.

2. And what have we to do with talk about genus and species! He to whom the Eternal Word speaketh is free from multiplied questionings. From this One Word are all things, and all things

[1] Psalm xciv. 12; Numbers xii. 8.

speak of Him; and this is the Beginning which also speaketh unto us.[2] No man without Him understandeth or rightly judgeth. The man to whom all things are one, who bringeth all things to one, who seeth all things in one, he is able to remain steadfast of spirit, and at rest in God. O God, who art the Truth, make me one with Thee in everlasting love. It wearieth me oftentimes to read and listen to many things; in Thee is all that I wish for and desire. Let all the doctors hold their peace; let all creation keep silence before Thee: speak Thou alone to me.

3. The more a man hath unity and simplicity in himself, the more things and the deeper things he understandeth; and that without labour, because he receiveth the light of understanding from above. The spirit which is pure, sincere, and steadfast, is not distracted though it hath many works to do, because it doth all things to the honour of God, and striveth to be free from all thoughts of self-seeking. Who is so full of hindrance and annoyance to thee as thine own undisciplined heart? A man who is good and devout arrangeth beforehand within his own heart the works which he hath to do abroad; and so is not drawn away by the desires of his evil will, but subjecteth everything to the judgment of right reason. Who hath a harder battle to fight than he who striveth for self-mastery? And this should be our endeavour, even to master self, and thus daily to grow stronger than self, and go on unto perfection.

4. All perfection hath some imperfection joined to it in this life, and all our power of sight is not without some darkness. A lowly knowledge of thyself is a surer way to God than the deep searchings of man's learning. Not that learning is to be blamed, nor the taking account of anything that is good; but a good conscience and a holy life is better than all. And because many seek knowledge rather than good living, therefore they go astray, and bear little or no fruit.

5. O if they would give that diligence to the rooting out of vice and the planting of virtue which they give unto vain questionings: there had not been so many evil doings and stumbling-blocks among the laity, nor such ill living among houses of religion. Of a surety, at the Day of Judgment it will be demanded of us, not what we have read, but what we have done; not how well we have spoken, but

[2] John viii. 25 (Vulg.).

how holily we have lived. Tell me, where now are all those masters and teachers, whom thou knewest well, whilst they were yet with you, and flourished in learning? Their stalls are now filled by others, who perhaps never have one thought concerning them. Whilst they lived they seemed to be somewhat, but now no one speaks of them.

6. Oh how quickly passeth the glory of the world away! Would that their life and knowledge had agreed together! For then would they have read and inquired unto good purpose. How many perish through empty learning in this world, who care little for serving God. And because they love to be great more than to be humble, therefore they *"have become vain in their imaginations."* He only is truly great, who hath great charity. He is truly great who deemeth himself small, and counteth all height of honour as nothing. He is the truly wise man, who counteth all earthly things as dung that he may win Christ. And he is the truly learned man, who doeth the will of God, and forsaketh his own will.

CHAPTER IV

OF PRUDENCE IN ACTION

WE must not trust every word of others or feeling within ourselves, but cautiously and patiently try the matter, whether it be of God. Unhappily we are so weak that we find it easier to believe and speak evil of others, rather than good. But they that are perfect, do not give ready heed to every news-bearer, for they know man's weakness that it is prone to evil and unstable in words.

2. This is great wisdom, not to be hasty in action, or stubborn in our own opinions. A part of this wisdom also is not to believe every word we hear, nor to tell others all that we hear, even though we believe it. Take counsel with a man who is wise and of a good conscience; and seek to be instructed by one better than thyself, rather than to follow thine own inventions. A good life maketh a man wise toward God, and giveth him experience in many things. The more humble a man is in himself, and the more obedient towards God, the wiser will he be in all things, and the more shall his soul be at peace.

CHAPTER V

OF THE READING OF HOLY SCRIPTURES

It is Truth which we must look for in Holy Writ, not cunning of words. All Scripture ought to be read in the spirit in which it was written. We must rather seek for what is profitable in Scripture, than for what ministereth to subtlety in discourse. Therefore we ought to read books which are devotional and simple, as well as those which are deep and difficult. And let not the weight of the writer be a stumbling-block to thee, whether he be of little or much learning, but let the love of the pure Truth draw thee to read. Ask not, who hath said this or that, but look to what he says.

2. Men pass away, but the truth of the Lord endureth for ever. Without respect of persons God speaketh to us in divers manners. Our own curiosity often hindereth us in the reading of holy writings, when we seek to understand and discuss, where we should pass simply on. If thou wouldst profit by thy reading, read humbly, simply, honestly, and not desiring to win a character for learning. Ask freely, and hear in silence the words of holy men; nor be displeased at the hard sayings of older men than thou, for they are not uttered without cause.

CHAPTER VI

OF INORDINATE AFFECTIONS

Whensoever a man desireth aught above measure, immediately he becometh restless. The proud and the avaricious man are never at rest; while the poor and lowly of heart abide in the multitude of peace. The man who is not yet wholly dead to self, is soon tempted, and is overcome in small and trifling matters. It is hard for him who is weak in spirit, and still in part carnal and inclined to the pleasures of sense, to withdraw himself altogether from earthly desires. And therefore, when he withdraweth himself from these, he is often sad, and easily angered too if any oppose his will.

2. But if, on the other hand, he yield to his inclination, immediately he is weighed down by the condemnation of his conscience;

for that he hath followed his own desire, and yet in no way attained the peace which he hoped for. For true peace of heart is to be found in resisting passion, not in yielding to it. And therefore there is no peace in the heart of a man who is carnal, nor in him who is given up to the things that are without him, but only in him who is fervent towards God and living the life of the Spirit.

CHAPTER VII

OF FLEEING FROM VAIN HOPE AND PRIDE

Vain is the life of that man who putteth his trust in men or in any created Thing. Be not ashamed to be the servant of others for the love of Jesus Christ, and to be reckoned poor in this life. Rest not upon thyself, but build thy hope in God. Do what lieth in thy power, and God will help thy good intent. Trust not in thy learning, nor in the cleverness of any that lives, but rather trust in the favour of God, who resisteth the proud and giveth grace to the humble.

2. Boast not thyself in thy riches if thou hast them, nor in thy friends if they be powerful, but in God, who giveth all things, and in addition to all things desireth to give even Himself. Be not lifted up because of thy strength or beauty of body, for with only a slight sickness it will fail and wither away. Be not vain of thy skilfulness or ability, lest thou displease God, from whom cometh every good gift which we have.

3. Count not thyself better than others, lest perchance thou appear worse in the sight of God, who knoweth what is in man. Be not proud of thy good works, for God's judgments are of another sort than the judgments of man, and what pleaseth man is ofttimes displeasing to Him. If thou hast any good, believe that others have more, and so thou mayest preserve thy humility. It is no harm to thee if thou place thyself below all others; but it is great harm if thou place thyself above even one. Peace is ever with the humble man, but in the heart of the proud there is envy and continual wrath.

CHAPTER VIII

OF THE DANGER OF TOO MUCH FAMILIARITY

OPEN not thine heart to every man, but deal with one who is wise and feareth God. Be seldom with the young and with strangers. Be not a flatterer of the rich; nor willingly seek the society of the great. Let thy company be the humble and the simple, the devout and the gentle, and let thy discourse be concerning things which edify. Be not familiar with any woman, but commend all good women alike unto God. Choose for thy companions God and His Angels only, and flee from the notice of men.

2. We must love all men, but not make close companions of all. It sometimes falleth out that one who is unknown to us is highly regarded through good report of him, whose actual person is nevertheless unpleasing to those who behold it. We sometimes think to please others by our intimacy, and forthwith displease them the more by the faultiness of character which they perceive in us.

CHAPTER IX

OF OBEDIENCE AND SUBJECTION

IT is verily a great thing to live in obedience, to be under authority, and not to be at our own disposal. Far safer is it to live in subjection than in a place of authority. Many are in obedience from necessity rather than from love; these take it amiss, and repine for small cause. Nor will they gain freedom of spirit, unless with all their heart they submit themselves for the love of God. Though thou run hither and thither, thou wilt not find peace, save in humble subjection to the authority of him who is set over thee. Fancies about places and change of them have deceived many.

2. True it is that every man willingly followeth his own bent, and is the more inclined to those who agree with him. But if Christ is amongst us, then it is necessary that we sometimes yield up our own opinion for the sake of peace. Who is so wise as to have perfect knowledge of all things? Therefore trust not too much to thine own opinion, but be ready also to hear the opinions of others.

Though thine own opinion be good, yet if for the love of God thou foregoest it, and followest that of another, thou shalt the more profit thereby.

3. Ofttimes I have heard that it is safer to hearken and to receive counsel than to give it. It may also come to pass that each opinion may be good; but to refuse to hearken to others when reason or occasion requireth it, is a mark of pride or wilfulness.

CHAPTER X

OF THE DANGER OF SUPERFLUITY OF WORDS

AVOID as far as thou canst the tumult of men; for talk concerning worldly things, though it be innocently undertaken, is a hindrance, so quickly are we led captive and defiled by vanity. Many a time I wish that I had held my peace, and had not gone amongst men. But why do we talk and gossip so continually, seeing that we so rarely resume our silence without some hurt done to our conscience? We like talking so much because we hope by our conversations to gain some mutual comfort, and because we seek to refresh our wearied spirits by variety of thoughts. And we very willingly talk and think of those things which we love or desire, or else of those which we most dislike.

2. But alas! it is often to no purpose and in vain. For this outward consolation is no small hindrance to the inner comfort which cometh from God. Therefore must we watch and pray that time pass not idly away. If it be right and desirable for thee to speak, speak things which are to edification. Evil custom and neglect of our real profit tend much to make us heedless of watching over our lips. Nevertheless, devout conversation on spiritual things helpeth not a little to spiritual progress, most of all where those of kindred mind and spirit find their ground of fellowship in God.

CHAPTER XI

OF SEEKING PEACE OF MIND AND OF SPIRITUAL PROGRESS

WE may enjoy abundance of peace if we refrain from busying ourselves with the sayings and doings of others, and things which concern not ourselves. How can he abide long time in peace who occupieth himself with other men's matters, and with things without himself, and meanwhile payeth little or rare heed to the self within? Blessed are the single-hearted, for they shall have abundance of peace.

2. How came it to pass that many of the Saints were so perfect, so contemplative of Divine things? Because they steadfastly sought to mortify themselves from all worldly desires, and so were enabled to cling with their whole heart to God, and be free and at leisure for the thought of Him. We are too much occupied with our own affections, and too anxious about transitory things. Seldom, too, do we entirely conquer even a single fault, nor are we zealous for daily growth in grace. And so we remain lukewarm and unspiritual.

3. Were we fully watchful of ourselves, and not bound in spirit to outward things, then might we be wise unto salvation, and make progress in Divine contemplation. Our great and grievous stumbling-block is that, not being freed from our affections and desires, we strive not to enter into the perfect way of the Saints. And when even a little trouble befalleth us, too quickly are we cast down, and fly to the world to give us comfort.

4. If we would quit ourselves like men, and strive to stand firm in the battle, then should we see the Lord helping us from Heaven. For He Himself is alway ready to help those who strive and who trust in Him; yea, He provideth for us occasions of striving, to the end that we may win the victory. If we look upon our progress in religion as a progress only in outward observances and forms, our devoutness will soon come to an end. But let us lay the axe to the very root of our life, that, being cleansed from affections, we may possess our souls in peace.

5. If each year should see one fault rooted out from us, we should go quickly on to perfection. But on the contrary, we often feel that we were better and holier in the beginning of our conversion than after many years of profession. Zeal and progress ought to increase day by day; yet now it seemeth a great thing if one is able to retain some portion of his first ardour. If we would put some slight stress on ourselves at the beginning, then afterwards we should be able to do all things with ease and joy.

6. It is a hard thing to break through a habit, and a yet harder

thing to go contrary to our own will. Yet if thou overcome not slight and easy obstacles, how shalt thou overcome greater ones? Withstand thy will at the beginning, and unlearn an evil habit, lest it lead thee little by little into worse difficulties. Oh, if thou knewest what peace to thyself thy holy life should bring to thyself, and what joy to others, methinketh thou wouldst be more zealous for spiritual profit.

CHAPTER XII

OF THE USES OF ADVERSITY

It is good for us that we sometimes have sorrows and adversities, for they often make a man lay to heart that he is only a stranger and sojourner, and may not put his trust in any worldly thing. It is good that we sometimes endure contradictions, and are hardly and unfairly judged, when we do and mean what is good. For these things help us to be humble, and shield us from vain-glory. For then we seek the more earnestly the witness of God, when men speak evil of us falsely, and give us no credit for good.

2. Therefore ought a man to rest wholly upon God, so that he needeth not seek much comfort at the hand of men. When a man who feareth God is afflicted or tried or oppressed with evil thoughts, then he seeth that God is the more necessary unto him, since without God he can do no good thing. Then he is heavy of heart, he groaneth, he crieth out for the very disquietness of his heart. Then he groweth weary of life, and would fain depart and be with Christ. By all this he is taught that in the world there can be no perfect security or fulness of peace.

CHAPTER XIII

OF RESISTING TEMPTATION

So long as we live in the world, we cannot be without trouble and trial. Wherefore it is written in Job, *The life of man upon the earth is a trial.*[1] And therefore ought each of us to give heed concerning

[1] Job vii. 1 (Vulg.).

trials and temptations, and watch unto prayer, lest the devil find occasion to deceive; for he never sleepeth, but goeth about seeking whom he may devour. No man is so perfect in holiness that he hath never temptations, nor can we ever be wholly free from them.

2. Yet, notwithstanding, temptations turn greatly unto our profit, even though they be great and hard to bear; for through them we are humbled, purified, instructed. All Saints have passed through much tribulation and temptation, and have profited thereby. And they who endured not temptation became reprobate and fell away. There is no position so sacred, no place so secret, that it is without temptations and adversities.

3. There is no man wholly free from temptations so long as he liveth, because we have the root of temptation within ourselves, in that we are born in concupiscence. One temptation or sorrow passeth, and another cometh; and always we shall have somewhat to suffer, for we have fallen from perfect happiness. Many who seek to fly from temptations fall yet more deeply into them. By flight alone we cannot overcome, but by endurance and true humility we are made stronger than all our enemies.

4. He who only resisteth outwardly and pulleth not up by the root, shall profit little; nay, rather temptations will return to him the more quickly, and will be the more terrible. Little by little, through patience and longsuffering, thou shalt conquer by the help of God, rather than by violence and thine own strength of will. In the midst of temptation often seek counsel; and deal not hardly with one who is tempted, but comfort and strengthen him as thou wouldest have done unto thyself.

5. The beginning of all temptations to evil is instability of temper and want of trust in God; for even as a ship without a helm is tossed about by the waves, so is a man who is careless and infirm of purpose tempted, now on this side, now on that. As fire testeth iron, so doth temptation the upright man. Oftentimes we know not what strength we have; but temptation revealeth to us what we are. Nevertheless, we must watch, especially in the beginnings of temptation; for then is the foe the more easily mastered, when he is not suffered to enter within the mind, but is met outside the door as soon as he hath knocked. Wherefore one saith,

> Check the beginnings; once thou might'st have cured,
> But now 'tis past thy skill, too long hath it endured.

For first cometh to the mind the simple suggestion, then the strong imagination, afterwards pleasure, evil affection, assent. And so little by little the enemy entereth in altogether, because he was not resisted at the beginning. And the longer a man delayeth his resistance, the weaker he groweth, and the stronger groweth the enemy against him.

6. Some men suffer their most grievous temptations in the beginning of their conversion, some at the end. Some are sorely tried their whole life long. Some there are who are tempted but lightly, according to the wisdom and justice of the ordering of God, who knoweth the character and circumstances of men, and ordereth all things for the welfare of His elect.

7. Therefore we ought not to despair when we are tempted, but the more fervently should cry unto God, that He will vouchsafe to help us in all our tribulation; and that He will, as St. Paul saith, *with the temptation make a way to escape that we may be able to bear it.*[2] Let us therefore humble ourselves under the mighty hand of God in all temptation and trouble, for He will save and exalt such as are of an humble spirit.

8. In temptations and troubles a man is proved, what progress he hath made, and therein is his reward the greater, and his virtue doth the more appear. Nor is it a great thing if a man be devout and zealous so long as he suffereth no affliction; but if he behave himself patiently in the time of adversity, then is there hope of great progress. Some are kept safe from great temptations, but are overtaken in those which are little and common, that the humiliation may teach them not to trust to themselves in great things, being weak in small things.

CHAPTER XIV

ON AVOIDING RASH JUDGMENT

Look well unto thyself, and beware that thou judge not the doings of others. In judging others a man laboureth in vain; he often

[2] 1 Corinthians x. 13.

erreth, and easily falleth into sin; but in judging and examining himself he always laboureth to good purpose. According as a matter toucheth our fancy, so oftentimes do we judge of it; for easily do we fail of true judgment because of our own personal feeling. If God were always the sole object of our desire, we should the less easily be troubled by the erring judgment of our fancy.

2. But often some secret thought lurking within us, or even some outward circumstance, turneth us aside. Many are secretly seeking their own ends in what they do, yet know it not. They seem to live in good peace of mind so long as things go well with them, and according to their desires, but if their desires be frustrated and broken, immediately they are shaken and displeased. Diversity of feelings and opinions very often brings about dissensions between friends, between countrymen, between religious and godly men.

3. Established custom is not easily relinquished, and no man is very easily led to see with the eyes of another. If thou rest more upon thy own reason or experience than upon the power of Jesus Christ, thy light shall come slowly and hardly; for God willeth us to be perfectly subject unto Himself, and all our reason to be exalted by abundant love towards Him.

CHAPTER XV

OF WORKS OF CHARITY

For no worldly good whatsoever, and for the love of no man, must anything be done which is evil, but for the help of the suffering a good work must sometimes be postponed, or be changed for a better; for herein a good work is not destroyed, but improved. Without charity no work profiteth, but whatsoever is done in charity, however small and of no reputation it be, bringeth forth good fruit; for God verily considereth what a man is able to do, more than the greatness of what he doth.

2. He doth much who loveth much. He doth much who doth well. He doth well who ministereth to the public good rather than to his own. Oftentimes that seemeth to be charity which is rather carnality, because it springeth from natural inclination, self-will, hope of repayment, desire of gain.

3. He who hath true and perfect charity, in no wise seeketh his own good, but desireth that God alone be altogether glorified. He envieth none, because he longeth for no selfish joy; nor doth he desire to rejoice in himself, but longeth to be blessed in God as the highest good. He ascribeth good to none save to God only, the Fountain whence all good proceedeth, and the End, the Peace, the joy of all Saints. Oh, he who hath but a spark of true charity, hath verily learned that all worldly things are full of vanity.

CHAPTER XVI

OF BEARING WITH THE FAULTS OF OTHERS

THOSE things which a man cannot amend in himself or in others, he ought patiently to bear, until God shall otherwise ordain. Bethink thee that perhaps it is better for thy trial and patience, without which our merits are but little worth. Nevertheless thou oughtest, when thou findeth such impediments, to beseech God that He would vouchsafe to sustain thee, that thou be able to bear them with a good will.

2. If one who is once or twice admonished refuse to hearken, strive not with him, but commit all to God, that His will may be done and His honour be shown in His servants, for He knoweth well how to convert the evil unto good. Endeavour to be patient in bearing with other men's faults and infirmities whatsoever they be, for thou thyself also hast many things which have need to be borne with by others. If thou canst not make thine own self what thou desireth, how shalt thou be able to fashion another to thine own liking. We are ready to see others made perfect, and yet we do not amend our own shortcomings.

3. We will that others be straitly corrected, but we will not be corrected ourselves. The freedom of others displeaseth us, but we are dissatisfied that our own wishes shall be denied us. We desire rules to be made restraining others, but by no means will we suffer ourselves to be restrained. Thus therefore doth it plainly appear how seldom we weigh our neighbour in the same balance with ourselves. If all men were perfect, what then should we have to suffer from others for God?

4. But now hath God thus ordained, that we may learn to bear one another's burdens, because none is without defect, none without a burden, none sufficient of himself, none wise enough of himself; but it behoveth us to bear with one another, to comfort one another, to help, instruct, admonish one another. How much strength each man hath is best proved by occasions of adversity: for such occasions do not make a man frail, but show of what temper he is.

CHAPTER XVII

OF A RELIGIOUS LIFE

It behoveth thee to learn to mortify thyself in many things, if thou wilt live in amity and concord with other men. It is no small thing to dwell in a religious community or congregation, and to live there without complaint, and therein to remain faithful even unto death. Blessed is he who hath lived a good life in such a body, and brought it to a happy end. If thou wilt stand fast and wilt profit as thou oughtest, hold thyself as an exile and a pilgrim upon the earth. Thou wilt have to be counted as a fool for Christ, if thou wilt lead a religious life.

2. The clothing and outward appearance are of small account; it is change of character and entire mortification of the affections which make a truly religious man. He who seeketh aught save God and the health of his soul, shall find only tribulation and sorrow. Nor can he stand long in peace, who striveth not to be least of all and servant of all.

3. Thou art called to endure and to labour, not to a life of ease and trifling talk. Here therefore are men tried as gold in the furnace. No man can stand, unless with all his heart he will humble himself for God's sake.

CHAPTER XVIII

OF THE EXAMPLE OF THE HOLY FATHERS

Consider now the lively examples of the holy fathers, in whom shone forth real perfectness and religion, and thou shalt see how little, even as nothing, is all that we do. Ah! What is our life when compared to theirs? They, saints and friends of Christ as they were, served the Lord in hunger and thirst, in cold and nakedness, in labour and weariness, in watchings and fastings, in prayer and holy meditations, in persecutions and much rebuke.

2. O how many and grievous tribulations did the Apostles, Martyrs, Confessors, Virgins, endure; and all others who would walk in the footsteps of Christ. For they hated their souls in this world that they might keep them unto life eternal. O how strict and retired a life was that of the holy fathers who dwelt in the desert! what long and grievous temptations they did suffer! how often were they assaulted by the enemy! what frequent and fervid prayers did they offer unto God! what strict fasts did they endure! what fervent zeal and desire after spiritual profit did they manifest! how bravely did they fight that their vices might not gain the mastery! how entirely and steadfastly did they reach after God! By day they laboured, and at night they gave themselves ofttimes unto prayer; yea, even when they were labouring they ceased not from mental prayer.

3. They spent their whole time profitably; every hour seemed short for retirement with God; and through the great sweetness of contemplation, even the need of bodily refreshment was forgotten. They renounced all riches, dignities, honours, friends, kinsmen; they desired nothing from the world; they ate the bare necessaries of life; they were unwilling to minister to the body even in necessity. Thus were they poor in earthly things, but rich above measure in grace and virtue. Though poor to the outer eye, within they were filled with grace and heavenly benedictions.

4. They were strangers to the world, but unto God they were as kinsmen and friends. They seemed unto themselves as of no reputation, and in the world's eyes contemptible; but in the sight of God they were precious and beloved. They stood fast in true humility, they lived in simple obedience, they walked in love and patience; and thus they waxed strong in spirit, and obtained great favour before God. To all religious men they were given as an example, and they ought more to provoke us unto good livings than the number of the lukewarm tempteth to carelessness of life.

5. O how great was the love of all religious persons at the beginning of this sacred institution! O what devoutness of prayer!

what rivalry in holiness! what strict discipline was observed! what reverence and obedience under the rule of the master showed they in all things! The traces of them that remain until now testify that they were truly holy and perfect men, who fighting so bravely trod the world underfoot. Now a man is counted great if only he be not a transgressor, and if he can only endure with patience what he hath undertaken.

6. O the coldness and negligence of our times, that we so quickly decline from the former love, and it is become a weariness to live, because of sloth and lukewarmness. May progress in holiness not wholly fall asleep in thee, who many times hast seen so many examples of devout men!

CHAPTER XIX

OF THE EXERCISES OF A RELIGIOUS MAN

THE life of a Christian ought to be adorned with all virtues, that he may be inwardly what he outwardly appeareth unto men. And verily it should be yet better within than without, for God is a discerner of our heart, Whom we must reverence with all our hearts wheresoever we are, and walk pure in His presence as do the angels. We ought daily to renew our vows, and to kindle our hearts to zeal, as if each day were the first day of our conversion, and to say, "Help me, O God, in my good resolutions, and in Thy holy service, and grant that this day I may make a good beginning, for hitherto I have done nothing!"

2. According to our resolution so is the rate of our progress, and much diligence is needful for him who would make good progress. For if he who resolveth bravely oftentimes falleth short, how shall it be with him who resolveth rarely or feebly? But manifold causes bring about abandonment of our resolution, yet a trivial omission of holy exercises can hardly be made without some loss to us. The resolution of the righteous dependeth more upon the grace of God than upon their own wisdom; for in Him they always put their trust, whatsoever they take in hand. For man proposeth, but God disposeth; and *the way of a man is not in himself.*[1]

[1] Jeremiah x. 23.

3. If a holy exercise be sometimes omitted for the sake of some act of piety, or of some brotherly kindness, it can easily be taken up afterwards; but if it be neglected through distaste or slothfulness, then is it sinful, and the mischief will be felt. Strive as earnestly as we may, we shall still fall short in many things. Always should some distinct resolution be made by us; and, most of all, we must strive against those sins which most easily beset us. Both our outer and inner life should be straitly examined and ruled by us, because both have to do with our progress.

4. If thou canst not be always examining thyself, thou canst at certain seasons, and at least twice in the day, at evening and at morning. In the morning make thy resolves, and in the evening inquire into thy life, how thou hast sped to-day in word, deed, and thought; for in these ways thou hast often perchance offended God and thy neighbour. Gird up thy loins like a man against the assaults of the devil; bridle thine appetite, and thou wilt soon be able to bridle every inclination of the flesh. Be thou never without something to do; be reading, or writing, or praying, or meditating, or doing something that is useful to the community. Bodily exercises, however, must be undertaken with discretion, nor are they to be used by all alike.

5. The duties which are not common to all must not be done openly, but are safest carried on in secret. But take heed that thou be not careless in the common duties, and more devout in the secret; but faithfully and honestly discharge the duties and commands which lie upon thee, then afterwards, if thou hast still leisure, give thyself to thyself as thy devotion leadeth thee. All cannot have one exercise, but one suiteth better to this man and another to that. Even for the diversity of season different exercises are needed, some suit better for feasts, some for fasts. We need one kind in time of temptations and others in time of peace and quietness. Some are suitable to our times of sadness, and others when we are joyful in the Lord.

6. When we draw near the time of the great feasts, good exercises should be renewed, and the prayers of holy men more fervently besought. We ought to make our resolutions from one Feast to another, as if each were the period of our departure from this

world, and of entering into the eternal feast. So ought we to prepare ourselves earnestly at solemn seasons, and the more solemnly to live, and to keep straightest watch upon each holy observance, as though we were soon to receive the reward of our labours at the hand of God.

7. And if this be deferred, let us believe ourselves to be as yet ill-prepared, and unworthy as yet of the glory which shall be revealed in us at the appointed season; and let us study to prepare ourselves the better for our end. *Blessed is that servant,* as the Evangelist Luke hath it, *whom, when the Lord cometh He shall find watching. Verily I say unto you He will make him ruler over all that He hath.*[2]

CHAPTER XX

OF THE LOVE OF SOLITUDE AND SILENCE

SEEK a suitable time for thy meditation, and think frequently of the mercies of God to thee. Leave curious questions. Study such matters as bring thee sorrow for sin rather than amusement. If thou withdraw thyself from trifling conversation and idle goings about, as well as from novelties and gossip, thou shalt find thy time sufficient and apt for good meditation. The greatest saints used to avoid as far as they could the company of men, and chose to live in secret with God.

2. One hath said, "As oft as I have gone among men, so oft have I returned less a man." This is what we often experience when we have been long time in conversation. For it is easier to be altogether silent than it is not to exceed in word. It is easier to remain hidden at home than to keep sufficient guard upon thyself out of doors. He, therefore, that seeketh to reach that which is hidden and spiritual, must go with Jesus "apart from the multitude." No man safely goeth abroad who loveth not to rest at home. No man safely talketh but he who loveth to hold his peace. No man safely ruleth but he who loveth to be subject. No man safely commandeth but he who loveth to obey.

3. No man safely rejoiceth but he who hath the testimony of a good

[2] Luke xii. 43, 44

conscience within himself. The boldness of the Saints was always full of the fear of God. Nor were they the less earnest and humble in themselves, because they shone forth with great virtues and grace. But the boldness of wicked men springeth from pride and presumption, and at the last turneth to their own confusion. Never promise thyself security in this life, howsoever good a monk or devout a solitary thou seemest.

4. Often those who stand highest in the esteem of men, fall the more grievously because of their over great confidence. Wherefore it is very profitable unto many that they should not be without inward temptation, but should be frequently assaulted, lest they be over confident, lest they be indeed lifted up into pride, or else lean too freely upon the consolations of the world. O how good a conscience should that man keep, who never sought a joy that passeth away, who never became entangled with the world! O how great peace and quiet should he possess, who would cast off all vain care, and think only of healthful and divine things, and build his whole hope upon God!

5. No man is worthy of heavenly consolation but he who hath diligently exercised himself in holy compunction. If thou wilt feel compunction within thy heart, enter into thy chamber and shut out the tumults of the world, as it is written, *Commune with your own heart in your own chamber and be still*.[1] In retirement thou shalt find what often thou wilt lose abroad. Retirement, if thou continue therein, groweth sweet, but if thou keep not in it, begetteth weariness. If in the beginning of thy conversation thou dwell in it and keep it well, it shall afterwards be to thee a dear friend, and a most pleasant solace.

6. In silence and quiet the devout soul goeth forward and learneth the hidden things of the Scriptures. Therein findeth she a fountain of tears, wherein to wash and cleanse herself each night, that she may grow the more dear to her Maker as she dwelleth the further from all worldly distraction. To him who withdraweth himself from his acquaintance and friends God with His holy angels will draw nigh. It is better to be unknown and take heed to oneself

[1] Psalm iv. 4.

than to neglect oneself and work wonders. It is praiseworthy for a religious man to go seldom abroad, to fly from being seen, to have no desire to see men.

7. Why wouldest thou see what thou mayest not have? *The world passeth away and the lust thereof.* The desires of sensuality draw thee abroad, but when an hour is past, what dost thou bring home, but a weight upon thy conscience and distraction of heart? A merry going forth bringeth often a sorrowful return, and a merry evening maketh a sad morning? So doth all carnal joy begin pleasantly, but in the end it gnaweth away and destroyeth. What canst thou see abroad which thou seest not at home? Behold the heaven and the earth and the elements, for out of these are all things made.

8. What canst thou see anywhere which can continue long under the sun? Thou believest perchance that thou shalt be satisfied, but thou wilt never be able to attain unto this. If thou shouldest see all things before thee at once, what would it be but a vain vision? Lift up thine eyes to God on high, and pray that thy sins and negligences may be forgiven. Leave vain things to vain men, and mind thou the things which God hath commanded thee. Shut thy door upon thee, and call unto thyself Jesus thy beloved. Remain with Him in thy chamber, for thou shalt not elsewhere find so great peace. If thou hadst not gone forth nor listened to vain talk, thou hadst better kept thyself in good peace. But because it sometimes delighteth thee to hear new things, thou must therefore suffer trouble of heart.

CHAPTER XXI

OF COMPUNCTION OF HEART

IF thou wilt make any progress keep thyself in the fear of God, and long not to be too free, but restrain all thy senses under discipline and give not thyself up to senseless mirth. Give thyself to compunction of heart and thou shalt find devotion. Compunction openeth the way for many good things, which dissoluteness is wont quickly to lose. It is wonderful that any man can ever rejoice heartily in this life who considereth and weigheth his banishment, and the manifold dangers which beset his soul.

2. Through lightness of heart and neglect of our shortcomings we feel not the sorrows of our soul, but often vainly laugh when we have good cause to weep. There is no true liberty nor real joy, save in the fear of God with a good conscience. Happy is he who can cast away every cause of distraction and bring himself to the one purpose of holy compunction. Happy is he who putteth away from him whatsoever may stain or burden his conscience. Strive manfully; custom is overcome by custom. If thou knowest how to let men alone, they will gladly let thee alone to do thine own works.

3. Busy not thyself with the affairs of others, nor entangle thyself with the business of great men. Keep always thine eye upon thyself first of all, and give advice to thyself specially before all thy dearest friends. If thou hast not the favour of men, be not thereby cast down, but let thy concern be that thou holdest not thyself so well and circumspectly, as becometh a servant of God and a devout monk. It is often better and safer for a man not to have many comforts in this life, especially those which concern the flesh. But that we lack divine comforts or feel them rarely is to our own blame, because we seek not compunction of heart, nor utterly cast away those comforts which are vain and worldly.

4. Know thyself to be unworthy of divine consolation, and worthy rather of much tribulation. When a man hath perfect compunction, then all the world is burdensome and bitter to him. A good man will find sufficient cause for mourning and weeping; for whether he considereth himself, or pondereth concerning his neighbour, he knoweth that no man liveth here without tribulation, and the more thoroughly he considereth himself, the more thoroughly he grieveth. Grounds for just grief and inward compunction there are in our sins and vices, wherein we lie so entangled that we are but seldom able to contemplate heavenly things.

5. If thou thoughtest upon thy death more often than how long thy life should be, thou wouldest doubtless strive more earnestly to improve. And if thou didst seriously consider the future pains of hell, I believe thou wouldest willingly endure toil or pain and fear not discipline. But because these things reach not the heart, and we still love pleasant things, therefore we remain cold and miserably indifferent.

6. Oftentimes it is from poverty of spirit that the wretched body is so easily led to complain. Pray therefore humbly unto the Lord that He will give thee the spirit of compunction and say in the language of the prophet, *Feed me, O Lord, with bread of tears, and give me plenteousness of tears to drink.*[1]

CHAPTER XXII

ON THE CONTEMPLATION OF HUMAN MISERY

Thou art miserable wheresoever thou art, and whithersoever thou turnest, unless thou turn thee to God. Why art thou disquieted because it happeneth not to thee according to thy wishes and desires? Who is he that hath everything according to his will? Neither I, nor thou, nor any man upon the earth. There is no man in the world free from trouble or anguish, though he were King or Pope. Who is he who hath the happiest lot? Even he who is strong to suffer somewhat for God.

2. There are many foolish and unstable men who say, "See what a prosperous life that man hath, how rich and how great he is, how powerful, how exalted." But lift up thine eyes to the good things of heaven, and thou shalt see that all these worldly things are nothing, they are utterly uncertain, yea, they are wearisome, because they are never possessed without care and fear. The happiness of man lieth not in the abundance of temporal things but a moderate portion sufficeth him. Our life upon earth is verily wretchedness. The more a man desireth to be spiritual, the more bitter doth the present life become to him; because he the better understandeth and seeth the defects of human corruption. For to eat, to drink, to watch, to sleep, to rest, to labour, and to be subject to the other necessities of nature, is truly a great wretchedness and affliction to a devout man, who would fain be released and free from all sin.

3. For the inner man is heavily burdened with the necessities of the body in this world. Wherefore the prophet devoutly prayeth to be freed from them, saying, *Deliver me from my necessities, O Lord.*[2] But woe to those who know not their own misery, and yet greater woe to those who love this miserable and corruptible life.

[1] Psalm lxxv. 5.　　[2] Psalm xxv. 17.

For to such a degree do some cling to it (even though by labouring or begging they scarce procure what is necessary for subsistence) that if they might live here always, they would care nothing for the Kingdom of God.

4. Oh foolish and faithless of heart, who lie buried so deep in worldly things, that they relish nothing save the things of the flesh! Miserable ones! they will too sadly find out at the last, how vile and worthless was that which they loved. The saints of God and all loyal friends of Christ held as nothing the things which pleased the flesh, or those which flourished in this life, but their whole hope and affection aspired to the things which are above. Their whole desire was borne upwards to everlasting and invisible things, lest they should be drawn downwards by the love of things visible.

5. Lose not, brother, thy loyal desire of progress to things spiritual. There is yet time, the hour is not past. Why wilt thou put off thy resolution? Arise, begin this very moment, and say, "Now is the time to do: now is the time to fight, now is the proper time for amendment." When thou art ill at ease and troubled, then is the time when thou art nearest unto blessing. Thou must *go through fire and water that God may bring thee into a wealthy place.* Unless thou put force upon thyself, thou wilt not conquer thy faults. So long as we carry about with us this frail body, we cannot be without sin, we cannot live without weariness and trouble. Gladly would we have rest from all misery; but because through sin we have lost innocence, we have lost also the true happiness. Therefore must we be patient, and wait for the mercy of God, *until this tyranny be overpast,* and this *mortality be swallowed up of life.*

6. O how great is the frailty of man, which is ever prone to evil! To-day thou confessest thy sins, and to-morrow thou committest again the sins thou didst confess. Now dost thou resolve to avoid a fault, and within an hour thou behavest thyself as if thou hadst never resolved at all. Good cause have we therefore to humble ourselves, and never to think highly of ourselves, seeing that we are so frail and unstable. And quickly may that be lost by our negligence, which by much labour was hardly attained through grace.

7. What shall become of us at the end, if at the beginning we are lukewarm and idle? Woe unto us, if we choose to rest, as though

it were a time of peace and security, while as yet no sign appeareth in our life of true holiness. Rather had we need that we might begin yet afresh, like good novices, to be instructed unto good living, if haply there might be hope of some future amendment and greater spiritual increase.

CHAPTER XXIII

OF MEDITATION UPON DEATH

VERY quickly will there be an end of thee here; take heed therefore how it will be with thee in another world. To-day man is, and to-morrow he will be seen no more. And being removed out of sight, quickly also he is out of mind. O the dulness and hardness of man's heart, which thinketh only of the present, and looketh not forward to the future. Thou oughtest in every deed and thought so to order thyself, as if thou wert to die this day. If thou hadst a good conscience thou wouldst not greatly fear death. It were better for thee to watch against sin, than to fly from death. If to-day thou art not ready, how shalt thou be ready to-morrow? To-morrow is an uncertain day; and how knowest thou that thou shalt have a to-morrow?

2. What doth it profit to live long, when we amend so little? Ah! long life doth not always amend, but often the more increaseth guilt. Oh that we might spend a single day in this world as it ought to be spent! Many there are who reckon the years since they were converted, and yet oftentimes how little is the fruit thereof. If it is a fearful thing to die, it may be perchance a yet more fearful thing to live long. Happy is the man who hath the hour of his death always before his eyes, and daily prepareth himself to die. If thou hast ever seen one die, consider that thou also shalt pass away by the same road.

3. When it is morning reflect that it may be thou shalt not see the evening, and at eventide dare not to boast thyself of the morrow. Always be thou prepared, and so live that death may never find thee unprepared. Many die suddenly and unexpectedly. For *at such an hour as ye think not, the Son of Man cometh*.[1] When that last hour

[1] Matthew xxiv. 44.

shall come, thou wilt begin to think very differently of thy whole life past, and wilt mourn bitterly that thou hast been so negligent and slothful.

4. Happy and wise is he who now striveth to be such in life as he would fain be found in death! For a perfect contempt of the world, a fervent desire to excel in virtue, the love of discipline, the painfulness of repentance, readiness to obey, denial of self, submission to any adversity for love of Christ; these are the things which shall give great confidence of a happy death. Whilst thou art in health thou hast many opportunities of good works; but when thou art in sickness I know not how much thou wilt be able to do. Few are made better by infirmity: even as they who wander much abroad seldom become holy.

5. Trust not thy friends and kinsfolk, nor put off the work of thy salvation to the future, for men will forget thee sooner than thou thinkest. It is better for thee now to provide in time, and to send some good before thee, than to trust to the help of others. If thou art not anxious for thyself now, who, thinkest thou, will be anxious for thee afterwards? Now the time is most precious. *Now is the accepted time, now is the day of salvation.* But, alas! that thou spendest not well this time, wherein thou mightest lay up treasure which should profit thee everlastingly. The hour will come when thou shalt desire one day, yea, one hour, for amendment of life, and I know not whether thou shalt obtain.

6. Oh, dearly beloved, from what danger thou mightest free thyself, from what great fear, if only thou wouldst always live in fear, and in expectation of death! Strive now to live in such wise that in the hour of death thou mayest rather rejoice than fear. Learn now to die to the world, so shalt thou begin to live with Christ. Learn now to contemn all earthly things, and then mayest thou freely go unto Christ. Keep under thy body by penitence, and then shalt thou be able to have a sure confidence.

7. Ah, foolish one! why thinkest thou that thou shalt live long, when thou art not sure of a single day? How many have been deceived, and suddenly have been snatched away from the body! How many times hast thou heard how one was slain by the sword, another was drowned, another falling from on high broke his neck,

another died at the table, another whilst at play! One died by fire, another by the sword, another by the pestilence, another by the robber. Thus cometh death to all, and the life of men swiftly passeth away like a shadow.

8. Who will remember thee after thy death? And who will entreat for thee? Work, work now, oh dearly beloved, work all that thou canst. For thou knowest not when thou shalt die, nor what shall happen unto thee after death. While thou hast time, lay up for thyself undying riches. Think of nought but of thy salvation; care only for the things of God. *Make to thyself friends,* by venerating the saints of God and walking in their steps, *that when thou failest, thou mayest be received into everlasting habitations.*[2]

9. Keep thyself as a stranger and a pilgrim upon the earth, to whom the things of the world appertain not. Keep thine heart free, and lifted up towards God, *for here have we no continuing city.*[3] To Him direct thy daily prayers with crying and tears, that thy spirit may be found worthy to pass happily after death unto its Lord. Amen.

CHAPTER XXIV

OF THE JUDGMENT AND PUNISHMENT OF THE WICKED

In all that thou doest, remember the end, and how thou wilt stand before a strict judge, from whom nothing is hid, who is not bribed with gifts, nor accepteth excuses, but will judge righteous judgment. O most miserable and foolish sinner, who art sometimes in fear of the countenance of an angry man, what wilt thou answer to God, who knoweth all thy misdeeds? Why dost thou not provide for thyself against the day of judgment, when no man shall be able to be excused or defended by means of another, but each one shall bear his burden himself alone? Now doth thy labour bring forth fruit, now is thy weeping acceptable, thy groaning heard, thy sorrow well pleasing to God, and cleansing to thy soul.

2. Even here on earth the patient man findeth great occasion of purifying his soul. When suffering injuries he grieveth more for the other's malice than for his own wrong; when he prayeth heart-

[2] Luke xvi. 9.   [3] Hebrews xiii. 14.

ily for those that despitefully use him, and forgiveth them from his heart; when he is not slow to ask pardon from others; when he is swifter to pity than to anger; when he frequently denieth himself and striveth altogether to subdue the flesh to the spirit. Better is it now to purify the soul from sin, than to cling to sins from which we must be purged hereafter. Truly we deceive ourselves by the inordinate love which we bear towards the flesh.

3. What is it which that fire shall devour, save thy sins? The more thou sparest thyself and followest the flesh, the more heavy shall thy punishment be, and the more fuel art thou heaping up for the burning. For wherein a man hath sinned, therein shall he be the more heavily punished. There shall the slothful be pricked forward with burning goads, and the gluttons be tormented with intolerable hunger and thirst. There shall the luxurious and the lovers of pleasure be plunged into burning pitch and stinking brimstone, and the envious shall howl like mad dogs for very grief.

4. No sin will there be which shall not be visited with its own proper punishment. The proud shall be filled with utter confusion, and the covetous shall be pinched with miserable poverty. An hour's pain there shall be more grievous than a hundred years here of the bitterest penitence. No quiet shall be there, no comfort for the lost, though here sometimes there is respite from pain, and enjoyment of the solace of friends. Be thou anxious now and sorrowful for thy sins, that in the day of judgment thou mayest have boldness with the blessed. For *then shall the righteous man stand in great boldness before the face of such as have afflicted him and made no account of his labours.*[1] Then shall he stand up to judge, he who now submitteth himself in humility to the judgments of men. Then shall the poor and humble man have great confidence, while the proud is taken with fear on every side.

5. Then shall it be seen that he was the wise man in this world who learned to be a fool and despised for Christ. Then shall all tribulation patiently borne delight us, while the mouth of the ungodly shall be stopped. Then shall every godly man rejoice, and every profane man shall mourn. Then the afflicted flesh shall more rejoice than if it had been alway nourished in delights. Then the

[1] Wisd. v. 1.

humble garment shall put on beauty, and the precious robe shall hide itself as vile. Then the little poor cottage shall be more commended than the gilded palace. Then enduring patience shall have more might than all the power of the world. Then simple obedience shall be more highly exalted than all worldly wisdom.

6. Then a pure and good conscience shall more rejoice than learned philosophy. Then contempt of riches shall have more weight than all the treasure of the children of this world. Then shalt thou find more comfort in having prayed devoutly than in having fared sumptuously. Then thou wilt rather rejoice in having kept silence than in having made long speech. Then holy deeds shall be far stronger than many fine words. Then a strict life and sincere penitence shall bring deeper pleasure than all earthly delight. Learn now to suffer a little, that then thou mayest be enabled to escape heavier sufferings. Prove first here, what thou art able to endure hereafter. If now thou art able to bear so little, how wilt thou be able to endure eternal torments? If now a little suffering maketh thee so impatient, what shall hell-fire do then? Behold of a surety thou art not able to have two Paradises, to take thy fill or delight here in this world, and to reign with Christ hereafter.

7. If even unto this day thou hadst ever lived in honours and pleasures, what would the whole profit thee if now death came to thee in an instant? All therefore is vanity, save to love God and to serve Him only. For he who loveth God with all his heart feareth not death, nor punishment, nor judgment, nor hell, because perfect love giveth sure access to God. But he who still delighteth in sin, no marvel if he is afraid of death and judgment. Nevertheless it is a good thing, if love as yet cannot restrain thee from evil, that at least the fear of hell should hold thee back. But he who putteth aside the fear of God cannot long continue in good, but shall quickly fall into the snares of the devil.

CHAPTER XXV

OF THE ZEALOUS AMENDMENT OF OUR WHOLE LIFE

BE thou watchful and diligent in God's service, and bethink thee often why thou hast renounced the world. Was it not that thou mightest live to God and become a spiritual man? Be zealous, therefore, for thy spiritual profit, for thou shalt receive shortly the reward of thy labours, and neither fear nor sorrow shall come any more into thy borders. Now shalt thou labour a little, and thou shalt find great rest, yea everlasting joy. If thou shalt remain faithful and zealous in labour, doubt not that God shall be faithful and bountiful in rewarding thee. It is thy duty to have a good hope that thou wilt attain the victory, but thou must not fall into security lest thou become slothful or lifted up.

2. A certain man being in anxiety of mind, continually tossed about between hope and fear, and being on a certain day overwhelmed with grief, cast himself down in prayer before the altar in a church, and meditated within himself, saying, "Oh! if I but knew that I should still persevere," and presently heard within him a voice from God, "And if thou didst know it, what wouldst thou do? Do now what thou wouldst do then, and thou shalt be very secure." And straightway being comforted and strengthened, he committed himself to the will of God and the perturbation of spirit ceased, neither had he a mind any more to search curiously to know what should befall him hereafter, but studied rather to inquire what was the good and acceptable will of God, for the beginning and perfecting of every good work.

3. *Hope in the Lord and be doing good,* saith the Prophet; *dwell in the land and thou shalt be fed*[1] with its riches. One thing there is which holdeth back many from progress and fervent amendment, even the dread of difficulty, or the labour of the conflict. Nevertheless they advance above all others in virtue who strive manfully to conquer those things which are most grievous and contrary to them, for there a man profiteth most and meriteth greater grace where he most overcometh himself and mortifieth himself in spirit.

4. But all men have not the same passions to conquer and to mortify, yet he who is diligent shall attain more profit, although he have stronger passions, than another who is more temperate of disposition, but is withal less fervent in the pursuit of virtue. Two things specially avail unto improvement in holiness, namely firmness to withdraw ourselves from the sin to which by nature we are most

[1] Psalm xxxvii. 3.

inclined, and earnest zeal for that good in which we are most lacking. And strive also very earnestly to guard against and subdue those faults which displease thee most frequently in others.

5. Gather some profit to thy soul wherever thou art, and wherever thou seest or hearest good examples, stir thyself to follow them, but where thou seest anything which is blameworthy, take heed that thou do not the same; or if at any time thou hast done it, strive quickly to amend thyself. As thine eye observeth others, so again are the eyes of others upon thee. How sweet and pleasant is it to see zealous and godly brethren temperate and of good discipline; and how sad is it and grievous to see them walking disorderly, not practising the duties to which they are called. How hurtful a thing it is to neglect the purpose of their calling, and turn their inclinations to things which are none of their business.

6. Be mindful of the duties which thou hast undertaken, and set always before thee the remembrance of the Crucified. Truly oughtest thou to be ashamed as thou lookest upon the life of Jesus Christ, because thou hast not yet endeavoured to conform thyself more unto Him, though thou hast been a long time in the way of God. A religious man who exercises himself seriously and devoutly in the most holy life and passion of our Lord shall find there abundantly all things that are profitable and necessary for him, neither is there need that he shall seek anything better beyond Jesus. Oh! if Jesus crucified would come into our hearts, how quickly, and completely should we have learned all that we need to know!

7. He who is earnest receiveth and beareth well all things that are laid upon him. He who is careless and lukewarm hath trouble upon trouble, and suffereth anguish upon every side, because he is without inward consolation, and is forbidden to seek that which is outward. He who is living without discipline is exposed to grievous ruin. He who seeketh easier and lighter discipline shall always be in distress, because one thing or another will give him displeasure.

8. O! if no other duty lay upon us but to praise the Lord our God with our whole heart and voice! Oh! if thou never hadst need to eat or drink, or sleep, but wert always able to praise God, and to give thyself to spiritual exercises alone; then shouldst thou be far happier than now, when for so many necessities thou must serve the

flesh. O! that these necessities were not, but only the spiritual refreshments of the soul, which alas we taste too seldom.

9. When a man hath come to this, that he seeketh comfort from no created thing, then doth he perfectly begin to enjoy God, then also will he be well contented with whatsoever shall happen unto him. Then will he neither rejoice for much nor be sorrowful for little, but he committeth himself altogether and with full trust unto God, who is all in all to him, to whom nothing perisheth nor dieth, but all things live to Him and obey His every word without delay.

10. Remember always thine end, and how the time which is lost returneth not. Without care and diligence thou shalt never get virtue. If thou beginnest to grow cold, it shall begin to go ill with thee, but if thou givest thyself unto zeal thou shalt find much peace, and shalt find thy labour the lighter because of the grace of God and the love of virtue. A zealous and diligent man is ready for all things. It is greater labour to resist sins and passions than to toil in bodily labours. He who shunneth not small faults falleth little by little into greater. At eventide thou shalt always be glad if thou spend the day profitably. Watch over thyself, stir thyself up, admonish thyself, and howsoever it be with others, neglect not thyself. The more violence thou dost unto thyself, the more thou shall profit. Amen.

THE SECOND BOOK

ADMONITIONS CONCERNING THE INNER LIFE

CHAPTER I

OF THE INWARD LIFE

*T*HE *kingdom of God is within you,*[1] saith the Lord. Turn thee with all thine heart to the Lord and forsake this miserable world, and thou shalt find rest unto thy soul. Learn to despise outward things and to give thyself to things inward, and thou shalt see the kingdom of God come within thee. For the kingdom of God is peace and joy in the Holy Ghost, and it is not given to the wicked. Christ will come to thee, and show thee His consolation, if thou prepare a worthy mansion for Him within thee. All His glory and beauty is from within, and there it pleaseth Him to dwell. He often visiteth the inward man and holdeth with him sweet discourse, giving him soothing consolation, much peace, friendship exceeding wonderful.

2. Go to, faithful soul, prepare thy heart for this bridegroom that he may vouchsafe to come to thee and dwell within thee, for so He saith, *if any man loveth me he will keep my words: and my Father will love him, and we will come unto him and make our abode with him.*[2] Give, therefore, place to Christ and refuse entrance to all others. When thou hast Christ, thou art rich, and hast sufficient. He shall be thy provider and faithful watchman in all things, so that thou hast no need to trust in men, for men soon change and swiftly pass away, but Christ remaineth for ever and standeth by us firmly even to the end.

3. There is no great trust to be placed in a frail and mortal man, even though he be useful and dear to us, neither should much sor-

[1] Luke xvii. 21. [2] John xiv. 23.

row arise within us if sometimes he oppose and contradict us. They who are on thy side to-day, may to-morrow be against thee, and often are they turned round like the wind. Put thy whole trust in God and let Him be thy fear and thy love, He will answer for thee Himself, and will do for thee what is best. *Here hast thou no continuing city,*[3] and wheresoever thou art, thou art a stranger and a pilgrim, and thou shalt never have rest unless thou art closely united to Christ within thee.

4. Why dost thou cast thine eyes hither and thither, since this is not the place of thy rest? In heaven ought thy habitation to be, and all earthly things should be looked upon as it were in the passing by. All things pass away and thou equally with them. Look that thou cleave not to them lest thou be taken with them and perish. Let thy contemplation be on the Most High, and let thy supplication be directed unto Christ without ceasing. If thou canst not behold high and heavenly things, rest thou in the passion of Christ and dwell willingly in His sacred wounds. For if thou devoutly fly to the wounds of Jesus, and the precious marks of the nails and the spear, thou shalt find great comfort in tribulation, nor will the slights of men trouble thee much, and thou wilt easily bear their unkind words.

5. Christ also, when He was in the world, was despised and rejected of men, and in His greatest necessity was left by His acquaintance and friends to bear these reproaches. Christ was willing to suffer and be despised, and darest thou complain of any? Christ had adversaries and gainsayers, and dost thou wish to have all men thy friends and benefactors? Whence shall thy patience attain her crown if no adversity befall thee? If thou art unwilling to suffer any adversity, how shalt thou be the friend of Christ? Sustain thyself with Christ and for Christ if thou wilt reign with Christ.

6. If thou hadst once entered into the mind of Jesus, and hadst tasted yea even a little of his tender love, then wouldst thou care nought for thine own convenience or inconvenience, but wouldst rather rejoice at trouble brought upon thee, because the love of Jesus maketh a man to despise himself. He who loveth Jesus, and is inwardly true and free from inordinate affections, is able to turn

[3] Hebrews xiii. 14.

himself readily unto God, and to rise above himself in spirit, and to enjoy fruitful peace.

7. He who knoweth things as they are and not as they are said or seem to be, he truly is wise, and is taught of God more than of men. He who knoweth how to walk from within, and to set little value upon outward things, requireth not places nor waiteth for seasons, for holding his intercourse with God. The inward man quickly recollecteth himself, because he is never entirely given up to outward things. No outward labour and no necessary occupations stand in his way, but as events fall out, so doth he fit himself to them. He who is rightly disposed and ordered within careth not for the strange and perverse conduct of men. A man is hindered and distracted in so far as he is moved by outward things.

8. If it were well with thee, and thou wert purified from evil, all things would work together for thy good and profiting. For this cause do many things displease thee and often trouble thee, that thou art not yet perfectly dead to thyself nor separated from all earthly things. Nothing so defileth and entangleth the heart of man as impure love towards created things. If thou rejectest outward comfort thou wilt be able to contemplate heavenly things and frequently to be joyful inwardly.

CHAPTER II

OF LOWLY SUBMISSION

Make no great account who is for thee or against thee, but mind only the present duty and take care that God be with thee in whatsoever thou doest. Have a good conscience and God will defend thee, for he whom God will help no man's perverseness shall be able to hurt. If thou knowest how to hold thy peace and to suffer, without doubt thou shalt see the help of the Lord. He knoweth the time and the way to deliver thee, therefore must thou resign thyself to Him. To God it belongeth to help and to deliver from all confusion. Oftentimes it is very profitable for keeping us in greater humility, that others know and rebuke our faults.

2. When a man humbleth himself for his defects, he then easily pacifieth others and quickly satisfieth those that are angered against

him. God protecteth and delivereth the humble man, He loveth and comforteth the humble man, to the humble man He inclineth Himself, on the humble He bestoweth great grace, and when he is cast down He raiseth him to glory: to the humble He revealeth His secrets, and sweetly draweth and inviteth him to Himself. The humble man having received reproach, is yet in sufficient peace, because he resteth on God and not on the world. Reckon not thyself to have profited in anywise unless thou feel thyself to be inferior to all.

CHAPTER III

OF THE GOOD, PEACEABLE MAN

First keep thyself in peace, and then shalt thou be able to be a peacemaker towards others. A peaceable man doth more good than a well-learned. A passionate man turneth even good into evil and easily believeth evil; a good, peaceable man converteth all things into good. He who dwelleth in peace is suspicious of none, but he who is discontented and restless is tossed with many suspicions, and is neither quiet himself nor suffereth others to be quiet. He often saith what he ought not to say, and omitteth what it were more expedient for him to do. He considereth to what duties others are bound, and neglecteth those to which he is bound himself. Therefore be zealous first over thyself, and then mayest thou righteously be zealous concerning thy neighbour.

2. Thou knowest well how to excuse and to colour thine own deeds, but thou wilt not accept the excuses of others. It would be more just to accuse thyself and excuse thy brother. If thou wilt that others bear with thee, bear thou with others. Behold how far thou art as yet from the true charity and humility which knows not how to be angry or indignant against any save self alone. It is no great thing to mingle with the good and the meek, for this is naturally pleasing to all, and every one of us willingly enjoyeth peace and liketh best those who think with us: but to be able to live peaceably with the hard and perverse, or with the disorderly, or those who oppose us, this is a great grace and a thing much to be commended and most worthy of a man.

3. There are who keep themselves in peace and keep peace also with others, and there are who neither have peace nor suffer others to have peace; they are troublesome to others, but always more troublesome to themselves. And there are who hold themselves in peace, and study to bring others unto peace; nevertheless, all our peace in this sad life lieth in humble suffering rather than in not feeling adversities. He who best knoweth how to suffer shall possess the most peace; that man is conqueror of himself and lord of the world, the friend of Christ, and the inheritor of heaven.

CHAPTER IV

OF A PURE MIND AND SIMPLE INTENTION

By two wings is man lifted above earthly things, even by simplicity and purity. Simplicity ought to be in the intention, purity in the affection. Simplicity reacheth towards God, purity apprehendeth Him and tasteth Him. No good action will be distasteful to thee if thou be free within from inordinate affection. If thou reachest after and seekest, nothing but the will of God and the benefit of thy neighbour, thou wilt entirely enjoy inward liberty. If thine heart were right, then should every creature be a mirror of life and a book of holy doctrine. There is no creature so small and vile but that it showeth us the goodness of God.

2. If thou wert good and pure within, then wouldst thou look upon all things without hurt and understand them aright. A pure heart seeth the very depths of heaven and hell. Such as each one is inwardly, so judgeth he outwardly. If there is any joy in the world surely the man of pure heart possesseth it, and if there is anywhere tribulation and anguish, the evil conscience knoweth it best. As iron cast into the fire loseth rust and is made altogether glowing, so the man who turneth himself altogether unto God is freed from slothfulness and changed into a new man.

3. When a man beginneth to grow lukewarm, then he feareth a little labour, and willingly accepteth outward consolation; but when he beginneth perfectly to conquer himself and to walk manfully in the way of God, then he counteth as nothing those things which aforetime seemed to be so grievous unto him.

CHAPTER V

OF SELF-ESTEEM

WE cannot place too little confidence in ourselves, because grace and understanding are often lacking to us. Little light is there within us, and what we have we quickly lose by negligence. Oftentimes we perceive not how great is our inward blindness. We often do ill and excuse it worse. Sometimes we are moved by passion and count it zeal; we blame little faults in others and pass over great faults in ourselves. Quickly enough we feel and reckon up what we bear at the hands of others, but we reflect not how much others are bearing from us. He who would weigh well and rightly his own doings would not be the man to judge severely of another.

2. The spiritually-minded man putteth care of himself before all cares; and he who diligently attendeth to himself easily keepeth silence concerning others. Thou wilt never be spiritually minded and godly unless thou art silent concerning other men's matters and take full heed to thyself. If thou think wholly upon thyself and upon God, what thou seest out of doors shall move thee little. Where art thou when thou art not present to thyself? and when thou hast overrun all things, what hath it profited thee, thyself being neglected? If thou wouldst have peace and true unity, thou must put aside all other things, and gaze only upon thyself.

3. Then thou shalt make great progress if thou keep thyself free from all temporal care. Thou shalt lamentably fall away if thou set a value upon any worldly thing. Let nothing be great, nothing high, nothing pleasing, nothing acceptable unto thee, save God Himself or the things of God. Reckon as altogether vain whatsoever consolation comes to thee from a creature. The soul that loveth God looketh not to anything that is beneath God. God alone is eternal and incomprehensible, filling all things, the solace of the soul, and the true joy of the heart.

CHAPTER VI

OF THE JOY OF A GOOD CONSCIENCE

THE testimony of a good conscience is the glory of a good man. Have a good conscience and thou shalt ever have joy. A good conscience is able to bear exceeding much, and is exceeding joyful in the midst of adversities; an evil conscience is ever fearful and unquiet. Thou shalt rest sweetly if thy heart condemn thee not. Never rejoice unless when thou hast done well. The wicked have never true joy, nor feel internal peace, for *there is no peace, saith my God, to the wicked*.[1] And if they say "we are in peace, there shall no harm happen unto us, and who shall dare to do us hurt?" believe them not, for suddenly shall the wrath of God rise up against them, and their deeds shall be brought to nought, and their thoughts shall perish.

2. To glory in tribulation is not grievous to him who loveth; for such glorying is glorying in the Cross of Christ. Brief is the glory which is given and received of men. Sadness always goeth hand in hand with the glory of the world. The glory of the good is in their conscience, and not in the report of men. The joy of the upright is from God and in God, and their joy is in the truth. He who desireth true and eternal glory careth not for that which is temporal; and he who seeketh temporal glory, or who despiseth it from his heart, is proved to bear little love for that which is heavenly. He who careth for neither praises nor reproaches hath great tranquillity of heart.

3. He will easily be contented and filled with peace, whose conscience is pure. Thou art none the holier if thou art praised, nor the viler if thou art reproached. Thou art what thou art; and thou canst not be better than God pronounceth thee to be. If thou considerest well what thou art inwardly, thou wilt not care what men will say to thee. *Man looketh on the outward appearance, but the Lord looketh on the heart:*[2] man looketh on the deed, but God considereth the intent. It is the token of a humble spirit always to do well, and

---

[1] Isaiah lvii. 21.   [2] 1 Samuel xvi. 7.

to set little by oneself. Not to look for consolation from any created thing is a sign of great purity and inward faithfulness.

4. He that seeketh no outward witness on his own behalf, showeth plainly that he hath committed himself wholly to God. *For not he that commendeth himself is approved,* as St. Paul saith, *but whom the Lord commendeth.*[3] To walk inwardly with God, and not to be held by any outer affections, is the state of a spiritual man.

CHAPTER VII

OF LOVING JESUS ABOVE ALL THINGS

BLESSED is he who understandeth what it is to love Jesus, and to despise himself for Jesus' sake. He must give up all that he loveth for his Beloved, for Jesus will be loved alone above all things. The love of created things is deceiving and unstable, but the love of Jesus is faithful and lasting. He who cleaveth to created things will fall with their slipperiness; but he who embraceth Jesus will stand upright for ever. Love Him and hold Him for thy friend, for He will not forsake thee when all depart from thee, nor will he suffer thee to perish at the last. Thou must one day be separated from all, whether thou wilt or wilt not.

2. Cleave thou to Jesus in life and death, and commit thyself unto His faithfulness, who, when all men fail thee, is alone able to help thee. Thy Beloved is such, by nature, that He will suffer no rival, but alone will possess thy heart, and as a king will sit upon His own throne. If thou wouldst learn to put away from thee every created thing, Jesus would freely take up His abode with thee. Thou wilt find all trust little better than lost which thou hast placed in men, and not in Jesus. Trust not nor lean upon a reed shaken with the wind, because *all flesh is grass, and the goodliness thereof falleth as the flower of the field.*[1]

3. Thou wilt be quickly deceived if thou lookest only upon the outward appearance of men, for if thou seekest thy comfort and profit in others, thou shalt too often experience loss. If thou seekest Jesus in all things thou shalt verily find Jesus, but if thou seekest

[3] 2 Corinthians x. 18.   [1] Isaiah xl. 6.

thyself thou shalt also find thyself, but to thine own hurt. For if a man seeketh not Jesus he is more hurtful to himself than all the world and all his adversaries.

CHAPTER VIII

OF THE INTIMATE LOVE OF JESUS

WHEN Jesus is present all is well and nothing seemeth hard, but when Jesus is not present everything is hard. When Jesus speaketh not within, our comfort is nothing worth, but if Jesus speaketh but a single word great is the comfort we experience. Did not Mary Magdalene rise up quickly from the place where she wept when Martha said to her, *The Master is come and calleth for thee?*[1] Happy hour when Jesus calleth thee from tears to the joy of the spirit! How dry and hard art thou without Jesus! How senseless and vain if thou desirest aught beyond Jesus! Is not this greater loss than if thou shouldst lose the whole world?

2. What can the world profit thee without Jesus? To be without Jesus is the nethermost hell, and to be with Jesus is sweet Paradise. If Jesus were with thee no enemy could hurt thee. He who findeth Jesus findeth a good treasure, yea, good above all good; and he who loseth Jesus loseth exceeding much, yea, more than the whole world. Most poor is he who liveth without Jesus, and most rich is he who is much with Jesus.

3. It is great skill to know how to live with Jesus, and to know how to hold Jesus is great wisdom. Be thou humble and peaceable and Jesus shall be with thee. Be godly and quiet, and Jesus will remain with thee. Thou canst quickly drive away Jesus and lose His favour if thou wilt turn away to the outer things. And if thou hast put Him to flight and lost Him, to whom wilt thou flee, and whom then wilt thou seek for a friend? Without a friend thou canst not live long, and if Jesus be not thy friend above all thou shalt be very sad and desolate. Madly therefore doest thou if thou trusteth or findest joy in any other. It is preferable to have the whole world against thee, than Jesus offended with thee. Therefore of all that are dear to thee, let Jesus be specially loved.

[1] John xi. 28.

4. Let all be loved for Jesus' sake, but Jesus for His own. Jesus Christ alone is to be specially loved, for He alone is found good and faithful above all friends. For His sake and in Him let both enemies and friends be dear to thee, and pray for them all that they may all know and love Him. Never desire to be specially praised or loved, because this belongeth to God alone, who hath none like unto Himself. Nor wish thou that any one set his heart on thee, nor do thou give thyself up to the love of any, but let Jesus be in thee and in every good man.

5. Be pure and free within thyself, and be not entangled by any created thing. Thou oughtest to bring a bare and clean heart to God, if thou desirest to be ready to see how gracious the Lord is. And in truth, unless thou be prevented and drawn on by His grace, thou wilt not attain to this, that having cast out and dismissed all else, thou alone art united to God. For when the grace of God cometh to a man, then he becometh able to do all things, and when it departeth then he will be poor and weak and given up unto troubles. In these thou art not to be cast down nor to despair, but to rest with calm mind on the will of God, and to bear all things which come upon thee unto the praise of Jesus Christ; for after winter cometh summer, after night returneth day, after the tempest a great calm.

CHAPTER IX

OF THE LACK OF ALL COMFORT

It is no hard thing to despise human comfort when divine is present. It is a great thing, yea very great, to be able to bear the loss both of human and divine comfort; and for the love of God willingly to bear exile of heart, and in nought to seek oneself, nor to look to one's own merit. What great matter is it, if thou be cheerful of heart and devout when favour cometh to thee? That is an hour wherein all rejoice. Pleasantly enough doth he ride whom the grace of God carrieth. And what marvel, if he feeleth no burden who is carried by the Almighty, and is led onwards by the Guide from on high?

2. We are willing to accept anything for comfort, and it is diffi-

cult for a man to be freed from himself. The holy martyr Laurence overcame the love of the world and even of his priestly master, because he despised everything in the world which seemed to be pleasant; and for the love of Christ he calmly suffered even God's chief priest, Sixtus, whom he dearly loved, to be taken from him. Thus by the love of the Creator he overcame the love of man, and instead of human comfort he chose rather God's good pleasure. So also learn thou to resign any near and beloved friend for the love of God. Nor take it amiss when thou hast been deserted by a friend, knowing that we must all be parted from one another at last.

3. Mightily and long must a man strive within himself before he learn altogether to overcome himself, and to draw his whole affection towards God. When a man resteth upon himself, he easily slippeth away unto human comforts. But a true lover of Christ, and a diligent seeker after virtue, falleth not back upon those comforts, nor seeketh such sweetnesses as may be tasted and handled, but desireth rather hard exercises, and to undertake severe labours for Christ.

4. When, therefore, spiritual comfort is given by God, receive it with giving of thanks, and know that it is the gift of God, not thy desert. Be not lifted up, rejoice not overmuch nor foolishly presume, but rather be more humble for the gift, more wary and more careful in all thy doings; for that hour will pass away, and temptation will follow. When comfort is taken from thee, do not straightway despair, but wait for the heavenly visitation with humility and patience, for God is able to give thee back greater favour and consolation. This is not new nor strange to those who have made trial of the way of God, for with the great saints and the ancient prophets there was often this manner of change.

5. Wherefore one said when the favour of God was present with him, *I said in my prosperity I shall never be moved,*[1] but he goeth on to say what he felt within himself when the favour departed: *Thou didst turn Thy face from me, and I was troubled.* In spite whereof he in no wise despaireth, but the more instantly entreateth God, and saith, *Unto Thee, O Lord, will I cry, and will pray unto my God;* and then he receiveth the fruit of his prayer, and testifieth

[1] Psalm xxx. 6.

how he hath been heard, saying, *The Lord heard me and had mercy upon me, the Lord was my helper*. But wherein? *Thou hast turned my heaviness into joy, Thou hast put off my sackcloth and girded me with gladness*. If it was thus with the great saints, we who are poor and needy ought not to despair if we are sometimes in the warmth and sometimes in the cold, for the Spirit cometh and goeth according to the good pleasure of His will. Wherefore holy Job saith, *Thou dost visit him in the morning, and suddenly Thou dost prove him*.[2]

6. Whereupon then can I hope, or wherein may I trust, save only in the great mercy of God, and the hope of heavenly grace? For whether good men are with me, godly brethren or faithful friends, whether holy books or beautiful discourses, whether sweet hymns and songs, all these help but little, and have but little savour when I am deserted by God's favour and left to mine own poverty. There is no better remedy, then, than patience and denial of self, and an abiding in the will of God.

7. I have never found any man so religious and godly, but that he felt sometimes a withdrawal of the divine favour, and lack of fervour. No saint was ever so filled with rapture, so enlightened, but that sooner or later he was tempted. For he is not worthy of the great vision of God, who, for God's sake, hath not been exercised by some temptation. For temptation is wont to go before as a sign of the comfort which shall follow, and heavenly comfort is promised to those who are proved by temptation. As it is written, *To him that overcometh I will give to eat of the tree of life*.[3]

8. Divine comfort is given that a man may be stronger to bear adversities. And temptation followeth, lest he be lifted up because of the benefit. The devil sleepeth not; thy flesh is not yet dead; therefore, cease thou not to make thyself ready unto the battle, for enemies stand on thy right hand and on thy left, and they are never at rest.

[2] Job vii. 18.   [3] Revelation ii. 7.

CHAPTER X

OF GRATITUDE FOR THE GRACE OF GOD

WHY seekest thou rest when thou art born to labour? Prepare thyself for patience more than for comforts, and for bearing the cross more than for joy. For who among the men of this world would not gladly receive consolation and spiritual joy if he might always have it? For spiritual comforts exceed all the delights of the world, and all the pleasures of the flesh. For all worldly delights are either empty or unclean, whilst spiritual delights alone are pleasant and honourable, the offspring of virtue, and poured forth by God into pure minds. But no man can always enjoy these divine comforts at his own will, because the season of temptation ceaseth not for long.

2. Great is the difference between a visitation from above and false liberty of spirit and great confidence in self. God doeth well in giving us the grace of comfort, but man doeth ill in not immediately giving God thanks thereof. And thus the gifts of grace are not able to flow unto us, because we are ungrateful to the Author of them, and return them not wholly to the Fountain whence they flow. For grace ever becometh the portion of him who is grateful and that is taken away from the proud, which is wont to be given to the humble.

3. I desire no consolation which taketh away from me compunction, I love no contemplation which leadeth to pride. For all that is high is not holy, nor is everything that is sweet good; every desire is not pure; nor is everything that is dear to us pleasing unto God. Willingly do I accept that grace whereby I am made humbler and more wary and more ready to renounce myself. He who is made learned by the gift of grace and taught wisdom by the stroke of the withdrawal thereof, will not dare to claim any good thing for himself, but will rather confess that he is poor and needy. *Give unto God the thing which is God's*,[1] and ascribe to thyself that which is thine; that is, give thanks unto God for His grace, but for thyself alone confess thy fault, and that thy punishment is deserved for thy fault.

4. Sit thou down always in the lowest room and thou shalt be

[1] Matthew xxii. 21.

given the highest place.[2] For the highest cannot be without the lowest. For the highest saints of God are least in their own sight, and the more glorious they are, so much the lowlier are they in themselves; full of grace and heavenly glory, they are not desirous of vainglory; resting on God and strong in His might, they cannot be lifted up in any wise. And they who ascribe unto God all the good which they have received, "seek not glory one of another, but the glory which cometh from God only," and they desire that God shall be praised in Himself and in all His Saints above all things, and they are always striving for this very thing.

5. Be thankful, therefore, for the least benefit and thou shalt be worthy to receive greater. Let the least be unto thee even as the greatest, and let that which is of little account be unto thee as a special gift. If the majesty of the Giver be considered, nothing that is given shall seem small and of no worth, for that is not a small thing which is given by the Most High God. Yea, though He gave punishment and stripes, we ought to be thankful, because He ever doth for our profit whatever He suffereth to come upon us. He who seeketh to retain the favour of God, let him be thankful for the favour which is given, and patient in respect of that which is taken away. Let him pray that it may return; let him be wary and humble that he lose it not.

CHAPTER XI

OF THE FEWNESS OF THOSE WHO LOVE THE CROSS OF JESUS

JESUS hath many lovers of His heavenly kingdom, but few bearers of His Cross. He hath many seekers of comfort, but few of tribulation. He findeth many companions of His table, but few of His fasting. All desire to rejoice with Him, few are willing to undergo anything for His sake. Many follow Jesus that they may eat of His loaves, but few that they may drink of the cup of His passion. Many are astonished at His Miracles, few follow after the shame of His Cross. Many love Jesus so long as no adversities happen to them. Many praise Him and bless Him, so long as they receive any comforts from Him. But if Jesus hide Himself and withdraw from

[2] Luke xiv. 10.

them a little while, they fall either into complaining or into too great dejection of mind.

2. But they who love Jesus for Jesus' sake, and not for any consolation of their own, bless Him in all tribulation and anguish of heart as in the highest consolation. And if He should never give them consolation, nevertheless they would always praise Him and always give Him thanks.

3. Oh what power hath the pure love of Jesus, unmixed with any gain or love of self! Should not all they be called mercenary who are always seeking consolations? Do they not prove themselves lovers of self more than of Christ who are always seeking their own gain and advantage? Where shall be found one who is willing to serve God altogether for nought?

4. Rarely is any one found so spiritual as to be stripped of all selfish thoughts, for who shall find a man truly poor in spirit and free of all created things? "His value is from afar, yea from the ends of the earth." A man may give away all his goods, yet that is nothing; and if he do many deeds of penitence, yet that is a small thing; and though he understand all knowledge, yet that is afar off; and if he have great virtue and zealous devotion, yet much is lacking unto him, yea, one thing which is the most necessary to him of all. What is it then? That having given up all things besides, he give up himself and go forth from himself utterly, and retain nothing of self-love; and having done all things which he knoweth to be his duty to do, that he feel that he hath done nothing. Let him not reckon that much which might be much esteemed, but let him pronounce himself to be in truth an unprofitable servant, as the Truth Himself saith, *When ye have done all things that are commanded you, say, we are unprofitable servants.*[1] Then may he be truly poor and naked in spirit, and be able to say with the Prophet, *As for me, I am poor and needy.*[2] Nevertheless, no man is richer than he, no man stronger, no man freer. For he knoweth both how to give up himself and all things, and how to be lowly in his own eyes.

[1] Luke xvii. 10.   [2] Psalm xxv. 16.

CHAPTER XII

OF THE ROYAL WAY OF THE HOLY CROSS

THAT seemeth a hard saying to many, *If any man will come after Me, let him deny himself and take up his Cross and follow Me.*[1] But it will be much harder to hear that last sentence, *Depart from me, ye wicked, into eternal fire.*[2] For they who now willingly hear the word of the Cross and follow it, shall not then fear the hearing of eternal damnation. This sign of the Cross shall be in heaven when the Lord cometh to Judgment. Then all servants of the Cross, who in life have conformed themselves to the Crucified, shall draw nigh unto Christ the Judge with great boldness.

2. Why fearest thou then to take up the cross which leadeth to a kingdom? In the Cross is health, in the Cross is life, in the Cross is protection from enemies, in the Cross is heavenly sweetness, in the Cross strength of mind, in the Cross joy of the spirit, in the Cross the height of virtue, in the Cross perfection of holiness. There is no health of the soul, no hope of eternal life, save in the Cross. Take up therefore, thy cross and follow Jesus and thou shalt go into eternal life. He went before thee bearing His Cross and died for thee upon the Cross, that thou also mayest bear thy cross and mayest love to be crucified upon it. For if thou be dead with Him, thou shalt also live with Him, and if thou be a partaker of His sufferings thou shalt be also of His glory.

3. Behold everything dependeth upon the Cross, and everything lieth in dying; and there is none other way unto life and to true inward peace, except the way of the Holy Cross and of daily mortification. Go where thou wilt, seek whatsoever thou wilt, and thou shalt find no higher way above nor safer way below, than the way of the Holy Cross. Dispose and order all things according to thine own will and judgment, and thou shalt ever find something to suffer either willingly or unwillingly, and thus thou shalt ever find thy cross. For thou shalt either feel pain of body, or tribulation of spirit within thy soul.

4. Sometimes thou wilt be forsaken of God, sometimes thou wilt

[1] Matthew xvi. 24.   [2] Matthew xxv. 41.

be tried by thy neighbour, and which is more, thou wilt often be wearisome to thyself. And still thou canst not be delivered nor eased by any remedy or consolation, but must bear so long as God will. For God will have thee learn to suffer tribulation without consolation, and to submit thyself fully to it, and by tribulation be made more humble. No man understandeth the Passion of Christ in his heart so well as he who hath had somewhat of the like suffering himself. The Cross therefore is always ready, and every where waiteth for thee. Thou canst not flee from it whithersoever thou hurriest, for whithersoever thou comest, thou bearest thyself with thee, and shalt ever find thyself. Turn thee above, turn thee below, turn thee without, turn thee within, and in them all thou shalt find the Cross; and needful is it that thou everywhere possess patience if thou wilt have internal peace and gain the everlasting crown.

5. If thou willingly bear the Cross, it will bear thee, and will bring thee to the end which thou seekest, even where there shall be the end of suffering; though it shall not be here. If thou bear it unwillingly, thou makest a burden for thyself and greatly increaseth thy load, and yet thou must bear it. If thou cast away one cross, without doubt thou shalt find another and perchance a heavier.

6. Thinkest thou to escape what no mortal hath been able to avoid? Which of the saints in the world hath been without the cross and tribulation? For not even Jesus Christ our Lord was one hour without the anguish of His Passion, so long as He lived. *It behooved,* He said, *Christ to suffer and to rise from the dead, and so enter into his glory.*[3] And how dost thou seek another way than this royal way, which is the way of the Holy Cross?

7. The whole life of Christ was a cross and martyrdom, and dost thou seek for thyself rest and joy? Thou art wrong, thou art wrong, if thou seekest aught but to suffer tribulations, for this whole mortal life is full of miseries, and set round with crosses. And the higher a man hath advanced in the spirit, the heavier crosses he will often find, because the sorrow of his banishment increaseth with the strength of his love.

8. But yet the man who is thus in so many wise afflicted, is not

[3] Luke xxiv. 46.

without refreshment of consolation, because he feeleth abundant fruit to be growing within him out of the bearing of his cross. For whilst he willingly submitteth himself to it, every burden of tribulation is turned into an assurance of divine comfort, and the more the flesh is wasted by affliction, the more is the spirit strengthened mightily by inward grace. And ofttimes so greatly is he comforted by the desire for tribulation and adversity, through love of conformity to the Cross of Christ, that he would not be without sorrow and tribulation; for he believeth that he shall be the more acceptable to God, the more and the heavier burdens he is able to bear for His sake. This is not the virtue of man, but the grace of Christ which hath such power and energy in the weak flesh, that what it naturally hateth and fleeth from, this it draweth to and loveth through fervour of spirit.

9. It is not in the nature of man to bear the cross, to love the cross, to keep under the body and to bring it into subjection, to fly from honours, to bear reproaches meekly, to despise self and desire to be despised, to bear all adversities and losses, and to desire no prosperity in this world. If thou lookest to thyself, thou wilt of thyself be able to do none of this; but if thou trustest in the Lord, endurance shall be given thee from heaven, and the world and the flesh shall be made subject to thy command. Yea, thou shalt not even fear thine adversary the devil, if thou be armed with faith and signed with the Cross of Christ.

10. Set thyself, therefore, like a good and faithful servant of Christ, to the manful bearing of the Cross of thy Lord, who out of love was crucified for thee. Prepare thyself for the bearing many adversities and manifold troubles in this wretched life; because so it shall be with thee wheresoever thou art, and so in very deed thou shalt find it, wherever thou hide thyself. This it must be; and there is no means of escaping from tribulation and sorrow, except to bear them patiently. Drink thou lovingly thy Lord's cup if thou desirest to be His friend and to have thy lot with Him. Leave consolations to God, let Him do as seemeth best to Him concerning them. But do thou set thyself to endure tribulations, and reckon them the best consolations; for *the sufferings of this present time are not worthy*

to be compared with the glory which shall be revealed in us,[4] nor would they be even if thou wert to endure them all.

11. When thou hast come to this, that tribulation is sweet and pleasant to thee for Christ's sake, then reckon that it is well with thee, because thou hast found paradise on earth. So long as it is hard to thee to suffer and thou desirest to escape, so long it will not be well with thee, and tribulations will follow thee everywhere.

12. If thou settest thyself to that thou oughtest, namely, to suffer and to die, it shall soon go better with thee, and thou shalt find peace. Though thou shouldest be caught up with Paul unto the third heaven,[5] thou art not on that account secure from suffering evil. *I will show him,* saith Jesus, *what great things he must suffer for My Name's sake.*[6] It remaineth, therefore, to thee to suffer, if thou wilt love Jesus and serve Him continually.

13. Oh that thou wert worthy to suffer something for the name of Jesus, how great glory should await thee, what rejoicing among all the saints of God, what bright example also to thy neighbour! For all men commend patience, although few be willing to practise it. Thou oughtest surely to suffer a little for Christ when many suffer heavier things for the world.

14. Know thou of a surety that thou oughtest to lead the life of a dying man. And the more a man dieth to himself, the more he beginneth to live towards God. None is fit for the understanding of heavenly things, unless he hath submitted himself to bearing adversities for Christ. Nothing more acceptable to God, nothing more healthful for thyself in this world, than to suffer willingly for Christ. And if it were thine to choose, thou oughtest rather to wish to suffer adversities for Christ, than to be refreshed with manifold consolations, for thou wouldest be more like Christ and more conformed to all saints. For our worthiness and growth in grace lieth not in many delights and consolations, but rather in bearing many troubles and adversities.

15. If indeed there had been anything better and more profitable to the health of men than to suffer, Christ would surely have shown it by word and example. For both the disciples who followed Him, and all who desire to follow Him, He plainly exhorteth to bear

[4] Romans viii. 18.   [5] 2 Corinthians xii. 2.   [6] Acts. ix. 16.

their cross, and saith, *If any man will come after Me, let him deny himself and take up his cross, and follow Me.*[7] So now that we have thoroughly read and studied all things, let us hear the conclusion of the whole matter. *We must through much tribulation enter into the kingdom of God.*[8]

[7] Luke ix. 23.   [8] Acts xiv. 21.

THE THIRD BOOK

ON INWARD CONSOLATION

CHAPTER I

OF THE INWARD VOICE OF CHRIST TO THE FAITHFUL SOUL

I WILL *hearken what the Lord God shall say within me.*[1] Blessed is the soul which heareth the Lord speaking within it, and receiveth the word of consolation from His mouth. Blessed are the ears which receive the echoes of the soft whisper of God, and turn not aside to the whisperings of this world. Blessed truly are the ears which listen not to the voice that soundeth without, but to that which teacheth truth inwardly. Blessed are the eyes which are closed to things without, but are fixed upon things within. Blessed are they who search inward things and study to prepare themselves more and more by daily exercises for the receiving of heavenly mysteries. Blessed are they who long to have leisure for God, and free themselves from every hindrance of the world. Think on these things, O my soul, and shut the doors of thy carnal desires, so mayest thou hear what the Lord God will say within thee.

2. These things saith thy Beloved, "I am thy salvation, I am thy peace and thy life. Keep thee unto Me, and thou shalt find peace." Put away thee all transitory things, seek those things that are eternal. For what are all temporal things but deceits, and what shall all created things help thee if thou be forsaken by the Creator? Therefore put all things else away, and give thyself to the Creator, to be well pleasing and faithful to Him, that thou mayest be able to attain true blessedness.

[1] Psalm lxxxv. 8.

CHAPTER II

WHAT THE TRUTH SAITH INWARDLY WITHOUT NOISE OF WORDS

SPEAK Lord, for thy servant heareth.[1] *I am Thy servant; O give me understanding that I may know Thy testimonies. Incline my heart unto the words of Thy mouth.*[2] *Let thy speech distil as the dew.* The children of Israel spake in old time to Moses, *Speak thou unto us and we will hear, but let not the Lord speak unto us lest we die.*[3] Not thus, O Lord, not thus do I pray, but rather with Samuel the prophet, I beseech Thee humbly and earnestly, *Speak, Lord, for Thy servant heareth.* Let not Moses speak to me, nor any prophet, but rather speak Thou, O Lord, who didst inspire and illuminate all the prophets; for Thou alone without them canst perfectly fill me with knowledge, whilst they without Thee shall profit nothing.

2. They can indeed utter words, but they give not the spirit. They speak with exceeding beauty, but when Thou art silent they kindle not the heart. They give us scriptures, but Thou makest known the sense thereof. They bring us mysteries, but Thou revealest the things which are signified. They utter commandments, but Thou helpest to the fulfilling of them. They show the way, but Thou givest strength for the journey. They act only outwardly, but Thou dost instruct and enlighten the heart. They water, but Thou givest the increase. They cry with words, but Thou givest understanding to the hearer.

3. Therefore let not Moses speak to me, but Thou, O Lord my God, Eternal Truth; lest I die and bring forth no fruit, being outwardly admonished, but not enkindled within; lest the word heard but not followed, known but not loved, believed but not obeyed, rise up against me in the judgment. *Speak, Lord, for Thy servant heareth; Thou hast the words of eternal life.*[4] Speak unto me for some consolation unto my soul, for the amendment of my whole life, and for the praise and glory and eternal honour of Thy Name.

---

[1] I Samuel iii. 9.   [2] Psalm cxix. 125.   [3] Exodus xx. 19.   [4] John vi. 68.

CHAPTER III

HOW ALL THE WORDS OF GOD ARE TO BE HEARD WITH HUMILITY, AND HOW MANY CONSIDER THEM NOT

"My Son, hear My words, for My words are most sweet, surpassing all the knowledge of the philosophers and wise men of this world. *My words are spirit, and they are life,*[1] and are not to be weighed by man's understanding. They are not to be drawn forth for vain approbation, but to be heard in silence, and to be received with all humility and with deep love."

2. And I said, *"Blessed is the man whom Thou teachest, O Lord, and instructest him in Thy law, that Thou mayest give him rest in time of adversity,*[2] and that he be not desolate in the earth."

3. "I," saith the Lord, "taught the prophets from the beginning, and even now cease I not to speak unto all; but many are deaf and hardened against My voice; many love to listen to the world rather than to God, they follow after the desires of the flesh more readily than after the good pleasure of God. The world promiseth things that are temporal and small, and it is served with great eagerness. I promise things that are great and eternal, and the hearts of mortals are slow to stir. Who serveth and obeyeth Me in all things, with such carefulness as he serveth the world and its rulers?

> Be thou ashamed, O Sidon, saith the sea;[3]
> And if thou reason seekest, hear thou me.

For a little reward men make a long journey; for eternal life many will scarce lift a foot once from the ground. Mean reward is sought after; for a single piece of money sometimes there is shameful striving; for a thing which is vain and for a trifling promise, men shrink not from toiling day and night."

4. "But, O shame! for an unchangeable good, for an inestimable reward, for the highest honour and for a glory that fadeth not away, it is irksome to them to toil even a little. Be thou ashamed therefore, slothful and discontented servant, for they are found readier unto perdition than thou unto life. They rejoice more heartily in vanity than thou in the truth. Sometimes, indeed, they are disap-

[1] John vi. 63.   [2] Psalm xciv. 13.   [3] Isaiah xxiii. 4.

pointed of their hope, but my promise faileth no man, nor sendeth away empty him who trusteth in Me. What I have promised I will give; what I have said I will fulfil; if only a man remain faithful in My love unto the end. Therefore am I the rewarder of all good men, and a strong approver of all who are godly.

5. "Write My words in thy heart and consider them diligently, for they shall be very needful to thee in time of temptation. What thou understandest not when thou readest, thou shalt know in the time of thy visitation. I am wont to visit Mine elect in twofold manner, even by temptation and by comfort, and I teach them two lessons day by day, the one in chiding their faults, the other in exhorting them to grow in grace. He who hath My words and rejecteth them, hath one who shall judge him at the last day."

A PRAYER FOR THE SPIRIT OF DEVOTION

6. O Lord my God, Thou art all my good, and who am I that I should dare to speak unto Thee? I am the very poorest of Thy servants, an abject worm, much poorer and more despicable than I know or dare to say. Nevertheless remember, O Lord, that I am nothing, I have nothing, and can do nothing. Thou only art good, just and holy; Thou canst do all things, art over all things, fillest all things, leaving empty only the sinner. Call to mind Thy tender mercies, and fill my heart with Thy grace, Thou who wilt not that Thy work should return to Thee void.

7. How can I bear this miserable life unless Thy mercy and grace strengthen me? Turn not away Thy face from me, delay not Thy visitation. Withdraw not Thou Thy comfort from me, lest my soul "gasp after thee as a thirsty land." Lord, teach me to do Thy will, teach me to walk humbly and uprightly before Thee, for Thou art my wisdom, who knowest me in truth, and knewest me before the world was made and before I was born into the world.

CHAPTER IV

HOW WE MUST WALK IN TRUTH AND HUMILITY BEFORE GOD

"My Son! walk before Me in truth, and in the simplicity of thy heart seek Me continually. He who walketh before Me in the truth shall be safe from evil assaults, and the truth shall deliver him from the wiles and slanders of the wicked. If the truth shall make thee free, thou shalt be free indeed, and shalt not care for the vain words of men."

2. Lord, it is true as Thou sayest; let it, I pray Thee, be so with me; let Thy truth teach me, let it keep me and preserve me safe unto the end. Let it free me from all evil and inordinate affection, and I will walk before Thee in great freedom of heart.

3. "I will teach thee," saith the Truth, "the things which are right and pleasing before Me. Think upon thy sins with great displeasure and sorrow, and never think thyself anything because of thy good works. Verily thou art a sinner, liable to many passions, yea, tied and bound with them. Of thyself thou always tendest unto nothing, thou wilt quickly fall, quickly be conquered, quickly disturbed, quickly undone. Thou hast nought whereof to glory, but many reasons why thou shouldest reckon thyself vile, for thou art far weaker than thou art able to comprehend.

4. "Let, therefore, nothing which thou doest seem to thee great; let nothing be grand, nothing of value or beauty, nothing worthy of honour, nothing lofty, nothing praiseworthy or desirable, save what is eternal. Let the eternal truth please thee above all things, let thine own great vileness displease thee continually. Fear, denounce, flee nothing so much as thine own faults and sins, which ought to be more displeasing to thee than any loss whatsoever of goods. There are some who walk not sincerely before me, but being led by curiosity and pride, they desire to know my secret things and to understand the deep things of God, whilst they neglect themselves and their salvation. These often fall into great temptations and sins because of their pride and curiosity, for I am against them.

5. "Fear thou the judgments of God, fear greatly the wrath of the Almighty. Shrink from debating upon the works of the Most High, but search narrowly thine own iniquities into what great sins thou hast fallen, and how many good things thou hast neglected. There are some who carry their devotion only in books, some in pictures, some in outward signs and figures; some have Me in their mouths, but little in their hearts. Others there are who, being enlightened in their understanding and purged in their affections, con-

tinually long after eternal things, hear of earthly things with unwillingness, obey the necessities of nature with sorrow. And these understand what the Spirit of truth speaketh in them; for He teacheth them to despise earthly things and to love heavenly; to neglect the world and to desire heaven all the day and night."

CHAPTER V

OF THE WONDERFUL POWER OF THE DIVINE LOVE

I BLESS Thee, O Heavenly Father, Father of my Lord Jesus Christ, for that Thou hast vouchsafed to think of me, poor that I am. *O, Father of Mercies and God of all comfort*,[1] I give thanks unto Thee, who refreshest me sometimes with thine own comfort, when I am unworthy of any comfort. I bless and glorify Thee continually, with thine only begotten Son and the Holy Ghost, the Paraclete, for ever and ever. O Lord God, Holy lover of my soul, when Thou shalt come into my heart, all my inward parts shall rejoice. Thou art my glory and the joy of my heart. Thou art my hope and my refuge in the day of my trouble.

2. But because I am still weak in love and imperfect in virtue, I need to be strengthened and comforted by Thee; therefore visit Thou me often and instruct me with Thy holy ways of discipline. Deliver me from evil passions, and cleanse my heart from all inordinate affections, that, being healed and altogether cleansed within, I may be made ready to love, strong to suffer, steadfast to endure.

3. Love is a great thing, a good above all others, which alone maketh every heavy burden light, and equaliseth every inequality. For it beareth the burden and maketh it no burden, it maketh every bitter thing to be sweet and of good taste. The surpassing love of Jesus impelleth to great works, and exciteth to the continual desiring of greater perfection. Love willeth to be raised up, and not to be held down by any mean thing. Love willeth to be free and aloof from all worldly affection, lest its inward power of vision be hindered, lest it be entangled by any worldly prosperity or overcome by adversity. Nothing is sweeter than love, nothing stronger, nothing loftier, nothing broader, nothing pleasanter, nothing fuller or better

[1] 2 Corinthians i. 3.

in heaven nor on earth, for love was born of God and cannot rest save in God above all created things.

4. He who loveth flyeth, runneth, and is glad; he is free and not hindered. He giveth all things for all things, and hath all things in all things, because he resteth in One who is high above all, from whom every good floweth and proceedeth. He looketh not for gifts, but turneth himself to the Giver above all good things. Love oftentimes knoweth no measure, but breaketh out above all measure; love feeleth no burden, reckoneth not labours, striveth after more than it is able to do, pleadeth not impossibility, because it judgeth all things which are lawful for it to be possible. It is strong therefore for all things, and it fulfilleth many things, and is successful where he who loveth not faileth and lieth down.

5. Love is watchful, and whilst sleeping still keepeth watch; though fatigued it is not weary, though pressed it is not forced, though alarmed it is not terrified, but like the living flame and the burning torch, it breaketh forth on high and securely triumpheth. If a man loveth, he knoweth what this voice crieth. For the ardent affection of the soul is a great clamour in the ears of God, and it saith: My God, my Beloved! Thou art all mine, and I am all Thine.

6. Enlarge Thou me in love, that I may learn to taste with the innermost mouth of my heart how sweet it is to love, to be dissolved, and to swim in love. Let me be holden by love, mounting above myself through exceeding fervour and admiration. Let me sing the song of love, let me follow Thee my Beloved on high, let my soul exhaust itself in Thy praise, exulting with love. Let me love Thee more than myself, not loving myself except for Thy sake, and all men in Thee who truly love Thee, as the law of love commandeth which shineth forth from Thee.

7. Love is swift, sincere, pious, pleasant, gentle, strong, patient, faithful, prudent, long-suffering, manly, and never seeking her own; for wheresoever a man seeketh his own, there he falleth from love. Love is circumspect, humble, and upright; not weak, not fickle, nor intent on vain things; sober, chaste, steadfast, quiet, and guarded in all the senses. Love is subject and obedient to all that are in authority, vile and lowly in its own sight, devout and grateful towards

God, faithful and always trusting in Him even when God hideth His face, for without sorrow we cannot live in love.

8. He who is not ready to suffer all things, and to conform to the will of the Beloved, is not worthy to be called a lover of God. It behoveth him who loveth to embrace willingly all hard and bitter things for the Beloved's sake, and not to be drawn away from Him because of any contrary accidents.

CHAPTER VI

OF THE PROVING OF THE TRUE LOVER

"My Son, thou art not yet strong and prudent in thy love."

2. Wherefore, O my Lord?

3. "Because for a little opposition thou fallest away from thy undertakings, and too eagerly seekest after consolation. The strong lover standeth fast in temptations, and believeth not the evil persuasions of the enemy. As in prosperity I please him, so in adversity I do not displease.

4. "The prudent lover considereth not the gift of the lover so much as the love of the giver. He looketh for the affection more than the value, and setteth all gifts lower than the Beloved. The noble lover resteth not in the gift, but in Me above every gift.

5. "All is not lost, though thou sometimes think of Me or of My saints, less than thou shouldest desire. That good and sweet affection which thou sometimes perceivest is the effect of present grace and some foretaste of the heavenly country; but hereon thou must not too much depend, for it goeth and cometh. But to strive against the evil motions of the mind which come to us, and to resist the suggestions of the devil, is a token of virtue and great merit.

6. "Therefore let not strange fancies disturb thee, whencesoever they arise. Bravely observe thy purpose and thy upright intentions towards God. It is not an illusion when thou art sometimes suddenly carried away into rapture, and then suddenly art brought back to the wonted vanities of thy heart. For thou dost rather unwillingly undergo them than cause them; and so long as they displease thee and thou strivest against them, it is a merit and no loss.

7. "Know thou that thine old enemy altogether striveth to hinder

thy pursuit after good, and to deter thee from every godly exercise, to wit, the contemplation of the Saints, the pious remembrance of My passion, the profitable recollection of sin, the keeping of thy own heart, and the steadfast purpose to grow in virtue. He suggesteth to thee many evil thoughts, that he may work in thee weariness and terror, and so draw thee away from prayer and holy reading. Humble confession displeaseth him, and if he were able he would make thee to cease from Communion. Believe him not, nor heed him, though many a time he hath laid for thee the snares of deceit. Account it to be from him, when he suggesteth evil and unclean thoughts. Say unto him, 'Depart unclean spirit; put on shame, miserable one; horribly unclean art thou, who bringest such things to mine ears. Depart from me, detestable deceiver; thou shalt have no part in me; but Jesus shall be with me, as a strong warrior, and thou shalt stand confounded. Rather would I die and bear all suffering, than consent unto thee. Hold thy peace and be dumb; I will not hear thee more, though thou plottest more snares against me. *The Lord is my light and my salvation: whom then shall I fear? Though a host of men should rise up against me, yet shall not my heart be afraid. The Lord is my strength and my Redeemer.'*[1]

8. "Strive thou like a good soldier; and if sometimes thou fail through weakness, put on thy strength more bravely than before, trusting in My more abundant grace, and take thou much heed of vain confidence and pride. Because of it many are led into error, and sometimes fall into blindness well-nigh irremediable. Let this ruin of the proud, who foolishly lift themselves up, be to thee for a warning and a continual exhortation to humility."

CHAPTER VII

OF HIDING OUR GRACE UNDER THE GUARD OF HUMILITY

"My Son, it is better and safer for thee to hide the grace of devotion, and not to lift thyself up on high, nor to speak much thereof, nor to value it greatly; but rather to despise thyself, and to fear as though this grace were given to one unworthy thereof. Nor must thou depend too much upon this feeling, for it can very quickly be

[1] Psalms xxvii. 1-3; xix 14.

turned into its opposite. Think when thou art in a state of grace how miserable and poor thou art wont to be without grace. Nor is there advance in spiritual life in this alone, that thou hast the grace of consolation, but that thou humbly and unselfishly and patiently takest the withdrawal thereof; so that thou cease not from the exercise of prayer, nor suffer thy other common duties to be in anywise neglected; rather do thy task more readily, as though thou hadst gained more strength and knowledge; and do not altogether neglect thyself because of the dearth and anxiety of spirit which thou feelest.

2. "For there are many who, when things have not gone prosperous with them, become forthwith impatient or slothful. *For the way of a man is not in himself,*[1] but it is God's to give and to console, when He will, and as much as He will, and whom He will, as it shall please Him, and no further. Some who were presumptuous because of the grace of devotion within them, have destroyed themselves, because they would do more than they were able, not considering the measure of their own littleness, but rather following the impulse of the heart than the judgment of the reason. And because they presumed beyond what was well-pleasing unto God, therefore they quickly lost grace. They became poor and were left vile, who had built for themselves their nest in heaven; so that being humbled and stricken with poverty, they might learn not to fly with their own wings, but to put their trust under My feathers. They who are as yet new and unskilled in the way of the Lord, unless they rule themselves after the counsel of the wise, may easily be deceived and led away.

3. "But if they wish to follow their own fancies rather than trust the experience of others, the result will be very dangerous to them if they still refuse to be drawn away from their own notion. Those who are wise in their own conceits, seldom patiently endure to be ruled by others. It is better to have a small portion of wisdom with humility, and a slender understanding, than great treasures of sciences with vain self-esteem. It is better for thee to have less than much of what may make thee proud. He doeth not very discreetly who giveth himself entirely to joy, forgetting his former helplessness and the chaste fear of the Lord, which feareth to lose the grace

[1] Jeremiah x. 23.

offered. Nor is he very wise, after a manly sort, who in time of adversity, or any trouble whatsoever, beareth himself too despairingly, and feeleth concerning Me less trustfully than he ought.

4. "He who in time of peace willeth to be oversecure shall be often found in time of war overdispirited and full of fears. If thou knewest always how to continue humble and moderate in thyself, and to guide and rule thine own spirit well, thou wouldest not so quickly fall into danger and mischief. It is good counsel that when fervour of spirit is kindled, thou shouldest meditate how it will be with thee when the light is taken away. Which when it doth happen, remember that still the light may return again, which I have taken away for a time for a warning to thee, and also for mine own glory. Such a trial is often more useful than if thou hadst always things prosperous according to thine own will.

5. "For merits are not to be reckoned by this, that a man hath many visions or consolations, or that he is skilled in the Scriptures, or that he is placed in a high situation; but that he is grounded upon true humility and filled with divine charity, that he always purely and uprightly seeketh the honour of God, that he setteth not by himself, but unfeignedly despiseth himself, and even rejoiceth to be despised and humbled by others more than to be honoured."

CHAPTER VIII

OF A LOW ESTIMATION OF SELF IN THE SIGHT OF GOD

I WILL speak unto my Lord who am but dust and ashes. If I count myself more, behold Thou standest against me, and my iniquities bear true testimony, and I cannot gainsay it. But if I abase myself, and bring myself to nought, and shrink from all self-esteem, and grind myself to dust, which I am, Thy grace will be favourable unto me, and Thy light will be near unto my heart; and all self-esteem, how little soever it be, shall be swallowed up in the depths of my nothingness, and shall perish for ever. There Thou showest to me myself, what I am, what I was, and whither I have come: *so foolish was I and ignorant*.[1] If I am left to myself, behold I am

[1] Psalm lxxiii. 22.

nothing, I am all weakness; but if suddenly Thou look upon me, immediately I am made strong, and filled with new joy. And it is great marvel that I am so suddenly lifted up, and so graciously embraced by Thee, since I am always being carried to the deep by my own weight.

2. This is the doing of Thy love which freely goeth before me and succoureth me in so many necessities, which guardeth me also in great dangers and snatcheth me, as I may truly say, from innumerable evils. For verily, by loving myself amiss, I lost myself, and by seeking and sincerely loving Thee alone, I found both myself and Thee, and through love I have brought myself to yet deeper nothingness: because Thou, O most sweet Lord, dealest with me beyond all merit, and above all which I dare ask or think.

3. Blessed be Thou, O my God, because though I be unworthy of all Thy benefits, Thy bountiful and infinite goodness never ceaseth to do good even to ingrates and to those who are turned far from Thee. Turn Thou us unto Thyself, that we may be grateful, humble, and godly, for Thou art our salvation, our courage, and our strength.

CHAPTER IX

THAT ALL THINGS ARE TO BE REFERRED TO GOD, AS THE FINAL END

"My Son, I must be thy Supreme and final end, if thou desirest to be truly happy. Out of such purpose thy affection shall be purified, which too often is sinfully bent upon itself and upon created things. For if thou seekest thyself in any matter, straightway thou wilt fail within thyself and grow barren. Therefore refer everything to Me first of all, for it is I who gave thee all. So look upon each blessing as flowing from the Supreme Good, and thus all things are to be attributed to Me as their source.

2. "From Me the humble and great, the poor and the rich, draw water as from a living fountain, and those who serve Me with a free and faithful spirit shall receive grace for grace. But he who will glory apart from Me, or will be delighted with any good which lieth in himself, shall not be established in true joy, nor shall be enlarged in heart, but shall be greatly hindered and thrown into tribulation.

Therefore thou must not ascribe any good to thyself, nor look upon virtue as belonging to any man, but ascribe it all unto God, without whom man hath nothing. I gave all, I will receive all again, and with great strictness require I the giving of thanks.

3. "This is the Truth, and by it the vanity of boasting is put to flight. And if heavenly grace and true charity shall enter into thee, there shall be no envy, nor straitening of the heart, nor shall any self-love take possession of thee. For divine charity conquereth all things, and enlargeth all the powers of the soul. If thou art truly wise, thou wilt rejoice in Me alone, thou wilt hope in Me alone; for there is *none good but one, that is God,*[1] Who is to be praised above all things, and in all things to receive blessing."

CHAPTER X

THAT IT IS SWEET TO DESPISE THE WORLD AND TO SERVE GOD

Now will I speak again, O my Lord, and hold not my peace; I will say in the ears of my God, my Lord, and my King, who is exalted above all, *Oh how plentiful is Thy goodness which Thou hast laid up for them that fear Thee!*[2] But what art Thou to those who love Thee? What to those who serve Thee with their whole heart? Truly unspeakable is the sweetness of the contemplation of Thee, which Thou bestowest upon those who love Thee. In this most of all Thou hast showed me the sweetness of Thy charity, that when I was not, Thou madest me, and when I wandered far from Thee, Thou broughtest me back that I might serve Thee, and commandedst me to love Thee.

2. O Fountain of perpetual love, what shall I say concerning Thee? How shall I be unmindful of Thee, who didst vouchsafe to remember me, even after I pined away and perished? Thou hast had mercy beyond all hope upon Thy servant, and hast showed Thy grace and friendship beyond all deserving. What reward shall I render Thee for this Thy grace? For it is not given unto all to renounce this world and its affairs, and to take up a religious life. For is it a great

[1] Luke xviii. 19.   [2] Psalm xxxi. 21.

thing that I should serve Thee, whom every creature ought to serve? It ought not to seem a great thing to me to serve Thee; but rather this appeareth to me a great and wonderful thing, that Thou vouchsafest to receive as Thy servant one so poor and unworthy, and to join him unto Thy chosen servants.

3. Behold all things which I have are Thine, and with them I serve Thee. And yet verily it is Thou who servest me, rather than I Thee. Behold the heaven and the earth which Thou hast created for the service of men; they are at Thy bidding, and perform daily whatsoever Thou dost command. Yea, and this is little; for Thou hast even ordained the Angels for the service of man. But it surpasseth even all these things, that Thou Thyself didst vouchsafe to minister unto man, and didst promise that Thou wouldest give Thyself unto him.

4. What shall I render unto Thee for all these Thy manifold mercies? Oh that I were able to serve Thee all the days of my life! Oh that even for one day I were enabled to do Thee service worthy of Thyself! For verily Thou art worthy of all service, all honour, and praise without end. Verily Thou art my God, and I am Thy poor servant, who am bound to serve Thee with all my strength, nor ought I ever to grow weary of Thy praise. This is my wish, this is my exceeding great desire, and whatsoever is lacking to me, vouchsafe Thou to supply.

5. It is great honour, great glory to serve Thee, and to despise all for Thy sake. For they shall have great grace who of their own will shall submit themselves to Thy most holy service. They who for Thy love have cast away every carnal delight shall find the sweetest consolation of the Holy Ghost. They who enter the narrow way of life for Thy Name's sake, and have put away all worldly cares, shall attain great liberty of spirit.

6. Oh grateful and delightsome service of God, whereby man is made truly free and holy! Oh sacred condition of the religious servant, which maketh man equal to the Angels, well-pleasing unto God, terrible to evil spirits, and acceptable to all faithful ones! Oh service to be embraced and ever desired, in which the highest good is promised, and joy is gained which shall remain for evermore!

CHAPTER XI

THAT THE DESIRES OF THE HEART ARE TO BE EXAMINED AND GOVERNED

"My Son, thou hast still many things to learn, which thou hast not well learned yet."

2. What are they, Lord?

3. "To place thy desire altogether in subjection to My good pleasure, and not to be a lover of thyself, but an earnest seeker of My will. Thy desires often excite and urge thee forward; but consider with thyself whether thou art not more moved for thine own objects than for My honour. If it is Myself that thou seekest, thou shalt be well content with whatsoever I shall ordain; but if any pursuit of thine own lieth hidden within thee, behold it is this which hindereth and weigheth thee down.

4. "Beware, therefore, lest thou strive too earnestly after some desire which thou hast conceived, without taking counsel of Me; lest haply it repent thee afterwards, and that displease thee which before pleased, and for which thou didst long as for a great good. For not every affection which seemeth good is to be forthwith followed; neither is every opposite affection to be immediately avoided. Sometimes it is expedient to use restraint even in good desires and wishes, lest through importunity thou fall into distraction of mind, lest through want of discipline thou become a stumbling-block to others, or lest by the resistance of others thou be suddenly disturbed and brought to confusion.

5. "Sometimes, indeed, it is needful to use violence, and manfully to strive against the sensual appetite, and not to consider what the flesh may or not will; but rather to strive after this, that it may become subject, however unwillingly, to the spirit. And for so long it ought to be chastised and compelled to undergo slavery, even until it be ready for all things, and learn to be contented with little, to be delighted with things simple, and never to murmur at any inconvenience."

CHAPTER XII

OF THE INWARD GROWTH OF PATIENCE, AND OF THE STRUGGLE
AGAINST EVIL DESIRES

O LORD God, I see that patience is very necessary unto me; for many things in this life fall out contrary. For howsoever I may have contrived for my peace, my life cannot go on without strife and trouble.

2. "Thou speakest truly, My Son. For I will not that thou seek such a peace as is without trials, and knoweth no adversities; but rather that thou shouldest judge thyself to have found peace, when thou art tried with manifold tribulations, and proved by many adversities. If thou shalt say that thou art not able to bear much, how then wilt thou sustain the fire hereafter? Of two evils we should always choose the less. Therefore, that thou mayest escape eternal torments hereafter, strive on God's behalf to endure present evils bravely. Thinkest thou that the children of this world suffer nought, or but little? Thou wilt not find it so, even though thou find out the most prosperous.

3. "'But,' thou wilt say, 'they have many delights, and they follow their own wills, and thus they bear lightly their tribulations.'

4. "Be it so, grant that they have what they list; but how long, thinkest thou, will it last? Behold, like the smoke those who are rich in this world will pass away, and no record shall remain of their past joys. Yea, even while they yet live, they rest not without bitterness and weariness and fear. For from the very same thing wherein they find delight, thence they oftentimes have the punishment of sorrow. Justly it befalleth them, that because out of measure they seek out and pursue pleasures, they enjoy them not without confusion and bitterness. Oh how short, how false, how inordinate and wicked are all these pleasures! Yet because of their sottishness and blindness men do not understand; but like brute beasts, for the sake of a little pleasure of this corruptible life, they incur death of the soul. *Thou therefore, my son, go not after thy lusts, but refrain thyself from thine appetites.*[1] *Delight thou in the Lord, and He shall give thee thy heart's desire.*[2]

[1] Ecclesiastes xviii. 30.   [2] Psalm xxxvii. 4.

5. "For if thou wilt truly find delight, and be abundantly comforted of Me, behold in the contempt of all worldly things and in the avoidance of all worthless pleasures shall be thy blessing, and fulness of consolation shall be given thee. And the more thou withdrawest thyself from all solace of creatures, the more sweet and powerful consolations shalt thou find. But at the first thou shalt not attain to them, without some sorrow and hard striving. Long-accustomed habit will oppose, but it shall be overcome by better habit. The flesh will murmur again and again, but will be restrained by fervour of spirit. The old serpent will urge and embitter thee, but will be put to flight by prayer; moreover, by useful labour his entrance will be greatly obstructed."

CHAPTER XIII

OF THE OBEDIENCE OF ONE IN LOWLY SUBJECTION AFTER THE EXAMPLE OF JESUS CHRIST

"My Son, he who striveth to withdraw himself from obedience, withdraweth himself also from grace, and he who seeketh private advantages, loseth those which are common unto all. If a man submit not freely and willingly to one set over him, it is a sign that his flesh is not yet perfectly subject to himself, but often resisteth and murmureth. Learn therefore quickly to submit thyself to him who is over thee, if thou seekest to bring thine own flesh into subjection. For the outward enemy is very quickly overcome if the inner man have not been laid low. There is no more grievous and deadly enemy to the soul than thou art to thyself, if thou art not led by the Spirit. Thou must not altogether conceive contempt for thyself, if thou wilt prevail against flesh and blood. Because as yet thou inordinately lovest thyself, therefore thou shrinkest from yielding thyself to the will of others.

2. "But what great thing is it that thou, who art dust and nothingness, yieldest thyself to man for God's sake, when I, the Almighty and the Most High, who created all things out of nothing, subjected Myself to man for thy sake? I became the most humble and despised of men, that by My humility thou mightest overcome thy pride. Learn to obey, O dust! Learn to humble thyself, O earth and

clay, and to bow thyself beneath the feet of all. Learn to crush thy passions, and to yield thyself in all subjection.

3. "Be zealous against thyself, nor suffer pride to live within thee, but so show thyself subject and of no reputation, that all may be able to walk over thee, and tread thee down as the clay in the streets. What hast thou, O foolish man, of which to complain? What, O vile sinner, canst thou answer those who speak against thee, seeing thou hast so often offended God, and many a time hast deserved hell? But Mine eye hath spared thee, because thy soul was precious in My sight; that thou mightest know My love, and mightest be thankful for My benefits; and that thou mightest give thyself altogether to true subjection and humility, and patiently bear the contempt which thou meritest."

CHAPTER XIV

OF MEDITATION UPON THE HIDDEN JUDGMENTS OF GOD, THAT WE MAY NOT BE LIFTED UP BECAUSE OF OUR WELL-DOING

THOU sendest forth Thy judgments against me, O Lord, and shakest all my bones with fear and trembling, and my soul trembleth exceedingly. I stand astonished, and remember that *the heavens are not clean in thy sight.*[1] If *Thou chargest Thine angels with folly,* and didst spare them not, how shall it be unto me? Stars have fallen from heaven, and what shall I dare who am but dust? They whose works seemed to be praiseworthy, fell into the lowest depths, and they who did eat Angels' food, them have I seen delighted with the husks that the swine do eat.

2. There is therefore no holiness, if Thou O Lord, withdraw Thine hand. No wisdom profiteth, if Thou leave off to guide the helm. No strength availeth, if Thou cease to preserve. No purity is secure, if Thou protect it not. No self-keeping availeth, if Thy holy watching be not there. For when we are left alone we are swallowed up and perish, but when we are visited, we are raised up, and we live. For indeed we are unstable, but are made strong through Thee; we grow cold, but are rekindled by Thee.

[1] Job xv. 15.

3. Oh, how humbly and abjectly must I reckon of myself, how must I weigh it as nothing, if I seem to have nothing good! Oh, how profoundly ought I to submit myself to Thy unfathomable judgments, O Lord, when I find myself nothing else save nothing, and again nothing! Oh weight unmeasurable, oh ocean which cannot be crossed over, where I find nothing of myself save nothing altogether! Where, then, is the hiding-place of glory, where the confidence begotten of virtue? All vain-glory is swallowed up in the depths of Thy judgments against me.

4. What is all flesh in Thy sight? *For how shall the clay boast against Him that fashioned it?*[2] How can he be lifted up in vain speech whose heart is subjected in truth to God? The whole world shall not lift him up whom Truth hath subdued; nor shall he be moved by the mouth of all who praise him, who hath placed all his hope in God. For they themselves who speak, behold, they are all nothing; for they shall cease with the sound of their words, *but the truth of the Lord endureth for ever.*[3]

CHAPTER XV

HOW WE MUST STAND AND SPEAK, IN EVERYTHING THAT WE DESIRE

"My Son, speak thou thus in every matter, 'Lord, if it please Thee, let this come to pass. Lord, if this shall be for Thine honour, let it be done in Thy Name. Lord, if thou see it good for me, and approve it as useful, then grant me to use it for Thy honour. But if thou knowest that it shall be hurtful unto me, and not profitable for the health of my soul, take the desire away from me'! For not every desire is from the Holy Ghost, although it appear to a man right and good. It is difficult to judge with certainty whether a good or an evil spirit move thee to desire this or that, or whether thou art moved by thine own spirit. Many have been deceived at the last, who seemed at the beginning to be moved by a good spirit.

2. "Therefore, whatsoever seemeth to thee desirable, thou must always desire and seek after it with the fear of God and humility of heart, and most of all, must altogether resign thyself, and com-

[2] Psalm xxix. 16.   [3] Psalm cxvii. 2.

mit all unto Me and say, 'Lord, thou knowest what is best; let this or that be, according as Thou wilt. Give what Thou wilt, so much as Thou wilt, when Thou wilt. Do with me as Thou knowest best, and as best shall please Thee, and as shall be most to Thine honour. Place me where Thou wilt, and freely work Thy will with me in all things. I am in Thine hand, and turn me in my course. Behold, I am Thy servant, ready for all things; for I desire to live not to myself but to Thee. Oh, that I might live worthily and perfectly.'"

A PRAYER TO BE ENABLED TO DO GOD'S WILL PERFECTLY

3. Grant me Thy grace, most merciful Jesus, that it may be with me, and work in me, and persevere with me, even unto the end. Grant that I may ever desire and wish whatsoever is most pleasing and dear unto Thee. Let Thy will be mine, and let my will alway follow Thine, and entirely accord with it. May I choose and reject whatsoever Thou dost; yea, let it be impossible for me to choose or reject except according to Thy will.

4. Grant that I may die to all worldly things, and for Thy sake love to be despised and unknown in this world. Grant unto me, above all things that I can desire, to rest in Thee, and that in Thee my heart may be at peace. Thou art the true peace of the heart, Thou alone its rest; apart from Thee all things are hard and unquiet. In Thee alone, the supreme and eternal God, *I will lay me down in peace and take my rest.*[1] Amen.

CHAPTER XVI

THAT TRUE SOLACE IS TO BE SOUGHT IN GOD ALONE

WHATSOEVER I am able to desire or to think of for my solace, I look for it not here, but hereafter. For if I alone had all the solaces of this world, and were able to enjoy all its delights, it is certain that they could not endure long. Wherefore, O my soul, thou canst be fully comforted and perfectly refreshed, only in God, the Comforter of the poor, and the lifter up of the humble. Wait but a little while, my soul, wait for the Divine promise, and thou shalt have abundance

[1] Psalm iv. 9.

of all good things in heaven. If thou longest too inordinately for the things which are now, thou shalt lose those which are eternal and heavenly. Let temporal things be in the use, eternal things in the desire. Thou canst not be satisfied with any temporal good, for thou wast not created for the enjoyment of these.

2. Although thou hadst all the good things which ever were created, yet couldst not thou be happy and blessed; all thy blessedness and thy felicity lieth in God who created all things; not such felicity as seemeth good to the foolish lover of the world, but such as Christ's good and faithful servants wait for, and as the spiritual and pure in heart sometimes taste, whose *conversation is in heaven.*[1] All human solace is empty and short-lived; blessed and true is that solace which is felt inwardly, springing from the truth. The godly man everywhere beareth about with him his own Comforter, Jesus, and saith unto Him: "Be with me, Lord Jesus, always and everywhere. Let it be my comfort to be able to give up cheerfully all human comfort. And if Thy consolation fail me, let Thy will and righteous approval be alway with me for the highest comfort. *For Thou wilt not always be chiding, neither keepest Thou Thine anger for ever."*[2]

CHAPTER XVII

THAT ALL CARE IS TO BE CAST UPON GOD

"My Son, suffer me to do with thee what I will; I know what is expedient for thee. Thou thinkest as a man, in many things thou judgest as human affection persuadeth thee."

2. Lord, what Thou sayest is true. Greater is Thy care for me than all the care which I am able to take for myself. For too insecurely doth he stand who casteth not all his care upon Thee. Lord, so long as my will standeth right and firm in Thee, do with me what Thou wilt, for whatsoever Thou shalt do with me cannot be aught but good. Blessed be Thou if Thou wilt leave me in darkness: blessed also be Thou if Thou wilt leave me in light. Blessed be Thou if Thou vouchsafe to comfort me, and always blessed be Thou if Thou cause me to be troubled.

[1] Philippians iii. 20.   [2] Psalm cii. 9.

3. "My Son! even thus thou must stand if thou desirest to walk with Me. Thou must be ready alike for suffering or rejoicing. Thou must be poor and needy as willingly as full and rich."

4. Lord, I will willingly bear for Thee whatsoever Thou wilt have to come upon me. Without choice I will receive from Thy hand good and evil, sweet and bitter, joy and sadness, and will give Thee thanks for all things which shall happen unto me. Keep me from all sin, and I will not fear death nor hell. Only cast me not away for ever, nor blot me out of the book of life. Then no tribulation which shall come upon me shall do me hurt.

CHAPTER XVIII

THAT TEMPORAL MISERIES ARE TO BE BORNE PATIENTLY AFTER THE EXAMPLE OF CHRIST

"My Son! I came down from heaven for thy salvation; I took upon Me thy miseries not of necessity, but drawn by love that thou mightest learn patience and mightest bear temporal miseries without murmuring. For from the hour of My birth, until My death upon the Cross, I ceased not from bearing of sorrow; I had much lack of temporal things; I oftentimes heard many reproaches against Myself; I gently bore contradictions and hard words; I received ingratitude for benefits, blasphemies for My miracles, rebukes for My doctrine."

2. Lord, because Thou wast patient in Thy life, herein most of all fulfilling the commandment of Thy Father, it is well that I, miserable sinner, should patiently bear myself according to Thy will, and as long as Thou wilt have it so, should bear about with me for my salvation, the burden of this corruptible life. For although the present life seemeth burdensome, it is nevertheless already made very full of merit through Thy grace, and to those who are weak it becometh easier and brighter through Thy example and the footsteps of Thy saints; but it is also much more full of consolation than it was of old, under the old Testament, when the gate of heaven remained shut; and even the way to heaven seemed more obscure when so few cared to seek after the heavenly kingdom. But not even

those who were then just and in the way of salvation were able, before Thy Passion and the ransom of Thy holy Death, to enter the kingdom of heaven.

3. Oh what great thanks am I bound to give Thee, who hast vouchsafed to show me and all faithful people the good and right way to Thine eternal kingdom, for Thy way is our way, and by holy patience we walk to Thee who art our Crown. If Thou hadst not gone before and taught us, who would care to follow? Oh, how far would they have gone backward if they had not beheld Thy glorious example! Behold we are still lukewarm, though we have heard of Thy many signs and discourses; what would become of us if we had not such a light to help us follow Thee?

CHAPTER XIX

OF BEARING INJURIES, AND WHO SHALL BE APPROVED
AS TRULY PATIENT

"What sayest thou, My Son? Cease to complain; consider My suffering and that of My saints. *Thou hast not yet resisted unto blood*.[1] It is little which thou sufferest in comparison with those who have suffered so many things, have been so strongly tempted, so grievously troubled, so manywise proved and tried. Thou oughtest therefore to call to mind the more grievous sufferings of others that thou mightest bear thy lesser ones more easily, and if they seem not to thee little, see that it is not thy impatience which is the cause of this. But whether they be little or whether they be great, study to bear them all with patience.

2. "So far as thou settest thyself to bear patiently, so far thou dost wisely and art deserving of the more merit; thou shalt also bear the more easily if thy mind and habit are carefully trained hereunto. And say not 'I cannot bear these things from such a man, nor are things of this kind to be borne by me, for he hath done me grievous harm and imputeth to me what I had never thought: but from another I will suffer patiently, such things as I see I ought to suffer.' Foolish is such a thought as this, for it considereth not the

[1] Hebrews xii. 4.

virtue of patience, nor by whom that virtue is to be crowned, but it rather weigheth persons and offences against self.

3. "He is not truly patient who will only suffer as far as seemeth right to himself and from whom he pleaseth. But the truly patient man considereth not by what man he is tried, whether by one above him, or by an equal or inferior, whether by a good and holy man, or a perverse and unworthy; but indifferently from every creature, whatsoever or how often soever adversity happeneth to him, he gratefully accepteth all from the hand of God and counteth it great gain: for with God nothing which is borne for His sake, however small, shall lose its reward.

4. "Be thou therefore ready for the fight if thou wilt have the victory. Without striving thou canst not win the crown of patience; if thou wilt not suffer thou refusest to be crowned. But if thou desirest to be crowned, strive manfully, endure patiently. Without labour thou drawest not near to rest, nor without fighting comest thou to victory."

5. Make possible to me, O Lord, by grace what seemeth impossible to me by nature. Thou knowest how little I am able to bear, and how quickly I am cast down when a like adversity riseth up against me. Whatsoever trial of tribulation may come to me, may it become unto me pleasing and acceptable, for to suffer and be vexed for Thy sake is exceeding healthful to the soul.

CHAPTER XX

OF CONFESSION OF OUR INFIRMITY AND OF THE MISERIES OF THIS LIFE

I WILL *acknowledge my sin unto Thee;*[1] I will confess to Thee, Lord, my infirmity. It is often a small thing which casteth me down and maketh me sad. I resolve that I will act bravely, but when a little temptation cometh, immediately I am in a great strait. Wonderfully small sometimes is the matter whence a grievous temptation cometh, and whilst I imagine myself safe for a little space; when I am not considering, I find myself often almost overcome by a little puff of wind.

2. Behold, therefore, O Lord, my humility and my frailty, which

[1] Psalm xxxii. 5.

is altogether known to Thee. Be merciful unto me, and *draw me out of the mire that I sink not*,[2] lest I ever remain cast down. This is what frequently throweth me backward and confoundeth me before Thee, that I am so liable to fall, so weak to resist my passions. And though their assault is not altogether according to my will, it is violent and grievous, and it altogether wearieth me to live thus daily in conflict. Herein is my infirmity made known to me, that hateful fancies always rush in far more easily than they depart.

3. Oh that Thou, most mighty God of Israel, Lover of all faithful souls, wouldst look upon the labour and sorrow of Thy servant, and give him help in all things whereunto he striveth. Strengthen me with heavenly fortitude, lest the old man, this miserable flesh, not being yet fully subdued to the spirit, prevail to rule over me; against which I ought to strive so long as I remain in this most miserable life. Oh what a life is this, where tribulations and miseries cease not, where all things are full of snares and of enemies, for when one tribulation or temptation goeth, another cometh, yea, while the former conflict is yet raging others come more in number and unexpected.

4. And how can the life of man be loved, seeing that it hath so many bitter things, that it is subjected to so many calamities and miseries. How can it be even called life, when it produces so many deaths and plagues? The world is often reproached because it is deceitful and vain, yet notwithstanding it is not easily given up, because the lusts of the flesh have too much rule over it. Some draw us to love, some to hate. The lust of the flesh, the lust of the eyes, and the pride of life, these draw to love of the world; but the punishments and miseries which righteously follow these things, bring forth hatred of the world and weariness.

5. But, alas! an evil desire conquereth a mind given to the world, and thinketh it happiness to be under the nettles[3] because it savoureth not nor perceiveth the sweetness of God nor the inward gracefulness of virtue. But they who perfectly despise the world and strive to live unto God in holy discipline, these are not ignorant of the divine sweetness promised to all who truly deny themselves and see clearly how grievously the world erreth, and in how many ways it is deceived.

[2] Psalm lix. 16.   [3] Job xxx. 7.

CHAPTER XXI

THAT WE MUST REST IN GOD ABOVE ALL GOODS AND GIFTS

ABOVE all things and in all things thou shalt rest alway in the Lord, O my soul, for he himself is the eternal rest of the saints. Grant me, most sweet and loving Jesus, to rest in Thee above every creature, above all health and beauty, above all glory and honour, above all power and dignity, above all knowledge and skilfulness, above all riches and arts, above all joy and exultation, above all fame and praise, above all sweetness and consolation, above all hope and promise, above all merit and desire, above all gifts and rewards which Thou canst give and pour forth, above all joy and jubilation which the mind is able to receive and feel; in a word, above Angels and Archangels and all the army of heaven, above all things visible and invisible, and above everything which Thou, O my God, art not.

2. For Thou, O Lord, my God, art best above all things; Thou only art the Most High, Thou only the Almighty, Thou only the All-sufficient, and the Fulness of all things; Thou only the All-delightsome and the All-comforting; Thou alone the altogether lovely and altogether loving; Thou alone the Most Exalted and Most Glorious above all things; in Whom all things are, and were, and ever shall be, altogether and all-perfect. And thus it falleth short and is insufficient whatsoever Thou givest to me without Thyself or whatsoever Thou revealest or dost promise concerning Thyself, whilst Thou art not seen or fully possessed: since verily my heart cannot truly rest nor be entirely content, except it rest in Thee, and go beyond all gifts and every creature.

3. O my most beloved Spouse, Jesus Christ, most holy lover of my soul, Ruler of this whole Creation, who shall give me the wings of true liberty, that I may flee to Thee and find rest? Oh when shall it be given me to be open to receive Thee to the full, and to see how sweet Thou art, O Lord my God? When shall I collect myself altogether in Thee, that because of Thy love I may not feel myself at all, but may know Thee only above every sense and measure, in measure not known to others. But now I ofttimes groan, and bear my sad estate with sorrow; because many evils befall me in this vale

of miseries which continually disturb and fill me with sorrow, and encloud me, continually hinder and fill me with care, allure and entangle me, that I cannot have free access to Thee, nor enjoy that sweet intercourse which is always near at hand to the blessed spirits. Let my deep sighing come before Thee, and my manifold desolation on the earth.

4. O Jesus, Light of Eternal Glory, solace of the wandering soul, before Thee my mouth is without speech, and my silence speaketh to Thee. How long will my Lord delay to come unto me? Let Him come unto me, His poor and humble one, and make me glad. Let Him put forth His hand, and deliver His holy one from every snare. Come, Oh come; for without Thee shall be no joyful day or hour, for Thou art my joy, and without Thee is my table empty. I am miserable, and in a manner imprisoned and loaded with fetters, until Thou refresh me by the light of Thy presence, and give me liberty, and show Thy loving countenance.

5. Let others seek some other thing instead of Thee, whatsoever it shall please them; but for my part nothing else pleaseth or shall please, save Thou, my God, my hope, my eternal salvation. I will not hold my peace, nor cease to implore, until Thy grace return, and until Thou speak to me within.

6. "Behold, here I am! Behold, I come to thee, for thou didst call Me. Thy tears and the longing of thy soul, thy humbleness and contrition of heart have inclined Me, and brought Me to thee."

7. And I said Lord, I have called upon Thee, and I have longed to enjoy Thee, being ready to reject everything for Thy sake. For Thou didst first move me to seek Thee. Therefore, blessed be Thou, O Lord, who has wrought this good work upon Thy servant, according to the multitude of Thy mercy. What then hath Thy servant to say in Thy presence, save to humble himself greatly before Thee, being alway mindful of his own iniquity and vileness. For there is none like unto Thee in all marvels of heaven and earth. Excellent are Thy works, true are Thy judgments, and by Thy Providence are all things governed. Therefore praise and glory be unto Thee, O Wisdom of the Father, let my mouth and my soul and all created things praise and bless Thee together.

CHAPTER XXII

OF THE RECOLLECTION OF GOD'S MANIFOLD BENEFITS

OPEN, O Lord, my heart in Thy law, and teach me to walk in the way of Thy commandments. Grant me to understand Thy will and to be mindful of Thy benefits, both general and special, with great reverence and diligent meditation, that thus I may be able worthily to give Thee thanks. Yet I know and confess that I cannot render Thee due praises for the least of Thy mercies. I am less than the least of all the good things which Thou gavest me; and when I consider Thy majesty, my spirit faileth because of the greatness thereof.

2. All things which we have in the soul and in the body, and whatsoever things we possess, whether outwardly or inwardly, naturally or supernaturally, are Thy good gifts, and prove Thee, from whom we have received them all, to be good, gentle, and kind. Although one receiveth many things, and another fewer, yet all are Thine, and without Thee not even the least thing can be possessed. He who hath received greater cannot boast that it is of his own merit, nor lift himself up above others, nor contemn those beneath him; for he is the greater and the better who ascribeth least to himself, and in giving thanks is the humbler and more devout; and he who holdeth himself to be viler than all, and judgeth himself to be the more unworthy, is the apter for receiving greater things.

3. But he who hath received fewer gifts, ought not to be cast down, nor to take it amiss, nor to envy him who is richer; but rather ought he to look unto Thee, and to greatly extol Thy goodness, for Thou pourest forth Thy gifts so richly, so freely and largely, without respect of persons. All things come of Thee; therefore in all things shalt thou be praised. Thou knowest what is best to be given to each; and why this man hath less, and that more, is not for us but for Thee to understand, for unto Thee each man's deservings are fully known.

4. Wherefore, O Lord God, I reckon it even a great benefit, not to have many things, whence praise and glory may appear outwardly, and after the thought of men. For so it is that he who considereth his own poverty and vileness, ought not only to draw therefrom no grief

or sorrow, or sadness of spirit, but rather comfort and cheerfulness; because Thou, Lord, hast chosen the poor and humble, and those who are poor in this world, to be Thy friends and acquaintance. So give all Thine apostles witness whom Thou hast made princes in all lands. Yet they had their conversation in this world blameless, so humble and meek, without any malice or deceit, *that they even rejoiced to suffer rebukes for Thy Name's sake,*[1] and what things the world hateth, they embraced with great joy.

5. Therefore ought nothing so much to rejoice him who loveth Thee and knoweth Thy benefits, as Thy will in him, and the good pleasure of Thine eternal Providence, wherewith he ought to be so contented and comforted, that he would as willingly be the least as any other would be the greatest, as peaceable and contented in the lowest as in the highest place, and as willingly held of small and low account and of no name or reputation as to be more honourable and greater in the world than others. For Thy will and the love of Thine honour ought to go before all things, and to please and comfort him more, than all benefits that are given or may be given to himself.

CHAPTER XXIII

OF FOUR THINGS WHICH BRING GREAT PEACE

"My Son, now will I teach thee the way of peace and of true liberty."

2. Do, O my Lord, as Thou sayest, for this is pleasing unto me to hear.

3. "Strive, My Son, to do another's will rather than thine own. Choose always to have less rather than more. Seek always after the lowest place, and to be subject to all. Wish always and pray that the will of God be fulfilled in thee. Behold, such a man as this entereth into the inheritance of peace and quietness."

4. O my Lord, this Thy short discourse hath in itself much of perfectness. It is short in words but full of meaning, and abundant in fruit. For if it were possible that I should fully keep it, disturbance would not so easily arise within me. For as often as I feel myself

[1] Acts v. 41.

disquieted and weighed down, I find myself to have gone back from this teaching. But Thou, Who art Almighty, and always lovest progress in the soul, vouchsafe more grace, that I may be enabled to fulfil Thy exhortation, and work out my salvation.

A PRAYER AGAINST EVIL THOUGHTS

5. *O Lord my God, be not Thou far from me, my God, haste Thee to help me,*[1] for many thoughts and great fears have risen up against me, afflicting my soul. How shall I pass through them unhurt? how shall I break through them?

6. *"I,"* saith He, *"will go before thee, and make the crooked places straight."*[2] I will open the prison doors, and reveal to thee the secret places.

7. Do, Lord, as Thou sayest; and let all evil thoughts fly away before Thy face. This is my hope and my only comfort, to fly unto Thee in all tribulation, to hope in Thee, to call upon Thee from my heart and patiently wait for Thy loving kindness.

A PRAYER FOR ENLIGHTENMENT OF THE MIND

8. Enlighten me, Blessed Jesus, with the brightness of Thy inner light, and cast forth all darkness from the habitation of my heart. Restrain my many wandering thoughts, and carry away the temptations which strive to do me hurt. Fight Thou mightily for me, and drive forth the evil beasts, so call I alluring lusts, that *peace may be within Thy walls and plenteousness of praise within Thy palaces,*[3] even in my pure conscience. Command Thou the winds and the storms, say unto the sea, "Be still," say unto the stormy wind, "Hold thy peace," so shall there be a great calm.

9. *Oh send forth Thy light and Thy truth,*[4] that they may shine upon the earth; for I am but earth without form and void until Thou give me light. Pour forth Thy grace from above; water my heart with the dew of heaven; give the waters of devotion to water the face of the earth, and cause it to bring forth good and perfect fruit. Lift up my mind which is oppressed with the weight of sins, and raise my whole desire to heavenly things; that having tasted the

[1] Psalm lxxi. 12.   [2] Isaiah xlv. 2.   [3] Psalm cxxii. 7.   [4] Psalm xliii. 3.

sweetness of the happiness which is from above, it may take no pleasure in thinking of things of earth.

10. Draw me and deliver me from every unstable comfort of creatures, for no created thing is able to satisfy my desire and to give me comfort. Join me to Thyself by the inseparable bond of love, for Thou alone art sufficient to him that loveth Thee, and without Thee all things are vain toys.

CHAPTER XXIV

OF AVOIDING OF CURIOUS INQUIRY INTO THE LIFE OF ANOTHER

"My Son, be not curious, nor trouble thyself with vain cares. *What is that to thee? Follow thou Me.*[1] For what is it to thee whether a man be this or that, or say or do thus or thus? Thou hast no need to answer for others, but thou must give an answer for thyself. Why therefore dost thou entangle thyself? Behold, I know all men, and I behold all things which are done under the sun; and I know how it standeth with each one, what he thinketh, what he willeth, and to what end his thoughts reach. All things therefore are to be committed to Me; watch thou thyself in godly peace, and leave him who is unquiet to be unquiet as he will. Whatsoever he shall do or say, shall come unto him, for he cannot deceive Me.

2. "Trouble not thyself about the shadow of a great name, nor about the friendship of many, nor about the love of men towards thee. For these things beget distraction and great sorrows of heart. My word should speak freely unto thee, and I would reveal secrets, if only thou didst diligently look for My appearing, and didst open unto Me the gates of thy heart. *Be sober and watch unto prayer,*[2] and humble thyself in all things."

CHAPTER XXV

WHEREIN FIRM PEACE OF HEART AND TRUE PROFIT CONSIST

"My Son, I have said, *Peace I leave with you, My peace I give unto you, not as the world giveth give I unto you.*[3] All men desire peace, but all do not care for the things which belong unto true

---

[1] John xxi. 12.　　　[2] 1 Peter iv. 7.　　　[3] John xiv. 27.

peace. My peace is with the humble and lowly in heart. Thy peace shall be in much patience. If thou heardest Me, and didst follow My voice, thou shouldest enjoy much peace."

2. What then shall I do, Lord?

3. "In everything take heed to thyself what thou doest, and what thou sayest; and direct all thy purpose to this, that thou please Me alone, and desire or seek nothing apart from Me. But, moreover, judge nothing rashly concerning the words or deeds of others, nor meddle with matters which are not committed to thee; and it may be that thou shalt be disturbed little or rarely. Yet never to feel any disquiet, nor to suffer any pain of heart or body, this belongeth not to the present life, but is the state of eternal rest. Therefore count not thyself to have found true peace, if thou hast felt no grief; nor that then all is well if thou hast no adversary; nor that this is perfect if all things fall out according to thy desire. Nor then reckon thyself to be anything great, or think that thou art specially beloved, if thou art in a state of great fervour and sweetness of spirit; for not by these things is the true lover of virtue known, nor in them doth the profit and perfection of man consist."

4. In what then, Lord?

5. "In offering thyself with all thy heart to the Divine Will, in not seeking the things which are thine own, whether great or small, whether temporal or eternal; so that thou remain with the same steady countenance in giving of thanks between prosperity and adversity, weighing all things in an equal balance. If thou be so brave and long-suffering in hope that when inward comfort is taken from thee, thou even prepare thy heart for the more endurance, and justify not thyself, as though thou oughtest not to suffer these heavy things, but dost justify Me in all things that I appoint, and dost bless My Holy Name, then dost thou walk in the true and right way of peace, and shalt have a sure hope that thou shalt again behold My face with joy. For if thou come to an utter contempt of thyself, know that then thou shalt enjoy abundance of peace, as much as is possible where thou art but a wayfaring man."

CHAPTER XXVI

OF THE EXALTATION OF A FREE SPIRIT, WHICH HUMBLE PRAYER MORE
DESERVETH THAN DOTH FREQUENT READING

LORD, this is the work of a perfect man, never to slacken his mind
from attention to heavenly things, and among many cares to pass
along as it were without care, not after the manner of one indifferent, but rather with the privilege of a free mind, cleaving to no
creature with inordinate affection.

2. I beseech Thee, my most merciful Lord God, preserve me from
the cares of this life, lest I become too much entangled; from many
necessities of the body, lest I be taken captive by pleasure; from all
obstacles of the spirit, lest I be broken and cast down with cares. I
say not from those things which the vanity of the world goeth about
after with all eagerness, but from those miseries, which by the uni-
versal curse of mortality weigh down and hold back the soul of thy
servant in punishment, that it cannot enter into liberty of spirit, so
often as it would.

3. O my God, sweetness unspeakable, turn into bitterness all my
fleshly consolation, which draweth me away from the love of eternal
things, and wickedly allureth toward itself by setting before me some
present delight. Let not, O my God, let not flesh and blood prevail
over me, let not the world and its short glory deceive me, let not the
devil and his craftiness supplant me. Give me courage to resist,
patience to endure, constancy to persevere. Grant, in place of all consolations of the world, the most sweet unction of Thy Spirit, and in
place of carnal love, pour into me the love of Thy Name.

4. Behold, food and drink and clothing, and all the other needs
appertaining to the support of the body, are burdensome to the
devout spirit. Grant that I may use such things with moderation,
and that I be not entangled with inordinate affection for them. To
cast away all these things is not lawful, because nature must be sustained, but to require superfluities and things which merely minister
delight, the holy law forbiddeth; for otherwise the flesh would wax
insolent against the spirit. In all these things, I beseech Thee, let
Thy hand guide and teach me, that I in no way exceed.

CHAPTER XXVII

THAT PERSONAL LOVE GREATLY HINDERETH FROM THE HIGHEST GOOD

"My Son, thou must give all for all, and be nothing of thine own. Know thou that the love of thyself is more hurtful to thee than anything in the world. According to the love and inclination which thou hast, everything more or less cleaveth to thee. If thy love be pure, sincere, well-regulated, thou shalt not be in captivity to anything. Do not covet what thou mayest not have; do not have what is able to hinder thee, and to rob thee of inward liberty. It is wonderful that thou committest not thyself to Me from the very bottom of thy heart, with all things which thou canst desire or have.

2. "Why art thou consumed with vain sorrow? Why art thou wearied with superfluous cares? Stand thou by My good pleasure, and thou shalt suffer no loss. If thou seekest after this or that, and wilt be here or there, according to thine own advantage or the fulfilling of thine own pleasure, thou shalt never be in quiet, nor free from care, because in everything somewhat will be found lacking, and everywhere there will be somebody who opposeth thee.

3. "Therefore it is not gaining or multiplying of this thing or that which advantageth thee, but rather the despising it and cutting it by the root out of thy heart; which thou must not only understand of money and riches, but of the desire after honour and vain praise, things which all pass away with the world. The place availeth little if the spirit of devotion is wanting; nor shall that peace stand long which is sought from abroad, if the state of thy heart is without the true foundation, that is, if it abide not in Me. Thou mayest change, but thou canst not better thyself; for when occasion ariseth and is accepted thou shalt find what thou didst fly from, yea more."

A PRAYER FOR CLEANSING OF THE HEART AND FOR HEAVENLY WISDOM

4. Strengthen me, O God, by the grace of Thy Holy Spirit. Give me virtue to be strengthened with might in the inner man, and to free my heart from all fruitless care and trouble, and that I be not drawn away by various desires after any things whatsoever, whether

of little value or great, but that I may look upon all as passing away, and myself as passing away with them; because there is *no profit under the sun, and all is vanity* and *vexation of spirit.*[1] Oh how wise is he that considereth thus!

5. Give me, O Lord, heavenly wisdom, that I may learn to seek Thee above all things and to find Thee; to relish Thee above all things and to love Thee; and to understand all other things, even as they are, according to the order of Thy wisdom. Grant me prudently to avoid the flatterer, and patiently to bear with him that opposeth me; for this is great wisdom, not to be carried by every wind of words, nor to give ear to the wicked flattering Siren; for thus do we go safely on in the way we have begun.

CHAPTER XXVIII

AGAINST THE TONGUES OF DETRACTORS

"My Son, take it not sadly to heart, if any think ill of thee, and say of thee what thou art unwilling to hear. Thou oughtest to think worse of thyself, and to believe no man weaker than thyself. If thou walkest inwardly, thou wilt not weigh flying words above their value. It is no small prudence to keep silence in an evil time and to turn inwardly unto Me, and not to be troubled by human judgment.

2. "Let not thy peace depend upon the word of men; for whether they judge well or ill of thee, thou art not therefore any other man than thyself. Where is true peace or true glory? Is it not in Me? And he who seeketh not to please men, nor feareth to displease, shall enjoy abundant peace. From inordinate love and vain fear ariseth all disquietude of heart, and all distraction of the senses."

CHAPTER XXIX

HOW WHEN TRIBULATION COMETH WE MUST CALL UPON AND BLESS GOD

Blessed be thy name, O Lord, for evermore, who hast willed this temptation and trouble to come upon me. I cannot escape it, but have need to flee unto Thee, that Thou mayest succour me and turn

[1] Ecclesiastes ii. 11.

it unto me for good. Lord, now am I in tribulation, and it is not well within my heart, but I am sore vexed by the suffering which lieth upon me. And now, O dear Father, what shall I say? I am taken among the snares. *Save me from this hour, but for this cause came I unto this hour,*[1] that Thou mightest be glorified when I am deeply humbled and am delivered through Thee. *Let it be Thy pleasure to deliver me;*[2] for what can I do who am poor, and without Thee whither shall I go? Give patience this time also. Help me, O Lord my God, and I will not fear how much soever I be weighed down.

2. And now amid these things what shall I say? Lord, Thy will be done. I have well deserved to be troubled and weighed down. Therefore I ought to bear, would that it be with patience, until the tempest be overpast and comfort return. Yet is Thine omnipotent arm able also to take this temptation away from me, and to lessen its power that I fall not utterly under it, even as many a time past thou has helped me, O God, my merciful God. And as much as this deliverance is difficult to me, so much is it easy to Thee, O right hand of the most Highest.

CHAPTER XXX

OF SEEKING DIVINE HELP, AND THE CONFIDENCE OF OBTAINING GRACE

"My Son, I the Lord am *a stronghold in the day of trouble.*[3] Come unto Me, when it is not well with thee.

"This it is which chiefly hindereth heavenly consolation, that thou too slowly betakest thyself unto prayer. For before thou earnestly seekest unto Me, thou dost first seek after many means of comfort, and refresheth thyself in outward things: so it cometh to pass that all things profit thee but little until thou learn that it is I who deliver those who trust in Me; neither beside Me is there any strong help, nor profitable counsel, nor enduring remedy. But now, recovering courage after the tempest, grow thou strong in the light of My mercies, for I am nigh, saith the Lord, that I may restore all things not only as they were at the first, but also abundantly and one upon another.

[1] John xii. 27. [2] Psalm xl. 16. [3] Nahum i. 7.

2. "For is anything too hard for Me, or shall I be like unto one who saith and doeth not? Where is thy faith? Stand fast and with perseverance. Be long-suffering and strong. Consolation will come unto thee in its due season. Wait for Me; yea, wait; I will come and heal thee. It is temptation which vexeth thee, and a vain fear which terrifieth thee. What doth care about future events bring thee, save sorrow upon sorrow? *Sufficient for the day is the evil thereof.*[4] It is vain and useless to be disturbed or lifted up about future things which perhaps will never come.

3. "But it is the nature of man to be deceived by fancies of this sort, and it is a sign of a mind which is still weak to be so easily drawn away at the suggestion of the enemy. For he careth not whether he deceive and beguile by true means or false; whether he throw thee down by the love of the present or fear of the future. Therefore let not thy heart be troubled, neither let it be afraid. Believe in Me, and put thy trust in My mercy.[5] When thou thinkest thyself far removed from Me, I am often the nearer. When thou reckonest that almost all is lost, then often is greater opportunity of gain at hand. All is not lost when something goeth contrary to thy wishes. Thou oughtest not to judge according to present feeling, nor so to take or give way to any grief which befalleth thee, as if all hope of escape were taken away.

4. "Think not thyself totally abandoned, although for the time I have sent to thee some tribulation, or have even withdrawn some cherished consolation; for this is the way to the Kingdom of Heaven. And without doubt it is better for thee and for all My other servants, that ye should be proved by adversities, than that ye should have all things as ye would. I know thy hidden thoughts: and that it is very needful for thy soul's health that sometimes thou be left without relish, lest perchance thou be lifted up by prosperity, and desirous to please thyself in that which thou art not. What I have given I am able to take away, and to restore again at My good pleasure.

5. "When I shall have given, it is Mine; when I shall have taken away, I have not taken what is thine; *for every good gift and every perfect gift*[6] is from me. If I shall have sent upon thee grief or

---

[4] Matthew vi. 34.   [5] John xiv. 27; Psalm xiii. 5.   [6] James i. 17.

any vexation, be not angry, nor let thy heart be sad; I am able quickly to lift thee up and to change every burden into joy. But I am just and greatly to be praised, when I do thus unto thee.

6. "If thou rightly consider, and look upon it with truth, thou oughtest never to be so sadly cast down because of adversity, but rather shouldst rejoice and give thanks; yea, verily to count it the highest joy that I afflict thee with sorrows and spare thee not. *As My Father hath loved Me, so love I you;*[7] thus have I spoken unto My beloved disciples: whom I sent forth not unto worldly joys, but to great strivings; not unto honours, but unto contempt; not unto ease, but to labours; not unto rest, but to bring forth much fruit with patience. My son, remember these words."

CHAPTER XXXI

OF THE NEGLECT OF EVERY CREATURE, THAT THE CREATOR MAY BE FOUND

O LORD, I still need more grace, if I would arrive where neither man nor any other creature may hinder me. For so long as anything keepeth me back, I cannot freely fly unto Thee. He desired eagerly thus to fly, who cried, saying, *Oh that I had wings like a dove, for then would I flee away and be at rest.* What is more peaceful than the single eye? And what more free than he that desireth nothing upon earth? Therefore must a man rise above every creature, and perfectly forsake himself, and with abstracted mind to stand and behold that Thou, the Creator of all things, hast among Thy creatures nothing like unto Thyself. And except a man be freed from all creatures, he will not be able to reach freely after Divine things. Therefore few are found who give themselves to contemplation, because few know how to separate themselves entirely from perishing and created things.

2. For this much grace is necessary, which may lift up the soul and raise it above itself. And except a man be lifted up in the spirit, and freed from all creatures, and altogether united to God, whatsoever he knoweth, whatsoever even he hath, it mattereth but little. He who esteemeth anything great save the one only incomprehensible, eternal, good, shall long time be little and lie low. For

[7] John xv. 9.

whatsoever is not God is nothing, and ought to be counted for nothing. Great is the difference between a godly man, illuminated with wisdom, and a scholar learned in knowledge and given to books. Far nobler is that doctrine which floweth down from the divine fulness above, than that which is acquired laboriously by human study.

3. Many are found who desire contemplation, but they do not strive to practice those things which are required thereunto. It is also a great impediment, that much is made of symbols and external signs, and too little of thorough mortification. I know not how it is, and by what spirit we are led, and what we who would be deemed spiritual are aiming at, that we give so great labour and so eager solicitude for transitory and worthless things, and scarcely ever gather our senses together to think at all of our inward condition.

4. Ah, me! Forthwith after a little recollection we rush out of doors, and do not subject our actions to a strict examination. Where our affections are set we take no heed, and we weep not that all things belonging to us are so defiled. For because *all flesh had corrupted itself upon the earth,* the great deluge came. Since therefore our inmost affections are very corrupt, it followeth of necessity that our actions also are corrupt, being the index of a deficient inward strength. Out of a pure heart proceedeth the fruit of good living.

5. We demand, how much a man hath done; but from how much virtue he acted, is not so narrowly considered. We ask if he be strong, rich, handsome, clever, whether he is a good writer, good singer, good workman; but how poor he may be in spirit, how patient and gentle, how devout and meditative, on these things many are silent. Nature looketh upon the outward appearance of a man, grace turneth its thought to the heart. The former frequently judgeth amiss; the latter trusteth in God, that it may not be deceived.

CHAPTER XXXII

OF SELF-DENIAL AND THE CASTING AWAY ALL SELFISHNESS

"My *Son,* thou canst not possess perfect liberty unless thou altogether deny thyself. All they are enslaved who are possessors of riches, they who love themselves, the selfish, the curious, the restless; those who ever seek after soft things, and not after the things of Jesus Christ; those who continually plan and devise that which will not stand. For whatsoever cometh not of God shall perish. Hold fast the short and complete saying, 'Renounce all things, and thou shalt find all things; give up thy lust, and thou shalt find rest.' Dwell upon this in thy mind, and when thou art full of it, thou shalt understand all things."

2. O Lord, this is not the work of a day, nor children's play; verily in this short saying is enclosed all the perfection of the religious.

3. "My son, thou oughtest not to be turned aside, nor immediately cast down, because thou hast heard the way of the perfect. Rather oughtest thou to be provoked to higher aims, and at the least to long after the desire thereof. Oh that it were so with thee, and that thou hadst come to this, that thou wert not a lover of thine own self, but wert ready always to My nod, and to his whom I have placed over thee as thy father. Then shouldest thou please Me exceedingly, and all thy life should go on in joy and peace. Thou hast still many things to renounce, which if thou resign not utterly to Me, thou shalt not gain what thou seekest. *I counsel thee to buy of Me gold tried in the fire, that thou mayest be rich,*[1] that is heavenly wisdom, which despiseth all base things. Put away from thee earthly wisdom, and all pleasure, whether common to men, or thine own.

4. "I tell thee that thou must buy vile things with those which are costly and great in the esteem of men. For wonderfully vile and small, and almost given up to forgetfulness, doth true heavenly wisdom appear, which thinketh not high things of itself, nor seeketh to be magnified upon the earth; many honour it with their lips, but in heart are far from it; it is indeed the precious pearl, which is hidden from many."

CHAPTER XXXIII

OF INSTABILITY OF THE HEART, AND OF DIRECTING THE AIM TOWARDS GOD

"My Son, trust not thy feeling, for that which is now will be quickly changed into somewhat else. As long as thou livest thou art

[1] Revelation iii. 18.

subject to change, howsoever unwilling; so that thou art found now joyful, now sad; now at peace, now disquieted; now devout, now indevout; now studious, now careless; now sad, now cheerful. But the wise man, and he who is truly learned in spirit, standeth above these changeable things, attentive not to what he may feel in himself, or from what quarter the wind may blow, but that the whole intent of his mind may carry him on to the due and much-desired end. For thus will he be able to remain one and the same and unshaken, the single eye of his desire being steadfastly fixed, through the manifold changes of the world, upon Me.

2. "But according as the eye of intention be the more pure, even so will a man make his way steadfastly through the manifold storms. But in many the eye of pure intention waxeth dim; for it quickly resteth itself upon anything pleasant which occurreth, and rarely is any man found altogether free from the blemish of self-seeking. So the Jews of old came to Bethany, to the house of Martha and Mary, that they might see not Jesus, but Lazarus, whom he had raised from the dead.[1] Therefore must the eye of the intention be cleansed, that it may be single and right, and above all things which come in its way, may be directed unto Me."

CHAPTER XXXIV

THAT TO HIM WHO LOVETH GOD IS SWEET ABOVE ALL THINGS AND IN ALL THINGS

BEHOLD, God is mine, and all things are mine! What will I more, and what more happy thing can I desire? O delightsome and sweet world! that is, to him that loveth the Word, *not the world, neither the things that are in the world*.[2] My God, my all! To him that understandeth, that word sufficeth, and to repeat it often is pleasing to him that loveth it. When Thou art present all things are pleasant; when Thou art absent, all things are wearisome. Thou makest the heart to be at rest, givest it deep peace and festal joy. Thou makest it to think rightly in every matter, and in every matter to give Thee praise; neither can anything please long without Thee but if it would be pleasant and of sweet savour, Thy grace must be there, and it is Thy wisdom which must give unto it a sweet savour.

[1] John xii. 9.   [2] 1 John ii. 15.

2. To him who tasteth Thee, what can be distasteful? And to him who tasteth Thee not, what is there which can make him joyous? But the worldly wise, and they who enjoy the flesh, these fail in Thy wisdom; for in the wisdom of the world is found utter vanity, and to be carnally minded is death. But they who follow after Thee through contempt of worldly things, and mortification of the flesh, are found to be the truly wise because they are carried from vanity to verity, from the flesh to the spirit. They taste that the Lord is good, and whatsoever good they find in creatures, they count it all unto the praise of the Creator. Unlike, yea, very unlike is the enjoyment of the Creator to enjoyment of the Creature, the enjoyment of eternity and of time, of light uncreated and of light reflected.

3. O Light everlasting, surpassing all created lights, dart down Thy ray from on high which shall pierce the inmost depths of my heart. Give purity, joy, clearness, life to my spirit that with all its powers it may cleave unto Thee with rapture passing man's understanding. Oh when shall that blessed and longed-for time come when Thou shalt satisfy me with Thy presence, and be unto me All in all? So long as this is delayed, my joy shall not be full. Still, ah me! the old man liveth in me: he is not yet all crucified, not yet quite dead; still he lusteth fiercely against the spirit, wageth inward wars, nor suffereth the soul's kingdom to be in peace.

4. But *Thou who rulest the raging of the sea, and stillest the waves thereof when they arise,* rise up and help me. *Scatter the people that delight in war.*[3] Destroy them by Thy power. Show forth, I beseech Thee, Thy might, and let Thy right hand be glorified, for I have no hope, no refuge, save in Thee, O Lord my God.

CHAPTER XXXV

THAT THERE IS NO SECURITY AGAINST TEMPTATION IN THIS LIFE

"My Son, thou art never secure in this life, but thy spiritual armour will always be needful for thee as long as thou livest. Thou dwellest among foes, and art attacked on the right hand and on the left. If therefore thou use not on all sides the shield of patience, thou wilt not remain long unwounded. Above all, if thou keep not thy

[3] Psalm lxviii. 30.

heart fixed upon Me with steadfast purpose to bear all things for My
sake, thou shalt not be able to bear the fierceness of the attack, nor
to attain to the victory of the blessed. Therefore must thou struggle
bravely all thy life through, and put forth a strong hand against
those things which oppose thee. For to him that overcometh is the
hidden manna given,[1] but great misery is reserved for the slothful.

2. "If thou seek rest in this life, how then wilt thou attain unto the
rest which is eternal? Set not thyself to attain much rest, but much
patience. Seek the true peace, not in earth but in heaven, not in
man nor in any created thing, but in God alone. For the love of
God thou must willingly undergo all things, whether labours or
sorrows, temptations, vexations, anxieties, necessities, infirmities, injuries, gainsayings, rebukes, humiliations, confusions, corrections,
despisings; these things help unto virtue, these things prove the
scholar of Christ; these things fashion the heavenly crown. I will
give thee an eternal reward for short labour, and infinite glory for
transient shame.

3. "Thinkest thou that thou shalt always have spiritual consolations at thy will? My Saints had never such, but instead thereof
manifold griefs, and divers temptations, and heavy desolations. But
patiently they bore themselves in all, and trusted in God more than
in themselves, knowing that *the sufferings of this present time are
not worthy to be compared with the glory which shall be revealed
in us.*[2] Wouldst thou have that immediately which many have
hardly attained unto after many tears and hard labours? Wait for
the Lord, quit thyself like a man and be strong; be not faint-
hearted, nor go aside from Me, but constantly devote thy body and
soul to the glory of God. I will reward thee plenteously, *I will be
with thee in trouble.*"[3]

CHAPTER XXXVI

AGAINST VAIN JUDGMENTS OF MEN

"My Son, anchor thy soul firmly upon God, and fear not man's
judgment, when conscience pronounceth thee pious and innocent. It
is good and blessed thus to suffer; nor will it be grievous to the

[1] Revelation ii. 17.   [2] Romans viii. 17.   [3] Psalm xci. 15.

heart which is humble, and which trusteth in God more than in itself. Many men have many opinions, and therefore little trust is to be placed in them. But moreover it is impossible to please all. Although Paul studied to please all men in the Lord, and *to become all things to all men,*[1] yet nevertheless *with him it was a very small thing that he should be judged by man's judgment."*[2]

2. He laboured abundantly, as much as in him lay, for the building up and the salvation of others; but he could not avoid being sometimes judged and despised by others. Therefore he committed all to God, who knew all, and by patience and humility defended himself against evil speakers, or foolish and false thinkers, and those who accused him according to their pleasure. Nevertheless, from time to time he replied, lest his silence should become a stumbling-block to those who were weak.

3. *"Who art thou, that thou shouldst be afraid of a man that shall die?* To-day he is, and to-morrow his place is not found. Fear God and thou shalt not quail before the terrors of men. What can any man do against thee by words or deeds? He hurteth himself more than thee, nor shall he escape the judgment of God, whosoever he may be. Have thou God before thine eyes, and do not contend with fretful words. And if for the present thou seem to give way, and to suffer confusion which thou hast not deserved, be not angry at this, nor by impatience diminish thy reward; but rather look up to Me in heaven, for I am able to deliver thee from all confusion and hurt, and to render to every man according to his works."

CHAPTER XXXVII

OF PURE AND ENTIRE RESIGNATION OF SELF, FOR THE OBTAINING LIBERTY OF HEART

"My Son, lose thyself and thou shalt find Me. Stand still without all choosing and all thought of self, and thou shalt ever be a gainer. For more grace shall be added to thee, as soon as thou resignest thyself, and so long as thou dost not turn back to take thyself again."

2. O Lord, how often shall I resign myself, and in what things shall I lose myself?

[1] 1 Corinthians ix. 22.   [2] 1 Corinthians iv. 3.

3. "Always; every hour: in that which is little, and in that which is great. I make no exception, but will that thou be found naked in all things. Otherwise how canst thou be Mine and I thine, unless thou be inwardly and outwardly free from every will of thine own? The sooner thou dost this, the better shall it be with thee; and the more fully and sincerely, the more thou shalt please Me, and the more abundantly shalt thou be rewarded.

4. "Some resign themselves, but with certain reservations, for they do not fully trust in God, therefore they think that they have some provision to make for themselves. Some again at first offer everything; but afterwards being pressed by temptation they return to their own devices, and thus make no progress in virtue. They will not attain to the true liberty of a pure heart, nor to the grace of My sweet companionship, unless they first entirely resign themselves and daily offer themselves up as a sacrifice; without this the union which bringeth forth fruit standeth not nor will stand.

5. "Many a time I have said unto thee, and now say again, Give thyself up, resign thyself, and thou shalt have great inward peace. Give all for all; demand nothing, ask nothing in return; stand simply and with no hesitation in Me, and thou shalt possess Me. Thou shalt have liberty of heart, and the darkness shall not overwhelm thee. For this strive thou, pray for it, long after it, that thou mayest be delivered from all possession of thyself, and nakedly follow Jesus who was made naked for thee; mayest die unto thyself and live eternally to Me. Then shall all vain fancies disappear, all evil disturbings, and superfluous cares. Then also shall immoderate fear depart from thee, and inordinate love shall die."

CHAPTER XXXVIII

OF A GOOD GOVERNMENT IN EXTERNAL THINGS, AND OF HAVING RECOURSE TO GOD IN DANGERS

"My Son, for this thou must diligently make thy endeavour, that in every place and outward action or occupation thou mayest be free within, and have power over thyself; and that all things be under thee, not thou under them; that thou be master and ruler of thy actions, not a slave or hireling, but rather a free and true He-brew, entering into the lot and the liberty of the children of God, who stand above the present and look upon the eternal, who with the left eye behold things transitory, and with the right things heavenly; whom temporal things draw not to cleave unto, but who rather draw temporal things to do them good service, even as they were ordained of God to do, and appointed by the Master Workman, who hath left nought in His creation without aim and end.

2. "And if in any chance of life thou stand not in outward ap-pearances, nor judgest things which are seen and heard by the fleshy sense, but straightway in every cause enterest with Moses into the tabernacle to ask counsel of God; thou shalt hear a divine response and come forth instructed concerning many things that are and shall be. For always Moses had recourse to the tabernacle for the solving of all doubts and questionings; and fled to the help of prayer to be delivered from the dangers and evil deeds of men. Thus also oughtest thou to fly to the secret chamber of thy heart, and earnestly implore the divine succour. For this cause we read that Joshua and the children of Israel were deceived by the Gibeon-ites, that they *asked not counsel at the mouth of the Lord*,[1] but being too ready to listen to fair speeches, were deceived by pretended piety."

CHAPTER XXXIX

THAT MAN MUST NOT BE IMMERSED IN BUSINESS

"MY Son, always commit thy cause to Me; I will dispose it aright in due time. Wait for My arrangement of it, and then thou shalt find it for thy profit."

2. O Lord, right freely I commit all things to Thee; for my plan-ning can profit but little. Oh that I did not dwell so much on future events, but could offer myself altogether to Thy pleasures without delay.

3. "My Son, a man often striveth vehemently after somewhat which he desireth; but when he hath obtained it he beginneth to be of another mind, because his affections towards it are not lasting,

[1] Joshua ix. 14.

but rather rush on from one thing to another. Therefore it is not really a small thing, when in small things we resist self."

4. The true progress of man lieth in self-denial, and a man who denieth himself is free and safe. But the old enemy, opposer of all good things, ceaseth not from temptation; but day and night setteth his wicked snares, if haply he may be able to entrap the unwary. *Watch and pray,* saith the Lord, *lest ye enter into temptation.*[1]

CHAPTER XL

THAT MAN HATH NO GOOD IN HIMSELF, AND NOTHING WHEREOF TO GLORY

LORD, what is man that Thou art mindful of him, or the son of man that Thou visitest him?[2] What hath man deserved, that Thou shouldest bestow thy favour upon him? Lord, what cause can I have of complaint, if Thou forsake me? Or what can I justly allege, if Thou refuse to hear my petition? Of a truth, this I may truly think and say, Lord, I am nothing, I have nothing that is good of myself, but I fall short in all things, and ever tend unto nothing. And unless I am helped by Thee and inwardly supported, I become altogether lukewarm and reckless.

2. But Thou, O Lord, art always the same, and endurest for ever, always good, righteous, and holy; doing all things well, righteously, and holily, and disposing all in Thy wisdom. But I who am more ready to go forward than backward, never continue in one stay, because changes sevenfold pass over me. Yet it quickly becometh better when it so pleaseth Thee, and Thou puttest forth Thy hand to help me; because Thou alone canst aid without help of man, and canst so strengthen me that my countenance shall be no more changed, but my heart shall be turned to Thee, and rest in Thee alone.

3. Wherefore, if I but knew well how to reject all human consolations, whether for the sake of gaining devotion, or because of the necessity by which I was compelled to seek Thee, seeing there is no man who can comfort me; then could I worthily trust in Thy grace, and rejoice in the gift of new consolation.

[1] Matthew xxvi. 41.   [2] Psalm viii. 4.

4. Thanks be to Thee, from whom all cometh, whensoever it goeth well with me! But I am vanity and nothing in Thy sight, a man inconstant and weak. What then have I whereof to glory, or why do I long to be held in honour? Is it not for nought? This also is utterly vain. Verily vain glory is an evil plague, the greatest of vanities, because it draweth us away from the true glory, and robbeth us of heavenly grace. For whilst a man pleaseth himself he displeaseth Thee; whilst he gapeth after the praises of man, he is deprived of true virtues.

5. But true glory and holy rejoicing lieth in glorying in Thee and not in self; in rejoicing in Thy Name, not in our own virtue; in not taking delight in any creature, save only for Thy sake. Let thy Name, not mine be praised; let Thy work, not mine be magnified; let Thy holy Name be blessed, but to me let nought be given of the praises of men. Thou art my glory, Thou art the joy of my heart. In Thee will I make my boast and be glad all the day long, but for myself let me not glory *save only in my infirmities.*[3]

6. Let the Jews seek *the honour which cometh from one another;* but I will ask for that which *cometh from God only.*[4] Truly all human glory, all temporal honour, all worldly exultation, compared to Thy eternal glory, is but vanity and folly. O God my Truth and my Mercy, Blessed Trinity, to Thee alone be all praise, honour, power, and glory for ever and for ever. Amen.

CHAPTER XLI

OF CONTEMPT OF ALL TEMPORAL HONOUR

"My Son, make it no matter of thine, if thou see others honoured and exalted, and thyself despised and humbled. Lift up thine heart to Me in heaven, and then the contempt of men upon earth will not make thee sad."

2. O Lord, we are in blindness, and are quickly seduced by vanity. If I look rightly within myself, never was injury done unto me by any creature, and therefore I have nought whereof to complain before Thee. But because I have many times and grievously

[3] 2 Corinthians xii. 5.   [4] John v. 44.

sinned against Thee, all creatures do justly take arms against me. Therefore to me confusion and contempt are justly due, but to Thee praise and honour and glory. And except I dispose myself for this, namely, to be willing that every creature should despise and desert me, and that I should be esteemed altogether as nothing, I cannot be inwardly filled with peace and strength, nor spiritually enlightened, nor fully united to Thee.

CHAPTER XLII

THAT OUR PEACE IS NOT TO BE PLACED IN MEN

"My Son, if thou set thy peace on any person because thou hast high opinion of him, and art familiar with him, thou shalt be unstable and entangled. But if thou betake thyself to the ever-living and abiding Truth, the desertion or death of a friend shall not make thee sad. In Me ought the love of thy friend to subsist, and for My sake is every one to be loved, whosoever he be, who appeareth to thee good, and is very dear to thee in this life. Without Me friendship hath no strength or endurance, neither is that love true and pure, which I unite not. Thou oughtest to be so dead to such affections of beloved friends, that as far as in thee lieth, thou wouldst rather choose to be without any companionship of men. The nearer a man approacheth to God, the further he recedeth from all earthly solace. The deeper also he descendeth into himself, and the viler he appeareth in his own eyes, the higher he ascendeth towards God.

2. "But he who attributeth anything good to himself, hindereth the grace of God from coming to him, because the grace of the Holy Ghost ever seeketh the humble heart. If thou couldst make thyself utterly nothing, and empty thyself of the love of every creature, then should it be My part to overflow unto thee with great grace. When thou settest thine eyes upon creatures, the face of the Creator is withdrawn from thee. Learn in all things to conquer thyself for thy Creator's sake, then shalt thou be able to attain unto divine knowledge. How small soever anything be, if it be loved and regarded inordinately, it holdeth us back from the highest good, and corrupteth."

CHAPTER XLIII

AGAINST VAIN AND WORLDLY KNOWLEDGE

"My Son, let not the fair and subtle sayings of men move thee. *For the kingdom of God is not in word, but in power.*[1] Give ear to My words, for they kindle the heart and enlighten the mind, they bring contrition, and they supply manifold consolations. Never read thou the word that thou mayest appear more learned or wise; but study for the mortification of thy sins, for this will be far more profitable for thee than the knowledge of many difficult questions.

2. "When thou hast read and learned many things, thou must always return to one first principle. I am *He that teacheth man knowledge*,[2] and I give unto babes clearer knowledge than can be taught by man. He to whom I speak will be quickly wise and shall grow much in the spirit. Woe unto them who inquire into many curious questions from men, and take little heed concerning the way of My service. The time will come when Christ will appear, the Master of masters, the Lord of the Angels, to hear the lessons of all, that is to examine the consciences of each one. And then will He *search Jerusalem with candles*,[3] and the *hidden things of darkness*[4] shall be made manifest, and the arguings of tongues shall be silent.

3. "I am He who in an instant lift up the humble spirit, to learn more reasonings of the Eternal Truth, than if a man had studied ten years in the schools. I teach without noise of words, without confusion of opinions, without striving after honour, without clash of arguments. I am He who teach men to despise earthly things, to loathe things present, to seek things heavenly, to enjoy things eternal, to flee honours, to endure offences, to place all hope in Me, to desire nothing apart from Me, and above all things to love Me ardently.

4. "For there was one, who by loving Me from the bottom of his heart, learned divine things, and spake things that were wonderful; he profited more by forsaking all things than by studying

[1] I Corinthians iv. 20.   [2] Psalm xciv. 10.
[3] Zephaniah i. 12.   [4] I Corinthians iv. 5.

subtleties. But to some I speak common things, to others special; to some I appear gently in signs and figures, and again to some I reveal mysteries in much light. The voice of books is one, but it informeth not all alike; because I inwardly am the Teacher of truth, the Searcher of the heart, the Discerner of the thoughts, the Mover of actions, distributing to each man, as I judge meet."

CHAPTER XLIV

OF NOT TROUBLING OURSELVES ABOUT OUTWARD THINGS

"My Son, in many things it behoveth thee to be ignorant, and to esteem thyself as one dead upon the earth, and as one to whom the whole world is crucified. Many things also thou must pass by with deaf ear, and must rather think upon those things which belong unto thy peace. It is more profitable to turn away thine eyes from those things that displease, and to leave each man to his own opinion, than to give thyself to discourses of strife. If thou stand well with God and hast His judgment in thy mind, thou wilt verily easily bear to be as one conquered."

2. O Lord, to what have we come? Behold a temporal loss is mourned over; for a trifling gain we labour and hurry; and spiritual loss passeth away into forgetfulness, and we rarely recover it. That which profiteth little or nothing is looked after, and that which is altogether necessary is negligently passed by; because the whole man slideth away to outward things, and unless he quickly recovereth himself in outward things he willingly lieth down.

CHAPTER XLV

THAT WE MUST NOT BELIEVE EVERYONE, AND THAT WE ARE PRONE TO FALL IN OUR WORDS

LORD, *be thou my help in trouble, for vain is the help of man.*[1] How often have I failed to find faithfulness, where I thought I possessed it. How many times I have found it where I least expected. Vain therefore is hope in men, but the salvation of the

[1] Psalm lx. 11.

just, O God, is in Thee. Blessed be thou, O Lord my God, in all things which happen unto us. We are weak and unstable, we are quickly deceived and quite changed.

2. Who is the man who is able to keep himself so warily and circumspectly as not sometimes to come into some snare of perplexity? But he who trusteth in Thee, O Lord, and seeketh Thee with an unfeigned heart, doth not so easily slip. And if he fall into any tribulation, howsoever he may be entangled, yet very quickly he shall be delivered through Thee, or by Thee shall be comforted, because Thou wilt not forsake him that trusteth in Thee unto the end. A friend who continueth faithful in all the distresses of his friend is rare to be found. Thou, O Lord, Thou alone art most faithful in all things, and there is none other like unto Thee.

3. Oh, how truly wise was that holy soul which said, "My mind is steadfastly fixed, and it is grounded in Christ."[2] If thus it were with me, the fear of man should not so easily tempt me, nor the arrows of words move me. Who is sufficient to foresee all things, who to guard beforehand against future ills? If even things which are foreseen sometimes hurt us, what can things which are not foreseen do, but grievously injure? But wherefore have I not better provided for myself, miserable that I am? Why, too, have I given such heed to others? But we are men, nor are we other than frail men, even though by many we are reckoned and called angels. Whom shall I trust, O Lord, whom shall I trust but Thee? Thou art the Truth, and deceivest not, nor canst be deceived. And on the other hand, *Every man is a liar*,[3] weak, unstable and frail, especially in his words, so that one ought scarcely ever to believe what seemeth to sound right on the face of it.

4. With what wisdom hast thou warned us beforehand to *beware of men*, and that *a man's foes are they of his own household*,[4] and that we must not believe if one say unto us *Lo here, or Lo there*.[5] I have been taught by my loss, and O that I may prove more careful and not foolish hereby. "Be cautious," saith some one: "be cautious, keep unto thyself what I tell thee." And whilst I am silent and believe that it is hid with me, he himself cannot keep silence concern-

[2] St. Agatha.   [3] Psalm cxvi. 11; Romans iii. 4.   [4] Matthew x. 17, 36.
[5] Matthew xxiv. 23.

ing it, but straightway betrayeth me and himself, and goeth his way. Protect me, O Lord, from such mischief-making and reckless men; let me not fall into their hands, nor ever do such things myself. Put a true and steadfast word into my mouth, and remove a deceitful tongue far from me. What I would not suffer, I ought by all means to beware of doing.

5. Oh, how good and peacemaking a thing it is to be silent concerning others, and not carelessly to believe all reports, nor to hand them on further; how good also to lay one's self open to few, to seek ever to have Thee as the beholder of the heart; not to be carried about with every wind of words, but to desire that all things inward and outward be done according to the good pleasure of Thy will! How safe for the preserving of heavenly grace to fly from human approval, and not to long after the things which seem to win admiration abroad, but to follow with all earnestness those things which bring amendment of life and heavenly fervour! How many have been injured by their virtue being made known and too hastily praised. How truly profitable hath been grace preserved in silence in this frail life, which, as we are told, is all temptation and warfare.

CHAPTER XLVI

OF HAVING CONFIDENCE IN GOD WHEN EVIL WORDS ARE CAST AT US

"My Son, stand fast and believe in Me. For what are words but words? They fly through the air, but they bruise no stone. If thou are guilty, think how thou wouldst gladly amend thyself; if thou knowest nothing against thyself, consider that thou wilt gladly bear this for God's sake. It is little enough that thou sometimes hast to bear hard words, for thou art not yet able to bear hard blows. And wherefore do such trivial matters go to thine heart, except that thou art yet carnal, and regardest men more than thou oughtest? For because thou fearest to be despised, thou art unwilling to be reproved for thy faults, and seekest paltry shelters of excuses.

2. "But look better into thyself, and thou shalt know that the world is still alive in thee, and the vain love of pleasing men. For when thou fleest away from being abased and confounded for thy

faults, it is plain that thou art neither truly humble nor truly dead to the world, and that the world is not crucified to thee. But hearken to My word, and thou shalt not care for ten thousand words of men. Behold, if all things could be said against thee which the utmost malice could invent, what should it hurt thee if thou wert altogether to let it go, and make no more account of it than of a mote? Could it pluck out a single hair of thy head?

3. "But he that hath no heart within him, and hath not God before his eyes, is easily moved by a word of reproach; but he who trusteth in Me, and seeketh not to abide by his own judgment, shall be free from the fear of men. For I am the Judge and the Discerner of all secrets; I know how the thing hath been done; I know both the injurer and the bearer. From Me went forth that word, by My permission this hath happened, *that the thoughts of many hearts may be revealed*.[1] I shall judge the guilty and the innocent; but beforehand I have willed to try them both by a secret judgment.

4. "The testimony of men often deceiveth. My judgment is true; it will stand, and it shall not be overturned. It commonly lieth hid, and only to few in certain cases is it made known; yet it never erreth, nor can err, although it seem not right to the eyes of foolish men. To Me, therefore, must men have recourse in all judgment, and must not lean to their opinion. For *there shall no evil happen to the just*,[2] whatsoever may be sent to him by God. Even though some unjust charge be brought against him, he will care little; nor, again, will he exult above measure, if through others he be clearly vindicated. For he considereth that I am *He who try the hearts and reins*,[3] who judge not outwardly and according to human appearance; for often in Mine eyes that is found blameworthy which in the judgment of men is held worthy of praise."

5. O Lord God, O Judge, just, strong, and patient, who knowest the frailty and sinfulness of men, be Thou my strength and my whole confidence; for my own conscience sufficeth me not. Thou knowest what I know not; and therefore ought I under all rebuke to humble myself, and to bear it meekly. Therefore mercifully forgive me as often as I have not done this, and grant me the next time the grace of greater endurance. For better unto me is Thine

[1] Luke ii. 35.   [2] Proverbs xii. 21.   [3] Psalm vii. 9.

abundant pity for the attainment of Thy pardon, than the righteous-ness which I believe myself to have for defence against my con-science, which lieth wait against me. Although *I know nothing against myself, yet am I not hereby justified,*[4] because if Thy mercy were removed away, *in Thy sight should no man living be justified.*[5]

CHAPTER XLVII

THAT ALL TROUBLES ARE TO BE ENDURED FOR THE SAKE OF ETERNAL LIFE

"My Son, let not the labours which thou hast undertaken for Me break thee down, nor let tribulations cast thee down in any wise, but let my promise strengthen and comfort thee in every event. I am sufficient to reward thee above all measure and extent. Not long shalt thou labour here, nor always be weighed down with sorrows. Wait yet a little while, and thou shalt see a speedy end of thine evils. An hour shall come when all labour and confusion shall cease. Little and short is all that passeth away with time.

2. "Do earnestly what thou dost; labour faithfully in My vine-yard; I will be thy reward. Write, read, sing, weep, be silent, pray, endure adversities manfully; eternal life is worthy of all these con-flicts, yea, and of greater. Peace shall come *in one day which is known to the Lord; which shall be neither day nor night,*[1] but light eternal, infinite clearness, steadfast peace, and undisturbed rest. Thou shalt not say then, *Who shall deliver me from the body of this death?*[2] nor cry out, *Woe is me, for my sojourning is prolonged,*[3] because death will be utterly destroyed, and there shall be salva-tion which can never fail, no more anxiety, happy delight, sweet and noble society.

3. "Oh, if thou sawest the unfading crowns of the Saints in heaven, and with what great glory they now rejoice, who aforetime were reckoned by this world contemptibly and as it were unworthy of life, truly thou wouldst immediately humble thyself even to the earth, and wouldst desire rather to be in subjection to all, than to

[4] I Corinthians iv. 4.   [5] Psalm cxliii. 2.   [1] Zechariah xiv. 7.   [2] Romans vii. 24.
[3] Psalm cxx.

have authority over one; nor wouldst thou long for pleasant days of this life, but wouldst more rejoice to be afflicted for God's sake, and wouldst esteem it gain to be counted for nought amongst men.

4. "Oh, if these things were sweet to thy taste, and moved thee to the bottom of thine heart, how shouldst thou dare even once to complain? Are not all laborious things to be endured for the sake of eternal life? It is no small thing, the losing or gaining the Kingdom of God. Lift up therefore thy face to heaven. Behold, I and all My Saints with Me, who in this world had a hard conflict, now rejoice, are now comforted, are now secure, are now at peace, and shall remain with Me evermore in the Kingdom of My Father."

CHAPTER XLVIII

OF THE DAY OF ETERNITY AND OF THE STRAITNESSES OF THIS LIFE

OH most blessed mansion of the City which is above! Oh most clear day of eternity which the night obscureth not, but the Supreme Truth ever enlighteneth! Day always joyful, always secure and never changing its state into those which are contrary. Oh would that this day might shine forth, and that all these temporal things would come to an end. It shineth indeed upon the Saints, glowing with unending brightness, but only from afar and through a glass, upon those who are pilgrims on the earth.

2. The citizens of heaven know how glorious that day is; the exiled sons of Eve groan, because this is bitter and wearisome. The days of this life are few and evil, full of sorrows and straits, where man is defiled with many sins, ensnared with many passions, bound fast with many fears, wearied with many cares, distracted with many questionings, entangled with many vanities, compassed about with many errors, worn away with many labours, weighed down with temptations, enervated by pleasures, tormented by poverty.

3. Oh when shall there be an end of these evils? When shall I be delivered from the wretched slavery of my sins? When shall I be mindful, O Lord, of Thee alone? When shall I rejoice in Thee to the full? When shall I be in true liberty without any impediment, without any burden on mind or body? When shall there be

solid peace, peace immovable and secure, peace within and without, peace firm on every side? Blessed Jesus, when shall I stand to behold Thee? When shall I gaze upon the glory of Thy kingdom? When shalt Thou be to me all in all? Oh when shall I be with Thee in Thy Kingdom which Thou hast prepared from the foundation of the world for them that love Thee? I am left destitute, an exile in a hostile land, where are daily wars and grievous misfortunes.

4. Console my exile, mitigate my sorrow, for towards Thee all my desire longeth. For all is to me a burden, whatsoever this world offereth for consolation. I yearn to enjoy Thee intimately, but I cannot attain unto it. I long to cleave to heavenly things, but temporal things and unmortified passions press me down. In my mind I would be above all things, but in my flesh I am unwillingly compelled to be beneath them. So, wretched man that I am, I fight with myself, and am made grievous even unto myself, while the spirit seeketh to be above and the flesh to be beneath.

5. Oh how I suffer inwardly, while with the mind I discourse on heavenly things, and presently a crowd of carnal things rusheth upon me whilst I pray. *My God, be not Thou far from me,* nor depart in wrath from Thy servant. *Cast forth Thy lightning and scatter them; send out Thine arrows,*[1] and let all delusions of my enemy be confounded. Recall my senses unto Thyself, cause me to forget all worldly things; grant me quickly to cast away and despise the imaginations of sin. Succour me, O Eternal Truth, that no vanity may move me. Come unto me, O Heavenly Sweetness, and let all impurity flee from before Thy face. Pardon me also, and of Thy mercy deal gently with me, whensoever in prayer I think on anything besides Thee; for truly I confess that I am wont to be continually distracted. For often and often, where in the body I stand or sit, there I myself am not; but rather am I there, whither I am borne by my thoughts. Where my thought is, there am I; and there commonly is my thought where that which I love is. That readily occurreth to me, which naturally delighteth, or pleaseth through custom.

6. Wherefore Thou, who art the Truth, hast plainly said, *Where your treasure is, there will your heart be also.*[2] If I love heaven, I

[1] Psalm lxxi. 12.   [2] Matthew vi. 21.

gladly meditate on heavenly things. If I love the world, I rejoice in the delights of the world, and am made sorry by its adversities. If I love the flesh, I am continually imagining the things which belong to the flesh; if I love the spirit, I am delighted by meditating on spiritual things. For whatsoever things I love, on these I readily converse and listen, and carry home with me the images of them. But blessed is that man who for Thy sake, O Lord, is willing to part from all creatures; who doth violence to his fleshly nature and crucifieth the lusts of the flesh by the fervour of his spirit, so that with serene conscience he may offer unto Thee a pure prayer, and be made worthy to enter into the angelic choirs, having shut out from himself, both outwardly and inwardly, all worldly things.

CHAPTER XLIX

OF THE DESIRE AFTER ETERNAL LIFE, AND HOW GREAT BLESSINGS ARE PROMISED TO THOSE WHO STRIVE

"My Son, when thou feelest the desire of eternal happiness to be poured into thee from above, and longest to depart from the tabernacle of this body, that thou mayest contemplate My glory without shadow of turning, enlarge thine heart, and take in this holy inspiration with all thy desire. Give most hearty thanks to the Supreme Goodness, who dealeth with thee so graciously, visiteth thee so lovingly, stirreth thee up so fervently, raiseth thee so powerfully, lest thou sink down through thine own weight, to earthly things. For not by thine own meditating or striving dost thou receive this gift, but by the sole gracious condescension of Supreme Grace and Divine regard; to the end that thou mayest make progress in virtue and in more humility, and prepare thyself for future conflicts, and cleave unto Me with all the affection of thy heart, and strive to serve Me with fervent will.

2. "My Son, often the fire burneth, but the flame ascendeth not without smoke. So also the desires of some men burn towards heavenly things, and yet they are not free from the temptation of carnal affection. Thus therefore they are not acting with an altogether simple desire for God's glory when they pray to Him so earnestly.

Such, too, is oftentimes thy desire, when thou hast imagined it to be so earnest. For that is not pure and perfect which is tainted with thine own self-seeking.

3. "Seek thou not what is pleasant and advantageous to thyself, but what is acceptable and honourable unto Me; for if thou judgest rightly, thou must choose and follow after My appointment rather than thine own desire; yea, rather than anything that can be desired. I know thy desire, and I have heard thy many groanings. Already thou longest to be in the glorious liberty of the children of God; already the eternal home delighteth thee, and the heavenly country full of joy; but the hour is not yet come; there remaineth still another season, even a season of warfare, a season of labour and probation. Thou desirest to be filled with the Chief Good, but thou canst not attain it immediately. I am that Good; wait for Me, until the Kingdom of God shall come.

4. "Thou must still be tried upon earth, and be exercised in many things. Consolation shall from time to time be given thee, but abundant satisfying shall not be granted. Be strong therefore, and be thou brave both in working and in suffering things which are against thy nature. Thou must put on the new man, and be changed into another man. Thou must often do what thou wouldst not; and thou must leave undone what thou wouldst do. What pleaseth others shall have good success, what pleaseth thee shall have no prosperity. What others say shall be listened to; what thou sayest shall receive no heed. Others shall ask and receive; thou shalt ask and not obtain. Others shall be great in the report of men, but about thee shall nothing be spoken. To others this or that shall be entrusted; thou shalt be judged useful for nought.

5. "For this cause nature shall sometimes be filled with sadness; and it is a great thing if thou bear it silently. In this and many like things the faithful servant of the Lord is wont to be tried, how far he is able to deny himself and bring himself into subjection in all things. Scarcely is there anything in which thou hast need to mortify thyself so much as in seeing things which are adverse to thy will; especially when things are commanded thee to be done which seem to thee inexpedient or of little use to thee. And because thou darest not resist a higher power, being under authority, therefore it seem-

eth hard for thee to shape thy course according to the nod of another, and to forego thine own opinion.

6. "But consider, My Son, the fruit of these labours, the swift end, and the reward exceeding great; and thou shalt find it no pain to bear them then, but rather the strongest solace of thy patience. For even in exchange for this trifling desire which thou hast readily forsaken, thou shalt always have thy will in Heaven. There verily thou shalt find all that thou wouldst, all that thou canst long for. There thou shalt have all good within thy power without the fear of losing it. There thy will, ever at one with Mine, shall desire nothing outward, nothing for itself. There no man shall withstand thee, none shall complain of thee, none shall hinder, nothing shall stand in thy path; but all things desired by thee shall be present together, and shall refresh thy whole affection, and fill it up even to the brim. There I will glory for the scorn suffered here, the garment of praise for sorrow, and for the lowest place a throne in the Kingdom, for ever. There shall appear the fruit of obedience, the labour of repentance shall rejoice, and humble subjection shall be crowned gloriously.

7. "Now therefore bow thyself humbly under the hands of all men; nor let it trouble thee who said this or who ordered that; but take special heed that whether thy superior, thy inferior, or thy equal, require anything from thee, or even show a desire for it; take it all in good part, and study with a good will to fulfil the desire. Let one seek this, another that; let this man glory in this, and that man in that, and be praised a thousand thousand times, but rejoice thou only in the contempt of thyself, and in Mine own good pleasure and glory. This is what thou art to long for, even that whether *by life or by death God may be ever magnified in thee*."[1]

CHAPTER L

HOW A DESOLATE MAN OUGHT TO COMMIT HIMSELF INTO THE HANDS OF GOD

O LORD, Holy Father, be Thou blessed now and evermore; because as Thou wilt so it is done, and what Thou doest is good. Let

[1] Philippians i. 20.

Thy servant rejoice in Thee, not in himself, nor in any other; because Thou alone art the true joy, Thou art my hope and my crown, Thou art my joy and my honour, O Lord. What hath Thy servant, which he received not from Thee, even without merit of his own? Thine are all things which Thou hast given, and which Thou hast made. *I am poor and in misery even from my youth up,*[1] and my soul is sorrowful unto tears, sometimes also it is disquieted within itself, because of the sufferings which are coming upon it.

2. I long after the joy of peace; for the peace of Thy children do I beseech, for in the light of Thy comfort they are fed by Thee. If Thou give peace, if Thou pour into me holy joy, the soul of Thy servant shall be full of melody, and devout in Thy praise. But if Thou withdraw Thyself as too often Thou art wont, he will not be able to run in the way of Thy commandments, but rather he will smite his breast and will bow his knees; because it is not with him as yesterday and the day before, *when Thy candle shined upon his head,*[2] *and he walked under the shadow of Thy wings,*[3] from the temptations which beset him.

3. O Father, righteous and ever to be praised, the hour cometh when Thy servant is to be proved. O beloved Father, it is well that in this hour Thy servant suffer somewhat for Thy sake. O Father, evermore to be adored, as the hour cometh which Thou foreknewest from everlasting, when for a little while Thy servant should outwardly bow down, but always live inwardly with Thee; when for a little while he should be little regarded, humbled, and fail in the eyes of men; should be wasted with sufferings and weaknesses, to rise again with Thee in the dawn of the new light, and be glorified in the heavenly places. O Holy Father, thou hast ordained it so, and so hast willed it; and that is done which Thou Thyself hast commanded.

4. For this is Thy favour to Thy friend, that he should suffer and be troubled in the world for Thy love's sake, how often soever, and by whomsoever and whosoever Thou hast suffered it to be done. Without Thy counsel and providence, and without cause, nothing cometh to pass on the earth. *It is good for me, Lord, that I had been*

[1] Psalm lxxxviii. 15.   [2] Job xxix. 3.   [3] Psalm xvii. 8.

in trouble, that I may learn Thy statutes,[4] and may cast away all pride of heart and presumption. It is profitable for me that confusion hath covered my face, that I may seek to Thee for consolation rather than unto men. By this also I have learned to dread Thine unsearchable judgment, who afflictest the just with the wicked, but not without equity and justice.

5. Thanks be unto Thee, because Thou hast not spared my sins, but hast beaten me with stripes of love, inflicting pains, and sending troubles upon me without and within. There is none who can console me, of all things which are under heaven, but Thou only, O Lord my God, Thou heavenly Physician of souls, *who dost scourge and hast mercy, who leadest down to hell and bringest up again.*[5] Thy discipline over me, and Thy rod itself shall teach me.

6. Behold, O beloved Father, I am in Thy hands, I bow myself under the rod of Thy correction. Smite my back and my neck that I may bend my crookedness to Thy will. Make me a pious and lowly disciple, as Thou wert wont to be kind, that I may walk according to every nod of Thine. To Thee I commend myself and all that I have for correction; better is it to be punished here than hereafter. Thou knowest all things and each of them; and nothing remaineth hid from Thee in man's conscience. Before they are, thou knowest that they will be, and Thou needest not that any man teach Thee or admonish Thee concerning the things which are done upon the earth. Thou knowest what is expedient for my profit, and how greatly trouble serveth unto the scrubbing off the rust of sin. Do with me according to Thy desired good pleasure, and despise not my life which is full of sin, known to none so entirely and fully as to Thee alone.

7. Grant me, O Lord, to know that which ought to be known; to love that which ought to be loved; to praise that which pleaseth Thee most, to esteem that which is precious in Thy sight, to blame that which is vile in Thine eyes. Suffer me not to judge according to the sight of bodily eyes, nor to give sentence according to the hearing of the ears of ignorant men; but to discern in true judgment between visible and spiritual things, and above all things to be ever seeking after the will of Thy good pleasure.

[4] Psalm cxix. 71.   [5] Job xiii. 2.

8. Oftentimes the senses of men are deceived in judging; the lovers of the world also are deceived in that they love only visible things. What is a man better because by man he is reckoned very great? The deceiver deceiveth the deceiver, the vain man the vain, the blind man the blind, the weak man the weak, when they exalt one another; and in truth they rather put to shame, while they foolishly praise. For as humble St. Francis saith, "What each one is in Thine eyes, so much he is, and no more."

CHAPTER LI

THAT WE MUST GIVE OURSELVES TO HUMBLE WORKS WHEN WE ARE UNEQUAL TO THOSE THAT ARE LOFTY

"My Son, thou art not always able to continue in very fervent desire after virtues, nor to stand fast in the loftier region of contemplation; but thou must of necessity sometimes descend to lower things because of thine original corruption, and bear about the burden of corruptible life, though unwillingly and with weariness. So long as thou wearest a mortal body, thou shalt feel weariness and heaviness of heart. Therefore thou oughtest to groan often in the flesh because of the burden of the flesh, inasmuch as thou canst not give thyself to spiritual studies and divine contemplation unceasingly.

2. "At such a time it is expedient for thee to flee to humble and external works, and to renew thyself with good actions; to wait for My coming and heavenly visitation with sure confidence; to bear thy exile and drought of mind with patience, until thou be visited by Me again, and be freed from all anxieties. For I will cause thee to forget thy labours, and altogether to enjoy eternal peace. I will spread open before thee the pleasant pastures of the Scriptures, that with enlarged heart thou mayest begin to run in the way of My commandments. And thou shalt say, *'The sufferings of this present time are not worthy to be compared with the glory which shall be revealed in us.'* "[1]

[1] Romans viii. 18.

CHAPTER LII

THAT A MAN OUGHT NOT TO RECKON HIMSELF WORTHY OF CONSOLATION,
BUT MORE WORTHY OF CHASTISEMENT

O LORD, I am not worthy of Thy consolation, nor of any spiritual visitation; and therefore Thou dealest justly with me, when Thou leavest me poor and desolate. For if I were able to pour forth tears like the sea, still should I not be worthy of Thy consolation. Therefore am I nothing worthy save to be scourged and punished, because I have grievously and many a time offended Thee, and in many things have greatly sinned. Therefore, true account being taken, I am not worthy even of the least of Thy consolations. But Thou, gracious and merciful God, who willest not that Thy works should perish, to show forth the riches of Thy mercy upon the vessels of mercy,[1] vouchsafest even beyond all his own deserving, to comfort Thy servant above the measure of mankind. For Thy consolations are not like unto the discoursings of men.

2. What have I done, O Lord, that Thou shouldst bestow any heavenly comfort upon me? I remember not that I have done any good, but have been ever prone to sin and slow to amendment. It is true and I cannot deny it. If I should say otherwise, Thou wouldst rise up against me, and there would be none to defend me. What have I deserved for my sins but hell and everlasting fire? In very truth I confess that I am worthy of all scorn and contempt, nor is it fit that I should be remembered among Thy faithful servants. And although I be unwilling to hear this, nevertheless I will for the Truth's sake, accuse myself of my sins, that the more readily I may prevail to be accounted worthy of Thy mercy.

3. What shall I say, guilty that I am and filled with confusion? I have no mouth to utter, unless it be this word alone, "I have sinned, Lord, I have sinned; have mercy upon me, forgive me." *Let me alone, that I may take comfort a little before I go whence I shall not return even to the land of darkness and the shadow of death.*[2] What dost Thou so much require of a guilty and miserable sinner, as that he be contrite, and humble himself for his sins? In true con-

---

[1] Romans ix. 23.   [2] Job x. 20, 21.

trition and humiliation of heart is begotten the hope of pardon, the troubled conscience is reconciled, lost grace is recovered, a man is preserved from the wrath to come, and God and the penitent soul hasten to meet each other with a holy kiss.[3]

4. The humble contrition of sinners is an acceptable sacrifice unto Thee, O Lord, sending forth a smell sweeter far in Thy sight than the incense. This also is that pleasant ointment which Thou wouldst have poured upon Thy sacred feet, *for a broken and contrite heart Thou hast never despised.*[4] There is the place of refuge from the wrathful countenance of the enemy. There is amended and washed away whatsoever evil hath elsewhere been contracted.

CHAPTER LIII

THAT THE GRACE OF GOD DOTH NOT JOIN ITSELF TO THOSE WHO MIND EARTHLY THINGS

"My Son, precious is My grace, it suffereth not itself to be joined with outward things, nor with earthly consolations. Therefore thou oughtest to cast away all things which hinder grace, if thou longest to receive the inpouring thereof. Seek a secret place for thyself, love to dwell alone with thyself, desire the conversation of no one; but rather pour out thy devout prayer to God, that thou mayest possess a contrite mind and a pure conscience. Count the whole world as nought; seek to be alone with God before all outward things. For thou canst not be alone with Me, and at the same time be delighted with transitory things. Thou oughtest to be separated from thy acquaintances and dear friends, and keep thy mind free from all worldly comfort. So the blessed Apostle Peter beseecheth, that Christ's faithful ones bear themselves in this world as strangers and pilgrims.[1]

2. "Oh how great a confidence shall there be to the dying man whom no affection to anything detaineth in the world? But to have a heart so separated from all things, a sickly soul doth not yet comprehend, nor doth the carnal man know the liberty of the spiritual man. But if indeed he desire to be spiritually minded, he must renounce both those who are far off, and those who are near, and to

[3] Luke xv. 20.   [4] Psalm li. 17.   [1] I Peter ii. 11.

beware of no man more than himself. If thou perfectly conquer thyself, very easily shalt thou subdue all things besides. Perfect victory is the triumph over oneself. For whoso keepeth himself in subjection, in such manner that the sensual affections obey the reason, and the reason in all things obeyeth Me, he truly is conqueror of himself, and lord of the world.

3. "If thou desire to climb to this height, thou oughtest to start bravely, and to lay the axe to the root, to the end that thou mayest pull up and destroy the hidden inordinate inclination towards thyself, and towards all selfish and earthly good. From this sin, that a man loveth himself too inordinately, almost everything hangeth which needeth to be utterly overcome: when that evil is conquered and put under foot, there shall be great peace and tranquillity continually. But because few strive earnestly to die perfectly to themselves, and do not heartily go forth from themselves, therefore do they remain entangled in themselves, and cannot be raised in spirit above themselves. But he who desireth to walk at liberty with Me, must of necessity mortify all his evil and inordinate affections, and must cling to no creature with selfish love."

CHAPTER LIV

OF THE DIVERSE MOTIONS OF NATURE AND OF GRACE

"My Son, pay diligent heed to the motions of Nature and of Grace, because they move in a very contrary and subtle manner, and are hardly distinguished save by a spiritual and inwardly enlightened man. All men indeed seek good, and make pretence of something good in all that they say or do; and thus under the appearance of good many are deceived.

2. "Nature is deceitful and draweth away, ensnareth, and deceiveth many, and always hath self for her end; but Grace walketh in simplicity and turneth away from every appearance of evil, maketh no false pretences, and doeth all entirely for the sake of God, in whom also she finally resteth.

3. "Nature is very unwilling to die, and to be pressed down, and to be overcome, and to be in subjection, and to bear the yoke readily; but Grace studieth self-mortification, resisteth sensuality,

seeketh to be subdued, longeth to be conquered, and willeth not to use her own liberty. She loveth to be held by discipline, and not to have authority over any, but always to live, to remain, to have her being under God, and for God's sake is ready to be humbly subject to every ordinance of man.

4. "Nature laboureth for her own advantage, and considereth what profit she may gain from another; but Grace considereth more, not what may be useful and convenient to self, but what may be profitable to the many.

5. "Nature willingly receiveth honour and reverence; but Grace faithfully ascribeth all honour and glory to God.

6. "Nature feareth confusion and contempt, but Grace rejoiceth to suffer shame for the name of Jesus.

7. "Nature loveth ease and bodily quiet; Grace cannot be unemployed, but gladly embraceth labour.

8. "Nature seeketh to possess things curious and attractive, and abhorreth those which are rough and cheap; Grace is delighted with things simple and humble, despiseth not those which are rough, nor refuseth to be clothed with old garments.

9. "Nature hath regard to things temporal, rejoiceth in earthly lucre, is made sad by loss, vexed by any little injurious word; but Grace reacheth after things eternal, cleaveth not to those which are temporal, is not perturbed by losses, nor embittered by any hard words, because she hath placed her treasure and joy in heaven where nought perisheth.

10. "Nature is covetous, and receiveth more willingly than she giveth, loveth things that are personal and private to herself; while Grace is kind and generous, avoideth selfishness, is contented with a little, believeth that it is more blessed to give than to receive.

11. "Nature inclineth thee to created things, to thine own flesh, to vanities and dissipation; but Grace draweth to God and to virtues, renounceth creatures, fleeth from the world, hateth the desires of the flesh, restraineth vagaries, blusheth to be seen in public.

12. "Nature is glad to receive some outward solace in which the senses may have delight; but Grace seeketh to be comforted in God alone, and to have delight in the chief good above all visible things.

13. "Nature doeth everything for her own gain and profit, can do nothing as a free favour, but hopeth to attain something as good or better, or some praise or favour for her benefits; and she loveth that her own deeds and gifts should be highly valued; but Grace seeketh nothing temporal, nor requireth any other gift of reward than God alone; neither longeth she for more of temporal necessities than such as may suffice for the attaining of eternal life.

14. "Nature rejoiceth in many friends and kinsfolk, she boasteth of noble place and noble birth, she smileth on the powerful, flattereth the rich, applaudeth those who are like herself; but Grace loveth even her enemies, and is not lifted up by the multitude of friends, setteth no store upon high place or high birth, unless there be greater virtue therewith; favoureth the poor man more than the rich, hath more sympathy with the innocent than with the powerful; rejoiceth with the truthful, not with the liar; always exhorteth the good to strive after better gifts of grace, and to become by holiness like unto the Son of God.

15. "Nature quickly complaineth of poverty and of trouble; Grace beareth want with constancy.

16. "Nature looketh upon all things in reference to herself; striveth and argueth for self; but Grace bringeth back all things to God from whom they came at the beginning; ascribeth no good to herself nor arrogantly presumeth; is not contentious, nor preferreth her own opinion to others, but in every sense and understanding submitteth herself to the Eternal wisdom and the Divine judgment.

17. "Nature is eager to know secrets and to hear new things; she loveth to appear abroad, and to make experience of many things through the senses; she desireth to be acknowledged and to do those things which win praise and admiration; but Grace careth not to gather up new or curious things, because all this springeth from the old corruption, whereas there is nothing new or lasting upon earth. So she teacheth to restrain the senses, to shun vain complacency and ostentation, to hide humbly those things which merit praise and real admiration, and from everything and in all knowledge to seek after useful fruit, and the praise and honour of God. She desireth not to receive praise for herself or her own, but longeth that God be blessed in all His gifts, who out of unmingled love bestoweth all things."

18. This Grace is a supernatural light, and a certain special gift of God, and the proper mark of the elect, and the pledge of eternal salvation; it exalteth a man from earthly things to love those that are heavenly; and it maketh the carnal man spiritual. So far therefore as Nature is utterly pressed down and overcome, so far is greater Grace bestowed and the inner man is daily created anew by fresh visitations, after the image of God.

CHAPTER LV

OF THE CORRUPTION OF NATURE AND THE EFFICACY OF DIVINE GRACE

O LORD my God, who hast created me after thine own image and similitude, grant me this grace, which Thou hast shown to be so great and so necessary for salvation, that I may conquer my wicked nature, which draweth me to sin and to perdition. For I feel in my flesh the law of sin, contradicting the law of my mind, and bringing me into captivity to the obedience of sensuality in many things; nor can I resist its passions, unless Thy most holy grace assist me, fervently poured into my heart.

2. There is need of Thy grace, yea, and of a great measure thereof, that my nature may be conquered, which hath alway been prone to evil from my youth. For being fallen through the first man Adam, and corrupted through sin, the punishment of this stain descended upon all men; so that *Nature* itself, which was framed good and right by Thee, is now used to express the vice and infirmity of corrupted Nature; because its motion left unto itself draweth men away to evil and to lower things. For the little power which remaineth is as it were one spark lying hid in the ashes. This is Natural reason itself, encompassed with thick clouds, having yet a discernment of good and evil, a distinction of the true and the false, though it be powerless to fulfil all that it approveth, and possess not yet the full light of truth, nor healthfulness of its affections.

3. Hence it is, O my God, that *I delight in Thy law after the inward man,*[1] knowing that Thy *commandment is holy and just and good;* reproving also all evil, and the sin that is to be avoided: yet *with the flesh I serve the law of sin,* whilst I obey sensuality rather

[1] Romans vii. 12, 22. 25.

than reason. Hence it is that *to will to do good is present with me, but how to perform it I find not.*[2] Hence I ofttimes purpose many good things; but because grace is lacking to help mine infirmities, I fall back before a little resistance and fail. Hence it cometh to pass that I recognize the way of perfectness, and see very clearly what things I ought to do; but pressed down by the weight of my own corruption, I rise not to the things which are more perfect.

4. Oh how entirely necessary is Thy grace to me, O Lord, for a good beginning, for progress, and for bringing to perfection. For without it I can do nothing, but *I can do all things through Thy grace which strengtheneth me.*[3] O truly heavenly grace, without which our own merits are nought, and no gifts of Nature at all are to be esteemed. Arts, riches, beauty, strength, wit, eloquence, they all avail nothing before Thee, O Lord, without Thy grace. For the gifts of Nature belong to good and evil alike; but the proper gift of the elect is grace—that is, love—and they who bear the mark thereof are held worthy of everlasting life. So mighty is this grace, that without it neither the gift of prophecy nor the working of miracles, nor any speculation, howsoever lofty, is of any value at all. But neither faith, nor hope, nor any other virtue is accepted with Thee without love and grace.

5. O most blessed grace that makest the poor in spirit rich in virtues, and renderest him who is rich in many things humble in spirit, come Thou, descend upon me, fill me early with Thy consolation, lest my soul fail through weariness and drought of mind. I beseech thee, O Lord, that I may find grace in Thy sight, for *Thy grace is sufficient for me,*[4] when I obtain not those things which Nature longeth for. If I be tempted and vexed with many tribulations, I will fear no evil, while Thy grace remaineth with me. This alone is my strength, this bringeth me counsel and help. It is more powerful than all enemies, and wiser than all the wise men in the world.

6. It is the mistress of truth, the teacher of discipline, the light of the heart, the solace of anxiety, the banisher of sorrow, the deliverer from fear, the nurse of devotion, the drawer forth of tears. What am I without it, save a dry tree, a useless branch, worthy to be cast away!

[2] Romans vii. 18.   [3] Philippians iv. 13.   [4] 2 Corinthians xii. 9.

"Let Thy grace, therefore, O Lord, always prevent and follow me, and make me continually given to all good works, through Jesus Christ, Thy Son. Amen."

CHAPTER LVI

THAT WE OUGHT TO DENY OURSELVES, AND TO IMITATE CHRIST BY MEANS OF THE CROSS

MY Son, so far as thou art able to go out of thyself so far shalt thou be able to enter into Me. As to desire no outward thing worketh internal peace, so the forsaking of self inwardly joineth unto God. I will that thou learn perfect self-denial, living in My will without contradiction or complaint. Follow Me: *I am the way, the truth, and the life.*[1] Without the way thou canst not go, without the truth thou canst not know, without the life thou canst not live. I am the Way which thou oughtest to follow; the Truth which thou oughtest to believe; the Life which thou oughtest to hope for. I am the Way unchangeable; the Truth infallible; the Life everlasting. I am the Way altogether straight, the Truth supreme, the true Life, the blessed Life, the uncreated Life. If thou remain in My way thou shalt know the Truth, *and the truth shall make thee free,*[2] and thou shalt lay hold on eternal life.

2. "*If thou wilt enter into life, keep the commandments.*[3] If thou wilt know the truth, believe in Me. *If thou wilt be perfect, sell all that thou hast.* If thou wilt be My disciple, deny thyself. If thou wouldst possess the blessed life, despise the life which now is. If thou wilt be exalted in heaven, humble thyself in the world. If thou wilt reign with Me, bear the cross with Me; for only the servants of the cross find the way of blessedness and of true light."

3. O Lord Jesu, forasmuch as Thy life was straitened and despised by the world, grant unto me to imitate Thee in despising the world, *for the servant is not greater than his lord, nor the disciple above his master.*[4] Let Thy servant be exercised in Thy life, because there is my salvation and true holiness. Whatsoever I read or hear besides it, it refresheth me not, nor giveth me delight.

[1] John xiv. 6.   [2] John viii. 32.   [3] Matthew xix. 17, 21.   [4] Matthew x. 24.

4. "My son, because thou knowest these things and hast read them all, blessed shalt thou be if thou doest them. *He who hath My commandments and keepeth them, he it is that loveth Me, and I will love him, and will manifest Myself to him,*[5] and I will make him to sit down with Me in My Father's Kingdom."

5. O Lord Jesu, as Thou hast said and promised, even so let it be unto me, and grant me to prove worthy. I have received the cross at Thy hand; I have carried it, and will carry it even unto death, as Thou hast laid it upon me. Truly the life of a truly devoted servant is a cross, but it leadeth to paradise. I have begun; I may not return back nor leave it.

6. Come, my brothers, let us together go forward. Jesus shall be with us. For Jesus' sake have we taken up this cross, for Jesus' sake let us persevere in the cross. He will be our helper, who was our Captain and Forerunner. Behold our King entereth in before us, and He will fight for us. Let us follow bravely, let no man fear terrors; let us be prepared to die bravely in battle, *and let us not so stain our honour,*[6] as to fly from the cross.

CHAPTER LVII

THAT A MAN MUST NOT BE TOO MUCH CAST DOWN WHEN HE FALLETH INTO SOME FAULTS

"My Son, patience and humility in adversities are more pleasing to Me than much comfort and devotion in prosperity. Why doth a little thing spoken against thee make thee sad? If it had been more, thou still oughtest not to be moved. But now suffer it to go by; it is not the first, it is not new, and it will not be the last, if thou live long. Thou art brave enough, so long as no adversity meeteth thee. Thou givest good counsel also, and knowest how to strengthen others with thy words; but when tribulation suddenly knocketh at thine own door, thy counsel and strength fail. Consider thy great frailty, which thou dost so often experience in trifling matters nevertheless, for thy soul's health these things are done when they and such like happen unto thee.

[5] John xiv. 21.   [6] 1 Mac. ix. 10.

2. "Put them away from thy heart as well as thou canst, and if tribulation hath touched thee, yet let it not cast thee down nor entangle thee long. At the least, bear patiently, if thou canst not joyfully. And although thou be very unwilling to hear it, and feel indignation, yet check thyself, and suffer no unadvised word to come forth from thy lips, whereby the little ones may be offended. Soon the storm which hath been raised shall be stilled, and inward grief shall be sweetened by returning grace. I yet live, saith the Lord, ready to help thee, and to give thee more than wonted consolation if thou put thy trust in Me, and call devoutly upon Me.

3. "Be thou more calm of spirit, and gird thyself for greater endurance. All is not frustrated, though thou find thyself very often afflicted or grievously tempted. Thou art man, not God; thou art flesh, not an angel. How shouldst thou be able to remain alway in the same state of virtue, when an angel in heaven fell, and the first man in paradise? I am He who lifteth up the mourners to deliverance, and those who know their own infirmity I raise up to my own nature."

4. O Lord, blessed be Thy word, sweeter to my mouth than honey and the honeycomb. What should I do in my so great tribulations and anxieties, unless Thou didst comfort me with Thy holy words? If only I may attain unto the haven of salvation, what matter is it what things or how many I suffer? Give me a good end, give me a happy passage out of this world. Remember me, O my God, and lead me by the right way unto Thy Kingdom. Amen.

CHAPTER LVIII

OF DEEPER MATTERS, AND GOD'S HIDDEN JUDGMENTS WHICH ARE NOT TO BE INQUIRED INTO

"My Son, beware thou dispute not of high matters and of the hidden judgments of God; why this man is thus left, and that man is taken into so great favour; why also this man is so greatly afflicted, and that so highly exalted. These things pass all man's power of judging, neither may any reasoning or disputation have power to search out the divine judgments. When therefore the enemy suggesteth these things to thee, or when any curious people ask such questions, answer with that word of the Prophet, *Just art Thou, O Lord, and true is Thy judgment,*[1] and with this, *The judgments of the Lord are true, and righteous altogether.*[2] My judgments are to be feared, not to be disputed on, because they are incomprehensible to human understanding.

2. "And be not given to inquire or dispute about the merits of the Saints, which is holier than another, or which is the greater in the Kingdom of Heaven. Such questions often beget useless strifes and contentions: they also nourish pride and vain glory, whence envyings and dissensions arise, while one man arrogantly endeavoureth to exalt one Saint and another another. But to wish to know and search out such things bringeth no fruit, but it rather displeaseth the Saints; for I am not *the God of confusion but of peace;*[3] which peace consisteth more in true humility than in self-exaltation.

3. "Some are drawn by zeal of love to greater affection to these Saints or those; but this is human affection rather than divine. I am He Who made all the Saints: I gave them grace, I brought them glory; I know the merits of every one; *I prevented them with the blessings of My goodness.*[4] I foreknew my beloved ones from everlasting, *I chose them out of the world;*[5] they did not choose Me. I called them by My grace, drew them by My mercy, led them on through sundry temptations. I poured mighty consolations upon them, I gave them perseverance, I crowned their patience.

4. "I acknowledge the first and the last; I embrace all with inestimable love. I am to be praised in all My Saints; I am to be blessed above all things, and to be honoured in every one whom I have so gloriously exalted and predestined, without any preceding merits of their own. He therefore that shall despise one of the least of these My people, honoureth not the great; because I made both small and great.[6] And he who speaketh against any of My Saints speaketh against Me, and against all others in the Kingdom of Heaven."

They are all one through the bond of charity; they think the same thing, will the same thing, and all are united in love one to another.

---

[1] Psalm cxix. 137. [2] Psalm xix. 9. [3] Corinthians xiv. 33.
[4] Psalm xxi. 3. [5] John xv. 19. [6] Wisd. vi. 8.

5. "But yet (which is far better) they love Me above themselves and their own merits. For being caught up above themselves, and drawn beyond self-love, they go all straightforward to the love of Me, and they rest in Me in perfect enjoyment. There is nothing which can turn them away or press them down; for being full of Eternal Truth, they burn with the fire of inextinguishable charity. Therefore let all carnal and natural men hold their peace concerning the state of the Saints, for they know nothing save to love their own personal enjoyment. They take away and add according to their own inclination, not as it pleaseth the Eternal Truth.

6. "In many men this is ignorance, chiefly is it so in those who, being little enlightened, rarely learn to love any one with perfect spiritual love. They are still much drawn by natural affection and human friendship to these or to those: and as they reckon of themselves in lower matters, só also do they frame imaginations of things heavenly. But there is an immeasurable difference between those things which they imperfectly imagine, and these things which enlightened men behold through supernatural revelation.

7. "Take heed, therefore, My son, that thou treat not curiously those things which surpass thy knowledge, but rather make this thy business and give attention to it, namely, that thou seek to be found, even though it be the least, in the Kingdom of God. And even if any one should know who were holier than others, or who were held greatest in the Kingdom of Heaven; what should that knowledge profit him, unless through this knowledge he should humble himself before Me, and should rise up to give greater praise unto My name? He who considereth how great are his own sins, how small his virtues, and how far he is removed from the perfection of the Saints, doeth far more acceptably in the sight of God, than he who disputeth about their greatness or littleness.

8. "They are altogether well content, if men would learn to be content, and to refrain from vain babbling. They glory not of their own merits, seeing they ascribe no good unto themselves, but all unto Me, seeing that I of my infinite charity have given them all things. They are filled with so great love of the Divinity, and with such overflowing joy, that no glory is lacking to them, neither can any felicity be lacking. All the Saints, the higher they are exalted in

glory, the humbler are they in themselves, and the nearer and dearer are they unto Me. And so thou hast it written that they cast their crowns before God and fell on their faces before the Lamb, and worshipped Him that liveth for ever and ever.[7]

9. "Many ask who is greatest in the Kingdom of Heaven, who know not whether they shall be worthy to be counted among the least. It is a great thing to be even the least in Heaven, where all are great, because all shall be called, and shall be, the sons of God. *A little one shall become a thousand,* but *the sinner being an hundred years old shall be accursed.* For when the disciples asked *who should be the greatest in the Kingdom of Heaven,* they received no other answer than this, *Except ye be converted and become as little children, ye shall not enter into the Kingdom of Heaven. But whosoever shall humble himself as this little child, the same shall be greatest in the Kingdom of Heaven."* [8]

10. Woe unto them who disdain to humble themselves willingly with the little children; for the low gate of the kingdom of Heaven will not suffer them to enter in. Woe also to them who are rich, who have their consolation here;[9] because whilst the poor enter into the kingdom of God, they shall stand lamenting without. Rejoice ye humble, and exult ye poor, for yours is the kingdom of God if only ye walk in the truth.

CHAPTER LIX

THAT ALL HOPE AND TRUST IS TO BE FIXED IN GOD ALONE

O LORD, what is my trust which I have in this life, or what is my greatest comfort of all the things which are seen under Heaven? Is it not Thou, O Lord my God, whose mercies are without number? Where hath it been well with me without Thee? Or when could it be evil whilst Thou wert near? I had rather be poor for Thy sake, than rich without Thee. I choose rather to be a pilgrim upon the earth with Thee than without Thee to possess heaven. Where Thou art, there is heaven; and where Thou are not, behold there death and hell. Thou art all my desire, and therefore must I groan and cry and earnestly pray after Thee. In short I can con-

---

[7] Revelation iv. 10; v. 14.   [8] Matthew xviii. 3.   [9] Philippians ii. 21.

fide fully in none to give me ready help in necessities, save in Thee alone, O my God. Thou art my hope, Thou art my trust, Thou art my Comforter, and most faithful in all things.

2. *All men seek their own;*[1] Thou settest forward only my salvation and my profit, and turnest all things unto my good. Even though Thou dost expose me to divers temptations and adversities, Thou ordainest all this unto my advantage, for Thou are wont to prove Thy beloved ones in a thousand ways. In which proving Thou oughtest no less to be loved and praised, than if Thou wert filling me full of heavenly consolations.

3. In Thee, therefore, O Lord God, I put all my hope and my refuge, on Thee I lay all my tribulation and anguish; because I find all to be weak and unstable whatsoever I behold out of Thee. For many friends shall not profit, nor strong helpers be able to succour, nor prudent counsellors to give a useful answer, nor the books of the learned to console, nor any precious substance to deliver, nor any secret and beautiful place to give shelter, if Thou Thyself do not assist, help, strengthen, comfort, instruct, keep in safety.

4. For all things which seem to belong to the attainment of peace and felicity are nothing when Thou art absent, and bring no felicity at all in reality. Therefore art Thou the end of all good, and the fulness of Life, and the soul of eloquence; and to hope in Thee above all things is the strongest solace of Thy servants. *Mine eyes look unto Thee,*[2] in Thee is my trust, O my God, Father of mercies.

5. Bless and sanctify my soul with heavenly blessing that it may become Thy holy habitation, and the seat of Thy eternal glory; and let nothing be found in the Temple of Thy divinity which may offend the eyes of Thy majesty. According to the greatness of Thy goodness and the multitude of Thy mercies look upon me, and hear the prayer of Thy poor servant, far exiled from Thee in the land of the shadow of death. Protect and preserve the soul of Thy least servant amid so many dangers of corruptible life, and by Thy grace accompanying me, direct it by the way of peace unto its home of perpetual light. Amen.

[1] Luke vi.　　[2] Psalm cxli. 8.

THE FOURTH BOOK

OF THE SACRAMENT OF THE ALTAR

A DEVOUT EXHORTATION TO THE HOLY COMMUNION

The Voice of Christ

Come unto Me, all ye that labour and are heavy laden, and I will refresh you,[1] saith the Lord. *The bread that I will give is My flesh which I give for the life of the world.*[2] *Take, eat: this is My Body, which is given for you; this do in remembrance of Me.*[3] *He that eateth My flesh and drinketh My blood dwelleth in Me and I in him. The words that I speak unto you, they are spirit, and they are life.*[4]

CHAPTER I

WITH HOW GREAT REVERENCE CHRIST MUST BE RECEIVED

The Voice of the Disciple

THESE are Thy words, O Christ, Eternal Truth; though not uttered at one time nor written together in one place of Scripture. Because therefore they are Thy words and true, I must gratefully and faithfully receive them all. They are Thine, and Thou hast uttered them; and they are mine also, because Thou didst speak them for my salvation. Gladly I receive them from Thy mouth, that they may be more deeply implanted in my heart. Words of such great grace arouse me, for they are full of sweetness and love; but my own sins terrify me, and my impure conscience driveth me away from receiving so great mysteries. The sweetness of Thy words encourageth me, but the multitude of my faults presseth me down.

2. Thou commandest that I draw near to Thee with firm confidence, if I would have part with Thee, and that I receive the food

---

[1] Matthew xi. 28. [2] John vi. 51. [3] Matthew xxi. 26; Luke xxii. 19.
[4] John vi. 51. 63.

of immortality, if I desire to obtain eternal life and glory. *Come unto Me,* sayest Thou, *all that labour and are heavy laden, and I will refresh you.* Oh, sweet and lovely word in the ear of the sinner, that Thou, O Lord my God, dost invite the poor and needy to the Communion of Thy most holy body and blood. But who am I, O Lord, that I should presume to approach unto Thee? Behold *the heaven of heavens cannot contain Thee,* and yet Thou sayest, *Come ye all unto Me.*

3. What meaneth this most gracious condescension, this most lovely invitation? How shall I dare to come, who know no good thing of myself, whence I might be able to presume? How shall I bring Thee within my house, seeing that I so often have sinned in Thy most loving sight? Angels and Archangels stand in awe of Thee, the Saints and just men fear Thee, and Thou sayest, *Come unto Me!* Except Thou, Lord, hadst said it, who should believe it true? And except Thou hadst commanded, who should attempt to draw near?

4. Behold, Noah, that just man, laboured for a hundred years in building the ark, that he might be saved with the few; and I, how shall I be able in one hour to prepare myself to receive the Builder of the world with reverence? Moses, Thy servant, Thy great and especial friend, made an ark of incorruptible wood, which also he covered with purest gold, that he might lay up in it the tables of the law, and I, a corruptible creature, shall I dare thus easily to receive Thee, the Maker of the Law and the Giver of life? Solomon, the wisest of the kings of Israel, was seven years building his magnificent temple to the praise of Thy Name, and for eight days celebrated the feast of its dedication, offered a thousand peace offerings, and solemnly brought up the Ark of the Covenant to the place prepared for it, with the sound of trumpets and great joy, and I, unhappy and poorest of mankind, how shall I bring Thee into my house, who scarce know how to spend half an hour in devotion? And oh that it were even one half hour worthily spent!

5. O my God, how earnestly these holy men strove to please Thee! And alas! how little and trifling is that which I do! how short a time do I spend, when I am disposing myself to Communion. Rarely altogether collected, most rarely cleansed from all distraction. And

surely in the saving presence of Thy Godhead no unmeet thought ought to intrude, nor should any creature take possession of me, because it is not an Angel but the Lord of the Angels, that I am about to receive as my Guest.

6. Yet there is a vast difference between the Ark of the Covenant with its relics, and Thy most pure Body with its ineffable virtues, between those sacrifices of the law, which were figures of things to come, and the true sacrifice of Thy Body, the completion of all the ancient sacrifices.

7. Wherefore then do I not yearn more ardently after Thy adorable presence? Why do I not prepare myself with greater solicitude to receive Thy holy things, when those holy Patriarchs and Prophets of old, kings also and princes, with the whole people, manifested so great affection of devotion towards Thy Divine Service?

8. The most devout king David danced with all his might before the Ark of God, calling to mind the benefits granted to his forefathers in days past; he fashioned musical instruments of various sorts, put forth Psalms, and appointed them to be sung with joy, played also himself ofttimes on the harp, being inspired with the grace of the Holy Ghost; he taught the people of Israel to praise God with the whole heart, and with unity of voice to bless and praise Him every day. If so great devotion was then exercised, and celebration of divine praise was carried on before the Ark of the Testimony, how great reverence and devotion ought now to be shown by me and all Christian people at the ministering of the Sacrament, at receiving the most precious Body and Blood of Christ.

9. Many run to diverse places to visit the memorials of departed Saints, and rejoice to hear of their deeds and to look upon the beautiful buildings of their shrines. And behold, Thou art present here with me, O my God, Saint of Saints, Creator of men and Lord of the Angels. Often in looking at those memorials men are moved by curiosity and novelty, and very little fruit of amendment is borne away, especially when there is so much careless trifling and so little true contrition. But here in the Sacrament of the Altar, Thou art present altogether, My God, the Man Christ Jesus; where also abundant fruit of eternal life is given to every one soever that receiveth Thee worthily and devoutly. But to this no levity draweth, no curi-

osity, nor sensuality, only steadfast faith, devout hope, and sincere charity.

10. O God, invisible Creator of the world, how wondrously dost Thou work with us, how sweetly and graciously Thou dealest with Thine elect, to whom Thou offerest Thyself to be received in this Sacrament! For this surpasseth all understanding, this specially draweth the hearts of the devout and enkindleth their affections. For even thy true faithful ones themselves, who order their whole life to amendment, oftentimes gain from this most excellent Sacrament great grace of devotion and love of virtue.

11. Oh admirable and hidden grace of the Sacrament, which only Christ's faithful ones know, but the faithless and those who serve sin cannot experience! In this Sacrament is conferred spiritual grace, and lost virtue is regained in the soul, and the beauty which was disfigured by sin returneth again. So great sometimes is this grace that out of the fulness of devotion given, not only the mind but also the weak body feeleth that more strength is supplied unto it.

12. But greatly must we mourn and lament over our lukewarmness and negligence, that we are not drawn by greater affection to become partakers of Christ, in whom all the hope and the merit of those that are to be saved consist. For He Himself *is our sanctification and redemption*.[1] He is the consolation of pilgrims and the eternal fruition of the Saints. Therefore it is grievously to be lamented that many so little consider this health-giving mystery, which maketh heaven glad and preserveth the whole world. Alas for the blindness and hardness of man's heart, that he considereth not more this unspeakable gift, and even slippeth down through the daily use, into carelessness.

13. For if this most holy Sacrament were celebrated in one place only, and were consecrated only by one priest in the whole world, with what great desire thinkest thou, would men be affected towards that place and towards such a priest of God, that they might behold the divine mysteries celebrated? But now are many men made priests and in many places the Sacrament is celebrated, that the grace and love of God towards men might the more appear, the more widely the Holy Communion is spread abroad over all the world.

[1] 1 Corinthians i. 30.

Thanks be unto Thee, O good Jesus, Eternal Shepherd, who hast vouchsafed to refresh us, poor and exiled ones, with Thy precious Body and Blood, and to invite us to partake these holy mysteries by the invitation from Thine own mouth, saying, *Come unto Me, ye who labour and are heavy laden, and I will refresh you.*

CHAPTER II

THAT THE GREATNESS AND CHARITY OF GOD IS SHOWN TO MEN IN THE SACRAMENT

The Voice of the Disciple

TRUSTING in Thy goodness and great mercy, O Lord, I draw near, the sick to the Healer, the hungering and thirsting to the Fountain of life, the poverty-stricken to the King of heaven, the servant to the Lord, the creature to the Creator, the desolate to my own gentle Comforter. But whence is this unto me, that Thou comest unto me? Who am I that Thou shouldest offer me Thyself? How doth a sinner dare to appear before Thee? And how dost thou vouchsafe to come to the sinner? Thou knowest Thy servant, and Thou knowest that he hath in him no good thing for which Thou shouldest grant him this grace. I confess therefore mine own vileness, I acknowledge Thy goodness, I praise Thy tenderness, and I give Thee thanks for Thine exceeding great love. For Thou doest this for Thine own sake, not for my merits, that Thy goodness may be more manifest unto me, Thy charity more abundantly poured out upon me, and Thy humility more perfectly commended unto me. Therefore because this pleaseth Thee and Thou hast commanded that thus it shall be, Thy condescension pleaseth me also; and oh that mine iniquity hinder it not.

2. O most sweet and tender Jesus, what reverence, what giving of thanks is due to Thee with perpetual praise for the receiving of Thy sacred Body and Blood, the dignity whereof no man is found able to express. But what shall I think upon in this Communion in approaching my Lord, whom I am not able worthily to honour, and nevertheless whom I long devoutly to receive? What shall be better and more healthful meditation for me, than utter humiliation

of myself before Thee, and exaltation of Thine infinite goodness towards me? I praise Thee, O my God, and exalt Thee for evermore. I despise myself, and cast myself down before Thee into the deep of my vileness.

3. Behold, Thou art the Saint of saints and I the refuse of sinners; behold, Thou stoopest unto me who am not worthy to look upon Thee; behold, Thou comest unto me, Thou willest to be with me, Thou invitest me to Thy feast. Thou willest to give me the heavenly food and bread of angels to eat; none other, in truth, than Thyself, *The living bread, which didst descend from heaven; and givest life to the world.*[1]

4. Behold, whence this love proceedeth! what manner of condescension shineth forth herein. What great giving of thanks and praise is due unto Thee for these benefits! Oh how salutary and profitable Thy purpose when Thou didst ordain this! How sweet and pleasant the feast when Thou didst give Thyself for food! Oh how admirable is thy working, O Lord, how mighty Thy power, how unspeakable Thy truth! For Thou didst speak the word, and all things were made; and this is done which Thou hast commanded.

5. A thing wonderful, and worthy of faith, and surpassing all the understanding of man, that Thou, O Lord my God, very God and very man, givest Thyself altogether to us in a little bread and wine, and art so our inexhaustible food. Thou, O Lord of all, who hast need of nothing, hast willed to dwell in us through Thy Sacrament. Preserve my heart and my body undefiled, that with a joyful and pure conscience I may be able very often to [celebrate, and][2] receive to my perpetual health. Thy mysteries, which Thou hast consecrated and instituted both for Thine own honour, and for a perpetual memorial.

6. Rejoice, O my soul, and give thanks unto God for so great a gift and precious consolation, left unto thee in this vale of tears. For so oft as thou callest this mystery to mind and receivest the body of Christ, so often dost thou celebrate the work of thy redemption, and art made partaker of all the merits of Christ. For the charity of Christ never groweth less, and the greatness of His propitiation is

[1] John vi. 51.   [2] The words in brackets are only suitable for a priest.

never exhausted. Therefore, by continual renewal of thy spirit, thou oughtest to dispose thyself hereunto and to weigh the great mystery of salvation with attentive consideration. So great, new, and joyful ought it to appear to thee when thou comest to communion, as if on this self-same day Christ for the first time were descending into the Virgin's womb and becoming man, or hanging on the cross, suffering and dying for the salvation of mankind.

CHAPTER III

THAT IT IS PROFITABLE TO COMMUNICATE OFTEN

The Voice of the Disciple

BEHOLD I come unto Thee, O Lord, that I may be blessed through Thy gift, and be made joyful in Thy holy feast which *Thou, O God, of Thy goodness hast prepared for the poor*.[1] Behold in Thee is all that I can and ought to desire, Thou art my salvation and redemption, my hope and strength, my honour and glory. Therefore *rejoice the soul of Thy servant this day, for unto Thee*, O Lord Jesus, *do I lift up my soul*.[2] I long now to receive Thee devoutly and reverently, I desire to bring Thee into my house, so that with Zacchæus I may be counted worthy to be blessed by Thee and numbered among the children of Abraham. My soul hath an earnest desire for Thy Body, my heart longeth to be united with Thee.

2. Give me Thyself and it sufficeth, for besides Thee no consolation availeth. Without Thee I cannot be, and without Thy visitation I have no power to live. And therefore I must needs draw nigh unto Thee often, and receive Thee for the healing of my soul, lest haply I faint by the way if I be deprived of heavenly food. For so Thou, most merciful Jesus, preaching to the people and healing many sick, didst once say, *I will not send them away fasting to their own homes, lest they faint by the way*.[3] Deal therefore now to me in like manner, for Thou left Thyself for the consolation of the faithful in the Sacrament. For Thou art the sweet refreshment of the soul, and he who shall eat Thee worthily shall be partaker and inheritor of the eternal glory. Necessary indeed it is for me, who so

[1] Psalm lxviii. 10.   [2] Psalm lxxxvi. 4.   [3] Matthew xv. 32.

often slide backwards and sin, so quickly wax cold and faint, to renew, cleanse, enkindle myself by frequent prayers and penitences and receiving of Thy sacred Body and Blood lest haply by too long abstinence, I fall short of my holy resolutions.

3. *For the imaginations of man's heart are evil from his youth,*[4] and except divine medicine succour him, man slideth away continually unto the worse. The Holy Communion therefore draweth us back from evil, and strengtheneth us for good. For if I now be so negligent and lukewarm when I communicate [or celebrate], how should it be with me, if I receive not this medicine, and sought not so great a help? [And though I am not every day fit nor well prepared to celebrate, I will nevertheless give diligent heed at due season, to receive the divine mysteries, and to become partaker of so great grace]. For this is the one principal consolation of a faithful soul, so long as it is absent from Thee in mortal body, that being continually mindful of its God, it receiveth its Beloved with devout spirit.

4. Oh wonderful condescension of Thy pity surrounding us, that Thou, O Lord God, Creator and Quickener of all spirits, deignest to come unto a soul so poor and weak, and to appease its hunger with Thy whole Deity and Humanity. Oh happy mind and blessed soul, to which is granted devoutly to receive Thee its Lord God, and in so receiving Thee to be filled with all spiritual joy! Oh how great a Lord doth it entertain, how beloved a Guest doth it bring in, how delightful a Companion doth it receive, how faithful a Friend doth it welcome, how beautiful and exalted a Spouse, above every other Beloved, doth it embrace, One to be loved above all things that can be desired! Oh my most sweet Beloved, let heaven and earth and all the glory of them, be silent in Thy presence; seeing whatsoever praise and beauty they have it is of Thy gracious bounty; and they shall never reach unto the loveliness of Thy Name, *Whose Wisdom is infinite.*[5]

[4] Genesis viii. 21.   [5] Psalm cxlvii. 5.

CHAPTER IV

THAT MANY GOOD GIFTS ARE BESTOWED UPON THOSE WHO COMMUNICATE DEVOUTLY

The Voice of the Disciple

O LORD my God, prevent Thou Thy servant with the blessings of Thy sweetness, that I may be enabled to draw near worthily and devoutly to Thy glorious Sacrament. Awaken my heart towards Thee, and deliver me from heavy slumber. Visit me with Thy salvation that I may in spirit taste Thy sweetness, which plentifully lieth hid in this Sacrament as in a fountain. Lighten also mine eyes to behold this so great mystery, and strengthen me that I may believe it with undoubting faith. For it is Thy word, not human power; it is Thy holy institution, not the invention of man. For no man is found fit in himself to receive and to understand these things, which transcend even the wisdom of the Angels. What portion then shall I, unworthy sinner, who am but dust and ashes, be able to search into and comprehend of so deep a Sacrament?

2. O Lord, in the simplicity of my heart, in good and firm faith, and according to Thy will, I draw nigh unto Thee with hope and reverence, and truly believe that Thou art here present in the Sacrament, God and man. Thou willest therefore that I receive Thee and unite myself to Thee in charity. Wherefore I beseech Thy mercy, and implore Thee to give me Thy special grace, to this end, that I may be wholly dissolved and overflow with love towards Thee, and no more suffer any other consolation to enter into me. For this most high and most glorious Sacrament is the health of the soul and the body, the medicine of all spiritual sickness, whereby I am healed of my sins, my passions are bridled, temptations are conquered or weakened, more grace is poured into me, virtue begun is increased, faith is made firm, hope is strengthened, and charity is enkindled and enlarged.

3. For in this Sacrament Thou hast bestowed many good things and still bestowest them continually on Thine elect who communicate devoutly, O my God, Lifter up of my soul, Repairer of human infirmity, and Giver of all inward consolation. For Thou pourest

into them much consolation against all sorts of tribulation, and out of the deep of their own misery Thou liftest them up to the hope of Thy protection, and with ever new grace, dost inwardly refresh and enlighten them; so that they who felt themselves to be anxious and without affection before Communion, afterwards being refreshed with heavenly food and drink, find themselves changed for the better. And even in such wise Thou dealest severally with Thine elect, that they may truly acknowledge and clearly make proof that they have nothing whatsoever of their own, and what goodness and grace come to them from Thee; because being in themselves cold, hard of heart, indevout, through Thee they become fervent, zealous, and devout. For who is there coming humbly to the fountain of sweetness, carrieth not away thence at the least some little of that sweetness? Or who standing by a large fire, feeleth not from thence a little of its heat? And Thou art ever a full and overflowing fountain, a fire continually burning, and never going out.

4. Wherefore if it is not suffered to me to draw from the fulness of the fountain, nor to drink unto satisfying, yet will I set my lips to the mouth of the heavenly conduit, that at least I may receive a small drop to quench my thirst, that I dry not up within my heart. And if I am not yet able to be altogether heavenly and so enkindled as the Cherubim and Seraphim, yet will I endeavour to give myself unto devotion, and to prepare my heart, that I may gain if it be but a little flame of the divine fire, through the humble receiving of the life-giving Sacrament. But whatsoever is wanting unto me, O merciful Jesus, Most Holy Saviour, do Thou of Thy kindness and grace supply, who hast vouchsafed to call all unto Thee, saying, *Come unto me, all ye that are weary and heavy laden, and I will refresh you.*

5. I indeed labour in the sweat of my face, I am tormented with sorrow of heart, I am burdened with sins, I am disquieted with temptations, I am entangled and oppressed with many passions, and there is none to help me, there is none to deliver and ease me, but Thou, O Lord God, my Saviour, to whom I commit myself and all things that are mine, that Thou mayest preserve me and lead me unto life eternal.

Receive me unto the praise and glory of Thy name, who hast prepared Thy Body and Blood to be my meat and drink. Grant, O

Lord God my Saviour, that with coming often to Thy mysteries the zeal of my devotion may increase.

CHAPTER V

OF THE DIGNITY OF THIS SACRAMENT, AND OF THE OFFICE OF THE PRIEST

The Voice of the Beloved

IF thou hadst angelic purity and the holiness of holy John the Baptist, thou wouldest not be worthy to receive or to minister this Sacrament. For this is not deserved by merit of man that a man should consecrate and minister the Sacrament of Christ, and take for food the bread of Angels. Vast is the mystery, and great is the dignity of the priests, to whom is given what is not granted to Angels. For priests only, rightly ordained in the church, have the power of consecrating and celebrating the Body of Christ. The priest indeed is the minister of God, using the Word of God by God's command and institution; nevertheless God is there the principal Author and invisible Worker, that to whom all that He willeth is subject, and all He commandeth is obedient.

2. Therefore thou must believe God Almighty in this most excellent Sacrament, more than thine own sense or any visible sign at all. And therefore with fear and reverence is this work to be approached. Take heed therefore and see what it is of which the ministry is committed to thee by the laying on of the Bishop's hand. Behold thou art made a priest and art consecrated to celebrate. See now that thou do it before God faithfully and devoutly at due time, and shew thyself without blame. Thou hast not lightened thy burden, but art now bound with a straiter bond of discipline, and art pledged to a higher degree of holiness. A priest ought to be adorned with all virtues and to afford to others an example of good life. His conversation must not be with the popular and common ways of men, but with Angels in Heaven or with perfect men on earth.

3. A priest clad in holy garments taketh Christ's place that he may pray unto God with all supplication and humility for himself and for the whole people. He must always remember the Passion of

Christ. He must diligently look upon Christ's footsteps and fervently endeavour himself to follow them. He must bear meekly for God whatsoever ills are brought upon him by others. He must mourn for his own sins, and for the sins committed by others, and may not grow careless of prayer and holy oblation, until he prevail to obtain grace and mercy. When the priest celebrateth, he honoureth God, giveth joy to the Angels, buildeth up the Church, helpeth the living, hath communion with the departed, and maketh himself a partaker of all good things.

CHAPTER VI

AN INQUIRY CONCERNING PREPARATION FOR COMMUNION

The Voice of the Disciple

WHEN I consider Thy dignity, O Lord, and mine own vileness, I tremble very exceedingly, and am confounded within myself. For if I approach not, I fly from life; and if I intrude myself unworthily, I run into Thy displeasure. What then shall I do, O my God, Thou helper and Counsellor in necessities.

2. Teach Thou me the right way; propound unto me some short exercise befitting Holy Communion. For it is profitable to know how I ought to prepare my heart devoutly and reverently for Thee, to the intent that I may receive Thy Sacrament to my soul's health [or it may be also for the celebrating this so great and divine mystery].

CHAPTER VII

OF THE EXAMINATION OF CONSCIENCE, AND PURPOSE OF AMENDMENT

The Voice of the Beloved

ABOVE all things the priest of God must draw nigh, with all humility of heart and supplicating reverence, with full faith and pious desire for the honour of God, to celebrate, minister, and receive this Sacrament. Diligently examine thy conscience and with all thy might with true contrition and humble confession cleanse and purify it, so that thou mayest feel no burden, nor know anything which bringeth thee remorse and impedeth thy free approach. Have displeasure against all thy sins in general, and specially sorrow and mourn because of thy daily transgressions. And if thou have time, confess unto God in the secret of thine heart, all miseries of thine own passion.

2. Lament grievously and be sorry, because thou art still so carnal and worldly, so unmortified from thy passions, so full of the motion of concupiscence, so unguarded in thine outward senses, so often entangled in many vain fancies, so much inclined to outward things, so negligent of internal; so ready to laughter and dissoluteness, so unready to weeping and contrition; so prone to ease and indulgence of the flesh, so dull to zeal and fervour; so curious to hear novelties and behold beauties, so loth to embrace things humble and despised; so desirous to have many things, so grudging in giving, so close in keeping; so inconsiderate in speaking, so reluctant to keep silence; so disorderly in manners, so inconsiderate in actions; so eager after food, so deaf towards the Word of God; so eager after rest, so slow to labour; so watchful after tales, so sleepy towards holy watchings; so eager for the end of them, so wandering in attention to them; so negligent in observing the hours of prayer, so lukewarm in celebrating, so unfruitful in communicating; so quickly distracted, so seldom quite collected with thyself; so quickly moved to anger, so ready for displeasure at others; so prone to judging, so severe at reproving; so joyful in prosperity, so weak in adversity; so often making many good resolutions and bringing them to so little effect.

3. When thou hast confessed and bewailed these and thy other shortcomings, with sorrow and sore displeasure at thine own infirmity, make then a firm resolution of continual amendment of life and of progress in all that is good. Then moreover with full resignation and entire will offer thyself to the honour of My name on the altar of thine heart as a perpetual whole burnt-offering, even by faithfully presenting thy body and soul unto Me, to the end that thou mayest so be accounted worthy to draw near to offer this sacrifice of praise and thanksgiving to God, and to receive the Sacrament of My Body and Blood to thy soul's health. For there is no

oblation worthier, no satisfaction greater for the destroying of sin, than that a man offer himself to God purely and entirely with the oblation of the Body and Blood of Christ in the Holy Communion. If a man shall have done what in him lieth, and shall repent him truly, then how often soever he shall draw nigh unto Me for pardon and grace, *As I live, saith the Lord, I have no pleasure in the death of a sinner, but rather that he should be converted, and live. All his transgressions that he hath committed, they shall not be mentioned unto him.*[1]

CHAPTER VIII

OF THE OBLATION OF CHRIST UPON THE CROSS, AND OF RESIGNATION OF SELF

The Voice of the Beloved

As I of my own will offered myself unto God the Father on the Cross for thy sins with outstretched hands and naked body, so that nothing remained in Me that did not become altogether a sacrifice for the Divine propitiation; so also oughtest thou every day to offer thyself willingly unto Me for a pure and holy oblation with all thy strength and affections, even to the utmost powers of thine heart. What more do I require of thee than thou study to resign thyself altogether unto Me? Whatsoever thou givest besides thyself, I nothing care for, for I ask not thy gift, but thee.

2. As it would not be sufficient for thee if thou hadst all things except Me, even so whatsoever thou shalt give Me, if thou give Me not thyself, it cannot please Me. Offer thyself to Me, and give thyself altogether for God, so shall thy offering be accepted. Behold I offered Myself altogether to the Father for thee, I give also My whole body and blood for food, that thou mightest remain altogether Mine and I thine. But if thou stand in thyself, and offer not thyself freely to My will, thy offering is not perfect, neither shall the union betwixt us be complete. Therefore ought the freewill offering of thyself into the hands of God to go before all thy works, if thou wilt attain liberty and grace. For this is the cause that so few are inwardly enlightened and made free, that they know not how to

[1] Ezekiel xviii, 22, 23.

deny themselves entirely. My word standeth sure, *Except a man forsake all, he cannot be My disciple.*[1] Thou therefore, if thou wilt be My disciple, offer thyself to Me with all thy affections.

CHAPTER IX

THAT WE OUGHT TO OFFER OURSELVES AND ALL THAT IS OURS TO GOD, AND TO PRAY FOR ALL

The Voice of the Disciple

LORD, *all that is in the heaven and in the earth is Thine.*[2] I desire to offer myself up unto thee as a freewill offering, and to continue Thine for ever. Lord, *in the uprightness of mine heart I willingly offer*[3] myself to Thee to-day to be Thy servant for ever, in humble submission and for a sacrifice of perpetual praise. Receive me with this holy Communion of Thy precious Body, which I celebrate before Thee this day in the presence of the Angels invisibly surrounding, that it may be for the salvation of me and of all Thy people.

2. Lord, I lay before Thee at this celebration all my sins and offences which I have committed before Thee and Thy holy Angels, from the day whereon I was first able to sin even unto this hour; that Thou mayest consume and burn them every one with the fire of Thy charity, and mayest do away all the stains of my sins, and cleanse my conscience from all offence, and restore me to Thy favour which by sinning I have lost, fully forgiving me all, and mercifully admitting me to the kiss of peace.

3. What can I do concerning my sins, save humbly to confess and lament them and unceasingly to beseech Thy propitiation? I beseech Thee, be propitious unto me and hear me, when I stand before Thee, O my God. All my sins displease me grievously: I will never more commit them; but I grieve for them and will grieve so long as I live, steadfastly purposing to repent me truly, and to make restitution as far as I can. Forgive, O God, forgive me my sins for Thy holy Name's sake; save my soul, which Thou hast redeemed with Thy precious blood. Behold I commit myself to Thy mercy, I resign myself to Thy hands. Deal with me according to Thy lovingkindness, not according to my wickedness and iniquity.

[1] Luke xiv. 33.   [2] 1 Chronicles xxix. 11.   [3] 1 Chronicles xxix. 17.

4. I offer also unto Thee all my goodness, though it is exceedingly little and imperfect, that Thou mayest mend and sanctify it, that Thou mayest make it well pleasing and acceptable in Thy sight, and ever draw it on towards perfection; and furthermore bring me safely, slothful and useless poor creature that I am, to a happy and blessed end.

5. Moreover I offer unto Thee all pious desires of the devout, necessities of parents, friends, brothers, sisters, and all who are dear to me, and of those who have done good to me, or to others for Thy love; and those who have desired and besought my prayers for themselves and all belonging to them; that all may feel themselves assisted by Thy grace, enriched by consolation, protected from dangers, freed from pains; and that being delivered from all evils they may joyfully give Thee exceeding thanks.

6. I offer also to Thee prayers and Sacramental intercessions for those specially who have injured me in aught, made me sad, or spoken evil concerning me, or have caused me any loss or displeasure; for all those also whom I have at any time made sad, disturbed, burdened, and scandalized, by words or deeds, knowingly or ignorantly; that to all of us alike, Thou mayest equally pardon our sins and mutual offences. Take away, O Lord, from our hearts all suspicion, indignation, anger, and contention, and whatsoever is able to injure charity and diminish brotherly love. Have mercy, have mercy, Lord, on those who entreat Thy mercy; give grace to the needy; and make us such that we may be worthy to enjoy Thy grace, and go forward to the life eternal. Amen.

CHAPTER X

THAT HOLY COMMUNION IS NOT LIGHTLY TO BE OMITTED

The Voice of the Beloved

THOU must frequently betake thee to the Fountain of grace and divine mercy, to the Fountain of goodness and all purity; to the end that thou mayest obtain the healing of thy passions and vices, and mayest be made stronger and more watchful against all temptations and wiles of the devil. The enemy, knowing what profit and exceeding strong remedy lieth in the Holy Communion, striveth by all means and occasions to draw back and hinder the faithful and devout, so far as he can.

2. For when some set about to prepare themselves for Holy Communion, they suffer from the more evil suggestions of Satan. The very evil spirit himself (as is written in Job), cometh among the sons of God that he may trouble them by his accustomed evil dealing, or make them over timid and perplexed; to the intent that he may diminish their affections, or take away their faith by his attacks, if haply he may prevail upon them to give up Holy Communion altogether, or to come thereto with lukewarm hearts. But his wiles and delusions must not be heeded, howsoever wicked and terrible they be; but all his delusion must be cast back upon his own head. The wretch must be despised and laughed to scorn: neither must Holy Communion be omitted because of his insults and the inward troubles which he stirreth up.

3. Often also too much carefulness or some anxiety or other touching confession hindereth from obtaining devotion. Do thou according to the counsel of wise men, and lay aside anxiety and scruple, because it hindereth the grace of God and destroyeth devotion of mind. Because of some little vexation or trouble do not thou neglect Holy Communion, but rather hasten to confess it, and forgive freely all offences committed against thee. And if thou hast offended any man, humbly beg for pardon, and God shall freely forgive thee.

4. What profiteth it to put off for long time the confession of thy sins, or to defer Holy Communion? Cleanse thyself forthwith, spit out the poison with all speed, hasten to take the remedy, and thou shalt feel thyself better than if thou didst long defer it. If to-day thou defer it on one account, to-morrow perchance some greater obstacle will come, and so thou mayest be long time hindered from Communion and become more unfit. As soon as thou canst, shake thyself from thy present heaviness and sloth, for it profiteth nothing to be long anxious, to go long on thy way with heaviness of heart, and because of daily little obstacles to sever thyself from divine things: nay it is exceeding hurtful to defer thy Communion long, for this commonly bringeth on great torpor. Alas! there are some, lukewarm and undisciplined, who willingly find excuses for delay-

ing repentance, and desire to defer Holy Communion, lest they should be bound to keep stricter watch upon themselves.

5. Alas! how little charity, what flagging devotion, have they who so lightly put off Holy Communion. How happy is he, how acceptable to God, who so liveth, and in such purity of conscience keepeth himself, that any day he could be ready and well inclined to communicate, if it were in his power, and might be done without the notice of others. If a man sometimes abstaineth for the sake of humility or some sound cause, he is to be commended for his reverence. But if drowsiness have taken hold of him, he ought to rouse himself and to do what in him lieth; and the Lord will help his desire for the good will which he hath, which God specially approveth.

6. But when he is hindered by sufficient cause, yet will he ever have a good will and pious intention to communicate; and so he shall not be lacking in the fruit of the Sacrament. For any devout man is able every day and every hour to draw near to spiritual communion with Christ to his soul's health and without hindrance. Nevertheless on certain days and at the appointed time he ought to receive the Body and Blood of his Redeemer with affectionate reverence, and rather to seek after the praise and honour of God, than his own comfort. For so often doth he communicate mystically, and is invisibly refreshed, as he devoutly calleth to mind the mystery of Christ's incarnation and His Passion, and is inflamed with the love of Him.

7. He who only prepareth himself when a festival is at hand or custom compelleth, will too often be unprepared. Blessed is he who offereth himself to God for a whole burnt-offering, so often as he celebrateth or communicateth! Be not too slow nor too hurried in thy celebrating, but preserve the good received custom of those with whom thou livest. Thou oughtest not to produce weariness and annoyance in others, but to observe the received custom, according to the institution of the elders; and to minister to the profit of others rather than to thine own devotion or feeling.

CHAPTER XI

THAT THE BODY AND BLOOD OF CHRIST AND THE HOLY SCRIPTURES ARE MOST NECESSARY TO A FAITHFUL SOUL

The Voice of the Disciple

O MOST sweet Lord Jesus, how great is the blessedness of the devout soul that feedeth with Thee in Thy banquet, where there is set before it no other food than Thyself its only Beloved, more to be desired than all the desires of the heart? And to me it would verily be sweet to pour forth my tears in Thy presence from the very bottom of my heart, and with the pious Magdalene to water Thy feet with my tears. But where is this devotion? Where the abundant flowing of holy tears? Surely in Thy presence and in the presence of the holy Angels my whole heart ought to burn and to weep for joy; for I have Thee in the Sacrament verily present, although hidden under other form.

2. For in Thine own Divine brightness, mine eyes could not endure to behold Thee, neither could the whole world stand before the splendour of the glory of Thy Majesty. In this therefore Thou hast consideration unto my weakness, that Thou hidest Thyself under the Sacrament. I verily possess and adore Him whom the Angels adore in heaven; I yet for a while by faith, but they by sight and without a veil. It is good for me to be content with the light of true faith, and to walk therein until the day of eternal brightness dawn, and the shadows of figures flee away.[1] But when that which is perfect is come, the using of Sacraments shall cease, because the Blessed in heavenly glory have no need of Sacramental remedy. For they rejoice unceasingly in the presence of God, beholding His glory face to face, and *being changed from glory to glory*[2] of the infinite God, they taste the Word of God made flesh, as He was in the beginning and remaineth for everlasting.

3. When I think on these wondrous things, even spiritual comfort whatsoever it be becometh sore weariness to me; for so long as I see not openly my Lord in His own Glory, I count for nothing all which I behold and hear in the world. Thou, O God, art my wit-

[1] Cant. ii. 17.   [2] 2 Corinthians iii. 18.

ness that nothing is able to comfort me, no creature is able to give me rest, save Thou, O my God, whom I desire to contemplate everlastingly. But this is not possible, so long as I remain in this mortal state. Therefore ought I to set myself unto great patience, and submit myself unto Thee in every desire. For even Thy Saints, O Lord, who now rejoice with Thee in the kingdom of heaven, waited for the coming of Thy glory whilst they lived here, in faith and great glory. What they believed, that believe I; what they hoped, I hope; whither they have attained to, thither through Thy grace hope I to come. I will walk meanwhile in faith, strengthened by the examples of the Saints. I will have also holy books for comfort and for a mirror of life, and above them all Thy most holy Body and Blood shall be for me a special remedy and refuge.

4. For two things do I feel to be exceedingly necessary to me in this life, without which this miserable life would be intolerable to me; being detained in the prison of this body, I confess that I need two things, even food and light. Thou hast therefore given to me who am so weak, Thy sacred Body and Blood, for the refreshing of my soul and body, and hast set *Thy Word for a lantern to my feet.*[3] Without these two I could not properly live; for the Word of God is the light of my soul, and Thy Sacrament the bread of life. These may also be called the two tables, placed on this side and on that, in the treasury of Thy holy Church. One table is that of the Sacred Altar, bearing the holy bread, that is the precious Body and Blood of Christ; the other is the table of the Divine Law, containing holy doctrine, teaching the true faith, and leading steadfastly onwards even to that which is within the veil, where the Holy of Holies is.

5. Thanks be unto Thee, O Lord Jesus, Light of Light everlasting, for that table of holy doctrine which Thou has furnished unto us by Thy servants the Prophets and Apostles and other teachers. Thanks be to Thee, O Creator and Redeemer of men, who to make known Thy love to the whole world has prepared a great supper, in which Thou hast set forth for good not the typical lamb, but Thine own most Holy Body and Blood; making all Thy faithful ones joyful with this holy banquet and giving them to drink the

[3] Psalm cxix. 105.

cup of salvation, wherein are all the delights of Paradise, and the holy Angels do feed with us, and with yet happier sweetness.

6. Oh how great and honourable is the office of the priests, to whom it is given to consecrate the Sacrament of the Lord of majesty with holy words, to bless it with the lips, to hold it in their hands, to receive it with their own mouth, and to administer it to others! Oh how clean ought those hands to be, how pure the mouth, how holy the body, how unspotted the heart of the priest, to whom so often the Author of purity entereth in! From the mouth of the priest ought naught to proceed but what is holy, what is honest and profitable, because he so often receiveth the Sacrament of Christ.

7. His eyes ought to be single and pure, seeing they are wont to look upon the Body of Christ; the hands should be pure and lifted towards heaven, which are wont to hold within them the Creator of heaven and earth. To priests is it specially said in the Law, *Be ye holy, for I the Lord your God am holy.*[4]

8. Assist us with Thy grace, O Almighty God, that we who have taken upon us the priestly office, may be able to converse worthily and devoutly with Thee in all purity and good conscience. And if we are not able to have our conversation in such innocency of life as we ought, yet grant unto us worthily to lament the sins which we have committed, and in the spirit of humility and full purpose of a good will, to serve Thee more earnestly for the future.

CHAPTER XII

THAT HE WHO IS ABOUT TO COMMUNICATE WITH CHRIST OUGHT TO PREPARE HIMSELF WITH GREAT DILIGENCE

The Voice of the Beloved

I AM the Lover of purity, and Giver of sanctity. I seek a pure heart, and *there is the place of My rest.* Prepare for Me *the larger upper room furnished,* and *I will keep the Passover at thy house with my disciples.*[1] If thou wilt that I come unto thee and abide with thee, *purge out the old leaven,*[2] and cleanse the habitation of thy heart. Shut out the whole world, and all the throng of sins;

[4] Leviticus xix. 2. [1] Mark xiv. 14, 15. [2] 1 Corinthians v. 7.

sit *as a sparrow alone upon the house-top*,[3] and think upon thy transgressions with bitterness of thy soul. For everyone that loveth prepareth the best and fairest place for his beloved, because hereby the affection of him that entertaineth his beloved is known.

2. Yet know thou that thou canst not make sufficient preparation out of the merit of any action of thine, even though thou shouldest prepare thyself for a whole year, and hadst nothing else in thy mind. But out of My tenderness and grace alone art thou permitted to draw nigh unto My table; as though a beggar were called to a rich man's dinner, and had no other recompense to offer him for the benefits done unto him, but to humble himself and to give him thanks. Do therefore as much as lieth in thee, and do it diligently, not of custom, nor of necessity, but with fear, reverence, and affection, receive the Body of thy beloved Lord God, who vouchsafeth to come unto thee. I am He who hath called thee; I commanded it to be done; I will supply what is lacking to thee; come and receive Me.

3. When I give the grace of devotion, give thanks unto thy God; it is not because thou art worthy, but because I had mercy on thee. If thou hast not devotion, but rather feelest thyself dry, be instant in prayer, cease not to groan and knock; cease not until thou prevail to obtain some crumb or drop of saving grace. Thou hast need of Me, I have no need of thee. Nor dost thou come to sanctify Me, but I come to sanctify thee and make thee better. Thou comest that thou mayest be sanctified by Me, and be united to Me; that thou mayest receive fresh grace, and be kindled anew to amendment of life. See that thou neglect not this grace, but prepare thy heart with all diligence, and receive thy Beloved unto thee.

4. But thou oughtest not only to prepare thyself for devotion before Communion, thou must also keep thyself with all diligence therein after receiving the Sacrament; nor is less watchfulness needed afterwards, than devout preparation beforehand: for good watchfulness afterwards becometh in turn the best preparation for the gaining more grace. For hereby is a man made entirely indisposed to good, if he immediately return from Communion to give himself up to outward consolations. Beware of much speaking;

[3] Psalm cii. 7.

remain in a secret place, and hold communion with thy God; for thou hast Him whom the whole world cannot take away from thee. I am He to whom thou oughtest wholly to give thyself; so that now thou mayest live not wholly in thyself, but in Me, free from all anxiety.

CHAPTER XIII

THAT THE DEVOUT SOUL OUGHT WITH THE WHOLE HEART TO YEARN AFTER UNION WITH CHRIST IN THE SACRAMENT

The Voice of the Disciple

WHO shall grant unto me, O Lord, that I may find Thee alone, and open all my heart unto Thee, and enjoy Thee as much as my soul desireth; and that no man may henceforth look upon me, nor any creature move me or have respect unto me, but Thou alone speak unto me and I unto Thee, even as beloved is wont to speak unto beloved, and friend to feast with friend? For this do I pray, this do I long for, that I may be wholly united unto Thee, and may withdraw my heart from all created things, and by means of Holy Communion and frequent celebration may learn more and more to relish heavenly and eternal things. Ah, Lord God, when shall I be entirely united and lost in Thee, and altogether forgetful of myself? *Thou in me, and I in Thee*;[1] even so grant that we may in like manner continue together in one.

2. Verily Thou art my Beloved, the choicest among ten thousand,[2] in whom my soul delighteth to dwell all the days of her life. Verily Thou art my Peacemaker, in Whom is perfect peace and true rest, apart from Whom is labour and sorrow and infinite misery. Verily *Thou art a God that hidest Thyself*, and Thy counsel is not with the wicked, but Thy Word is with the humble and the simple. O how sweet, *O Lord, is Thy spirit*, who that Thou mightest manifest Thy sweetness towards Thy children, dost vouchsafe to refresh them with the bread which is full of sweetness, which cometh down from heaven. Verily *there is no other nation so great, which hath its gods drawing nigh to them, as Thou, our God, art present unto all Thy faithful ones*,[3] unto whom for their daily solace, and for

[1] John xv. 4.   [2] Cant. v. 10.   [3] Deuteronomy iv. 7.

lifting up their heart unto heaven, Thou givest Thyself for their food and delight.

3. For what other nation is there so renowned as the Christian people? Or what creature is so beloved under heaven as the devout soul to which God entereth in, that he may feed it with His glorious flesh? O unspeakable grace! O wonderful condescension! O immeasurable love specially bestowed upon men! But what reward shall I give unto the Lord for this grace, for charity so mighty? There is nothing which I am able to present more acceptable than to give my heart altogether unto God, and to join it inwardly to Him. Then all my inward parts shall rejoice, when my soul shall be perfectly united unto God. Then shall He say unto me, "If thou wilt be with Me, I will be with thee." And I will answer Him, "Vouchsafe, O Lord, to abide with me, I will gladly be with Thee; this is my whole desire, even that my heart be united unto Thee."

CHAPTER XIV

OF THE FERVENT DESIRE OF CERTAIN DEVOUT PERSONS TO RECEIVE THE BODY AND BLOOD OF CHRIST

The Voice of the Disciple

O HOW great is the abundance of Thy sweetness, O Lord, which Thou hast laid up for them that fear Thee. When I call to mind some devout persons who draw nigh to Thy Sacrament, O Lord, with the deepest devotion and affection, then very often I am confounded in myself and blush for shame, that I approach Thine altar and table of Holy Communion so carelessly and coldly, that I remain so dry and without affection, that I am not wholly kindled with love before Thee, my God, nor so vehemently drawn and affected as many devout persons have been, who out of the very earnest desire of the Communion, and tender affection of heart, could not refrain from weeping, but as it were with mouth of heart and body alike panted inwardly after Thee, O God, O Fountain of Life, having no power to appease or satiate their hunger, save by receiving Thy Body with all joyfulness and spiritual eagerness.

2. O truly ardent faith of those, becoming a very proof of Thy Sacred Presence! For they verily know their Lord *in the breaking*

of bread, whose heart so *ardently burneth within them*[1] when Jesus walketh with them by the way. Ah me! far from me for the most part is such love and devotion as this, such vehement love and ardour. Be merciful unto me, O Jesus, good, sweet, and kind, and grant unto Thy poor suppliant to feel sometimes, in Holy Communion, though it be but a little, the cordial affection of Thy love, that my faith may grow stronger, my hope in Thy goodness increase, and my charity, once kindled within me by the tasting of the heavenly manna, may never fail.

3. But Thy mercy is able even to grant me the grace which I long for, and to visit me most tenderly with the spirit of fervour when the day of Thy good pleasure shall come. For, although I burn not with desire so vehement as theirs who are specially devout towards Thee, yet, through Thy grace, I have a desire after that greatly inflamed desire, praying and desiring to be made partaker with all those who so fervently love Thee, and to be numbered among their holy company.

CHAPTER XV

THAT THE GRACE OF DEVOTION IS ACQUIRED BY HUMILITY AND SELF-DENIAL

The Voice of the Beloved

THOU oughtest to seek earnestly the grace of devotion, to ask it fervently, to wait for it patiently and faithfully, to receive it gratefully, to preserve it humbly, to work with it diligently, and to leave to God the time and manner of heavenly visitation until it come. Chiefly oughtest thou to humble thyself when thou feelest inwardly little or no devotion, yet not to be too much cast down, nor to grieve out of measure. God ofttimes giveth in one short moment what He hath long time denied; He sometimes giveth at the end what at the beginning of prayer He hath deferred to give.

2. If grace were always given immediately, and were at hand at the wish, it would be hardly bearable to weak man. Wherefore the grace of devotion is to be waited for with a good hope and with humble patience. Yet impute it to thyself and to thy sins when it

[1] Luke xxiv. 32.

is not given, or when it is mysteriously taken away. It is some-times a small thing which hindereth and hideth grace; (if indeed that ought to be called *small* and not rather *great,* which hindereth so great a good); but if thou remove this, be it small or great, and perfectly overcome it, thou wilt have what thou hast asked.

3. For immediately that thou hast given thyself unto God with all thine heart, and hast sought neither this nor that according to thine own will and pleasure, but hast altogether settled thyself in Him, thou shalt find thyself united and at peace; because nothing shall give thee so sweet relish and delight, as the good pleasure of the Divine will. Whosoever therefore shall have lifted up his will unto God with singleness of heart, and shall have delivered him-self from every inordinate love or dislike of any created thing, he will be the most fit for receiving grace, and worthy of the gift of devotion. For where the Lord findeth empty vessels,[1] there giveth He His blessing. And the more perfectly a man forsaketh things which cannot profit, and the more he dieth to himself, the more quickly doth grace come, the more plentifully doth it enter in, and the higher doth it lift up the free heart.

4. Then shall he see, and flow together, and wonder, and his heart shall be enlarged within him,[2] because the hand of the Lord is with him, and he hath put himself wholly in His hand, even for ever. Lo, thus shall the man be blessed, that seeketh God with all his heart, and receiveth not his soul in vain. This man in receiving the Holy Eucharist obtaineth the great grace of Divine Union; because he hath not regard to his own devotion and comfort, but, above all devotion and comfort, to the glory and honour of God.

CHAPTER XVI

THAT WE OUGHT TO LAY OPEN OUR NECESSITIES TO CHRIST AND TO REQUIRE HIS GRACE

The Voice of the Disciple

O most sweet and loving Lord, whom now I devoutly desire to receive, Thou knowest my infirmity and the necessity which I suffer, in what evils and vices I lie; how often I am weighed down,

[1] 2 Kings iv.   [2] Isaiah lx. 5.

tempted, disturbed, and defiled. I come unto Thee for remedy, I beseech of Thee consolation and support. I speak unto Thee who knowest all things, to whom all my secrets are open, and who alone art able perfectly to comfort and help me. Thou knowest what good thing I most stand in need of, and how poor I am in virtues.

2. Behold, I stand poor and naked before Thee, requiring grace, and imploring mercy. Refresh the hungry suppliant, kindle my coldness with the fire of Thy love, illuminate my blindness with the brightness of Thy presence. Turn thou all earthly things into bitterness for me, all grievous and contrary things into patience, all things worthless and created into contempt and oblivion. Lift up my heart unto Thee in Heaven, and suffer me not to wander over the earth. Be Thou alone sweet unto me from this day forward for ever, because Thou alone art my meat and drink, my love and joy, my sweetness and my whole good.

3. Oh that Thou wouldest altogether by Thy presence, kindle, consume, and transform me into Thyself; that I may be made one spirit with Thee, by the grace of inward union, and the melting of earnest love! Suffer me not to go away from Thee hungry and dry; but deal mercifully with me, as oftentimes Thou hast dealt wondrously with Thy saints. What marvel if I should be wholly kindled from Thee, and in myself should utterly fail, since Thou art fire always burning and never failing, love purifying the heart and enlightening the understanding.

CHAPTER XVII

OF FERVENT LOVE AND VEHEMENT DESIRE OF RECEIVING CHRIST

The Voice of the Disciple

WITH the deepest devotion and fervent love, with all affection and fervour of heart, I long to receive Thee, O Lord, even as many Saints and devout persons have desired Thee in communicating, who were altogether well pleasing to Thee by their sanctity of life, and dwelt in all ardent devotion. O my God, Eternal Love, my whole Good, Happiness without measure, I long to receive Thee with the most vehement desire and becoming reverence which any Saint ever had or could have.

2. And although I be unworthy to have all those feelings of devotion, yet do I offer Thee the whole affection of my heart, even as though I alone had all those most grateful inflamed desires. Yea, also, whatsoever things a pious mind is able to conceive and long for, all these with the deepest veneration and inward fervour do I offer and present unto Thee. I desire to reserve nothing unto myself, but freely and entirely to offer myself and all that I have unto Thee for a sacrifice. O Lord my God, my Creator and Redeemer! with such affection, reverence, praise, and honour, with such gratitude, worthiness, and love, with such faith, hope, and purity do I desire to receive Thee this day, as Thy most blessed Mother, the glorious Virgin Mary, received and desired Thee, when she humbly and devoutly answered the Angel who brought unto her the glad tidings of the mystery of the Incarnation. *Behold the handmaid of the Lord; be it unto me according to thy word.*[1]

3. And as Thy blessed forerunner, the most excellent of Saints, John Baptist, being full of joy in Thy presence, leapt while yet in the womb of his mother, for joy in the Holy Ghost; and afterwards discerning Jesus walking amongst men, humbled himself exceedingly, and said, with devout affection, *The friend of the bridegroom, who standeth and heareth him, rejoiceth greatly because of the bridegroom's voice;*[2] even so I wish to be inflamed with great and holy desires, and to present myself unto Thee with my whole heart. Whence also, on behalf of myself and of all commended to me in prayer, I offer and present unto Thee the jubilation of all devout hearts, their ardent affections, their mental ecstasies, and supernatural illuminations and heavenly visions, with all the virtues and praises celebrated and to be celebrated by every creature in heaven and earth; to the end that by all Thou mayest worthily be praised and glorified for ever.

4. Receive my prayers, O Lord my God, and my desires of giving Thee infinite praise and unbounded benediction, which, according to the multitude of Thine unspeakable greatness, are most justly due unto Thee. These do I give Thee, and desire to give every day and very moment; and with beseechings and affectionate desires I

[1] Luke i. 38.   [2] John iii. 29.

call upon all celestial spirits and all Thy faithful people to join with me in rendering Thee thanks and praises.

5. Let all peoples, nations, and tongues praise Thee, and magnify Thy holy and sweet-sounding Name, with highest jubilations and ardent devotion. And let all who reverently and devoutly celebrate Thy most high Sacrament, and receive it with full assurance of faith, be accounted worthy to find grace and mercy with Thee, and intercede with all supplication for me a sinner; and when they shall have attained unto their wished-for devotion and joyous union with Thee, and shall depart full of comfort and wondrously refreshed from Thy holy, heavenly table, let them vouchsafe to be mindful of me, for I am poor and needy.

CHAPTER XVIII

THAT A MAN SHOULD NOT BE A CURIOUS SEARCHER OF THE SACRAMENT, BUT A HUMBLE IMITATOR OF CHRIST, SUBMITTING HIS SENSE TO HOLY FAITH

The Voice of the Beloved

THOU must take heed of curious and useless searching into this most profound Sacrament, if thou wilt not be plunged into the abyss of doubt. *He that is a searcher of Majesty shall be oppressed by the glory thereof.*[1] God is able to do more than man can understand. A pious and humble search after truth is to be allowed, when it is always ready to be taught, and striving to walk after the wholesome opinions of the fathers.

2. Blessed is the simplicity which leaveth alone the difficult paths of questionings, and followeth the plain and firm steps of God's commandments. Many have lost devotion whilst they sought to search into deeper things. Faith is required of thee, and a sincere life, not loftiness of intellect, nor deepness in the mysteries of God. If thou understandest not nor comprehendest the things which are beneath thee, how shalt thou comprehend those which are above thee? Submit thyself unto God, and humble thy sense to faith, and the light of knowledge shall be given thee, as shall be profitable and necessary unto thee.   [1] Proverbs xxv. 27 (Vulg.).

3. There are some who are grievously tempted concerning faith and the Sacrament; but this is not to be imputed to themselves but rather to the enemy. Care not then for this, dispute not with thine own thoughts, nor make answer to the doubts which are cast into thee by the devil; but believe the words of God, believe His Saints and Prophets, and the wicked enemy shall flee from thee. Often it profiteth much, that the servant of God endureth such things. For the enemy tempteth not unbelievers and sinners, because he already hath secure possession of them; but he tempteth and harasseth the faithful and devout by various means.

4. Go forward therefore with simple and undoubting faith, and draw nigh unto the Sacrament with supplicating reverence. And whatsoever thou art not enabled to understand, that commit without anxiety to Almighty God. God deceiveth thee not; he is deceived who believeth too much in himself. God walketh with the simple, revealeth Himself to the humble, giveth understanding to babes, openeth the sense to pure minds, and hideth grace from the curious and proud. Human reason is weak and may be deceived; but true faith cannot be deceived.

5. All reason and natural investigation ought to follow faith, not to precede, nor to break it. For faith and love do here especially take the highest place, and work in hidden ways in this most holy and exceeding excellent Sacrament. God who is eternal and incomprehensible, and of infinite power, doth great and inscrutable things in heaven and in earth, and His wonderful works are past finding out. If the works of God were of such sort that they might easily be comprehended by human reason, they should no longer be called wonderful or unspeakable.

VE RI TAS

VE RI TAS

VE RI TAS